THE EARLY CISTERCIAN NUNS

Previously published by Gracewing

The Cistercians in the Early Middle Ages

The Welsh Cistercians

The Five Wounds of Jesus

The Tudor Cistercians

Cistercian Chronicles and Necrologies

The Early Cistercian Nuns 1098-1350

David H. Williams

Gracewing

First published in England in 2023
by
Gracewing
2 Southern Avenue
Leominster
Herefordshire HR6 0QF
United Kingdom
www.gracewing.co.uk

All rights reserved

No part of this publication may be reproduced,
stored in a retrieval system, or transmitted in any
form or by any means, electronic, mechanical,
photocopying, recording or otherwise,
without the written permission of the publisher.

© 2023, David H. Williams

The rights of David H. Williams to be identified
as the author of this work have been asserted
in accordance with the Copyright, Designs and Patents Act 1988.

The publishers have no responsibility
for the persistence or accuracy of URLs for websites
referred to in this publication, and do not guarantee
that any content on such websites is, or will remain,
accurate or appropriate.

ISBN 978 085244 995 0

Typeset by Word and Page, Chester, UK

Cover design by Bernardita Peña Hurtado

Cover images

Cistercian Nuns: Depicted on the Esholt Priory Charter of 1484 (England).
Courtesy of the West Yorkshire Archive Service, Leeds: WYL 1530

Llanllŷr, Wales: Matrix of the Seal of an Abbess (early 15th-century).
A die of weathered copper.; 46 x 25 mm.
Courtesy of Mrs Loveday Gee; Photo:National Museum of Wales

Contents

Acknowledgements — vii

Abbreviations for Country Names — viii

Map of Cistercian Nunneries before 1350 — x

1. The Growth of the Female Houses — 1
Preface, The Foundation of Tart, The General Chapter of 1147; The Later Twelfth Century; the Abbey of Las Huelgas; Other Notable Nunneries; Scotland and England; The Thirteenth Century: Throughout Europe and the Near East; Early Relations with the Male Order; The Religious Women's Movement; the Daughters of God and the Beguinages; the Hospitals; Incorporated Monasteries and Hermitages; Double Monasteries; the Founders and their Motives; the Backing of the Papacy

2. Nunnery Sites — 57
Introduction; Geographical Locations; Woodland Sites, Riverine Sites, Lacustrine and Island Sites; Upland Sites, Frontier Sites, Routeway Sites; Site Names; Urban Nunneries; Changes of Site; Ephemeral and United Sites; Parochial Compensation

3. Church and Cloister — 77
Nunnery Churches, Cloisters, Chapter-houses, Dorters, Infirmaries, Refectories and Diet, Pittances, Books, Manuscripts and Seals, Images and Relics

4. The Communities — 107
The Nuns and Their Purpose, the *Conversae*, Apparel, Recruitment, Evidence from Necrologies, Community Size, Enclosure, Visitation, Local Chapters, Disaffected Nuns, The Abbesses, the Claustral Officers, Visionaries and Mystics, The Male Community: the Provosts, *Conversi*, Chaplains and Confessors; Spiritual Fraternity, Other Residents and Guests, Pilgrims, the Departed

5. The Economy — 179
The Work Force, Charters and Benefactions, Benefactors and Their Motives, the Estates, Boundaries and Property Disputes, Criminal Jurisdiction, Arable Farming and the Milling Industry, Pastoralism, Fisheries, Woodland and Timber, Salt Extraction, Trade, Urban Property.

6. Epilogue: The Fourteenth Century — 227
Introduction; Yorkshire Visitation Charters; Private Income and Pocket Money, Poverty; the Effects of Conflict: the Migration to the Towns; Conclusion

Notes	241
Bibliography	303
Variant Names of Nunneries	323
Index of Nunneries	339

Acknowledgements

In preparing this work I have been much assisted by the publication of Bernard Peugniez's invaluable volume, *L'Europe cistercienne* (Éditions du Signe, 2012). I am very grateful to those who have answered queries or conveyed materials and photographs to me, as Professor Kateřina Charvátová of Prague; Yvonne Murphy of Keble College, Oxford; Dr Andreas Mölder of Nordwestdeutsche Forstliche Versuchsanstalt, Göttingen, Monsieur B. Detry of Villagesdemons, Belgium; Mr R Labhart, Kurator Museum im Turmhof, Steckborn.

I am also indebted to Sr. Marianne-Franziska Inhasly of Mariazell Abbey, Wurmsbach, Switzerland; Dr James D'Emilio, University of South Florida; Herr Hartmunt Haedrick, editor of the homepage of the Neuwerk Church, Goslar; Professor Anton Escher of the University of Mainz, Dr Constance Berman of Iowa University; Dr Andrzej Nienartowicz of Torun University; Professor Martin Uhrmachel of Luxembourg University; Tessa Vanpaeschen, registrar Het Stadsmuseum Hasselt, Belgium, and Marc Willems, Hasselt; Dr Volker Trugenberger Landesarchiv Baden-Württemberg; and Isabella Gabach, Maubuisson Abbey, the Sisters of Charity at Chelmno on my visit there, and above all to my willing translators: Rose Sillars for German, and Mariusz Bekasiak for Polish.

I am very grateful to the Very Revd. Andreas Abakuks for communicating to me the fine thesis of the late Fr Heinrich Trops regarding the convent in Rïga. My sincere apologies to any whom I have failed to mention. This work is a revised, enlarged and illustrated edition of an essay in the periodical *Analecta Sacra Ordinis Cisterciensis* in 2016.

Once again I express my thanks to Mr Tom Longford and Gracewing Publishing for the careful and fine presentation of my works over the last quarter of a century.

David H. Williams
College of St Barnabas
Lingfield, Surrey

Abbreviations for Country Names

A	Austria	It	Italy
B	Belgium	L	Luxembourg
C	Cyprus	La	Latvia
Cz	Czechoslovakia	Ln	Lebanon
D	Denmark	N	Norway
E	England	Pl	Poland
Es	Estonia	Pt	Portugal
F	France	S	Scotland
G	Germany	Sp	Spain
Gr	Greece	Sw	Sweden
H	Hungary	Swz	Switzerland
Ho	Holland	Sy	Syria
IOM	Isle of Man	W	Wales
Ir	Ireland		

Porta Coeli Abbey, Tišnov, Czech Republic

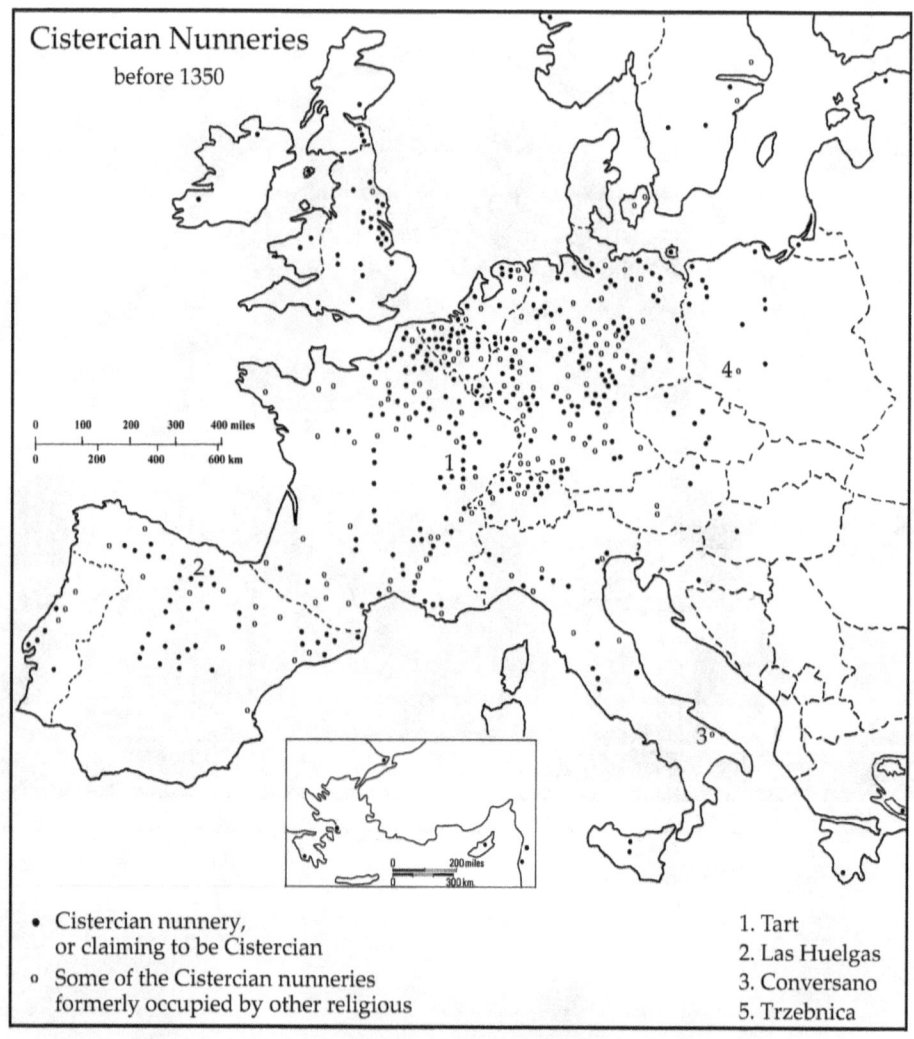

Fig. 1. Cistercian Nunneries before 1350 (David Williams/Colin Williams, 1989)

1

The Growth of the Female Houses

PREFACE

Some scholars dislike the nunneries of the Order receiving separate treatment in a work such as this; they feel that the sisters should be incorporated into each and every chapter of a general study on the same footing as their male counterparts. Unfortunately this is not really practicable: firstly, the nunneries were, by and large, much smaller both in terms of buildings, personnel and estates, than the male houses; secondly, the insistence from 1213 onwards of strict enclosure for the nuns made their participation in normal Cistercian agrarian and other economic activity impossible; thirdly, they had no personal representation at the annual General Chapter of the male Order. For these reasons, it is not possible to compare the male and female monasteries like-for-like. Moreover, the sheer number of nunneries which counted themselves Cistercian calls for separate and voluminous treatment, to which this essay can be but an introduction.

The appearance of nuns as members or associates or would-be followers of the Cistercian Order is shrouded in uncertainty, especially as the earliest document of the White Monks, the *Exordium Parvum*, compiled by perhaps 1150 makes no mention of them, nor indeed did the first codification of Cistercian statutes in 1202.[1] Yet, by the year 1200, in France alone some one hundred nunneries claimed to be Cistercian. In the early to mid-thirteenth century there was to be a rapid growth in the number of convents which was reminiscent of the speedy advance of the male houses of the Order a century before. By the time of the European Reformation estimates of the number of convents in Europe and the Near East, Cistercian or claiming to be Cistercian, vary widely between five and nine hundred.

The Early Cistercian Nuns, 1098–1350

The origins of many are obscure and, as often there is no record of their formal incorporation into the Order, it is not always certain which nunneries were truly Cistercian and which were simply endeavouring to follow the Cistercian way of life. Herman of Tournai (d. 1147) described the early Cistercian nuns as 'of their own free will embracing violently, nay joyfully, the Order of Cîteaux, which many robust men and youths fear to enter ... imitating in all things the monks of Clairvaux'.[2] A Welsh archdeacon and chronicler, Giraldus Cambrensis (fl. 1195/1220), writing of the nuns of Llanllŷr, described them as abiding from the start to the ideals, institutions, and habit, of the Cistercian Order, both interiorly and exteriorly, 'so far as it is lawful for the female sex'.[3]

Nunneries were expected to pay regular contributions to the coffers of the Order. The General Chapter (1336) ordered that those reluctant to pay were to be forced to do so, 'by deposition of the abbess, excommunication of the officials, and by interdict of the convent'.[4] The Cistercian Tax Book, as published and deriving from around 1354/1355, lists the 'medium' amounts expected of some thirty Cistercian nunneries, mostly of France. The highest rated was La Prée (£45), whilst £30 was expected of Élan, £23-6-8 of La Cour-Dieu, and £22 of Klaarkamp (Ho). Mostly the amounts expected ranged between £4 and £16.[5] Lilienthal (G; 1292) was excused from payment of a subsidy to the Holy See intended for business of the Holy Land.[6] Conversano (It; 1339) did however have the annual obligation of paying one ounce of gold to the Holy See, but only for four years.[7]

There were in the early-twelfth century perhaps more contacts between Cistercian abbots and nuns than previously supposed. St Aelred was not averse to writing a definite rule for anchorites, his *De Institutione Inclusarum* for his sister; he also praised the spirituality of the Gilbertine nuns of his day.[8] Of the surviving 547 letters of St Bernard, twenty-three were addressed to women, and he was well aware of the usefulness of mothers when it came to persuading their sons to join the Cistercian movement. He remained detached from women, but he was not 'anti-women' as such.[9] St Bernard played an active role at Jully (F), as when in 1142 he, with the bishop of Langres, 'solemnly received' two daughters into the holy community of nuns there.[10]

Some twentieth century authors, like Grundmann and Krenig, would deny that there were Cistercian women in the twelfth century, and that the eventual admission of women was forced upon reluctant abbots: far from the truth. They were 'imitators' but in real sense 'true followers': witness the papal confirmation of Tart and other houses in the wording used: 'following the rule of St Benedict and the customs of Cîteaux'.[11] Such terminology was commonplace, as witness a bull of Nicholas IV (1291) in favour of Sonnefeld (G), who saw its nuns as living 'for God, according to the Rule of Blessed Benedict, and the institutions of the Cistercian brothers'.[12]

THE FOUNDATION OF TART

The earliest Cistercian convents founded were so with the backing of senior figures in the Order: Tart (F) was established in 1125 by Elizabeth of Vergy, mother of its first abbess, with undoubtedly the blessing and consent, and perhaps the active encouragement, of Abbot Stephen Harding of Cîteaux, and it had also the backing of Bishop Josserant of Langres. Stephen Harding had the experience of the women living close to Molesme.[13] Its establishment was quickly followed by that in 1128 of Belfays by Abbot Gaucher of Morimond.[14]

These first houses were in part at least a solution as to what to do with the wives and other female relations of married men wishing to enter the Order, although the womenfolk of St Bernard and his companions entered the convent of Jully (founded in 1113) which remained Benedictine.[15] Even earlier than the foundation of Tart may have been the establishment of Laval-Bénite (F) specifically founded for the wives and daughters of Berlion de Moisanc, Arnaud de Rives and Amedeus de Clermont d'Hautrives, as all three became monks of Bonnevaux shortly after its establishment in 1119.[16]

The male Benedictine abbey at Molesme, established in 1075, had women: relatives of men who joined the community, living in small groups in houses close to the men's monastery, but eventually the women moved to Jully, following Cluniac traditions.[17] When St Bernard enlisted Guy, his eldest brother and a married man into the monastic life, he hesitated and his wife, Elizabeth, at first refused to give her consent, but then 'separated from her husband by the mutual vow of chastity according to the custom of the Church, she joined a group of religious women, and to this day she is serving God there as a nun': 'She' means the 'wife', and 'there' denotes Jully, which had been founded from Molesme around 1113 by Abbot Alberic.[18]

The part played by St Bernard in the foundation of Jully has been exaggerated (he was hardly on the scene!), but he was consulted when new usages were drawn up for the Jully nuns.[19] The first prioress of Jully was Elizabeth, sister-in-law of St Bernard, whilst his sister, Humbelina, later became prioress.[20] St Bernard himself arranged some property acquisition for Jully, and even took the vows of some of its nuns.[21] Some nuns from Jully, one account has it, dissatisfied with the religious life in that house, asked St Stephen Harding for help to follow a stricter vocation. Elizabeth of Vergy, the first abbess of Tart, was perhaps the daughter of a generous benefactor, of the same name.

There were, however, early divergences at Tart from Cistercian life, as in the ownership of the tithes of the church of Tart.[22] Tart stood close to the right bank of the river Ouche some twenty kilometres south-east of Dijon. The settlement of Tart was aided by major donations, including the tithes of Rouvres and of Tart itself, and the fisheries of Genlis; all these were confirmed by Duke Hugh of Burgundy who added the grange of Marmot.[23]

Critics have argued that Tart 'was not a daughter-house of Cîteaux but a personal intervention of Stephen Harding'.[24] A bull of Eugenius III (1145–53) made no mention of Tart being Cistercian. The first extant acknowledgement of that fact came only in the 1190s, when Abbot Guy of Cîteaux issued a charter stating that Tart was 'the house of Cîteaux's own daughter', and that the nuns followed the Institutes of the Order. He stressed that the abbots of Cîteaux had full jurisdiction in Tart, and that the abbesses of the eighteen communities related to Tart were obliged to participate in the regional chapter of Tart.[25]

A subsequent bull from Innocent III (1200) also showed that by that date Tart was the head of a mini-congregation of eighteen nunneries, of which more in a subsequent chapter.[26] This apparent late recognition may simply be a consequence of the General Chapter at the time of Tart's foundation being more of a pastoral than a legislative assembly, and one which contained no structure to enable it to authorise the foundation of Tart', but this is by no means certain.[27] At the very least, no statutes have survived from the twelfth century regarding the nunnery.

Belmont-aux-Nonnains (F) in the diocese of Langres and the first daughter-house of Tart, was founded in 1127 by the lords of Achey. The first abbess, Petronilla, was the daughter of Philip of Acey, one of the founders.[28] Another early daughter-house of Tart, Belfays (Beaufay; F), was effectively realised in 1128 by Gaucher, second abbot of Morimond, and the generosity of Count Simon III of Clefmont. The third abbot, Otto, placed thirty noble ladies from France and Germany there, and united to it the abbey of Chazeaux.[29] In Germany, the convent at Wechterswinkel, founded in 1134, became Cistercian in 1134, and itself settled new Cistercian nunneries at Ichtershausen in 1147, and at Bamberg in 1157. The proposed early date of foundation of 1125 for Marienau (G) has been queried, and it is suggested that it may only have come into existence in 1265.[30]

THE GENERAL CHAPTER OF 1147

A further impetus allowing the admission of nunneries to the Order was given when in 1147 (though this date has latterly been questioned), the General Chapter held that year in the presence of the Cistercian pope, Eugenius III, whilst rejecting the request of the Gilbertine double-houses to be admitted, did approve the incorporation of the relatively small French congregations of Savigny and of Obazine.[31] The congregation of Savigny included at that time three nunneries, the first of which was: Les Blanches (F), founded in 1105 by the hermit Vital with the support of the count of Mortain; Vital's sister, Adeline, was its first superior.

There followed Villers-Canivet (F), founded by Roger de Montbray between 1127 and 1140, and Bival (F), established by Count Hugh IV of Gournay certainly by 1140. Placed under the authority of the Savigniac abbot of Beaubec, it went on to settle nuns at Bondeville (F), a few years later, though this chronology is not absolutely certain. Bival and Bondeville were both dedicated to St Mary Magdalene, denoting women who wished to retire from the world, like the mother of the bishop of Sées, a nun at Villers-Canivet (F) in 1150.[32]

Also admitted into the Order at that General Chapter of 1147 were the abbey of Obazine (F), and its three dependent houses of Valette, Bonnaigue, and the nunnery of Coyroux. Around 1130

Stephen of Obazine had settled hermits, men and women, on same site but in different places. The influx of vocations led him about 1140 to found two separate monasteries and in 1142 this arrangement was confirmed by the bishop of Limoges, who took the houses under his oversight. The two communities were 600 metres apart, though latterly it has been postulated that the site of Coyroux nunnery was not obtained until 1159 or 1160.[33]

In 1147 when congregation of Obazine was admitted, there were dissentient voices at the General Chapter because Stephen of Obazine had accepted the government of women as well as men, but by then there were at least twenty Cistercian nunneries in existence, each under the regular care of a Cistercian abbot.[34] Indeed, in those early decades there appears to have been little or no hostility towards the female element. The nuns of those first decades were counselled and inspected by Cistercian abbots, but were seen not so much as 'members' of the Order, but rather as 'imitators' of it, though in the sense of being 'true followers'.

This phraseology was employed by Idung of Prufening (1154/55).[35] Regarding Obazine and Coyroux, Abbot Raynald of Cîteaux stipulated that everything contrary to Cistercian custom was to be removed, though gradually, and monks and *conversi* instructors were sent from Cîteaux to assure conformity in both houses.[36] Placed at first under the authority of the male abbey, Coyroux later came to have its own prioress.

Married couples, even entire families, were attracted to Obazine in pre-Cistercian days. Ademar Berenger (1143/1153) entered Obazine with 'his wife and all their children, relinquishing the world'. At much the same time Peter William and Almodis, his wife, 'renouncing the world for a happier existence in the celestial fields', gave themselves and their sons 'as devotees to Obazine to serve God perpetually as paupers there'.[37] The dates of these deeds, mentioning nuns at Obazine, must suggest that the final separation of Coyroux from Obazine was much later than 1147 as first thought.[38]

By 1150 there were some forty Cistercian convents, the existence of Cistercian nuns was well established, and thereafter nunneries began to appear in many parts of Europe. In Scotland, four Cistercian female houses appeared in the 1150s, though some of the dates are uncertain, as is any knowledge as to whether they were initially Benedictine houses: North Berwick, founded by Earl Duncan of

Fife; Manuel, where nuns were settled by King Malcolm IV; Eccles, the foundation of the countess of March, and Haddington, built on lands owned by the founder, Countess Ada de Warrene. This last house gave to the locality the name of *Nun*raw, now the location of a modern-day Trappist male abbey. All ranked as priories and were subject to visitation by their diocesan bishop.[39]

In England some eight of the Cistercian convents in Yorkshire may have dated from the 1150s.[40] A northern outpost was the convent of Nonneseter near Bergen, the only Cistercian nunnery in Norway, and first founded perhaps as a Benedictine nunnery by 1150.[41] Nuns following Cistercian practices inhabited the Benedictine male abbey of Semide in Portugal from 1183,[42] but the presence of Cistercian nuns in eastern Europe and much of Italy was to await the thirteenth century. By the year 1200 there were around one hundred and thirty five Cistercian nunneries, close on twenty of these being in Germany, but expansion in the Low Countries was also a feature of the thirteenth century.

In Spain there were to be some forty Cistercian nunneries, mostly in the north and east, rather than in the Muslim south.[43] The first Cistercian foundation in Spain on land offered by the king of Navarre, Garcia Ramirez, was that of Tulebras in 1147; nuns coming to found it from Favas/Fabas in Gascony. It prospered with privileges and donations given by kings, princes and papal endorsement. The sisters first settled at Tudela in Navarre in 1149 but transferred the next year to Tulebras.[44]

LAS HUELGAS

Forty years later some of the nuns of Tulebras moved to inhabit the most notable Spanish Cistercian convent, that of Las Huelgas, a kilometer from Burgos. They included Missol, the first abbess; she like the prioress and precentor, were natives of Burgos.[45] The new abbey was founded, perhaps on royal land, on 1 June 1187 by King Alfonso VIII of Castile on the insistence of 'his most serene wife', Eleanor of England and Aquitaine, daughter of Henry II, with the consent of their daughters, Berenguela and Urraca.[46]

The new foundation was backed by papal bulls granted by Urban III and Clement III (1187/1188), and also in 1187 by the king's Foundation Privilege. The papal bulls freed the nunnery from episcopal oversight, approved all donations, and made the nuns exempt from the payment of tithes; whilst, following the usual terminology, the abbess might receive free or freed women and girls notwithstanding any objections, and no sister could leave after profession without permission from the abbess. The nuns were reminded to follow the Rule of St Benedict and the Institutes of the Cistercian Order.[47] The Foundation Privilege stated that the Cistercian way of life was to be observed in perpetuity.[48]

Abbot Guy of Cîteaux came to Burgos in 1199 to receive in an impressive ceremony the donation of Las Huelgas to the Cistercian Order by Alfonso VIII; it was to be incorporated into the Order and become a 'special daughter' of Cîteaux.[49] Monarchs insisted it, a royal pantheon, should be the head of all Cistercian nunneries in their kingdom. Alfonso X and Alfonso XI were crowned at Las Huelgas, whilst in 1268 Ferdinand de la Cerde and Blanche of France, daughter of St Louis, were married there. The young and short-lived Henry I of Castile was crowned at Las Huelgas after his father's death in 1204; a temporary roof may have been constructed over the nave for this occasion.[50] The sarcophagus of Alfonso VIII in the choir at Las Huelgas depicts the first abbess, Dona Missol, kneeling before him to receive the foundation bull.[51]

The most important convent in Spain, a cardinal once said: 'If the pope were to marry, he would not find a wife more worthy than the abbess of Las Huelgas'.[52] Alfonso and Eleanor in their charter said they settled nuns at Las Huelgas not only so that 'holy virgins consecrated to God might sing psalms to God with praise day and night', but also so that 'they (the king and queen) might likewise find delight in contemplation and praise'.[53] Alfonso VIII also founded Arroyo convent by 1186, and its first abbess was a daughter of Alfonso VII.[54]

Alfonso VIII lobbied to free nunneries from allegiance of Tulebras and transfer them to submission to Las Huelgas, it thereby becoming the head house of a mini-congregation (of which more below). Royal political aims may have been a factor in Alfonso VIII wishing to subject Gradefes and Carrizo in Leon to Las Huelgas not their mother house of Tulebras, which was in Navarre. The freeing of the nunneries from dependence on the Navarrese nunnery of Tulebras must be seen against local politics after Sancho VII of Navarre had fled by 1199 into exile. Abbot Guy II of Cîteaux intervened personally to obtain the consent of Abbess Urrara of

The Growth of the Female Houses

Tulebras to the earlier agreement releasing her daughter-houses to submit to Las Huelgas.[55]

The abbess of Las Huelgas personally or by a delegate attended the election of abbesses in her daughter-houses, who then came to Las Huelgas for confirmation of their election. The abbess appointed the prioress, the sub-prioress, portress, sacristan, cellarer, and other nuns with special duties, in all the daughter-houses, and all their grants and leases had to be confirmed by her.[56] Alphonsus VIII built the earliest buildings at Las Huelgas, but the principal cloister was raised by the son of his daughter, Berenguela, St Ferdinand (1217–52), and the monumental three-naved church was consecrated on 20th September 1279 in the time of Alphonsus X. The actual foundation was in 1187, but work on the early buildings started in 1180.

One of the king's daughters, Princess Constance, became a member of the community. Another daughter, Berenguela, short-lived Queen of León and Castile, spent much of her life at Las Huelgas, and dying in 1246 was, like other royals buried there.[57] A monastery very much for the nobility, Mafaud, wife of Henry I and a daughter of King Henry I of Portugal was a nun at Las Huelgas in 1252.[58]

The royal charter of 1199 granting Las Huelgas to Cîteaux also pledged that Queen Leonor and her husband (Alfonso VIII) and their children would be buried there, and the king repeated this commitment in 1204. It is generally believed that the royal burials were in the Capilla de la Asunción at the north-east corner of the earliest cloister, and that the royal tombs were translated into the nuns' choir, the nave of the church, on its dedication in 1279.[59] The tomb of Alfonso VIII bears a striking relief depicting the act of foundation, he bestowing the deed into the hands of the abbess.[60]

Las Huelgas had the further privilege that a resident Castilian princess held from the mid-thirteenth to mid-fourteenth century the title of Lady of Las Huelgas; usually though not always a nun and never abbess, this afforded its community surety of royal patronage and protection. This nun or 'infanta' exercised the right of lordship over the patrimony of the abbey, whilst the abbess had the governance of the community in her hands.

The first Lady of Las Huelgas was Princess Constance, the daughter of the founder. A notable 'infanta', who died in 1279, was Berenguela, a daughter of Ferdinand III and sister of Alfonso X. Berenguela exercised a double role: professed as a nun she did much to assist the business of Las Huelgas – 'participated in economic transactions, and advocated for it before the king and the pope'. She also reorganised the abbey by establishing new statutes in 1257. She also acted as 'infanta' of Castile and became involved in politics, which led to her exile from 1282 for two years. During that period the nunnery suffered many infringements of its privileges, even the invasion of its lands, but when Sancho IV became king, he reconfirmed all the properties and privileges of Las Huelgas 'by request of the infanta Berenguela, our aunt'.

Berenguela died about 1286, and the next but one infanta from the Spanish royal family was Blanca, a niece of Sancho IV. At first she hesitated to take up her position for she was already possessed of substantial rights and holdings in Castile. After the accession of her cousin Fernando IV in 1295, she obtained from him confirmation and ratification of all the properties and privileges of Las Huelgas; she also obtained from the king and from Cîteaux confirmation of her position and status.[61] She was particularly active in enhancing the salt rights of the abbey, and in obtaining confirmation of its royal charters also from Alfonso XI (1317).[62].

A similar position was occupied at Ferreira de Pantón (Sp) by Doña Milia Gutiérrez, a member of a family who had show patronage to the convent. Titled its 'keeper and lady', and taking this position in 1238, between 1242 and 1264 she issued several demises of properties of the convent.[63] Two other convents in Spain bore the same name as Huelgas.[64]

OTHER NOTABLE NUNNERIES

Apart from Las Huelgas, Jully and Tart, there were several female abbeys of status, like Saint Antoine-des-Champs (incorporated in 1206) sited outside the east gate of Paris. St Louis took it under his wing, giving it the title 'royal',[65] and displaying there the Crown of Thorns on his return from the Crusades.[66] At Maubuisson, founded in 1236 by Queen Blanche of Castile, survives a fine 'day-room' and thirteenth-century barn.[67] Near Tišnov in Bohemia is the nunnery of 'Porta coeli' founded by Queen Constance, with the support of her two sons, and upon which she spared no expense. She was buried there in 1240, and later an ornate portal was added to the west front, its elaborate tympanum depicting Christ looking down

The Growth of the Female Houses

on the kneeling figures of Constance and her son, Margrave Přemysl (also interred there).⁶⁸ At Rostock (G), nuns were settled at the convent of the Holy Cross by Queen Margarethe of Denmark, with the consent of her cousin, Waldemar of Rostock.⁶⁹

SCOTLAND AND ENGLAND

On the Scottish border lay the nunnery of Coldstream, named as Cistercian in a papal bull of 1259 but described about 1418 as not being Cistercian because 'the nuns do not wear the Cistercian habit'. Were they Benedictines claiming to be Cistercian in order to gain the privileges of the Order?⁷⁰ When Edward I and his 8,000-strong army encamped at Coldstream in 1296, the nunnery was able to provide the troops with food valued at £118 [nearly £60,000 in modern value]; it received 700 sheep in recompense.⁷¹

The best endowed Cistercian convent in England was Tarrant in Dorset.⁷² It was founded towards the close of the twelfth century by Ralph, a member of the local Keines family, and hence was often known as Tarrant Kaines. The nunnery was taken under his wing by Richard le Poor, bishop of Salisbury, who may have had it in mind when he wrote his treatise, the *Ancrene Riwle*, and it may well have been the bishop who suggested its incorporation [at an unknown date] into the Cistercian Order. Unlike all but one of the other nunneries of England claiming to be Cistercian, it bore the status of 'abbey' rather than 'priory', and was acknowledged as being Cistercian by Henry III in a charter of 1265. In 1238 the nunnery had afforded burial to Joan, a sister of Henry III, and wife of Alexander II of Scotland. She bequeathed £20 to the convent.

Before he died Bishop Richard le Poor placed the house under the patronage of Queen Eleanor, Henry III's wife. It had the tithes of three churches, numerous grants of properties, and the right of free warren on its demesne lands, whilst William de Kahayes, the founder's son, gave it the tithe of all salt meat killed in his household each year, 'one barrel of his prime and good ale for Christmas with another barrel of second ale, or malt to make as much'. The bishop reminded the nuns that they must not hold any personal property. He told them: 'Ye shall not possess any beast, my dear sisters, only a cat', or, when seeking their pittance in the hall of their early founder, they were bidden 'be glad in your heart if ye suffer insolence from Slurry the cook's boy who washeth dishes in the kitchen'.

Several convents, at least quasi-Cistercian, were located in the county of Yorkshire, where one commentator has pointed out that 'few women were involved in the foundation of the male Yorkshire houses, but more so in the foundation of nunneries'.[73]

THE THIRTEENTH CENTURY THROUGHOUT EUROPE AND THE NEAR EAST

By the early-thirteenth century there were numerous existing nunneries wishing to enter the Order, as well as the many benefactors hoping to endow new ones. Apart from the personal motives of individual benefactors the reasons are not far to seek. In north-west Europe it was a time of spiritual fervour epitomised by the 'religious women's' movement, and a number of Cistercian nunnneries had their origins in the beguinages. Some convents may have wished to avail themselves of Cistercian privileges – such as exemption from the payment of tithes and from episcopal control.

The ban on any further acceptance of nunneries by the Premonstratensians in 1198, and hurdles in their path also raised for a time by the Dominicans and Franciscans, were other factors making membership of the Cistercian Order a sought after attraction.[74] Indeed, James de Vitry (c. 1230) also linked the later expansion of the Cistercian nunneries to the refusal of the Premonstratensians to admit any more women.[75] In France, the long reign of King Louis IX (St Louis; 1226–70), and the patronage of Queen Blanche of Castile (1223–52) and of Margaret of Constantinople (Countess of Flanders, 1244–78), created a spiritual policy which favoured the establishment of religious houses. Nor must be forgotten the active involvement of several Cistercian abbots, particularly those of Aulne, Salem and Villers.

Whatever the motives, especially between 1210 to1250 the number of Cistercian nunneries grew very rapidly. That first half of the thirteenth century saw the foundation or incorporation of sixty-six convents in Belgium and one hundred and fifty in Germany, thirty-three of them being in the diocese of Mainz alone.[76]

In those parts of northern Gemany being Christianised the foundation of nunneries such as Reinbek (1226), Itzehoe (1230), Uetersen

The Growth of the Female Houses

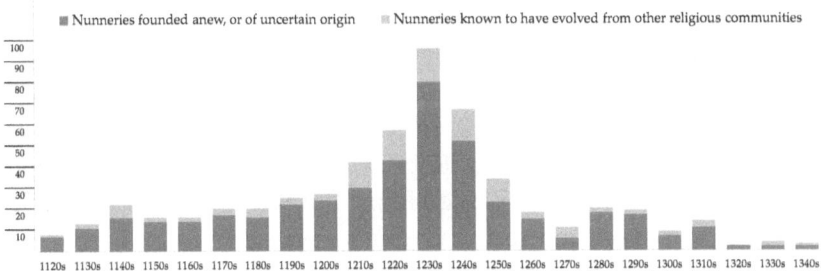

Fig. 2. The Growth of the Nunneries (by decade)

(1234) and Harvesthude (1245), cannot have been anything else but helpful.[77] New foundations continued there into the fourteenth century, as Himmelau at Geldshausen, with royal charters granted its nuns by King Heinrich VII in 1313, and King Ludvig in 1339.[78]

In France, between 1190 and 1250, eighty-eight female monasteries as opposed to fifteen male abbeys were created.[79] In the Rhône valley some houses of Cistercian nuns were founded with a view to their being a bulwark against the spread of heresy, including some dependent on Thoronet, whose reformed troubadour abbot, Fulk of Marseilles, bishop of Toulouse from 1205–31.

Such nunneries perhaps included Saint-Pons de Géménos (1205), its daughter-house of Mollèges (by 1213), and Saint-Pierre-du-Puy at Orange (1217).[80] The passion for founding a Cistercian house was shown in 1220 when a widow, Amice, lady of Creteuil, decided to found a Cistercian nunnery at Villiers-aux-Nonnains (F), instead of a Dominican priory as she had originally intended.[81]

In north-east Germany, Bergen, founded as a Benedictine house in 1193 on the island of Rügen, became Cistercian before 1250, and was peopled by nuns from Roskilde in Denmark. In a newly-evangelised area, where many inhabitants had been forced to accept Christianity, it unusually had a hill-top site at an altitude of ninety metres, and gained protection by being located only some 800 metres from the residence of Prince Jaroma.[82]

The nuns of the Order now also spread into Moravia with the foundation first of Oslavany (Mariental; 1224/5), and a decade later of Porta Coeli, close to Tišnov. This well endowed convent was founded on the initiative of Constance, widow of King Přemysl Otakar I of Bohemia, together with her son, Margrave Přemysl of Moravia, in atonement for the sins of her husband, Přemsyl Otakar I, and incorporated in 1234. Its father-abbot was the abbot of Velehrad. Constance was buried there in 1240.[83]

Poland shared in the growth of Cistercian nunneries during the first half of the thirteenth century. First came Ołobok (1213), then (1218) the incorporation of the Benedictine convent in Silesia of Trzebnica, to be followed by Żarnowiec (1235) and lastly Owińska (1245) with nuns from Trezbnica.[84] When the almost royal abbey of Trzebnica, founded by Duke Henry I of Silesia and his wife, St Hedwig, was admitted to the Order in 1218, it was by a charter sealed by the abbot of Cîteaux and the four proto-abbots, acting on 'the authority of the General Chapter and the entire Order'. It was said to be 'fully incorporated and united to our Order'.[85] Honorius III placed it under the care of the abbot of Pforta (January 1220), but soon afterwards (March 1220) under the oversight of the abbot of Lubiąż, a monastery much closer to the nunnery.[86]

Duke Henry invariably noted in the preamble to his charters that his daughter, Gertrude, was a nun of the house;[87] later, of course, she was its abbess.[88] Duke Henry was concerned for the well-being of the nuns, for their 'salt, clothing, meat [food], beer, bread, and all needs and necessities'.[89] He also saw that that they were well provided for on their patronal festival, St Bartholomew's Day (24 August).[90]

The charter of the Benedictine foundation which had been granted in 1203, 'to the honour of God and of blessed Bartholomew the apostle', by Duke Henry, was signed by no less than forty-four witnesses, including the bishop of Breslau, its dean and archdeacon, and two abbots'.[91] His daughter, Blessed Gertrude, became in 1218 its second abbess, and her family connections ensured that when she died in 1269 after an abbacy of fifty years, she left Trzebnica 'in full prosperity, as pilgrimage centre, and populous abbey with a well organised fortune'.[92]

Her mother, St Hedwig, was known for her holy life. After being widowed in 1238, she later came to reside at Trzebnica, dying and being buried there in 1243; her tomb becoming a shrine. As for Duke Henry, legend has it that once whilst out hunting he fell into a swamp from which he could not extricate himself. Rescued, he vowed to build the abbey.[93]

In northern Poland, some of the nuns of Wolin, founded in 1288, migrated in 1305 to settle a new monastery at Krummin on the island of Usedom. Both foundations were made by Duke Bogislaw IV of Pomerania, whose daughter, Jutta, a nun of Wolin, later became abbess of Krummin. It had scattered properties on neighbouring islands, including two millls, a sheep-fold, and an hostel at Ziemitz.[94] Bishop Herman of Camin (1277) confirmed the new foundation of Cistercian nuns from Itzehoe 'on the island of the Blessed Virgin Mary by Koszalin'. He confirmed also grants made to them and gave them fishing rights.[95]

Further afield came the foundation, possibly towards the close of the twelfth century of the convent of St Mary Magdalene in Riga, Latvia, forming part of the Baltic Crusade, and settled by nuns from Germany, who eventually became known as 'the singing sisters'! Further north, at Reval (Tallinn) in Estonia, St Michael's Cistercian nunnery was founded by 1255 by King Eric IV and Queen Margaret of Denmark; he being duke of Estonia and she 'lady of Estonia'. In 1282 King Eric V received from Pope Martin IV a bull of protection for the sisters.[96]

There were but ten Cistercian nunneries in Scandinavia. As they were mostly led by prioresses instead of abbesses, in some cases well into the fourteenth century, they were perhaps incorporations into the Cistercian Order well after their original foundation. It has been argued that there was a negative attitude to Cistercian nuns in the region, but there were positive signs. Certainly they were favoured by royalty, particularly in Sweden: King Karl Sverkerson (1161–7) is considered to have been the founder of Vreta nunnery, and his sister, Ingegerd, the first superior there.

Earl Birger Brose, father-in-law of King Severker Karlson (1195–1210) settled nuns at Riseberga; King Magnus Ladulâs assisted the final foundation of Sko, whilst earlier, in 1250, Queen Katarina had bequeathed to Gudhem, extensive estates in Denmark. She died at Gudhem and was buried there. In Denmark the nunnery of Slangerup was closely connected with that country's royal house. Norway had but one Cistercian nunnery at Bergen.[97]

Cistercian convents appeared in the Near East in the wake of the Crusades. James de Vitry, writing about 1230, told how the nunneries of the Order 'were multiplying like stars in the sky', and also 'newly constructed, in Constantinople and Cyprus, in Antioch, Tripoli and Acre'.[98] Those in Nicosia, Tripoli and Acre were, coincidentally or otherwise, all dedicated to St Mary Magdalene.[99] Their presence is also evidenced by a late-thirteenth-century Oxford manuscript listing the 'daughters' of Cîteaux, which refers to the nunnery of Percheyo in Constantinople, and to those 'beyond the sea': St Mary Magdalene in Acre, St Mary Magdalene in Tripoli (Lebanon today), and those of St Mary Magdalene and of St Theodore in Cyprus.[100]

The convent at Nicosia was settled by nuns from Acre in 1222.[101] Later Moslem incursion meant that those nunneries on the Lebanese and Syrian mainland were short-lived foundations.

In northern Italy Benedictine nuns settled at Rifreddo (1220), Marchese Manfred III of Saluzzo having sold to his aunt, the lady Agnes, for five hundred pounds of Genova money, the entire district of Rifreddo for the construction of a monastery, and at the General Council held at Lyons in 1245 it was incorporated into the Cistercian Order, Innocent IV granting them two bulls of protection. The abbot of Staffarda, but ten kilometres distant, was appointed as their Visitor, but in 1279, for at least a while and after a time of discord between Staffarda and Rifreddo, the abbot of Lucedio fulfilled this role. Urban IV, in 1262, had also confirmed their privileges as members of the Cistercian Order.[102]

In southern Italy a nunnery of note was at Conversano, an ancient ninth-century monastery deserted by 1266, when on the authority of Clement IV it was given to the Cistercian nuns of S.-Marie de Verge in 'la Romagne', who transferred there. The convent was said in 1271 to be 'united and incorporated' as a daughter of Cîteaux, but its position meant that the duty of its visitation was delegated to the abbot of Daphni, Greece. This may have been because the nuns originated in a monastery in the Peloponnese, but also because the abbot of Daphni was well-placed to visit Conversano on his journeying to and from General Chapter. There is note of that in 1271 and 1283, but even so annual visitations were impracticable.[103]

Conversano became an abbey nullius, and the land of Castellane depended totally upon it. The abbess exercised jurisdiction through a priest who was her vicar-general.[104] Much later, the abbesses of Conversano wore a mitre, whilst members of the clergy prostrated before them.[105] In Spain, despite strict enclosure, the nunnery of San Felices de los Barrios, founded in 1219, was attached to the Cistercian-governed military Order of Calatrava. The General Chapter (1220) allowed dispersed nunneries to be united in this foundation as 'Calatrava sisters'.[106]

Where a patron wished to establish a Cistercian nunnery, the benefactor would grant land to the mother-house for this purpose: as when in 1245 Beuren (G) was given land at Welderekeshusen

The Growth of the Female Houses

which became the site of became the site of Mariengarten.[107] Such foundations were often described as 'new plantations of nuns', as at Beuren (1208),[108] Marienkammer (G; 1234),[109] Dûsseren (G; 1237),[110] Leyme (F; 1246 – this twenty-five years after it became Cistercian),[111] Lichtenthal (Baden; 1248);[112] Harvestehude (Frauental, D; 1249);[113] Gotha (Heiligkreuz, G; 1251),[114] and Mariengarten; (Lower Saxony; 1256).[115]

The sisters at Wormeln (D; 1252) were described as being 'a plantation, new and of poverty'.[116] Duke Bogislaw IV of Pomerania (1278), described his father, Barnim I, as having 'planted the nunnery [of Szczecin] to the increase of the Cistercian Order'.[117] The archbishop of Mainz (1233) referred to the Cisterian nuns 'planted' at Neuwerk (Nordhausen).[118] John II, lord of Nesle, chose to be buried on his death in 1230 at Parc-aux-Bois (F) 'in the choir of the nuns at the place which I have planted'.[119] Such terminology suggests that the founders hoped that the convents they 'planted', would prove a godly influence in their localities or in the spiritual life of the Order as a whole. The term 'plantation' was also used when monks setled at Caczicze (? 1218), the first site of Polish Mogiła.[120] The nunnery at Wald (G) was frequently referred to as "God's House, Wald."[121]

When resources and the number of its nuns permitted, a convent would make a new foundation, often at the request of a would-be benefactor, and sometimes because a convent was full to overflowing, and could not support its large contingent. Ten years after its own foundation, Beuren (G; 1260) had sufficient nuns to send ten sisters to settle, with the support of the duke of Brunswick, a new convent at Teistungenburg. The archbishop of Mainz commented in 1265 that the reason for this was that 'on account of poverty Beuren could not sustain many people'.[122] A portion of church land at Teistungenburg was granted for the site by Günzel of Bodenstein, and later (1279) Günther of Hardenberg gave the nuns the third portion of the tithes of Teistungenburg. The provost of Beuren continued to handle the affairs of Teistungenburg, but by 1268 Teistungenburg had its own provost and difficulties arose between him and the mother house.[123]

The nuns of Les Îles, Burgundy, founded Marcilly in 1229, only ten years after moving to their own new site.[124] Blendecques (F), founded in 1182 knew six centuries of peaceful existence, and settled nuns at Woestine (1217) and Verger (1225).[125] St Pons-de-

Gémenos (F) had three daughter-houses in Provence: Lamanarre (1220, where a former Benedictine house was taken over), Mollèges (1235, its nuns moved in 1305 into Arles), and Mount Sion (1242, intended for the daughters of the nobility of the region).[126] The grant to Saint-Pons of Mount Sion consisted of a church and hospital donated by three brothers of the Roquefort family, their relative, Nicola, being the abbess.[127]

Fabas (F) settled Cistercian nuns at Goujon/Goion (by the nuns of Les Îles, Burgundy, founded Marcilly in 1229, only ten years after moving to their own new site.[128] Blendecques (F), founded in 1182 knew six centuries of peaceful existence, and settled nuns at Woestine (1217) and Verger (1225).[129] St Pons-de-Gémenos (F) had three daughter-houses in Provence: Lamanarre (1220, where a former Benedictine house was taken over), Mollèg es (1235, its nuns moved in 1305 into Arles), and Mount Sion 1167), Orthez and Salenques (1353).[130]

Leyme settled five nunneries: Castejean (1220), Les Bouysses (1232), Lazières (1272), Lissac (1286), and Vic-du-Cielac (1360), and others.[131] Founded in 1196, the nunnery of Brayelle-les-Aulnay was favoured by Blanche of Sicily (d. 1269) and Margaret of Constantinople (d. 1273); allowing it to settle four daughter-houses: Notre-Dame-des Prés (*c.* 1200), Beaupré-sur-Lys (1224), Saulchoir (1233) and Biache (1235).[132]

EARLY RELATIONS WITH THE MALE ORDER

The early statutes of the General Chapter virtually ignore the question of nuns and nunneries, and it was not until 1213 that a decree specifically dealt with them, placing their care and annual visitation under a father abbot, but are the records complete? In time this changed, and in 1241 twenty of the seventy-five statutes were concerned with the need and demands of religious ladies.[133] The 1257 codification of the statutes of the General Chapter contained but eleven chapters referring to the nuns.[134] These were:

Whoever made the canonical visitation of a nunnery was to write into the charter of visitation on whose authority the visitation took place; (2) restriction was placed on the number of nunneries wishing to be associated with the Order; (3) only the official Visitors were to enter the cloister; (4) arrangements outlined for the hearing

The Growth of the Female Houses

of nuns confessions; and the stipulation that no abbess or nun was to attend the General Chapter; (5) no nun was to talk with seculars save through the appointed window; Visitors were to determine the number of nuns; (6) formal visitation was always to be done by father-abbots; an abbess might visit her daughter houses in a less formal and charitable manner, but might not vary anything decreed by the father abbot; (7) strict enclosure, but an abbess or cellarer might go out on business of the house; (8) dealt with the habit; (9) of the blessing and profession of nuns, and when an abbess might use her pastoral staff; (10) of the expulsion and imprisonment of nuns; (11) the form of profession of chaplains and *conversi*.

Not all nuns were happy with a loss of independence. Around 1225 the nuns of Moncey were at odds with the neighbouring abbot of Fontaines-le-Blanche, whilst in 1321 the abbot of Loroux (F) complained that the nuns of Bonlieu rejected his authority, and refused to accept their appointed confessor.[135] In 1243 it was reported to the General Chapter of thirteen named convents that they locked out the official Visitors, or shouted or clapped hands to drown out the reading of their decrees.[136]

The bull, *Parvus Fons*, issued by Clement IV in 1265 constantly referred to the abbots and monks of the Order, but seemed oblivious to the presence of nuns; of them there is no mention.[137] He did take cognisance of them by fixing their maximum numbers in particular convents. Pope Clement also referred to nuns wandering abroad and staying in the houses of relatives under the pretext of seeking food.[138]

There were more contacts between Cistercian monks and nuns than often supposed as at Villers (B), where both abbots and even *conversi* of experience had a role to play. It was Goswin, precentor at Villers (d. 1238), who wrote the *Life of Ida of Nivelles* shortly before she died in 1231, following that up with an account of lay-brother Arnuf, who had died earlier in 1228. It was Goswin who coined the term 'religious women' for the perhaps less polite 'beguines'.[139]

Villers had several nunneries under its oversight, as Aywières, Salzinnes, La Ramée and Valduc.[140] Abbot Walter of Utrecht (1214–27) of Villers showed great zeal in attracting male and female vocations; the *Chronicle of Villers* says that 'he created many houses of our Order in the diocese of Liège, but he also resigned eight female communities into the hands of the abbot of Cîteaux', as he was concerned that the younger monks of his house might suffer if too many senior monks were absent as chaplains or confessors of nuns.[141]

Abbot William of Brussels (1221–37/38) saw the affiliation of six nunneries, and later 'supported beguines in their spiritual and economic needs, appearing after his death to a recluse with whom he had a spiritual friendship'.[142] He also was close to the Grand Beguinage at Louvain; and Abbot Arnulf de Ghisheles (1270–6) revised its statutes.[143] Abbot Arnulf of Louvain of Villers (1240–8) after his resignation 'only left the monastery to visit the recluses and pious souls''.[144] Abbot Robert de Blocquerie (1283–1302) was appointed by the bishop of Liège as Visitor of the beguinages in his diocese.[145] Another abbey significant in the care of Cistercian nuns was Camp (G), which had oversight of twenty-four convents.[146]

A notable mystic of the times was Arnulf, a *conversus* of Villers, whose duties for a time included that of waggoner. Entering the monastery when about twenty-years old in around 1202, and dying there in 1228, he had a special devotion to the joys of Mary. A poem written about 1600 concerning him said: 'An ascetic he was, brilliantly virtuous, sportimg the stigmata of Christ scorch-branded into his flesh'.[147]

Given to wearing a hair-shirt, and to performing penances, such as self-flagellaton, it was he who persuaded Blanche of Champagne to found a Cistercian convent at Argensolles, and Gilles Berthout, lord of Malines, to found another at Val-des-Roses. Furthermore, he helped a young poor girl to realise her vocation, built a cell for her and sought aid for her maintenance.[148]

A *conversus* of Villers, John de Witterzée, master of its Chênoit grange, seeing the poverty of the nuns of the beguines of Nivelles directed to them wheat meant for his abbey. He himself wore a shirt and a pair of leggings made of sack-cloth; when a beguine begged at the gate of Villers, the porter, Gobert, gave her a pair of shoes.[149]

Amongst the monks of Villers was Godfrey Pachôme, who would visit the 'holy saints' of Nivelles 'to know more heavenly conversation rather than earthly'.[150] Thomas, precentor, and brother and biographer of Godfrey, wrote letters full of ascetic and mystical subjects to his sister, Aleide, a nun of Parc-les-Dames.[151] The recluse, Ode de Namur, saw a globe of fire descend upon the head of a monk of Villers, Ultric, whilst he celebrated Mass.[152] The monks of Villers and of Aulne sought the prayers of the mystics in their

The Growth of the Female Houses

affairs.[153] Earlier, in 1176, Hildegarde of Bingen had addressed to the monks of Villers her *Liber vitae meritorum*.[154]

Godard, a well-travelled and experienced monk, and retired abbot of Newenham (E), around 1250 wrote a treatise for Abbess Matilda of Tarrant (E) giving advice for her duties and the way of life of her nuns. It opened with the words, 'So run that you may obtain' (1 Cor. 9, v. 24).[155] In the 1170s Roger of Ford had a copy of Elizabeth of Schönau's vision copied out and given to Baldwin of Ford's mother who had become a nun.[156] Adam of Perseigne (*c.* 1200) also wrote a treatise for nuns, and corresponded with Agnes, a nun of Fontevrault, she probably becoming first abbess of Cistercian Les Clairets under his influence.[157] Simon, a conversus of Aulne, had at the former double-monastery of Benedictine Maubeuge 'a spiritual daughter', while a nun, Lutgard of Aywières, knowing Simon's remarkable gifts, had recourse for his assistance in delivering a nun possessed by demons.[158]

THE RELIGIOUS WOMEN'S MOVEMENT: THE DAUGHTERS OF GOD AND THE BEGUINAGES

In the first half of the thirteenth century, throughout northern France and beyond significant numbers of women left the comforts of families and friends to live in granges, small chapels, hospices, hospitals and leper communities on the margins of urban centres, or alongside the major trade routes. Many of these women were penitents, known as 'religious women' or 'daughters of God'. They did not, in Champagne, take the title of beguines until canon law demanded it in the fourteenth century. Other women, also with a penitential mindset, cared for the sick and poor labouring within or near small *domus Dei*, hospices and leprosaria, where they put into practice the apostolic ideals of poverty and charity.[159]

Many of the Cistercian convents in Champagne began life as communities of such 'daughters of God' (Filles-Dieu), and before they became the convent of Notre-Dame-des-Près (1230) the women at Chichéry were referred to by that title. In 1229 a knight, Philip of Mécringes, who had supported thirteen young 'daughters of God' founded the convent of La Piété-Dieu, near Ramerupt, along the road from Troyes to Vitry-le-François. After becoming Cistercian such convents were to some extent transformed to some extent.

Two nearby convents, La Grâce and Le Jardin sent nuns to the beguinage of La Piété on its wish to join the Order, to guide the 'daughters of God' there into the Cistercian life and liturgy.[160] In 1234 Louis IX gave the 'daughters of God' of Orléans, to the west of Champagne, several acres of vineyard, and then a further donation. This encouraged the ladies who began to wear white habits, move to St.-Loup, and who a decade later were incorporated into the Order.[161]

In 1230 monks of Montier-la-Celle complained to Pope Gregory IX of certain women esconced in a farm-house at Chichéry, who wore white habits and committed themselves to a life of penance and piety. The monks grumbled because the ladies professed to be part of the Cistercian Order, but did not observe its customs; they were not cloistered but wandered about.[162] The farm-house, outside Troyes, had been given to the women by Stephen of Champagne, one of the rising burgher artisan class, and possibly a goldsmith. It became later Notre-Dame des-Prés.

Stephen's motives are hard to know; indeed patrons rarely spell out their motives, but members of the urban bourgeoisie were, with their wives, the most consistent supporters of the new communities of nuns. In 1236, after the nunnery had gained more lands and been incorporated into the Order, Stephen and his wife stood in front of the cathedral in Troyes and bequeathed to the nuns Chichéry and its appurtenances.[163]

Beuren (G) developed around 1200 from a 'Gotteshaus' established in Lower Beuren in the mid-12th Century by Rudolf von Bodenstein. Cistercian nuns were around 1200 given St Andrew's church there on the authority of Cardinal-Bishop Guy von Praeneste. The foundation was supported by Innocent III and the archbishop of Mainz.[164] The nunnery of La-Joie, Picardy, originated in an ancient lazar-house dedicated to St Claire.[165] Exceptionally within the Cistercian Order, the abbot of Villers took over the administration of the lazar-house of Ter Banck (B) in 1224 at the request of its founder, the duke of Brabant, but the nuns there continued to live according to the Augustinian rule.[166]

The term "religious women" also covered several sub-groups of nuns, recluses and virgins, living at home or in small groups, the latter being the 'beguines', and intent on a life of prayer and charitable works like caring for the sick.[167] From 1242 on the beguines grouped their numerous small houses (accommodating all told certainly over five thousand pious women) in walled-off beguinages, as a kind of city within a city.[168] The origin of the beguines, and of their name, has been the subject of several theories, and the religious life varied between the beguinages.

The beguines had no common habit nor common rule. They did not take solemn vows, but promised to observe chastity during their stay in a beguinage; without making a vow of poverty they lived a humble and modest life, with the expectation that they would attend Mass daily and make their confession monthly. They undertook manual work, as in the cloth industry of the times. The religious fervour of the beguines within the diocese of Liège saw not only the publication of devotional psalters for their use, but also led to the establishment of the feast of Corpus Christi.[169]

Initially under the protection of St Louis in France, beguines came to be found in the Low Countries, Germany and Switzerland, and there were even a few beguinages in Spain, Bohemia and Poland. There came to be sixty houses of beguines in Strasbourg and 141 in Cologne. They were a form of religious life more accessible to the urban populations. They recited the divine office in parish churches and by the mid-thirteenth century groups of beguines were uniting with an oratory or church, an infirmary, or a cemetery chapel. In 1264 St Louis constructed in Paris a beguinage accommodating 400 beguines, under the spiritual direction of the Dominicans. At the height of the movement there were ninety-four beguinages in Belgium and thirty-eight in Holland.

James of Vitry implied that beguines and 'religious women' preferred to follow the Cistercian way of life rather that of the older Orders, such as the Augustinians, Benedictines, and Premonstratensians. In the countries most affected by these movements the foundation and incorporation of Cistercian nunneries was high: in the first half of the thirteenth century over one hundred and fifty in Germany and sixty-six in in Belgium. Requests from the counts and countesses of Flanders to the General Chapter accounted for twenty-one in Belgium, one-third of them all.[170]

Jacques de Vitry was a great supporter of the beguines, though some suspected them of heresy. He wrote the biography of Maria d'Oignies, the Belgian beguine who achieved sanctity and died in 1213.[171] Beatrice of Nazareth (B) spent over one year with a group of beguines in Zoutleeuw before she joined the Cistercian nuns of Bloemendaal or Florica (B). Ida of Nivelles (B) lived for six or seven years with seven beguines in Nivelles, and Ida of Gorsleeuw before she went, as Ida of Nivelles did, to Rameya (La Ramée), had close contact with them. Ida of Leeuwen was a 'religious woman' before she became a nun in Roosendaal. Indeed, the Cistercian Roosendaal near Malines traces its origins back to four recluses.[172]

A 'community of devoted women' established by 1202 at Aywières (B) transferred to the Order after its principal benefactor obtained the approval of Pope Innocent III and local bishops by 1207, becoming the Cistercian house of Aywières. Its site vacillated between that date and 1215, because of a lack of water at an intermediate site at Lillois (1210–15). The papal bull of 1211 placed the nuns under the oversight of Aulne, and termed the convent St Mary's instead of the initial dedication to St Stephen.[173]

Notre-Dame-des-Prés (F) was a beguinage placed in 1186 by the abbot of Clairvaux under the tutelage of the abbot of Vaucelles, the chapter of Saint-Amé opposing this move. The leader of the beguinage, Frissent, made three journeys unaccompanied to Rome regarding the matter. In 1218 Honorius III permitted the beguinage to become a priory with it own chaplain, and the group then moved into the countryside. On her third journey to Rome in 1221 Honorius III elevated the priory into an abbey and placed it under the protection of the Holy See.[174]

In Baden the beguinage of Heggbach, founded in 1195, became Cistercian in 1234, due to the efforts of Cardinal Konrad von Urach, himself a Cistercian, and the abbot of Salem.[175] In Bavaria the beguinage of Ste Agnes, Lauingen, founded in 1270, was incorporated in 1319,[176] as had been the beguinage which became the Cistercian nunnery of Oberschönenfeld in 1248.[177] At Feldbach (Swz), a beguinage from 1252, four years later it was within the Cistercian fold.[178] Wettingen (Swz) received the care of Selnau (1256; outside the walls of Zurich). Gutenzell (G; 1237) sprang from a community of women who thanked and served God 'through prayer, reading, singing, fasting and vigils'.[179]

The nunnery of Baindt (G) developed from a 'pious association of beguines', whose spiritual direction had been undertaken by Abbot Everard of Salem; about 1232 they adopted the Rule of St Benedict with the usages of Cîteaux. They moved to Baindt from a site near Lake Constance, and once incorporated were placed under the oversight of Salem.[180] Incorporated in the Order in 1222, at the request of Honorius III, and also forming part of Salem's family, was a community of nuns at Rottheil, the new monastery being known as Marienal or Rottenmünster.[181] Other admissions of beguinages to the Order included Fontenelle (F; 1218) and Magdenau (Switzerland, 1244).[182] A late development of a Cistercian nunnery from a beguinage was Gnadenthal (Swz) in 1344.[183]

Later in the thirteenth century the beguines and 'religious women' were sometimes suspected of heresy. The Franciscan bishop of Tournai (1273) complained that 'there are among us women called beguines, some of whom blossom forth in subtleties and rejoice in novelties. They interpret in vernacular French idiom the mysteries of Scripture which are scarcely accessible to experts in divine writings. They read aloud in common irreverently and boldly, in convents and public squares'. This was one of three reports sent to Gregory II in preparation for the Council of Lyons II the next year.[184]

The flow of 'religious women' to the Order declined after 1251 when Innocent IV allowed the Cistercians to ignore papal letters recommending, at the request of others, the incorporation of nuns if these letters did not mention word by word the privilege *Paci et tranquillitati* given to them to that effect. In 1244 the General Chapter had made incorporations more difficult by demanding not only the explicit consent of the local bishop but also that of his cathedral chapter.[185] The movement faded further in the early fourteenth century with the condemnation of begardism by Clement V (1305–14), and in some places their goods were confiscated, but John XXII (1316–34) took a different and more appeasing attitude.

There were some continuing contacts between Cistercian women and the beguines. A beguine of Nil-St-Vincent, Ida (1277), seems to have handed over the beguinage to Val-St-Georges.[186] Another beguine, Helvis of Jambes (1291), gave Val-St-Georges (B) an annual grant of four measures of 'spelt corn' from four 'bonniers' of land, to provide twice a year a pittance of wine for its nuns.[187] Yet another beguine, Gertrude of Eussenheim (1306), gave the nuns of Himmelspforten (G) a vineyard close to another which the nuns already owned at the village of Eussenheim.[188]

THE HOSPITALS

In his visitation of his nunneries Stephen Lexington, Abbot of Savigny (1230s), urged them only to receive as guests 'the manifestly sick and truly poor'.[189] Some Cistercian nunneries in Flanders originated in congregations of women who cared for the sick and poor, as the hospital of Sint-Gillis by Dendermunde. After its incorporation into the Cistercian Order the community moved in 1228 to a more apt location at Zwijveke.[190]

Over half of those female communities in Champagne that became Cistercian in the 1230s began life as hospices (*domus dei*) or leper-houses. By 1191 a group of women outside the new town of Villuis, close to Sens, had started caring for lepers. In 1236 they were incorporated into the Order as La Cour Notre-Dame-de-Michery.[191]

It was perhaps a growth in numbers that caused a move to Michery, although some nuns remained at Villuis – where at the original convent nuns, around 1268, cared for eighteen children – perhaps the offspring of lepers, whilst at the nearby leper-house a further seven nuns cared for the lepers.[192]

Bishop Jacques de Bazoches of Soissons (1219–42) reformed the leper house of Berneuil, and it was incorporated La Joie Notre-Dame ino the Cistercian Order. The nunnery of St.-Jacques-de-Vitry was originally founded in the *domus dei* of Vitry in 1233 by Count Thibaut IV. Here the needs of the sick and poor continued to be catered for, and the income donated for the lepers administered. The bishop of Chalons (1289) was later to challenge the control of the sisters over another leper-house at Montmirail, but the rights of the nuns were upheld by Parisian judges. By 1290 'the connection between Cistercian nuns and lepers was enforced both in custom and by law'.[193]

Of the forty Cistercian nunneries founded in the dioceses of Sens and Rheims after 1200, about one-third were connected to hospitals and *domus dei*. Where existing hospitals continued to be maintained, it is probable that the lay sisters served their needs.[194] At Bonneweg (L), however, there is reference in 1238 to the leper-house which 'formerly' stood within the enclosure.[195]

La-Piété-Dieu (F) negotiated with interested parties to retain possession of the *domus dei* within its holdings and of the leper-house of Ramerupt. As well as the bishop of Troyes, the Cister-

The Growth of the Female Houses

cian abbots of Cîteaux, Clairvaux and Boulancourt played a part in these proceedings, as they had in mind 'the reception of the infirm and the works of charity that often take place in houses of this sort'. The nuns consented to pay a priest to care for the souls of sick and annual tithes to canons who had claimed certain rights.[196]

La Barre was a *domus dei*, a hospital for the poor. In 1235, after it had been a hospital for twenty-four years, Thibaut IV gave it to Cecilia d'Arcy who, with the community of women already in residence, converted it into the Cistercian nunnery of La Barre (F), which continued to maintain the original *domus dei*.[197]

Countess Jean of Flanders (1237) had intended that a hospital for the poor be constructed within the precincts at Marquette, but 'on the advice of wise men' released the nuns from any obligation towards it; the hospital was transferred to Lille, and the nuns renounced the large sums of money intended for it annually – no less than two hundred pounds for the use of the 'poor infirm' there, as well as forty pounds to maintain two chaplains in the hospital.[198]

After the nuns at Orchies moved to Flines (F) the first site became, by 1257, a hospital owned by the nunnery.[199] Charles V of France (king, 1364–80) gave the revenues of an eleven-bed hospital at Gaillefontaine to Bival (F), whilst the local lord granted timber from the forest there for the maintenance of the hospital buildings.[200] In 1327 Fraupriessnitz (G) set up the ten-bed Lorenz Hospital, but the care of it was too great, and ten years later it was given over to the Moritzhospital in Naumburg.[201] From 1253 to 1289 the short-lived nunnery at Grimma (G) had the care of the nearby Elisabeth Hospital, founded by the Margrave of Meissen in 1240.[202]

In Scotland St Leonard's Hospital, Perth, was reputedly a Cistercian nunnery.[203] In Italy, Rifreddo (1265) was granted the hospice of Bergondio Parasacco di Diano.[204] The account book of its abbesses refer to 'the hospital and nursing' maintained by the nuns of Frauenroth (G).[205] The nunnery of Mansfeld – later at Helfta (G; 1229), had amongst the earliest of the properties granted it 'the house of the hospital of St Catharine' at Ysleben.[206] The convent of St Agnes in Mainz originate in 1250 when the sisters withdrew from a double-community with nursing duties at Kilstock nearby.[207]

In 1232 Hugh of Châtillon and a knight, Philip of Mécringes founded the nunnery of L'Amour Dei in the *domus dei* of Troissy and, at the request of Blanche of Castille and supported by a papal bull, it was incorporated into the Cistercian Order in 1237/40. Its foundation charter asserted that 'it was, should be and always will be a hospital for the poor'.[208] A hospital of brothers and sisters tending reformed prostitutes, Saint-Antoine-des-Champs, near Paris, was incorporated in 1208, at the request of the bishop of Paris, the General Chapter ruling in 1213 that no monk or *conversus* was to eat or spend a night there,[209] but later its location meant that university students practised sermons there, whilst monks and *conversi* on business in the city sought food and lodging of it.[210]

Beutitz (Beuditz, Saxony) had its origins in a hospital founded in 1218 at Prissetz by Mechtild of Lobdabourg, it passed to the Cistercians in 1232 and transferred to Beuditz.[211] Ludmilla, countess of Bavaria, founded Seligenthal (1232) at the Hospital of the Holy Spirit close to the bridge in Landeshut.[212]

Around 1200 a noble lady Ermentrude de Utenhove founded a hospital in Ghent which became a small religious community. Many of its nuns desiring to be Cistercians migrated to a new abbey between Lokeren and Zeveneeken founded for them by Count Ferrand and Countess Jean of Flanders and Hainaut, at Bijloke on the bank of the river Lys, and to be known as Notre-Dame-au-Bois.

In 1215 this new abbey was incorporated into the Order, but the few hospitaller sisters who remained in Ghent regarded the abbey as their mother house and the abbess as their superior. As the abbey was a good distance away the situation was inconvenient, and so by 1229 a new abbey had been built at Bijloke and the hospital in Ghent made a dependency of it. Theoretically, only the lay sisters and servants were allowed to work in the hospital and have contact with lay people, while the nuns lived in the cloister and worked in the pharmacy preparing medicines.[213]

Different precincts enclosed the hospital and the convent in Ghent, and within the fine large brick complex erected during the thirteenth century, a hospital continued to be maintained. Its administration passed in 1234 from the nuns of Nieuwenbosch (Ter Bosch) who had settled sisters there, to the new community at Bijloke. That year the abbot of Clairvaux determined that the goods of the hospital and of the abbey be separated. In 1246 forty nuns formed the community at Byloque.[214] Between 1231 and 1251 numerous grants and privileges were made, whilst Abbess Maria Uten Hove (1249–85) constructed at Byloque a new precinct wall. Alas, in 1314, the sick of the hospital had occasion to complain of bad treatment.[215] The hall of the hospital, with its fine mid-thirteenth century timber roof, survives.

In Spain, in 1210, a hospice for pilgrims on route to Compostella, The King's Hospital (Hospital del Rey), was founded by Alfonso VIII at the front of the abbey court at Las Huelgas, some five hundred metres WNW of the conventual buildings. The monarch, at the request of his wife, placed it under the oversight of the abbess of Las Huelgas, and in 1235 Gregory IX confirmed it as a possession of the abbey.

It had a double-community to care for the pilgrims consisting of twelve 'freyles' and eight 'freylas', who made their profession before the abbess, promising obedience 'according to the Rule of our Father Saint Benedict, and the Institutes of the Order of Cîteaux'. They were headed by one of their number as 'mayor', whom they elected, subject to confirmation by the abbess. The other brethren held diverse positions within their community, as almoner, infirmarian and accountant.

In 1294, Sancho IV gave the Hospital to the Knights of Calatrava, but on the protestations of the abbess, the grant was revoked.[216] The hospital catered both for the very poor, and for pilgrims en route to Santiago de Compostella, to whom fixed amounts of food and drink were daily served.[217]

INCORPORATED MONASTERIES AND HERMITAGES

Whilst certain abbots, as Eberhard of Salem [1194–?1245][218] and Walter of Villers [1214–21], were to the fore in co-founding new monasteries, or encouraging existing convents to join the Order, the General Chapter tried repeatedly to stem the flow. Several of its injunctions, however, were not absolute, but left a loop-hole so that new additions were not barred altogether. In 1220 General Chapter determined that no convents already members of other Orders should be admitted, but this rule was soon to fall into abeyance.[219] In 1222 the Chapter stipulated that no house was to be incorporated *unless* sufficiently endowed; this it said was important as strict enclosure meant that the nuns would not be able to go out to beg.[220]

In 1225 the Chapter ruled that no new foundations were to be made, nor existing nunneries incorporated, *unless* suitable property and buildings could be assured. In 1228 the prohibition allowed of no qualification, *save* that if a convent wished to follow Cistercian usages the Chapter would not stop it, but would decline any responsibility for visitation and spiritual oversight.[221] The requirement of strict enclosure was repeatedly stressed.[222]

It is noteworthy that the statutes of General Chapter frequently avoided the word 'incorporate'; other expressions being used, such as being 'in the society of the Order' or 'associated' with it.[223] In 1235 the future incorporation of further nunneries was foreseen. The codification of statutes completed in 1240 contained intentional loop-holes: at the request of popes or when otherwise unavoidable new incorporations could be accepted, on the conditions stipulated in 1225 that the buildings be completed, self-support guaranteed, and cloister respected, but those enclosure stipulations were certainly not absolute.[224]

The wave of incorporations reached its peak in the 1230s and 1240s; indeed in one year alone, 1244, no less than twelve existing religious houses (or their patrons on their behalf) wished to be admitted to the Order; in 1247 the number was eleven. IIn 1251, Innocent IV issued a bull promising firmly that the papacy would not request any more incorporations. Only now did the numbers of would-be members slacken seriously, and by this time the Dominicans and Franciscans were accepting women into the religious life. There was still a trickle of known requests for Cistercian membership by nunneries until late in the thirteenth century and beyond.[225]

From 1244 new foundations and incorporations of nunneries could be made only *if* the diocesan bishop issued a charter freeing the nuns from all episcopal jurisdiction. In 1245 came the further provision that such a charter must have both the bishop's seal and that of his cathedral chapter attached.[226] In this vein, the General Chapter approved the incorporation of San Donato Polverosa (1281; Tuscany) 'so long as the assent and favour of the diocesan bishop was obtained'.[227]

The nuns of 'St James de Palude' (1255), experienced many problems in regard to their liberties after their incorporation from the bishop of Torcello, himself a Premonstratensian canon.[228] In 1258 the bishop of Prague approved the incorporation of the nunnery of Sifridsdorf; this became known as Mariental or Oslavany.[229] In 1279 the bishop and chapter of Merseburg, after a time of dissension,

The Growth of the Female Houses

agreed that as Grimma (Nimbschen; G) was incorporated into the Order, it enjoyed the rights and privileges thereunto pertaining.[230]

Many nunneries were never formally incorporated, although they claimed to be Cistercian and following Cistercian custom – this was certainly true in England and in North Germany – where of the many convents only one, Liliental in Lower Saxony, is known to have been incorporated. The rest came under the control of the archbishops of Bremen and Hamburg and their cathedral chapters.[231]

One of these was Himmelpforten, Lower Saxony, whose nuns were referred to in 1255 as 'handmaids of Christ; never incorporated but considered Cistercian'. It superiors were sometimes termed 'abbess', sometimes 'prioress'.[232] Himmelau, a Benedictine house established in 1313, followed Cistercian customs from 1323, but remained under the authority of the archbishops of Mainz.[233] Neukloster (Sonnenkamp), a Benedictine house founded in 1219, introduced Cistercian observances after 1245, but remained under the jurisdiction of the bishop of Schwerin. Its church pre-dates the Cistercian times.[234] Charter evidence is that it also came under the oversight of the abbot of Doberan.[235]

Heiligkreuz (Eisenberg; G) was under episcopal jurisdiction but followed Cistercian rule, habit and observances. Like others in Thuringia it grew out of a group of beguines. Late in the day, in 1337, it was incorporated into the Cistercian Order with the approval of Benedict XII[236] Mariengarten (Neuwerk), was founded a little before 1186 in Goslar, Lower Saxony, by a group of twelve Benedictine nuns of Ichtershausen, Thuringia; they followed the Cistercian rule but were also never fully incorporated. With generous grants of land the nunnery prospered; for the greater part the nuns were of noble stock.[237]

Sophie von Stolberg the chronicler of Helfta, writing in the later Middle Ages, asserted that it was Cistercian but not incorporated.[238] Holthausen (G; fd. c. 1253) was not incorporated but followed Cistercian customs and observances.[239] Lucius II (1144) referred to the nuns of Wechterswinkel (G; founded 1134/35) as following the Rule of St Benedict, but also as being Cistercian.[240]

Ichtershausen (G) followed Cistercian customs and observances, and was accounted Cistercian but not incorporated. It had bonds of fraternity with the abbots of Pforta and Volkenrode, but in 1157 two Benedictine abbots were appointed as its Visitors. Archbishop

Henry of Mainz blessed its first abbess in 1147, and the convent was assured of free election of abbess and provost.[241] Ilm (G), was never incorporated although it too followed Cistercian customs. Its regular visitation was undertaken some times by a Cistercian abbot, at other times by a Benedictine superior.[242]

Several of the English nunneries were never incorporated and were firmly under the oversight of their diocesans, chiefly the archbishops of York and the bishops of Lincoln.[243] There were fifteen Cistercian nunneries in medieval Poland, but only three – Trzebnica, Ołobok and Owinska, were formally incorporated into the Order. Together with Żarnowiec, Toruń and Kimbarówka, they were subject to visitation by abbots of the Order; the remainder under the jurisdiction of local bishops.[244]

BENEDICTINE MONASTERIES

It is impossible to count the number of incorporated nunneries as opposed to those simply following the Cistercian way of life. Certainly a number of Benedictine houses were amongst them, as Fürstenberg (G). A Benedictine abbey by 1144, in 1259, despite protests from some of the religious, the abbot of Siegburg ceded the monastery to Cistercian nuns from Horst. Until at least 1284 some Benedictine nuns appear to have continued to reside there, with a separate choir and a secular priest.

.The Cistercian nunnery of St John in Lübeck was founded as a male Benedictine abbey in 1177, but in the early thirteenth century nuns were allowed to become members, and in 1245, on it becoming Cistercian, the monks removed to a new location in Cismar.[245] Their move followed dissension within the community,[246] but for a decade problems regarding possessions arose between the outgoing monks and the incoming nuns.[247] In his bull of 1254, Innocent IV favoured the nuns.[248] At Isenhagen (G), Cistercian nuns replaced Cistercian monks who had moved elsewhere by 1265.[249]

Poulangy (F) had been founded in 637: firstly it was a Benedictine house then changed to Augustinian allegiance before its incorporation into the Cistercian Order at St Bernard's request in 1149. Indeed his young niece, Adeline, entered there and became abbess in 1157, after her uncle's death. A century on, in 1230, chafing at subjection to Tart, some of its community wished to place themselves under the bishop of Langres and their temporal goods under the protection of the count of Champagne.

The archbishop of Bar decided that the monastic life at Poulangy should continue according to the usages of Tart, and that the abbess of Poulangy should attend the annual chapter at Tart. In 1234, however, the nuns became Benedictine again, only to return to the Cistercian fold a hundred years later.[250] In like manner, Neuburg, Baden, became Cistercian in 1303 but returned to the Benedictine fold in 1460.[251] Another incorporated Benedictine filiation of Tart was Vauxbons, founded around 1181 by Thibaud of Saint-Loup, in favour of his daughter, Lucy, who became its first abbess.[252]

Other formerly Benedictine houses to become Cistercian included: St Felix de Montceau (Languedoc; founded around 1150, incorporated 1165);[253] Fontaine-Guérard (Normandy; founded in 1135, incorporated in 1189);[254] Le-Perray-aux-Nonnains (Loire valley; founded around 1185, incorporated 1246, and placed under the oversight of Loroux);[255] Soleilmont (B), founded 1088; (affiliated 1237/38, at the request of Countess Jean of Flanders and Hainaut, and of the bishop of Liège);[256] Eisenberg (G; 1337, with the approval of Benedict XII);[257] St-Annen (Ho), affiliated 1342);[258] Midwolda (Ho; around 1259);[259] After the Benedictines of Trimunt, Holland, were incorporated in 1339, and placed under the oversight of Aduard, it was not long before that nunnery became simply a grange of Aduard.[260]

Around 1196, a Benedictine nun of Brussels, Gisele, sought to embrace the Cistercian life. It was not easy, but she found a protector in Abbot Charles de Seyne of Villers, and benefactors in Duke Henry I of Brabant and his wife, Matilda, who gave the necessary donations for the foundation of La Cambre.[261] When Florival, previously Benedictine was incorporated, it was after Abbess Genta had travelled to Rome where Pope Honorius III (1217) confirmed the move. She died in 1247, and was buried in the choir of her abbey church. Genta was described on her tombstone as 'an ark of devout faith', and she strictly led the Cistercian life: 'she slept in the common dormitory and ate in the refectory'.[262]

In Germany, Sonnenkamp, founded as a Benedictine house in 1219, passed to the Cistercians in 1245; Althaldensleben, founded in 965, passed to the Order in in 1228,[263] Rohrbach, founded in 1117 was incorporated in around 1275;[264] Blankenau in Hesse, founded in 1265 for Benedictine nuns became Cistercian in 1331;[265] and

Marienkron by Mainz (Cistercian from 1250),[266] but Marienborn (Westphalia) may have been Cistercian from its inception.[267]

Disibodenberg, incorporated in 1259, had been a Benedictine foundation since the seventh century, and took its name from St Disibod who evangelised the region (Rhineland) in the sixth century.[268] Ramsen (Ramosa), Rhineland, Benedictine since 1146 passed to the Cistercians in 1267,[269] as did Rupertsberg, Benedictine since 1147, in 1215; and Sankt-Thomas-an-der-Kyll, also in the Rhineland, Benedictine from 1171 and named after St Thomas Becket; Cistercian from 1185.[270]

Olsberg (Swz), Benedictine from 1083, was occupied by Cistercians in 1172.[271] A charter of Innocent IV implies that the Benedictine nuns of Bergen (G) were already following Cistercian usages 'before the Council', i.e.: prior to 1215. This suggests that the nuns came to join the Order soon after their foundation in 1193. Their appointed father-abbot was the abbot of Eldena, at the time the only abbey within easy reach of Bergen. When, in 1306, the knight Pritbor of Vilmnitz wanted his daughter to become a nun at Bergen he had to seek permission from Abbot Henry of Eldena.[272]

In Tuscany, the Benedictine community of Santa Maria della Visitatione, Siena, adopted Cistercian statutes in 1213.[273] In Galicia, Ferreira del Pantón had been Benedictine since at least 924 when it was absorbed into the Cistercian Order in 1175.[274] In Navarre, the Benedictine nunnery of Cañas also became Cistercian.[275] In Castile, the Benedictine nunnery of Villamayor, Castile, became a Cistercian monastery soon after its foundation around 1224.[276]

In Portugal, the Benedictine nunnery of Semide was occupied by 'non-affiliated' Cistercian nuns from 1183.[277] In England, Rosedale was founded as a Benedictine house in 1189, perhaps becoming Cistercian ten years later. In Denmark, Slangerup was Benedictine at its foundation in 1170, but passed into the Cistercian Order only six years later.[278]

MONASTERIES OF OTHER ORDERS

Sites originally Premonstratensian which passed to the Cistercians included: Goion (F), settled by nuns from Fabas before 1167;[279] Abbenrode (G; perhaps in 1252);[280] Sko (Sw; in 1225;[281] and Ivanics (Hg; at an uncertain date).[282] Freisdorf/Freistroff (F; *fd.* 1130), a

The Growth of the Female Houses

monastery which at first housed canons regular, some decades later was occupied briefly by Cistercian nuns. About 1200 they were replaced by Premonstratensan canons, but in 1208, at the demand of Duke Matthew I of Lorraine, the Cistercian nuns regained possession.[283] The nunnery of Buenafuente (Sp) passed into Cistercian hands from canons regular in 1246.[284]

A house of Augustinan canons at Watten, founded in 1195 – was replaced in 1217 by nuns of Blendecques (F).[285] Other Augustinian nunneries which were incorporated included Vrouenpark (Parc-les-Dames (B; incorporated in 1215 under the direction of the abbot of Villers);[286] Robertmont (B; incorporated in 1215 at request of Bishop Robert of Verdun, the abbey now taking his name);[287] Vivegnis (B; received in 1236 at the request of the bishop of Liège and the duke of Lotharingia);[288] the duke also requesting the 'association' of Guldenberg (B) in 1237.[289]

Yet more Augustinian nunneries becoming Cistercian included Zissendorf (G; in 1247 on the instructions of the papal legate);[290] and Rossleben (G; in 1263)[291] Contrariwise, the Cistercian nunnery of Codenham, Suffolk (E), in existence by 1204, later passed to the Canons Regular of St Augustine.[292] Bickenkloster, near Villingen in the Black Forest, was founded as a Cistercian nunnery by 1238, but thirty years later, in 1268, it moved into the town of Villingen and became Franciscan, adopting the rule and habit of the Clarisses.[293]

Cistercian nuns of Gereuth in 1251 occupied a Dominican house in the town of Friesach, Austria.[294] In 1333 Cistercian nuns replaced Carthusian sisters at Buonluogo (Bonlieu), Italy.[295]. Unusually, in 1216, Cistercian nuns from Mont-St-Sauveur, Aix-la-Chapelle, took over in 1216 a site at Hocht abandoned by monks of the Order who had faced economic difficulty, and had moved to Val-Dieu. With generous grants of land, the new Cistercian sisters prospered there.[296] Similarly, in 1259, the Cistercian monks of Isenhagen having transferred to a new site, were replaced by nuns of the Order.[297]

Hermitages becoming Cistercian convents included Vallbona (Sp; 1173); Valldonzella (Sp; 1237);[298] Robertmont (B; 1180), Epinlieu (B; after 1216), Voisins (F; 1217);[299] Leyme (F; 1220),[300] and Tarrant Keynes (E; 1228).[301] Vallbona, like Valldonzella, in Catalonia, had been a double community of hermits, brothers and sisters, led by a notable hermit, Ramond de Vallbona, who died in 1176. King Alfonso I in 1178 required monks of Poblet to take oversight of the nunnery, whose first entrants came mostly from the nobility.[302]

The Early Cistercian Nuns, 1098–1350

MECHANICS OF INCORPORATION

The General Chapter in 1228 stipulated that whilst it had no objection to existing nuns of other allegiances emulating the institutions of the Cistercian Order, the latter could not take responsibility for them.[303] There were to be a number of instances of nunneries being formally incorporated into the Order after having followed Cistercian custom for many years: one was Saõ Benito de Castris, a Portuguese convent founded by Alcobaça in 1169 but not formally admitted to the Order until 1275.[304]

Some houses were incorporated without the proper procedures being followed: such was the Swiss nunnery of Fraubrunnen (1249) incorrectly admitted, though it remained so, by the abbots of Freinisberg and Hauterive.[305] The abbey of Val Virginal in Brittany was rejected four times and so, in 1253, became a Benedictine priory, despite having called itself 'Cistercian' for twenty years.[306] The nuns of Coton (E), some time after 1180, afraid that they might lose their Cistercian status because the bishop of Lincoln had visited them, petitioned that prelate to support their claim to be Cistercian.[307]

In South-West Germany a group of religious women were received into the Order by the General Chapter in 1233, with the abbot of Salem as Visitor, and the support of King Heinrich VII and, sited in a valley, the Latin name of their nunnery was *Valle Sancte Crucis*; colloquially Heiligkreuztal. An altar in their church was dedicated to the Holy Cross. The abbess in 1246, Agnes von Hornstein, was a thoughtful lady, requesting a copy of the bull of Innocent IV four years earlier listing the privileges of the Order. This was made for her by Heinrich Stolltz, prior of Bebenhausen, working in the infirmary of his monastery.[308]

The act of incorporation required a preliminary enquiry, with a personal inspection by two or more abbots of the Order of the nunnery concerned,[309] as those carried out by the abbots of Beaupré, Foucarmont and Mortemer, before the admission of La Trésor in the diocese of Rouen (1236),[310] and by the abbots of Schönau and Otterberg in respect of Patershusen (Marienkron) in the diocese of Mainz (1267).[311]

In 1244 the abbots of Buch and Dobrilugk were delegated to inspect the nunnery of Nimbschen (Grimma; G), and if found fitting it was to be incorporated at the request of the bishop of Meissen, and to become a daughter-house of Pforta.[312] If all was satisfactory such investigating abbots, if empowered to act on behalf of the General Chapter, would issue formal letters of incorporation – like those sealed by the abbots of Osek and Pforta (1264) in favour of Marienstern in Lusatia.[313]

Frequently in the 1230s the investigating abbots if they saw fit would in this way admit a nunnery to the Order without awaiting leave of the General Chapter – as in the case of Notre-Dame-de-Prés, Champagne (1235), when the investigating abbots were those of Boulancourt, L'Arrivour and Mores;[314] in the instance of Mont-Ste-Marie (Provins, F; 1235) when the duty fell to the superiors of Preuilly, Jouy and Les Sellières.[315]

The investigating abbots were sometimes required to report back their findings to the Chapter of the following year, as in the case of Olsberg, Switzerland (1234).[316] When the almost royal Silesian abbey of Trebznica was admitted in 1218, it was by a charter sealed by the abbot of Cîteaux and the four proto-abbots, acting on 'the authority of the General Chapter and the entire Order'. It was said to be 'fully incorporated and united to our Order'.[317]

As the numbers of abbots attending General Chapter diminished, it was often necessary for that body to instruct an abbot who was present to notify abbots chosen to carry out an inspection of their nomination: in 1236 the abbot of Locedio (It) who was at Chapter had to inform the abbots of Ripalta and Tiglieto of their duties regarding the incorporation of S. Sepulchro (possibly at Genoa).[318] In 1238 the abbot of Himmerod similarly had to pass on the Chapter's instructions regarding the incorporation of Machern (G) to the abbots of Villers-Betnach, Werschweiler and, perhaps, Baumgarten. It is difficult to see the logic of that command, as all these abbeys were well distant from Machern whilst Himmerod was very close, and indeed its abbot became that nunnery's father-immediate.[319]

When in England the incorporation of Marham nunnery (1251) was desired, the abbot of Stanley who was at Chapter that year was to convey their appointment as investigating abbots to the superiors of Beaulieu and Waverley.[320] Occasionally, leave for an incorporation was given without an inspection being commanded – unless certain of the published statutes have been redacted; this happened in the instance of Vivegnis (B; 1236).[321]

Not all new foundations or incorporations gave rise to unblemished success, and in 1239 – at a time when sought-after incorporations were at their maximum, the General Chapter had to command all investigating abbots to have strict regard to the needs of the Order, not to carelessly admit nunneries, and not to favour would-be patrons and founders like princes, for otherwise there could be 'grave scandal' for the Order. Abbots not performing their duties properly in these regards were to be deposed.[322] Such a command could well have been difficult to obey, as when in 1239 Conrad IV, 'king of the Romans', successfully sought the incorporation of Billigheim nunnery (Marienbrunn; G), founded by the bishop of Würzburg, Hermann I von Lobdeburg,[323] who also founded Mariental at that time,[324] and had previously founded Maidbronn (1232).[325]

A proposed incorporation was not always immediately agreed to: in 1254 the abbots of Strada and Cliente (Fiastra; It) reported back to the Chapter that whereas one of three nunneries they had inspected was suitable for incorporation, they had doubts concerning the other two. The first, and successful candidate, must have been Monte Favali, formerly Benedictine; the others, named as *Sta Maria in pleno Esine* and *Sancti Angeli* in the diocese of Camarina, cannot be positively identified.[326] One of the last nunneries whose incorporation is on record, 'Stunnemunster' in the diocese of Worms in 1293, was admitted 'for the good peace between the Order and the abbess and nuns'.[327]

The status of numerous female monasteries remained uncertain: like Billigheim (1238) whose bishop spoke of its nuns as having 'voluntarily received' the observances of the Order.[328] In Hungary the nuns of Poszony (Bratislava; 1235) were said to be 'associated' with the Cistercians, but those of Veszprém (1240) to be 'incorporated' into the Order.[329] In England, of some thirty nunneries only two ranked as abbeys: Marham and Tarrant, and in Wales: Llanllugan and Llanllŷr. Their abbatial status suggests that, although written evidence is lacking, they may have at some stage been properly incorporated.[330]

As for Stixwould and five other Lincolnshire nunneries, whom the king exempted from payment of a tenth in 1268 on account of their being Cistercian, the abbot of Cîteaux wrote two years later to the dean of Lincoln pointing out that they were not members of the Order – even though they wore the Cistercian habit. In the sixteenth century, however, the General Chapter did lay claim to many of the reputedly Cistercian English convents.[331]

The Growth of the Female Houses

A complicated case is that of the nunnery of Frauensee (G), often thought of as being Cistercian. In 1217 the Benedictine abbot of Hersfeld referred to Frauensee as 'our monastery', and five years later the abbot referred to 'divers necessities and various defects' at Frauensee. A century later an abbot of Hersfeld noted the 'penury and the needs' of Frauensee. Meanwhile, a papal visitation of the nunnery was led by the prior of Cistercian Walkenried (1233), and when in 1266 nuns went from Frauensee to settle a new convent at Kölleda they were described as being 'grey nuns of the Order of St Benedict'.[332] Benedictine nuns did replace the Cistercians at Frauensee in 1316.[333]

The nuns of Waterler (G; 1300) related that they followed 'the rule of St Benedict, our father', but were termed Cistercian thereafter.[334] Even when there was an association with a Cistercian monastery, it is not always clear that the nunneries followed Cistercian institutes. Terbank (B), for example, was linked to Villers but the nuns seem to have followed the Augustinian rule.[335] Nor is it certain when some convents previously of a different religious Order began to follow Cistercian ideals.

Rinteln was sometimes referred to as a Benedictine nunnery until 1268, though the nuns were 'of the grey Order',[336] when the archbishop of Magdeburg termed it Cistercian.[337] It was again referred to as Benedictine in 1312 and 1320.[338] The Dominican chronicler, Hermann von Lerbecke (d. 1410) implied that it came under the authority of the Benedictine abbot of Minden.[339]

Wormeln (G), indubitably Cistercian, was in one bull of John XXII in 1317 noted as being 'of the Order of St Benedict', but another bull of the same year described it as being Cistercian.[340] Neuwerk (Mariengarten, Goslar, G) was noted as Cistercian by Pope Boniface VIII (1295),[341] but adornment of its nuns' choir with Benedictine saints might suggest Benedictine leanings.[342] It was never apparently formally incorporated.[343] Eisenberg (G), described as a Benedictine house in 1268 and 1380, was noted as Cistercian by Clement VI (1348).[344] At its foundation in 1246 the archbishop of Cologne said that Sterkrade (G) was to be a Cistercian house, it was not formally incorporated into the Order until 1271.[345]

The Early Cistercian Nuns, 1098–1350

DOUBLE MONASTERIES

St Bernard had said that 'it was a fearful danger for monks and nuns to live under the same roof',[346] and the Cistercian Order did not allow of monasteries occupied by both monks and nuns. Not only, however, is there considerable evidence of womens' houses participating in the Order from its creation, but a number of the houses derived from double monasteries like Obazine and Coyroux (detailed above).

The consequence was that when the double Benedictine monastery of Menterwolde, Frisia, was incorporated in 1247, the monks stayed there at first though later moving to Termunten, but the nuns removed twelve kilometres south to establish their convent at Midwolde. The General Chapter noted that there would be two abbeys, 'one for men and one for women', and that both would come under the oversight of Aduard. Midwolde had to be abandoned in 1299 on account of flooding.[347]

Gottesgnaden, Saxony, was founded as a Premonstratensian double house in 1131. On transferring to the Cistercian Order by 1220, the nuns transferred to Magdebourg.[348] Valmagne was originally part of a double community that included the nuns of Le Vignogoul, both on the Languedoc coast near Montpellier. The latter had been a priory of Cistercian nuns since at least 1175, and was elevated to abbey status in 1245.[349] Navelgas (Sp) sprang from a double-monastery which had been separated by order of Pascal II.[350]

In some double houses, like Nonenque and Silvanès (Sp), the religious women may have had originally the leading role,[351] but when the foundation chronicle of Silvanès was written around 1170 it was made to look as it had founded Nonenque.[352] Nonenque was in many respects, including economic, the foremost of the two, and indeed Silvanès may have originated from priests looking after after the spiritual needs of Nonenque's nuns; those priests may have evolved into or joined the eremitical community of Pons of Léras. There is some charter evidence suggesting that the foundation of Nonenque preceded that Silvanès, but at the end of the thirteenth century Nonenque was made subject to visitation by Silvanès, despite an earlier challenge in this respect by the abbot of Mazan.[353]

Vallbona (Sp) was founded by the hermit, Ramon, in 1157, but incorporated in 1175 under Tulebras;[354] so too was Bonrepós

The Growth of the Female Houses

(founded here 1180, incorporated after 1215 as a dependancy of Vallbona);[355] Vallbona's foundation dates back to two communities, one male, one female, founded by the hermit, Ramon, who (in 1173) gave himself 'body and soul' to Poblet.[356] After La Cambre (B; 1201) had been established on a site given by the duke of Brabant, Henry I, and placed under the oversight of Villers, which provided chaplain, confessor and some *conversi*, it may be the presence of the latter which caused the duke in two charters of the year 1210 in favour of the house to refer to 'the brothers and sisters' and the 'monks and nuns' there. Abbess Marguerite (1245) referred to 'our brothers and sisters'.[357]

There were at least six 'brothers' at Coldstream nunnery (S) in 1296.[358] Bonrepós (Sp), founded in 1215, originated from a double monastery.[359] Leyme (F) was a hermitage until it became Cistercian in 1220; in 1233 comes a reference to 'the brothers and sisters there', and in 1237 to 'all the brothers and sisters who reside in the monastery.[360] Cotham (E; 1296), described itself as 'a convent of both sexes'.[361] In all these instances the term 'brothers' probably refers to the male *conversi* attached to a nunnery, but the phraseology suggests that in some instances they were seen as equal partners with the nuns and not simply as subordinate assistants.

A grant to Balerne (F) by two brothers on condition that their mother was made a nun, may refer to a dual-monastery there before its incorporation into the Order in 1136.[362] 'Brothers and sisters' were living at Bon Repós (Sp; 1204), but the monks ceded the property to a benefactor who established by 1215 a nunnery with his daughter as first abbess.[363] Other Cistercian nunneries which originated from dual-houses incuded Vivegnis (F; 1238, the nuns moving from Beaufays);[364] and Lübeck (G; incorporated 1245, the Benedictine monks moving out to Cismar).[365]

Gottesthal (Hesse), replaced in 1247 a monastery of Augustinian canons and nuns;[366] Dalheim (Bretzenheim, Mainz), originated in 1265 from a Benedictine double house at Zahlbach.[367] Stephen Lexington, abbot of Savigny (1228), was offended to find that in Ireland monks and nuns of his generation were sharing different sections of the same buildings at Jerpoint, Mellifont and Suir. This was in line with Celtic tradition, but he ordered the removal of the abbot's house at Mellifont from within 'the courtyard of the nuns'.[368]

In England, Greenfield also may have orginated as a double monastery following the traditions of Sempringham, but in the thirteenth century claimed to be Cistercian. In 1270 the abbot of Cîteaux wrote that although its nuns wore Cistercian habit, the nunnery (and five others) were not part of the Order. In the sixteenth-century a different attitude was taken when the General Chapter claimed it as its own, and ordered an abbatial inspection of it.[369]

Other initially double-houses in Lincolnshire perhaps included Legbourne and Stixwould which even into the thirteenth century, appears to have had some monks as well as nuns, holding the temporalities jointly with the nuns.[370] The mid-twelfth century foundation charter of Heynings (E) notes its establishment for 'brothers and sisters' – but there is no further mention of the 'brothers'.[371]

There is also some evidence from charters of the time of Henry II that Swine (E) commenced life as a double monastery of men and women.[372] The status of certain English nunneries was never clear: whilst pontiffs, bishops of Lincoln, and the Cistercian abbot of Kirkstall, all acknowledged St Michael's, Stamford, to be Cistercian, yet Abbot John of Cîteaux (1270) declared that neither it nor other Lincolnshire nunneries had been incorporated into the Order.[373]

THE FOUNDERS

When would-be founders of a Cistercian nunnery approached the General Chapter for leave to do so, two abbots were normally appointed to personally visit the location chosen, and report back the following year as to the suitability of the site and the endowment, as in 1219, when the count of Geldern wished to erect an abbey of nuns.

When, in 1234, the countess of Kärnten wished to do the same, the lot of inspection fell upon the abbots of La Cour-Dieu, L'Aumône and Olivet (F). They were instructed to report back their findings to the next year's Chapter.[374] In 1241 the General Chapter delegated the abbots of Lehnin and of Buch to personally inspect the site of the proposed nunnery of Medingen (G); seemingly they failed to do so, as the order was repeated the following year.[375]

In France the Order was especially favoured by Blanche of Castile (Queen of France, 1223–6; Queen Mother, 1226–52), and her son St Louis (King Louis IX, 1226–70); Blanche receiving papal permission both to have existing nunneries incorporated and to found new ones.[376] With St Louis she was responsible for the establishment in 1236 of Biaches-lès-Péronne nunnery in Picardy,[377] and she went on to found both Maubuisson (1242) where she took the veil and was buried, and Le Lys (1244), to which her heart was sent for interment.[378] Probably because of the Order's strictures, when the first nuns arrived at Maubuisson in 1241/1242 they found the building wholly completed, and in the foundation charter Blanche stated that 'all this was acquired with our own personal funds'.[379]

When Blanche petitioned the General Chapter for leave to erect Le Lys it was granted, but the work was not allowed to go ahead until the abbot of Cîteaux had conversed with the queen.[380] It was a joint effort with her son, and Le Lys came to possess as relics the king's hair shirt and discipline. It had abbesses of high standing, like its first superior, Alix, countess of Mâcon, a half cousin of Blanche. Alix had been a nun of Maubuisson, where her wealth had allowed her to give one hundred French pounds as an entrance gift, and from where she brought some of its nuns to settle the new foundation at Lys.[381]

Louis, aided by his mother, ensured the stability of Lys by generous financial aid, and also founded in 1228 the nunnery of Royaumont, for the repose of the soul of his father, Louis VIII; it was a foundation for whch no expense was spared. Well over five thousand pounds were spent on purchasing the site and constructing the magnificent abbey.[382] Berman points out that the establishment of Royaumont was 'a great political success', and that forty-four Cistercian nunneries were established during the lifetime of Blanche of Castile (1188–1252); her example and influence must have played a part.[383] As for Lys, Blanche augmented its financial resources nine months before her death in 1252.[384]

St Louis also endowed Port-Royal-des-Champs in the Île-de-France, and both mother and son ensured with their grants the prosperity of Le-Trésor, Normandy; indeed St Louis was considered there as a second founder. Established in 1228, it was affiliated to Cîteaux in 1237, and placed under the oversight of Vaux-de-Cernay.[385] The Cistercian nunnery of Notre-Dame-de-la Saussaye, Picardy, changed its name after Blanche of Castile received at its gate her son, St Louis, on his return from the Holy Land in 1254; hence forth it was known as Notre-Dame-de-la Joie.[386]

Royal patronage, including that of Philip Augustus, Blanche and St Louis was also afforded to Parc-aux-Dames, Picardy, founded in

1205 by the countess of Saint-Quentin, Eleanor of Vermandois.[387] Blanche's cousin Isabel, countess of Chartres, established three nunneries: Moncey (1209), Lieu-Notre-Dame (1222) and Eau-les-Chartres (1226).[388] Philip the Fair founded Lissac in 1286, on land given by the lord of Montbrun; it was settled by nuns of Leyme.[389]

In Portugal, the three daughters of Don Sancho I (1185–1211), encouraged by their father, are credited with the introduction of Cistercian nuns there; they were Teresa, Sancha and Mafalda. Lorvão was incorporated (1211) and Celas founded (1211), and five other nunneries later that century.[390] Dona Teresa (1176–1250), queen of Portugal until the annulment of her marriage to Alfonso IX, about 1210, removed the Benedictine monks from Lorvão abbey, near Coimbra, despite the reservations of Innocent III, alleging their monastery to be at a low ebb. She replaced them with Cistercian nuns drawn from the Portugese nobility, making the nunnery a refuge for unmarried women of the royal house, and set over them her former nurse as abbess![391]

Mafalda introduced Cistercian nuns into the ancient Benedictine monastery of Arouca, Portugal, by 1223, and her marriage to Henry I of Castile having been annulled by the Holy See, 'she had entered the convent of Arouca''.[392] How far did ladies of such high birth adapt to Cistercian rule and custom? Incorporation meant for the nuns concerned a change of habit. The bishop of Lamego, by 1223, authorised the nuns of Arouca to wear 'Cistercian white habits instead of Benedictine black', and Pope Honorious III acknowledged their change.[393] It was to become a place of royal burials.[394]

Frederick II of Swabia established Koenigsbrück in 1152; it was to become one of the wealthiest religious houses in Alsace.[395] Vreta (1162), perhaps the oldest monastery in Sweden, was founded by King Karl Sverkerson. His sister, Ingegerd, was the first abbess.[396]

After the death of her husband in 1319, Beatrix, a daughter of King Charles of Hungary, retired to the Cistercian nunnery in France of Laval-Bénite (Val-de-Bressieux), eventually becoming its abbess. She returned for a time to living in the world, but in 1349 her son, Humbert II, himself about to become a Dominican friar, built a small monastery for her close to Saint-Just, where she lived as a simple nun until her death in 1354.[397]

Ducal foundations included L'Éclache in the Auvergne (before 1159 by the dukes of Bourbon);[398] La-Joie, Brittany (by Blanche of

The Growth of the Female Houses

Champagne and her husband Jean Le Roux; 1260), and Marienfloss, Lorraine (1238, by Matthew II, duke of Lorraine).[399] Such nobles who settled Cistercian nuns frequently had in mind the making of a home for their unmarried female offspring.[400]

That a number of nunneries were founded primarily to provide such a home was attested by the General Chapter (1287) when it ruled that 'no nun is to have her own chamber, except those for whom the nunnery was founded'.[401] Duke Henry of Brabant established Valduc in 1232 in fulfilment of a vow,[402] but the first two abbesses were his daughters.[403]

Trasobares in Aragon was founded in 1168 by Alfonso II for religious coming from noble families.[404] Urraca, a daughter of the founder of Cañas, Navarre, Count Lopez Diaz, became abbess there,[405] and three of her sisters entered there.[406] The first abbess of Roermond (Ho), Richardis, was the mother of the founder, Count Gerhard IV of Geldern.[407] The first abbess of Flines was Ogive, a kinswoman of the founder, Margaret of Constantinople, and perhaps a nun of Marquette.[408]

The first abbess of Differdange (L; 1235) was Gertrude, the only daughter of the founder, Alexander, lord of Soleuvre, and that monastery became his family's burial place.[409] Between 1280 and 1360 four of the abbesses of Mollégès (F) were great-nieces of its foundress, Sacristane of the Porcelet family.[410] L'Étanche, Lorraine, was founded in 1148 by Duke Matthew I of Lorraine, and his mother, Adelaide, who was already a nun of Tart. The visit of St Bernard to Lorraine in 1246 also had an influence. Duchess Adelaide played an influential role in the new foundation, whilst noble families ensured it had a large estate.[411]

Two of the abbesses of Krummin (G) were Jutta – sister of Duke Wartislaw IV of Pomerania, and Elizabeth, the eldest daughter of Wartislaw IX.[412] Barnim I [Barnim the Good], Duke of Pomerania, was a generous founder of the convent close to Szczecin and his son, Bogislaw IV, made further grants to the nunnery in his memory, as well as granting in 1278 a full confirmatory charter.[413]

Barnim I (Duke of Pomerania from 1226 to 1278) favoured the nuns of Szczecin from 1265 to1277, granting them the vills of Zabelsdorf and Pyarch with their tithes, Güstow, Pomellin ('with its woods, fisheries, pastures'), Prislow and Warsoe;[414] the patronage of St Peter's church in Stettin, with the chapels of Blessed Mary and St Nicholas, with property worth ten marks for the restoration of the church and chapels; and a mill on the Vuelsnam stream,[415] with ten marks annually for the sisters to pray 'in vigils and in Masses' for the repose of his wife, Margaret.[416]

Barnim also made grants to the nuns of Ivenack in 1264-5, including the vill of Glendefin, one hundred other *mansos* of his lands, and the patronage of the church of Sophiehof,[417] and to Sonnencamp, one grant beng made whilst he stayed there.[418] His son, Bogislaw IV (1280), with the consent of his brothers, Barnim and Otto, confirmed the ownership of eight villages to Ivenack,[419] and Wizlaw II of Rügen gave Ivenack the vill of Neuendorf.[420]

Bogislaw confirmed the ownership by Ivenack of the vill and mill of Schönfeld, and also granted it the vill of Zollendorf[421], whilst in 1283 his confirmatory charter saw Bishop Hermann of Kamień list in detail the properties on Ivenack, which by 1304 possessed eleven vills.[422] He did the same for the sisters at Koszalin.[423] Barnim and Bogislaw both gave detailed confirmatory charters to Ivenack, which tell that its founders were 'the lords Reyburn and Rauen'.[424]

Bogislaw granted the nuns of Szczecin a confirmatory charter, and the vills of Colbisow and Golenzyn.[425] He was 'the pious founder', and a benefactor, of the Cistercian nunnery at Wolin where, by 1298, his daughter, Jutte, was a nun, and who by 1302 played a leading role in the community.[426] Other grantors favouring Wolin nunnery included the consuls of the city, who in order 'to drive away necessity', gave the nuns six *mansos*, at Wenkenhagen 'across the long bridge'.[427]

Counts and countesses as founders included: Guy, count of Auxerre (Les Îles, Burgundy, 1229);[428] Mahaut de Courtenay, countess of Nevers (Réconfort, Burgundy, 1235);[429] Christine de Zinneghem, daughter-in-law or step-daughter of Count Thierry of Alsace (Ravensberg, Pas-de-Calais, 1191;[430] Count Frederick of Beichlingen (Frankenhausen, Thuringia, 1215).[431] Count Albrecht of Orlamünde gave the land for the foundation of Reinbek (G; 1226), its prosperity assured by Count Adolf IV of Holstein, after his victory in that region.[432]

Notable was Jean, countess of Flanders, who died in 1244. In 1238 she declared that the lands of newly-founded Hemelsdaele (B) were 'to be free from all feudal and other services'. The foundress had been Elizabeth of Stainfort, but Countess Jean (1242), noting that many problems had arisen between the nuns and their foundress, stepped in and arranged matters justly. Later she herself became seen as the foundress, and it was at Hemelsdaele that two years later she was buried.[433]

She, with Margaret of Constantinople, was responsible in 1234 for the establishment of Ter Hagen (Ho) in the Zeeland polders,[434] and she also requested in 1236 the incorporation of Groeninghe (B) near Courtrai.[435] In that year she also sought the incorporation of Vrouwekamer, Zeeland;[436] and joined with Henry II, duke of Brabant, and the bishop of Liège, in seeking the incorporation of Soleilmont, Hainault, Nazareth, Zeeland, and Val-St Bernard, Brabant.[437] Earlier, in 1216, she had founded L'Épinlieu (B) on land given by a young noble lady from her marriage dowry.[438]

A convent was founded at Marke (Ho) before 1236, as two daughters of the local lord wished to embrace the Cistercian life. It was incorporated in 1236 at the request of Jean, Countess of Flanders, and later, in 1267, moved to Groeninge, three kilometers closer to Courtrai, and near that city's walls. The lady of Brabant provided land there for the nuns, and built herself a house within the enclosure.[439]

In the kingdom of León three Cistercian nunneries were founded or refounded between 1158 and 1176 by noble widows. Under the patronage of Countess Fronilde Fernández the ancient monastery of Ferreira de Pantón became Cistercian, with later her daughter, Guiomar, as abbess. Countess Estefania Ramirez, widow of Count Ponce de Minerva, gave the Cistercians the vill of Carrizo, one of her dowry possessions, for the construction of a nunnery.

Her daughter, Maria Ponce, was abbess by 1184 until at least 1192. She had been married to a Galician count, Rodrigo Alvarez. Countess Estefania had already settled Cistercian monks at Benavides and Sandoval. Gradefes was founded by another noblewoman, Teresa Pérez, she herself being the first abbess. Her descendants kept a firm grip of the convent for nearly seventy years. The wealth of Abbess Teresa and her family allowed Gradefes to make substantial purchases of lands in its opening decades.[440]

Count Otto II of Ravensberg and his wife, Sophia, founded Bersenbrück (G; 1231) 'in honour of Our Lord Jesus Christ', and substantially endowed it with four major properties and holdings in twenty other localities.[441] After Otto's death a grant of a house was made to Bersenbrück, in return for which the nuns had to maintain a perpetual light at his tomb there.[442]

In England the countess of Arundel ensured the incorporation of Marham abbey;[443] she had founded it on land given to her by her father as a marriage gift.[444] Dedicated in January 1249 by Bishop Richard of Chichester, it was in honour of the Blessed Virgin, St Barbara and St Edmund. On St Bartholomew's Day, 1252, Marham was incorporated under the oversight of the abbey of Waverley, the nuns making to its abbot a gift of four marks and a cask of wine.[445]

In Switzerland, when Count Hartman of Kyburg founded Fraubrunnen in 1246 as a Cistercian convent, 'for the remission of his sins and for the salvation of his soul and of his parents'. It was to be named *Fons Beate Marie*, and to have as Visitor the abbot of Frienisberg.[446] Count Otto II of Geldern gave a site to found Grafenthal (G) in 1248, and the monastery's official Latin name, *vallis comitis*, reflected its origins. Settled in 1250 by nuns from Roermond it became the mausoleum of his dynasty, commencing with his wife, Margaret of Cleves (*ob.* 1250), who was buried in the choir, and with the abbot of Camp as Visitor.[447]

Countess Sophia of Thuringia and Hesse (1250) gave the chapel and site of Caldern as a Cistercian nunnery;[448] she also played a part in the foundation of Mansfeld (1229);[449] Count Friedrich of Beichlingen settled Cistercian nuns at Kelbra (1251) giving them the church of St George there, a mill and some woodland.[450] Countess Estejanía Ramírez (1176) gave, 'for the soul of my husband and the remission of my sins', three villages and other lands for the erection of a Cistercian nunnery in Carrizo (Sp). The deed was witnessed by the archbishop of Compostella, six other bishops and four abbots. Gifts by others soon followed.[451] St Bernard-by-Horn (A), when founded in Old Melon in 1269/70, had for its first abbess, Hildeburg, daughter of Henry, count of Hardegg, one of its lay founders.[452]

Local bishops playing a part in the development of a number of Cistercian nunneries may reflect a lack of concern on the part of the General Chapter, and of individual abbots in the twelfth century.[453] Bishops settling Cistercian nuns included Geoffrey of Langres (Colonge, by 1140);[454] and Philip de Dreux, the crusading bishop of Beauvais (Pentemont; in the last year of his life, 1217).[455] The archbishop of Cologne reputedly founded Graurheindorf in 1149 following a visit to the region by St Bernard.[456]

Philip de Heinsberg, archbishop of Cologne, and local nobles, greatly facilitated the settlement at Hoven in 1188 of nuns from

The Growth of the Female Houses

S.-Thomas-sur-le-Kyll.[457] King Conrad II and Henry I, archbishop of Mainz, gave his blessing to the foundation by the margrave of Grumbach of Ichtershausen in 1147.[458] Although it had bonds of fraternity with Pforta and Volkenrode, Ichtershausen remained subject to the archbishop who sometimes delegated Benedictine abbots to visit it.[459]

Archbishop Gerhard II of Bremen (1231), with the consent of his cathedral chapter, gave the first site of the nuns of Lilienthal. He died in 1258, the year after he referred to Abbess Sophia as his 'dear sister'.[460] Four nuns from Walberberg led the initial community in the Cistercian way of life,[461] whilst Pope Gregory IX and Emperor Frederick II both took the new convent under their protection.[462]

Bishop Friedrich of Ratzeburg (1252) confirmed the foundation by Count Gunzelin of Schwerin, and grants given to the Cistercian nuns of Zarrentin, 'now and in the future, invoking the authority of the Lord, and of the apostles Peter and Paul'.[463] Zarrentin was a Slav village, and its founder endowed it with three churches.[464]

Successive bishops of Würzburg made many grants and privileges to Wechterswinkel, greatly aiding its prosperity.[465] Bishop Hermann 1 (1238) of that diocese, wishing to reform the ancient Benedictine monastery at Billigheim, orientated it towards Cîteaux, and at the request of Conrad IV, King of the Romans, it was incorporated in 1239.[466]

It was perhaps the influence of the local bishops like Absalon, bishop of Roskilde (1158) and later archbishop of Lund (1177–1201), that led to the foundation of Cistercian nunneries at Roskilde (before 1177) and Slangerup (before 1200), by the abbeys of Sorø and Esrum respectively.[467]

The nuns of Tarrant Kaines (E) find full mention above. The profession of its first abbess, Clarice, must ante-date the bishop's translation to Durham in 1228. Several 'professions' of its nuns are kept in the muniment room of Salisbury Cathedral. Bishop le Poor died at Tarrant on 13 April 1237 at the hour of Compline, having arranged for Queen Eleanor to be its patron, and so the house was later known as *Benedictus Locus Regine super Tarrant*.[468] Whilst there is record of Marham's formal incorporation into the Order, this does not survive for Tarrant, but it was accomplished by 1243, when the General Chapter appointed the abbots of Boxley and of Robertsbridge to have the care of it.[469]

The Early Cistercian Nuns, 1098–1350

THEIR MOTIVES

Nobles who settled Cistercian nuns frequently had in mind the making of a home for their unmarried female offspring,[470] like Floris IV, count of Holland, who founded Loosduinen in about 1229 with daughters of noble origin in mind.[471] Duke Henry of Brabant established Valduc in 1232 in fulfilment of a vow,[472] but the first two abbesses were his daughters.[473]

A local but powerful lord, Sicard Alaman, in the mid-thirteenth century helped Nonenque to found St-Sulpice (Mid-Pyrenees) specifically so that his daughter could become a nun there.[474] She, Esclarmunde Alaman, was already a professed nun of Nonenque and she became the first prioress of Saint-Sulpice, with a gift from Nonenque of 150 shillings of 'Melgorian money' for the construction and enlargement of the new nunnery. Further, Nonenque released to Saint-Sulpice the inheritance received by Aiceline Alaman when she had became a nun of Nonenque; it consisted of the entire village and territory called Vaissa Rabia.[475]

Nazareth (B) was founded in 1236 by Bl. Barthélémy; the first abbess was his daughter Beatrice (d. 1268).[476] Barthélémy also founded, around 1220, Maagdendaal, bringing there nuns from La Ramée.[477] Soon after it entered the Order, under the oversight of Maidbronn, Seligenporten (G; 1247) became an establishment reserved for the daughters of nobles.[478] The first abbess of Gravenhorst (G:), Oda, was the daughter of the founder, the knight, Conrad von Brochterbeck and his wife Amalgarde von Budde. Aged then only about twenty-five, she ruled for forty-two years.[479]

Also reserved for rich females who could bring a good endowment with them were Himmelkron (G),[480] and Guadalajara (Sp).[481] The first abbess of Heiligenthal (Bavaria), Jutta von Fuchsstadt, was the sister of Helebode de Fuchsstadt, who gave the site; Jutta was later beatified.[482] Katherine, the first abbess of Georgenbusch (St Joris, G; 1274) was the daughter of the founders, a knight, Winfried of Kinzweiler, and his wife Jutta.[483]

Not all parents were so willing to see their offspring embrace the religious life. Caesarius of Heisterbach told how when a nine year old daughter of a bailiff of Aix tried to enter Burtscheid (G), her father forcibly took her away. After the bishop of Liège intervened, the girl was restored to the convent and eventually became its abbess.[484]

The Growth of the Female Houses

In the thirteenth century many nuns did come from what would today be described as the 'middle-class'. Such were Alice and Alix daughters of local townsmen of substance who joined Notre-Dame-des-Près (F) during its early decades; Katherine, a niece of a canon of St.-Etienne (1275); and the four daughters of Beatrix, widow of Thomas of St.-Rémy, a townswoman of Reims, who entered Clairmarais. In each case gifts from their close relative accompanied their profession.[485] Sited in Paris, the community of Saint-Antoine-des-Champs, also had many bourgeois women amongst its nuns.[486]

Margaret of Savoy, daughter of Count Amedeus, who wished to retire from the world, founded Bons convent (F) for that purpose around 1155, whilst in 1171 William and Eustache of Poitiers founded Bonlieu nunnery (F) for their mother, Veronica.[487] Saint-Just (F) was founded by the Dauphin, Humbert II, in 1349 in favour of his mother, Beatrice, who became a religious there, dying in 1354.[488]

Many of those wishing to establish a Cistercian nunnery did so because they had it in mind as their burial place. On his return from the Holy Land around 1150 from the Second Crusade, Bertrand I, baron of the Tour d'Auvergne, chose a 'desolate rocky site' to found La Vassin; it became the burying-place of his family.[489]

Herkenrode, to become the most significant Cistercian nunnery in the Low Countries, was founded in 1182 by Count Gerard of Looz. Killed at the siege of Acre in 1194, he was buried at Herkenrode, and it became his family mausoleum. The convent was incorporated into the Cistercian Order in 1217.[490] Grafenthal in the Rhineland was founded in 1248 by Count Otto II of Gueldre, at the request of his wife, Margaret of Clèves, as a family burial-place, and she herself was interred in its newly constructed choir in 1251.[491]

Another monastery to become the last resting place of its founders and their families was Holthausen, Westphalia, settled about 1253 by Bertold II and III, lords of Büren.[492] William des Roches, steward of Anjou and Maine, founded Bonlieu in 1219 on land donated by Philip Augustus and Queen Berenger. He intended the monastery to be a family resting-place, and was himself interred in the choir there in 1222 in the presence of the bishops of Mans and Anjou and some twenty of his vassals; eventually his two daughters were buried to either side.[493]

The convent of Lichtental (1242/45) was founded by Irmengarde, the widow of Margrave Herman V of Baden, to serve as a family sepulchre. This it did, and at the close of the thirteenth century an elaborate mausoleum-chapel was built there for her later descendants.[494]

The desire to be interred in a monastery with which they had been associated was also exemplified when the remains of Jean de Trie – a benefactor of Gomerfontaine (F; initially buried in the early fourteenth century at the house of the Dominicans in Beauvais) and of his wife, Margaret (interred in the church of the Friars Minor there), were transported by 1330 for reburial in the nuns church at Gomerfontaine.[495] Machteld of Brabant, wife of Count Floris IV of Holland, founder of Loosduinen, was buried at Helfta.[496] Lichtenstern (G; 1242) was founded by Lutgarde Schenke, after the death of her husband, Engelhard III of Weinsberg. At the close of her life she took the veil at the nunnery and was buried there.[497]

Staré-Brno (Cz) was founded around 1323 by Elizabeth Richenza, successively spouse of Wenceslas II (1283–1305) and Radolph de Hapsbourg (1306–7), kings of Bohemia. Its new church was completed by 1333; she often visited the convent and was buried there in 1335; and this may have been in her mind when making the foundation.[498] By 1315 she had assembled nine liturgical books for the use of the nuns, and from 1319 to 1323 she built up their temporal holdings; she signed the act of foundation in 1328 and it was confirmed later that year by King John of Luxembourg.

The nuns, Abbess Christine and twelve others, had taken up residence on Easter Monday 1323. The site chosen was close to the walls of Brno and the residence of the queen dowager.[499] Similar considerations applied to the burial of Prince Jaromar I of Rügen in 1218, in the church of the nunnery of Bergen (G) which he had founded.[500]

Rudolf I of Hürnheim-Rauhhaus offered his property at Zimmern (G) for a Cistercian nunnery, on condition that it became the burial place of his family.[501] Roermond (Ho) abbey church was founded in 1218 by Count Gerard IV of Gelre and his wife, and primarily intended as funerary monument.[502] Margaret of Constantinople founded a nunnery at Orchies in 1234, it transferred to Flines (F) in 1251; its new church was consecrated in 1279, Margaret died and was buried there the next year in the new choir beneath

The Growth of the Female Houses

a marble sepulchre. So, later, too, were her husband and other members of her family.[503]

Jean of Flanders, and her husband Count Fernand founded Marquette (F; 1226/1236) and there spent her last days. In a deed of 1231 the count assured Marquette that the rent of four hundred pounds arising out of property at Damme and Le Quesnoy would be paid after his death.[504] In 1216 the abbots of Bonnevaux and Hautecombe were appointed to ensure that within a reasonable period of time the body of a 'countess' was returned by Le Betton (F), something the nuns there had declined to do.[505]

In Belgium, Ermesinde, countess of Luxembourg and marchioness of Arlon, played a part in the original foundation of Clairefontaine which passed to the Order in 1253; she died in 1247, but the monastery became the necropolis of the counts of Luxembourg.[506]

Vows made by, and practical considerations of pilgrims and crusaders, also played a part in the foundation and endowment of some nunneries. Foundation gifts that would support a community of nuns served as a penitential bequest before some donors left for the Holy Land. These new foundations also provided for the souls, and on occasion the bodies, of the crusaders' female kin, if they chose to profess within the community.

Baudouin of Constantinople (1202) about to depart for the crusade to Jerusalem, gave the tithes of Mont-Sainte-Geneviève to the newly founded nunnery of Val-Saint-Georges (B).[507] The nunneries of Port-Royal and Les Clairets (F) were founded by knights in recompense for their failure to participate in the Fourth Crusade.[508] Matthew, lord of Marly, died in 1205 before he could fulfil his crusading vow, and his widow used money given for prayers for him in order to found Port-Royal. Its supporters included knights who had taken part in the Albigensian Crusade, and Bishop Peter of Paris who in 1215 elevated the nunnery into an independent house, 'to be an abbey of white nuns, and that its abbesses be elected by its community'. Hitherto, it had been a priory subject to the monks of Vaux-de-Cernay.[509]

Enguerrand de Boves, before he departed on the Fifth Crusade in 1219, founded the Cistercian nunnery of La Paraclet, endowing it with a vast portion of his estate. He eventually, some four years later returned to France, but then died. Count Geoffrey IV of Perche died before he could fulfil his crusader vow, and so instructed his wife, Matilda of Brunswick, to found a religious house to redeem what he could not; so Les Clairets was settled, west of Chartres.[510] St Louis (Louis IX) in 1249 gave grants to Le Lys 'before we depart for the East, so that we may obtain divine aid for our endeavours'.[511]

A would-be female pilgrim to Jerusalem in about 1218, Sibyl of Habrough, made a grant to Cotham (E) in order to gain money for her venture.[512] Margaret of Beverley, one of whose brothers was a monk of Froidmont, after a long and troubled pilgrimage to the Holy Land, during which she knew spells of captivity in Muslim hands, joined the Cistercian nunnery of Montreuil-les-Dames (F) in about 1196 as a lay-sister. Her monastic brother, Thomas of Froidmont, composed after her death a life in prose and verse which reflected her spirituality of suffering and sacrifice for Christ.[513] On his return from a crusade, Otto von Bottenlauben, with his wife Beatrix, founded Frauenroth (G) in 1220.[514]

Underlying all these motives was very commonly a spiritual insurance policy: the hope that founding a nunnery might atone for sins committed in this life, not only of the founder but also of his or her ancestors and other family members.

Thus it was that the widowed Irmengarde, Marchioness of Bavaria, established the nunnery of Lichtental (1245) 'in remission of her sins, and for the honour of the glorious Virgin Mary and all the Saints'. Moreover, at her wish, her two sons, Herman and Rudolf, Marquesses of Bavaria, 'for the repose of the soul of their father', presented the nuns with the patronage of two churches, two further grants of tithe, and the possession of three villages.[515] Alfonso VIII and Eleanor of Castile, in founding Las Huelgas, wished for 'the remission of sins on earth, and to obtain a place after this life with the saints in heaven'.[516]

THE BACKING OF THE PAPACY

Very many Cistercian nunneries endeavoured to achieve a papal bull, within a very short time after their foundation, to confirm grants made them, but claims to property or even assaults on their lands and buildings, made it necessary for Catesby (E) to secure subsequent such bulls in succeeding years. Such bulls would be sought soon after a nunnery's inception: Rathausen (Swz; founded in 1245) received its bull of protection and of privileges from Innocent IV that same year,[517] as had Groeninge (B; 1244).[518]

The Growth of the Female Houses

Val-St-Georges (B), within a thirty year period, from 1228 to 1259, received no less than six bulls of protection and confirmation of privileges from Gregory IX, five from Innocent IV, and four from Alexander IV.[519]

Alexander IV was especially helpful granting the nuns of Marquette (F) sixteen bulls of confirmation, privileges and protection, between 1243 and 1246.[520] His bull in favour of Clairefontaine (B; 1256) included the usual terminology of freeing the nuns from attendance at ecclesiastcal synods, and forbidding any hindrance to the free election of an abbess.[521] Cotham (E) received ten papal privileges, ranging in date from that of Anastasius IV (1153/54) to that of Martin IV (1283).[522]

A papal charter granted to Burtscheid (G) by Honorius III (1224), detailed the nunnery's right to receive any wishing to join without hindrance, but once entered they might not leave save with the consent of the abbess; they were exempted from the payment of tithes and from summons to ecclesiastical synods; and in time of interdict they might recite the daily office. If the see of Cologne was vacant, any passing bishop might perform the episcopal duties they required.

Such bulls also normally included the privilege of not being summoned to ecclesiastical or secular synods, and of the free election of an abbess by the members of her community.[523] A typical bull, like that of Benedict XII (1335) to Lichtentlal (G), also extended papal protection to the property of the nuns: 'churches, lands, houses, possessions, vineyards, mills, meadows, pastures, law, jurisdiction, and other goods'.[524] Very frequently, a monastic cartulary groups the papal bulls together, and gives them pride of place.

The papal bulls normally included the sanction of excommunication for troublemakers, exemption from paying new tithes, and from attending diocesan synods and the like.[525] As for Saarn (Mariasaal, G; 1223),[526] Flines (F; 1236) and Gräfenthal (G; 1250),[527] such bulls also permitted people 'fleeing from the world in order to be converted' (i.e: professed), to be able to do so without contradiction, and once professed none could leave their monastery without their abbess's consent. None were to impede the regular election of an abbess, and divine service might be held in times of interdict. At Flines, in time of interdict, the bell was not to be rung, and the offices were to be chanted 'in a low voice'.[528]

2

Nunnery Sites

INTRODUCTION

Cistercian male abbeys were mostly sited by rivers, but the sites of their female counter-parts were much more varied, partly on account of the whim of their founders, and partly because a considerable number sprang from earlier religious establishments of one kind or another. Those sites to be definitely recognised by the Order were subject to the same inspection by at least two abbots of the Order, just as for the male monasteries. Such was the case when the abbots of Beaupré and Vaucelles (F) were sent to examine the location for a nunnery the countess of Champagne (1221) wished to erect.[1]

The rules of the Order also specified that the sites of nunneries newly founded were to be at least six 'leagues' away from a male monastery of the Order, and ten or more 'leagues' distant from another Cistercian nunnery.[2] There were historical factors when this was not feasible, as in the near proximity of the monks of Obazine and the nuns of Coyroux (F), both originating from a double monastery. A charter might describe the position of a nunnery, as when in 1302 Prince Wizlaw II of Rügen bequeathed to the nuns of Ryd (D), 'the wood which lies at the foot of the hill next to the cloister'.[3]

In England all Cistercian nunneries had a rural position, either in a village (like Marham) or more isolated (as Handale).[4] Abbot Stephen of Clairvaux (1244), having consulted four other abbots, allowed 'by a special grace' the nuns of Val-St-Georges (B) to retain their grange at Rhion, even though it was not within the permitted distance allowed from a grange of Villers at Dhuy.[5] In Pomerania more than one Cistercian nunnery had an urban setting, perhaps for reasons of security. Duke Barnim I in 1266 noted the nunnery of Szczecin (Stettin) as being 'before our city of Stettin'.[6]

It was because the convent of St Margaret [Coelestia] was very close to the abbey of St Thomas-by-Venice (It), that there was a dispute in the 1230s as to whether that nunnery should be moved to another site or closed down. The bishop of Torcello complained that their near proximity meant that there was 'notable frequenting of the monks with nuns and others'. Eventually, in 1235, the Chapter ruled that the nuns should move, that the abbots of Chiaravalle Milano, Sancta Maria della Colomba and Cerreto should approve their new site, and that the nuns were not to move back to their former location. This did not happen, so that in 1239 the abbot of Rosières, far distant in central France, was delegated to close down the offending nunnery of St Margaret, taking to the task neighbouring abbots with him.[7]. The order was repeated in 1242, when the help of the 'duke of Venice' was sought.[8]

When, in 1244, the nunnery of La-Paix Dieu (B) transferred from an earlier site; the move brought it too close allegedly to the existing convent nearby of Val-Notre-Dame. Both convents now stood south-west of Liège, and their final sites were extremely close.[9] Ter Hagen, first located at Axel in Flanders, transferred to Merelbeke on account of frequent flooding. This brought it too close to the Cistercian foundations in the neighbourhood of Ghent of Nieuwenbosch and Bijloke, and the General Chapter (1271) ordered the nuns to return to Axel. At first they were unwilling to do so, and the command had to be repeated, but in 1278 Countess Marguerite of Flanders authorised the construction of a dike to prevent the flooding, thus allowing the nuns to move back.[10] Also in close proximity to Ghent were the monks of Baudeloo; it had a problem with Nieuwenbosch nunnery (B) regarding ownership of the tithes of Lokeren; the Chapter (1271) ordered that they be divided equally between the two houses.[11]

A number of Cistercian convents were built on land afforded by another religious house, or converted from monastic granges: as Fulda's Moppen Grange in Bayern (G; *c.* 1189) which became Schönau convent, with the approval of Philip of Thuringia and the bishop of Würzburg,[12] and Argensolles (F; 1222) settled on a grange of Benedictine Hautvillers; the latter receiving in return surrender from Countess Blanche of certain rights she had in the local forest.[13] The foundress, Blanche de Navarre, widow of Count Thibaud III of Champagne, brought there Cistercian religious from Val-Notre-Dame in Belgium.[14] Aftholderbach, Rhineland, was founded about

Nunnery Sites

1220 on a grange of Eberbach.[15] In northern Italy, the nunnery of Brione stood on lands belonging to Casanova abbey.[16]

In Portugal the nunnery of Cós was founded in 1241 on land belonging to the male abbey of Alcobaça; it became one of the richest Cistercian nunneries.[17] The convent of Bethlehem at Damme, Belgium was established on a property in Zeeland belonging to the male Cistercian abbey of Ter Doest in Zeeland, which it had purchased from the Benedictines of Echternach.[18] In 1237 Abbess Jutta and the nuns of Heiligenthal (G; only founded in 1234) handed over to the bishop of Würzburg the villages of Sturs and Win which belonged to them with a plea that a Cistercian nunnery be founded at Sturs. The outcome is unknown.[19] Marquette (F) (1226) was founded on land belonging to Loos, and acquired for the purpose by the count and countess of Flanders.[20] The first site of Isenhagen (G; 1246) was on a property belonging to the male Cistercian abbey of Riddagshausen.[21]

GEOGRAPHICAL LOCATIONS

Woodland sites gave protection from severe gales and pannage for pigs, but also a ready supply of timber for building purposes and for fuel: such were the locations of Koenigsbrück, Alsace, placed in the heart of the forest of Hagenau;[22] and Droiteval, Limousin (an early daughter of Tart), in the forest of Darney [1128]).[23]

Other French forest sites included those of: Consolation in the Champagne (by 1274);[24] Mercoire (Limousin, early-twelfth century);[25] and Leyme (mid-Pyrenees; 1220).[26] Parc-aux-Bois, as its name indicates, stood in the heart of Bouvresse Forest in Picardy.[27] In Belgium Valduc stood on the edge of the forest of Summerdale, La Cambre on the border of the forest of Soignes,[28] whilst Herkenrode was encircled by a large wood.[29] German forest sites included Börstel, Lower Saxony – in the wood of that name at Berge,[30] and Gravenhorst, Westphalia – in the heart of the massif of Teutoburg.[31]

Riverine sites, so dear to the male Cistercians, offered the possibility of fishing, water-supply and of transport, whilst almost fifty nunnery sites incorporated the word *vallis* in their official Latin title. Divielle in Aquitaine stood within a loop of the river Louts;[32] Keldholme in Yorkshire stood on land almost entirely surrounded by a meander of the river Dove, so that in early deeds it was sometimes spoken of as 'Duva' rather than Keldholme.[33] In Scotland, Coldstream lay close to the river Tweed;[34] Haddington on the left bank of the Tyne.[35] In Spain, Gradafes and Sta. Colomba, were sited by the same river, the Esla.[36] In Portugal, Lorvão was built on the right bank of the river Mondego,[37] whilst Celas nunnery stood 'by the bridge of Coimbra'.[38]

Other riverine sites in France included those of: Maubuisson (on the left bank of the Oise (1236), at its confluence with the Liesse, on land given by Blanche of Castile – a two kilometre long aqueduct supplied the cloister lavabo with water;[39] La-Joie, Brittany (by the Blavet, 1260);[40] Beauvoir, Central France (by the Yèvre, 1234);[41] Blendecques, Pas-de-Calais, by the river Aa.[42] St-Hoïlde, Lorraine (1228, by the river Ornain); and Bondeville (Normandy; on the banks of the river Cailly, 1140).[43] Vernaison, founded about 1165 at Comiers on the right bank of the river Isère, transferred around 1220 to Vernaison on the other bank.[44] St Sulpice, mid-Pyrenees, was founded in the mid-thirteenth century near the confluence of the rivers Tarn and Agout, giving it the colloquial name of Saint-Sulpice-de-la-Pointe;[45] in Pas-de-Calais.

Beaupré had a like location at the confluence of the rivers Lys and Lawe.[46] A nunnery settled at Camp-Souverian was transferred in 1167 by the Empress Matilda to a location on the banks of the river Varenne, close to the entry of Saint-Saëns.[47] Canals provided the cloister, mill and fish-pond of Burtscheid (G, 1226) with a constant supply of water.[48]

Belgian riverine nunneries included several by the river Meuse: the first site of Dalheim at Ophoven stood on the left bank of the Meuse;[49] so, too, did Hemelsdaal (sited there before 1196), and Vivegnis (founded 1238);[50] Solières stood on its right bank – but this was an incorporated site of 1229.[51] The nuns at Hocht in 1215 also occupied a position on the left bank of the Meuse; it had just been vacated by monks moving to found Val-Dieu.[52] Blatzheim, Westphalia, was sited by 1247 on the eastern bank of the river Neffelbach;[53] Allerheiligen before the Cistercians came in 1259 was located on the left bank of the Rhine;[54] as was Marienkron (Mainz), previously Benedictine and incorporated in 1265.[55]

In Bohemia Pohled was founded in around 1266 on the right bank of the river Sázava, whilst Sezemice stood on the river Labe.[56] In Poland Owińska was sited on the banks of the river Varta.[57] The bounds of its home estate, as given in 1250, show the significance of waterways: 'From Preborowe where the Warta flows into the Noteć, as far as Lake Chomathouo, Kuchini, the island of Stbeuo, Lake Lype, Dluge, Plauno, Potrougnat and Rokythno and from the aforesaid lake as far as the Warta river'.[58]

Lacustrine and island sites served like purposes of fishing and transport. Le Lieu-Notre-Dame, Rhône, founded about 1150, stood near Lake Leman, though little is known of its history;[59] Wald (G) stood by Lake Constance. With the gift of the village of Ivenack (1252) the nuns there received also 'its lake, with the stream flowing to the mill'.[60]

The nuns of Wolin, Poland, migrated in 1305 to Krummin in Mecklenburg, Germany, to live on the island of Usedom.[61] Both foundations were made by Duke Bogislaw IV of Pomerania, whose daughter, Jutta, a nun of Wolin, later became abbess of Krummin (1323–36). Krummin had scattered properties on neighbouring islands, including two mills, a sheep-fold, and an hostel at Ziemitz.[62]

Solberga, first mentioned in 1246, was sited on the Baltic island of Gotland.[63] Frauensee was sited on an island in the lake of that name in Thuringia, but later backfilled soil joined it to the shore.[64] Bishop Herman of Camin (1277) confirmed the new foundation of Cistercian nuns from Itzehoe (G) 'on the island of the Blessed Virgin Mary by Koszalin'. He confirmed also gave them fishing rights.[65]

Friedland nunnery, founded about 1250, stood between two lakes at a German market settlement between two Slavic villages, and may have been intended to assist the process of germanisation.[66] Feldbach (Swz) stood just about 100 metres from a castle on the banks of Lake Constance; a site purchased for one hundred silver marks.[67] The location to which nuns moved in 1229 from the abbey of Notre-Dame de la Celle (F), encompassed four islands on the right bank of the river Yonne; hence it became known as the nunnery of Les Îles.[68] Villancourt (F), was founded in the late-twelfth century on the island of Senart, its nuns may have found this site restrictive, occasioning their move to Villancourt (Willencourt) in 1220.[69]

Upland sites resulted from the circumstance of a foundation, or on account of its position when incorporated. In the cases of at least fifteen convents their official name was prefixed by the Latin word, 'mons', indicating a situation on an eminence however slight, as *Mons Sancti Georgii* (Georgenberg; G). L'Éclache (F) was founded in the heart of the mountains of the Auvergne, at a high altitude with much marshland.[70] Battant (F) stood on a small plateau at the source of the river Battant; founded in 1227 it was affiliated to Cîteaux before 1300.[71]

Bergen was founded as a Benedictine house in 1193 on the island of Rügen in what is now north-east Germany, twenty-five years after its pagan inhabitants were forced to become Christians. Peopled by nuns of Roskilde (D), it had a hill-top site 800 metres from the residence of Prince Jaroma, and ninety metres high, affording it the Latin name of *Monasterium in Monte Ruga*.[72] When Bogislaw IV founded Wolin nunnery (Pl) in 1288, the consuls of Wolin noted its site as being 'on the great hill outside the walls of the city'.[73] Koszalin nunnery (Pl) also had a hill-top site, and maintained a light-house to help mariners on the adjacent Baltic Sea.[74]

Nunneries with *frontier sites* might experience consequential problems. When in 1296 King Edward I of England encamped at the nunnery of Coldstream on the Scottish border, with 5000 horses and 30,000 infantry, extensive damage was done to the priory and its orchard. The 'master' of the house demanded compensation claiming £50 for cereals consumed and £62 for animals killed for meat.[75] The war meant the temporary dispersal of the nuns; one of whom, Beatrix of Hodesale, was in 1315 still living as an anchoress in the house by the bridge of Doncaster.[76]

Routeway sites included that of Marquette, sited near the road from Lille to Courtrai, and a little way from the confluence of the Marque into the Deûle. This position was not helpful when in 1297 Philip the Bel assembled troops to attack Liège, and the nunnery was badly damaged.[77] L'Amour-Dieu (incorporated in 1237) sprang from a 'house of God', situated near Troissy and close to the road from Paris to Strasbourg; it was pillaged in the Hundred Years' War.[78] The Roman road from Arras to Compiègne passed by the gate-house of Parc-aux-Bois.[79] The nunnery of Bouchet (F) stood next to the 'public way', along which pilgrims came to the tomb of Blessed Bertrand of Garrigue in its church.[80]

Eustace of Coton, in the later twelfth century, gave Cotham (E) the use of a road leading from the nunnery's great gate westward to the 'common road'. It passed between his two tofts, and was to be wide enough for two wagons to pass.[81] The abbey of St Peter, Ghent (1262) gave Marquette (F) the use, though not exclusively, of a road between Saffelaere and Wachtebeke, at the request of

Nunnery Sites

Countess Margaret of Flanders.[82] Barnim I, Duke of Pomerania, insisted in 1278 – not long before his death, that the common way from the city of Szczecin to the mill of the nuns of Szczecin was a free way for those coming and going, it was not to be impeded, and that any hindrances were to be removed.[83] Adersleben (G; 1285) was given leave by Count Otto of Ascaria to build a bridge across 'the Boda'.[84]

Proximity to such routeways could detract from the ideal isolation of a Cistercian monastery, and so Evrard of Chartres (1241) gave to the nuns of L'Eau 'the way next to the convent' for their 'peace and quiet', with the right to obstruct the way and turn it to their own use.[85] Added seclusion was afforded when the nuns of L'Eau (1257) paid seventy Chartres shillings to buy up land located outside their abbey gate.[86] Count Heinrich of Gleichenstein (1294) gave to the nuns of Anrode (Thuringia), 'for their greater peace', the common way adjoining the convent so that it should no longer be a public thoroughfare.[87] The nuns of Mariengarten (Saxony) were given leave by the duke of Brunswick (1314) to close to the public the way which abutted on the upper part of their home grange, so long as they provided a similar way across their fields.[88]

SITE NAMES

The topographical or political origins of the names of several Cistercian nunneries have found mentioned in the preceding pages, like Bouchet (F) which took its Latin name, *Boscheto*, from the hunting lodge that previously occupied its site.[89] Four Cistercian nunneries in France, in the dioceses of Geneva, Lyons, Mans and Valence, bore the name of Bonlieu, literally praising their location as being 'a good place', perhaps not only on account of a perfect site, but also as being spiritually a good place to be.[90]

For the researcher such duplicity of names can occasionally present problems of easy identification, as in the instance of the references to Gnadenthal: there being one convent so called in the diocese of Wurzburg, one in the diocese of Cologne, and one in the diocese of Trèves. There was also a like named nunnery in Switzerland, in the diocese of Constance.[91] In Spain, three Cistercian nunneries bore the name of Las Huelgas, the chiefest by Burgos, another by Valladolid, and the third close to Avilés in Asturias.[92]

Apart from their localised colloquial name, nearly all Cistercian nunneries had an official Latin name, and the Keble list of the late-thirteenth century mostly gives these rather than their actual place-name. Again there can be occasion for confusion. James de Vitry said of certain convents of his acquaintance, that 'virgins throng there, widows hasten there, and married women with husbands' consent'.[93]

No wonder that three nunneries in Germany and one in Bohemia bore the official name of *Porta Coeli* ('gate of heaven').[94] The name of Our Lady was prefixed in at least nine Latin names, such as *Marienthron* (Grimma, G); at least seven bore the prefix of 'Fons' (as Fraubrunnen, Swz) – sometimes perhaps suggesting a source of spirituality rather than of flowing water, and at least five were prefixed by 'cella', referring to their monastic status, as *Cella Dei* (Gutenzell, G).

Medieval records and modern literature sometimes use not only the colloquial name but also the Latin name for the same monastery; again a potential means of confusion. This was reflected when in 1228 King Ottakar I of Bohemia noted that the nunnery at Oslavany (Cz) was commonly so called but that, transmuted, its equivalent was *Vallis Sancte Marie*.[95] In like vein, Counts Otto and John of Oldenburg noted in 1254 of the nunnery at Menslage (G) that 'the common name for the place was Borstel, but it is more laudable to refer to *Mons Sancte Marie*'.[96]

Another source of potential difficulty comes in the fact that several houses were known by alternative colloquial names, like Frauental by Hamburg, also known as Harvesthude, the existing name of the vill where it was founded in 1247.[97] Moving site in 1327 to Hankesbüttel, the nuns of Isenhagen (G) retained their old name.[98] The naming of Loosduinen (Ho) reflected its site, 'in the dunes of Loosduinem'.[99]

URBAN NUNNERIES

Some nunneries were sited in towns from their inception, perhaps because they developed from other religious houses already there. Others moved into towns later in their history, usually for reasons of peace and security. Town nunneries included Roskilde in Denmark and Bergen (Nonneseter) in Norway,[100] St George's, Kelbra, in

Thuringia,[101] Ivanics, in Hungary – given by the bishop of Zagreb 'all the tithes of the people of the new town of Ivanics';[102] St Clement's, Toledo, in Spain;[103] and St Agnes and St Laurence located 'in the new city of Magdeburg'.[104]

St-Antoine-des-Champs was founded in 1198 within the walls of Paris by Fulk of Neuilly (d. 1201), a preacher of renown, for women repenting of their sins and wishing to embrace the monastic life. It was attached to the Cistercian Order by the bishop of Paris in 1204. In 1215, Louis VIII after the birth of his second son, the future St Louis, gave a large site for the abbey which was enclosed with strong walls.[105]

The precincts of Chelmno nunnery (Pl; fd. 1266) were bordered by the town wall; its site incorporated Mestwin's Tower, formerly part of a Teutonic Knights' fortress.[106] The street-name of Selnau in Zurich bears witness to the position of that cloister adjacent to the city.[107] The nuns at Old Rinteln, originally settled near Stadthagen by 1208, were moved by Count Adolf IV of Holstein first to Old Rinteln in 1230 and then into New Rinteln when that settlement was raised in 1235.[108] The move to Old Rinteln had been occasioned by a dream the count had in his sleep.[109] At New Rinteln the nunnery stood so close to the town wall that the watchman on his rounds had to cross the cloister grounds.[110]

Location within a built-up area was not always conducive to the contemplative life. The Cistercian nunnery of the Holy Cross was founded in the town of Gotha (G) in 1216, but 'the noise and numbers of men there', meant that the nuns 'were hindered from a life of holy contemplation'. Alexander IV (1255) therefore authorised their move to a place outside the city, at the discretion of their father-abbot.[111] In 1233, the nunnery of Mariengarten in Cologne, close to the cathedral, was somewhat over-crowded, and the archbishop of Cologne felt that the restlessness of the city was not a suitable place for the contemplative vocation, so thirty-one of the nuns removed from there to found Burbach (Marienbrunn).[112]

At Magdeburg (G; 1243, c. 1250) the dorter of the nuns of the convent of St-Agnes lay by the city wall, whilst the wall at St-Lawrence nunnery also touched upon 'the angle of our court by the barn', and lay 'by the way to the cemetery'. Its nuns reported in 1266 that passers-by, sometimes a throng, had attempted to break into their precincts.[113] The nuns of Toruń (Pl; 1327), living close by the Hospital of the Holy Spirit in that city with 'many people coming and going', were offered a more peaceful site by the Grand Master of the Teutonic Knights.[114]

Initially it had been intended to settle Cistercian nuns at the church of St Peter, Brno, replacing the Teutonic Order brothers there, but as this would not be a suitable place the foundation was made at nearby Tišnov (Cz;1233) instead.[115] The nuns of Mariengarten sought in 1243 to change their location in Cologne with the local Friars Minor. This seems to have taken place, but three years on the Chapter ruled that a site must be found for them outside the city.[116]

Cistercian nuns were settled in Halberstadt (G) in 1199 by Count Siegfried of Blankenburg for his sister, Mechtild, but the site in the hospice of St James was unsuitable, being within the city walls, so Bishop Conrad of Halberstadt arranged an exchange with the Templars of Saint Burchard Abbey, just north of the city walls, to which the nuns moved.[117]

The nunnery of Ilm (G), founded in 1267 in the town of Saalfeld, experienced difficulties with the Franciscans there, and so transferred into the nearby town of Ilm in 1275. Their move had the assent of the bishop of Mayence, and they were given a church and site within the fortifications. By a charter of 1274 the abbesses of Priesnitz, Ichtershausen, Kelbra, Roda, Weimar, Kölleda and Greislau, promised a grant of spiritual fraternity to all those who aided the nuns of Ilm in accomplishing their transfer.[118]

Town houses could be safer places in time of war, though not always. The duke of Brabant allowed Swybeeck nunnery (1235) to build the monastery of 'Little Bigard' in Brussels,[119] whilst in 1274 the abbess of 'St Nicholas in Austria' (possibly Friesbach, or a house close to Vienna) sought permission for some of her nuns to abide in and care for a certain house they had in a 'certain city' – quite probably Vienna. She said that at times they fled there on account of 'pagans and ruffians'. The General Chapter agreed, providing that they did not stay there continuously.[120] On the other hand, Neuwerk (Mariengarten), sited in Goslar (G), suffered from its position when in 1205 the army of King Otto IV of Guelph attacked the town, and invaded the cloister.[121]

In Ireland, Ballymore was sited in an area of substantial settlement, and built but 300 feet (100 metres) from a motte and bailey castle of its founder, Walter de Lacy, and in clear sight of it – thus affording the convent protection by the garrison.[122] The nuns of

Nunnery Sites

Koszalin (Pl) in 1310, after a time of local conflict, agreed both to pay city taxes and also to build part of the city's defence walls.[123] In Wales, Llanllŷr nunnery stood remotely, and suffered during the Edwardian conquest of Wales, but received forty marks compensation in 1284.[124]

Several Cistercian nunneries lay close to a town wall but outside of it: such included Clairmarais, outside the walls of Rheims,[125] and Galilea and Nazaret, without the walls of Piacenza, Italy.[126] Mansfeld (G; 1229) was 'newly planted next to the castle' of the founder, Count Burchard of Mansfeld, but a few years later the nuns moved first to Rodersdorf (1234) and then to Helfta (1258).[127] Marienkammer was sited 'close to the walls of Halle', but not as close as that phrase suggests.[128] The nuns of Frauenberg (Neuwerk; 1254), which later became Cistercian, were sited 'outside the walls of Nordhausen',[129] and those of Solberga (Sw) were settled by the walls of Visby.[130] Notre-Dame de La Joie (F) was founded in 1260 by the gate of the town of Hennebont.[131] The first and later site of Lilienthal both lay close to Bremen.[132]

The founder, Duke Barnim I (1243), spelt out the bounds of the precinct of the nunnery at Szczecin: 'between the mountain and the Oder by the city bank to the fountain, which is at the eastern part of the monastery'.[133] Later, in 1261, he gave the nunnery the church of St Peter in Szczecin together with its chapel of St Mary and St Nicholas.[134] In 1304 the nunnery was described as being 'outside the walls of Szczecin'.[135] In 1256 the nuns of St John's abbey were 'within the city of Lübeck';[136] and in 1270 the nuns of Holy Cross abbey were 'within the walls of Rostock'.[137]

The nunnery of Bonneweg lay some way south of the walls of Luxemburg, across the river, and by two road junctions.[138] One of its early grantors gave it in 1235, 'all my fields, sited near the gate of Luxembourg'.[139] Marcilly (F) was founded one kilometre west of the village of Provency, and the Chapter ruled in 1241 that houses neighbouring the nunnery (and presumably on its lands) were to be removed, to avoid 'the ingress and egress of seculars causing scandal'.[140]

The Latin names of several nunneries spell out their location, as for: Eisenach (G), 'extra muros Isenach' (1338) and 'the cloister of God's-houses at St Katherine by Isenach' (1367).[141] Eisenberg (G) was described as being 'the cloister of the Cross outside the walls of Isenberg' (1346).[142]

Gnadenthal was 'the monastery of the Holy Cross outside the walls of Gotha' (G; 1275);[143] and Mariengarten 'the garden of St Martin by the walls of Erfurt (G; 1304)'.[144] The Erfurt nuns had originally found a home in a building of the Sachet friars (1288), but moved to the parish church of St Martin of Brühl and there united with a hospital, but still by the walls of Erfurt.[145]

Nunneries founded within or outside the walls of urban centres sustained ties with their burghers, frequently receiving grants and gifts from them, as well as vocations (Chapter 3).

Many such patrons were artisans and tradesmen. One of the major patrons of Port-Royal was a goldsmith, John of Lagny, and there were other such. Another was Urban IV (Pope from 1261), formerly a cathedral canon in Troyes, and son of a local shoemaker. In 1263 he gave Notre-Dame-des-Près a gift of 100 marks of silver for anniversary Masses for his mother, who may have been professed in that nunnery after his father's death.[146] In 1268 Renard of Bar, a baker, gave all his moveable goods and a vineyard to the convent of Val-des-Vignes, so that his sister and daughter could become nuns there, and he himself a *conversus*. Descendants of thirteenth-century benefactors might augment their original gifts; this was true of the family of Stephen of Champguyon in favour of Clairmarais.[147]

CHANGES OF SITE

In the thirteenth century a number of Cistercian nunneries found it expedient to remove from their original location to another site; indeed a few convents moved several times. The reasons were diverse, including a lack of space for expansion at the initial site; the realisation that a site was marshy or subject to flooding or poor weather; fire destroying a convent's buildings; pestering by local people or the effects of regional warfare.

The latter factor often causing a nunnery to migrate into or close to a town. The removal of a nunnery fully a member of the Order, required consent from the General Chapter, as when, in 1237, father-abbot of Lucelle pointed out that only twelve nuns remained at Olsberg, Switzerland, and sought leave for the nuns to move to a fresh location. The abbots of Frienisberg and Wettingen were appointed to visit the new site, and the change was to go ahead if they approved.[148]

Nunnery Sites

In 1238 it was reported to the Chapter that the nuns of Le Saulchoir, Belgium, wished to move elsewhere in order to have a better supply of water.[149] A site change was also mooted that year for Mariënhorst (Ter Hunnepe; Ho) in 1238, but no reason was given in the Chapter's decree.[150] The abbots of Aduard and of Ihlo were appointed to inspect the new site proposed for Mariënkamp (G), which removed in 1260 from Duurse to a location only six kilometres from Assen.[151]

Some nunneries moved more than once. The first site of Lilienthal (Lower Saxony) at Trupe where the archbishop of Bremen settled Cistercian nuns in 1231 was found to be badly affected by flooding, so the nuns moved to Wolda, then about 1238 set up their cloister at Lesum, before and not long after finally settling close to Bremen.[152] Hemelsdaele founded in 1237 at Esen near Dixmude was translated in 1270 to Zillebeke near Ypres, and then in 1295 to Wercken.[153]

When in 1237 a plague had killed all the nuns of Soleilmont (B), Baudoin of Constantinople re-peopled it with nuns from Flines.[154] Some proposed site changes did not take place: as in 1229 when Blessed Genta, abbess of Florival (B) wished to move her nuns to property owned at Ottenberg, but St Gertrude at Louvain resisted this and the transfer did not take place.[155]

The need for greater isolation may have been the reason for the nuns of Termonde (B) to move to the parish of Zwyveke-lez-Termonde. Mechtild, lady of Termonde, in 1223 gave the hospital of St Gilles on the outskirts of Termonde, with all its property, to become a Cistercian nunnery, but the transfer to the parish of Zwyveke appears to have been envisaged from the start. Mechtild died in 1224, and it was at the petition of her kinswoman, Margaret, lady of Termonde, that Godfrey, bishop of Cambrai, authorised the change of site.

The bishop delegated the abbots of Norbertine Ninove and Benedictine Afflighem, together with the archdeacons of Antwerp and Brabant to find a suitable site in that parish for the nuns to settle. This they did, and from 1228 the transfer was under way. Gregory IX ((1234) took the new house under his protection.[156] After Mechtild's death, her son, Robert de Béthune, lord of Termonde, gave an annual rent of eleven pounds to the nuns 'for his soul and that of his mother'.[157]

The first site of La Ramée (B) stood at Kerkom by 1207, where in 1212 Hugh de Pierpont took under his protection 'the sisters of Kerekom of the Order of Cîteaux'. The move to La Ramée by 1216 may have resulted from the feeling that the estate at Kerkom was too limited in size, or because of too close a proximity to the nunnery established at Maagdendaal in 1215.[158] Later in 1225, the nuns of La Ramée had to seek the support of Pope Honorius when Gosuin de Velp wanted to regain his territory of Velphoven on which the nunnery was now sited.[159]

The first site at Duisburg of Duissern (G) was found in 1243 to be 'unhelpful, poor and inconvenient', so the Roman Emperor gave the nuns leave to move to a site closer to the river Ruhr, but as firm foundations there were lacking, the sisters soon returned back to their original home.[160]

Hardly had a nunnery been founded at the gates of Haste (1230) when King Henry VII (1232) referred to its 'deficiency and poverty'. In 1233 the nuns were granted a 'court' in Rulle (G), and they moved there in 1246, although the cloister ponds were subject to overflow. The move may have been foreseen from the outset, since the chapter of Osnabruck (1232) ruled that if the nuns transferred elsewhere it would retain the parish.[161] The nuns retained Haste as a grange.[162]

The nuns of Neukloster (Sonnenkamp, G) likewise retained their first site at Parchow as a grange.[163] Wild animals might also necessitate a site transfer: the nuns of Suc-Ardu (F; c. 1200) in the Central Massif moved - on account of wolves, to Bellecombe – close to Yssingeaux.[164] The nuns of Vernaison (F), their abbey destroyed in 1221 when the river Isère overflowed it banks, also found a new site,[165] as did the nuns of Mègemont in the Auvergne after the rupture of a barrage early in the fourteenth century.[166]

Flooding of the polder site of Ter Hagen (Ho) caused its nuns to move in 1255, whilst the overflowing of the river Dollard forced the nuns of Midwolda (Ho) to do likewise in 1299.[167] The archbishop of Bremen-Hamburg in 1263 authorised the transfer of the nuns of Ivenfleth – sited where the river Stör joined the Elbe, to Itzehoe on account of the danger of flooding.[168] On the other hand, the Cistercian nuns of Marienborn (Hesse), originally settled at Haag moved to a new site at Büdingen (1275) 'on account of a deficiency of water'.[169]

The humidity and insalubrity of the site by the river Ise meant that the nuns settled there moved in 1327 to nearby Hankesbüttel (G), but the name of Isenhagen was retained. A further move to New Isenhagen was necessary in 1345 as the buildings of the nunnery had been burnt. The construction of the buildings here was delayed by the Black Death.[170] Isolation and a lack of water prompted nuns inhabiting a former Grandmontine cell in the forest of Bucy, central France, to transfer to Voisins in 1214.[171]

The raw humid climate in the valley of Old Melon forced the nuns of S. Bernard-by-Horn (A; *fd.* 1269/70) to transfer to the nearby valley of New Melon;[172] this proving equally unsuitable they removed again to Chrueg-by-Horn in 1277 where the climate was milder and the land more fertile.[173] The nuns of St Salvator (G) living on a hill-top almost 230 metres high by Aachen, moved down in 1220 to occupy the buildings of Burtscheid Abbey just vacated by Benedictine monks. The move was also dictated by the difficulties of life on the mountain: strong winds and severe winters.[174]

The nuns of St. Maria de Cambrón (Sp) moved in 1250 from the Benedictine site given them at Iguazzar in the Pyrenees in 1203 by Peter II of Aragon, down to the plain of the river Riguel, also on account of the coldness of the mountains.[175] The nuns of Mariensee (Lower Saxony) were first located on Mouunt Wedgenberg, then moved to a wooded site at Vorenhagen, then to the village of Todenham, and finally, at the instance of Count Bernard of Welpe, to their final site in 1215.[176]

External human pressures might also be responsible for a change of location. The nuns of Maagdendale, East Flanders (B), initially founded in 1233 near Flobecq, moved after a few decades closer to Oudenaarde, because of 'the dangers that they encountered night and day in the middle of such solitude'.[177] The nuns of Breitenbich, Thuringia, removed to Anrode in 1269 because 'on account of malicious insults and frequent attacks the divine office was not possible'. They were granted property there by the chamberlain of Mulhausen and had the support of the archbishop of Mainz.[178]

In Toruń (Pl), where the Cistercian convent lay close to the Hospital of the Holy Spirit, with many people coming and going, the Grand Master of the Teutonic Knights (1327) offered the nuns a more peaceful site.[179] The nuns of Himmelstadt (G), founded by the bishop of Würzburg in 1231, found it necessary to move to the proximity of the town of Schottenau in 1248, on account of troubles caused by malicious neighbours; thereafter the convent was named Himmelspforten.[180]

The nuns of Ichtershausen (G) made a temporary move in 1249 to the Cistercian nunnery of Kapellendorf (near Weimar), though not all that distance away, due to the War of Succession in Thuringia.[181] Twenty years after its foundation, Borwin, lord of Rostock, in 1252, had to obtain an assurance from Bernard Luscus, a citizen of Ribnitz, that he would no longer molest the nunnery at Bersenbrück in Lower Saxony.[182]

Fire was a constant hazard, especially where much timber had been employed in construction. After destruction of their abbey by fire around 1255, the Cistercian monks of Isenhagen (G) moved to Marienrode.[183] It was fire damage that also caused the nuns of Horst (Ho), near Deventer, to move in 1253 to Fürstenburg, near Xanten. The bishop of Utrecht, however, caused a new monastery to be built at Somersfoore, near the previous site of Horst. The nuns moved there in the early 1260s, and the convent became known as Marienhorst or Ter Hunnepe.[184] When the convent of Las Huelgas del Ezgueva (Sp) was destroyed by fire in 1282, the queen-mother, Maria de Molina, widow of Sanche IV of Castile and León, a few years later gave the nuns her palace close to Valladolid as their new home.[185]

Sonnefeld (G; 1287) offered spiritual fraternity, backed by indulgences from several bishops, to those who would assist it materially after it had been, in the words of the bishop of Bamberg, 'totally burnt',[186] and forced to move from Ebersdorf to Hofstädten.[187] A disastrous fire in 1296 destroyed completely a nunnery in the valley of Henares in Spain. It transferred to Guadalajara, on the other side of the Alamin valley, and was much favoured by Isabel and Beatrice, daughters of Sancho IV of Spain.[188]

Their nunnery in Old Medingen being burnt at night in the early-fourteenth century by the Slavs, the nuns moved into New Medingen.[189] Fire on Holy Saturday, 1252, damaged the convent at Bersenbrück, but it did not force the nuns to leave.[190] After the burning of their monastery in 1276, the bishop of Paderborn for 170 marks sold tithes and other property to the nuns of Brenkhausen (G), to yield long term income for the work of reparation.[191]

The wishes of benefactors were instrumental in some changes of site. When Le Refuge Notre-Dame, Hainaut (B), transferred to Ath in 1234 from an earlier site near Audenaerde, it was at the request of Countess Jean of Flanders.[192] When the nuns (later at Spermalie, B) moved from Slijpe to Sijsele in 1241 it was at the behest of a clerk,

Gilles de Bredene, who gave them a manor there; dying in 1270 he was buried under a marble tomb in the choir.[193]

When nuns moved after forty-seven years from Marcke to Groeninghe (B; by 1267), it was to a substantial property they already owned close by the walls of Courtrai. It was a transfer made possible by the generosity of Beatrice of Brasbant.[194] Earlier sites of nunneries which had changed location were frequently still possessed by the convent concerned, as Nunthorp in the case of Basedale (E),[195] and Parcowe in the instance of Sonnenkamp (Neukloster; G).[196]

EPHEMERAL AND UNITED SITES

Some sites were ephemeral: indeed it has been suggested that there were more of these than supposed.[197] Grana nunnery, Saxony, was only heard of between 1179 and 1181;[198] Kuernach, Lower Franconia, was in existence by 1279, but in 1291 had only four nuns and its site was ceded to the local parish priest.[199] In 1250 the abbey of Vesola, Italy, was said to be in 'a state of major collapse', and that it might not be possible to continue as an abbey.[200] In 1224, Beatrice, widow of Thomas of St-Remy gave a rent of sixty shillings to the incipient convent of Clairmarais, just outside the walls of Reims. Her daughter, Sarah, was one of the nuns, and she stipulated that if Clairmarais closed the rent would transfer to which-ever convent her daughter decided to transfer to.[201]

Another short-lived foundation was that of Łubnice, Poland, peopled in 1249 with nuns from Ołobok, they returned to their mother-house four years later.[202] The convent of Sancte Marie de Verge was founded at Modon (Methoni) in the Peloponnese, Greece, in 1254 but in 1267 Pope Clement III gave its nuns the decayed monastery of St Benedict, Conversano, southern Italy, and they removed there.[203] Berthe de Lutzerna founded a Cistercian nunnery at La-Voix-Dieu, Switzerland, in 1314; she herself was a religious, but the endowment was insufficient and the convent ceased with her death in 1323.[204]

Occasionally a Cistercian convent might pass into the hands of another Order: as when Divielle (F), an early foundation of 1132, became a Premonstratensian house in 1209.[205] The nuns of Pozsony, Slovakia, incorporated in 1235, were said in 1297 to have neglected their possessions for some twenty years and often to have been absent from the convent, so King Andrew III of Hungary gave everything to sisters of the Order of St Clare.[206]

The nunnery of Rute in Spain, emerging from a hermitage in 1162, was but an ephemeral Cistercian convent, passing into the possession of local monks twenty years later.[207] The nuns of La Peyrouse (F) seceded from the Order in 1254 to become regular canonesses, whilst the nuns of St-Felix-de-Monceau (F) left the Order in 1332 'presumably disaffected with the increasingly hostile attitude of the General Chapter to the Order's women'.[208]

Not all nunneries were well-endowed or well-peopled. Where this was the case the abbots of Cîteaux and of Clairvaux were permitted to unite two or more of the nunneries under their care and, if expedient, to transfer the new combined house to a more apt location.[209] In 1273 the General Chapter suggested the union of certain Belgian abbeys but, with one possible exception, this was not carried through.[210]

In 1269 father-abbots were reminded that they must not disperse a convent without leave of the General Chapter.[211] In 1276 they were bidden to determine whether their charges had sufficient possessions, income and revenue by which to live, without recourse to begging. Those who regularly did not should be cut off from the Order.[212] From 1294 any lesser nunnery could be united to another, if the respective father-abbot and the founder agreed; the nuns seemingly had little say in the matter.[213]

PAROCHIAL COMPENSATION

Wheresoever sited, the establishment of a Cistercian nunnery – given its tithe-free privileges, might affect the income of the local clergy. It was to compensate the parish priest of Löningen for this, that the nuns of Börstel (G), settling at their first site of Menslage, were required to pay him five shillings annually, and fixed amounts of malt, rye and barley 'by the measure of that place'.[214] The nuns had moved from Menslage in 1251 as Counts Otto and John of Oldenburg thought the new site at Börstel more advantageous.[215] The site cost one hundred marks, but Count Otto gave the nuns leave to take timber for fuel and building purposes.[216] The means by which the transaction was achieved was that the count and countess of Oldenburg placed 'the wood called Borstel in Berge' in the hands of their kinsman, the bishop-elect of Osnabruck, and he conferred it upon the nuns.[217]

When the nuns of Battant (F; 1227) commenced the building of their new church, the archbishop of Besançon ensured that the rights of the nearby collegiate church of St Mary Magdalene were not affected.[218] When the nuns of Flines (F; 1234) first settled at Orchies, they were required to pay thirty-three shillings, four pence, to the parish priest each Christmas, on account of loss in his income by their coming.[219]

When L'Amour-Dieu (F; 1237) was incorporated the chapter of Soissons drew up a deed to preserve the parochial rights.[220] Gravenhorst (G; 1272) made a payment of one hundred marks to the diocese of Osnabruck for parochial lands and rights lost since its foundation in 1256; Bishop Conrad requiring its nuns to pay the local parish priest three marks yearly: eighteen shillings in the octave of the Epiphany and eighteen shillings in the octave of Pentecost, and that without delay.[221]

3

Church and Cloister

NUNNERY CHURCHES

The churches of the Cistercian nunneries were usually, but not always, dedicated to Our Lady, as at Koszalin (Pl), its church 'constructed in honour of the Blessed Virgin Mary'.[1] There were a number of exceptions, especially when a convent had been incorporated. Different patrons included at Arouca, St Peter;[2] at Celas, St Anne;[3] at Ichtershausen, St George the Martyr;[4] at Odivelas, St Dinis, after King Dinis;[5] at Rostock and Gnadenthal, the Holy Cross;[6] at Trebnitz, St Bartholomew,[7] and at Waterler, the Precious Blood (Heiligenblut).[8]

The nuns churches do not lend themselves to easy classification, as those of their male counterparts. Only a few have been identified as corresponding in plan to a male abbey. Such included, it has been suggested: the church of SS James and Burchard, Halberstadt (G), in the style of Cîteaux 2 (of 1180 – cruciform with a rectangular east end);[9] though another authority would ascribe its plan to that of Walkenried 2.[10]

The plan of Flines (F), with its rounded east end with radiating chapels, is not dissimilar to that of Royaumont, built by 1235 by St Louis.[11] If these likenesses were deliberate, then they were the exception rather than the rule, and perhaps tenuous. The plan of the nunnery church at St Pons-de-Gémenos (F) for instance, as given in a recent work, does not correspond exactly to other suggested likenesses depicted.[12]

Scholars have endeavoured to make classifications of the nunnery churches of the Order. Coester distinguishes between those with (1) cruciform churches with one nave; (2) simple oblong churches without aisle; (3) aisle-less churches with a kind of chancel with chapels in echelon; (4) aisle-less churches with semi-circular or polygonal choirs.[13]

Kratzke, looking at the churches of Germany suggests a more detailed classification: (1) aisle-less church with rectangular ground-plan – as Lilenthal; (2) the same, with retracted flat choir – as Zarrentin; (3) the same, but with choir terminating in three parts – as Krummin; (4) rectangular ground-plan, with a polygonal choir – as Mariensee (5) double-nave church - as Rulle; (6) cruciform ground-plan as Neukloster; (7) basilica - as Rostock; (8) irregular – as Reinbek.[14] Elizabeth Freeman, however, makes the pertinent point that 'there was no uniform architectural style for Cistercian nunneries in theory, or in practice'.[15]

One of the best collection of plans of Cistercian monasteries, both male and female, remains that prepared by the late Fr Anselm Dimier in 1949, whom the present author was privileged once to meet. So far as the nunnery churches are concerned, his plans include those of simple one nave churches, as Beauvoir (F), Gigean (F) and Tannikon (Sw); cruciform churches as at Abbaye Blanche (F), Droiteval (F), and Port-Royal-des-Champs (F); churches with an absidal east end, like those of Arroyo (Sp), Carrizo (Sp), Corcelles (F), and Frauenberg (G); absidal – with three chevets, as Gradefes (Sp), and Ruremonde (Ho); absidal, with five chevets, as the church of Flines (F).

Unfortunately, Fr Dimier's plans, like so many others, do not usually depict clearly any division between the choir of the nuns and that of the lay sisters (the *converses*). They do, however, all bear a scale in metres, unlike a number of older and indeed some modern works relating to monastic churches.[16]

One reason for the disparity in plan between the nuns' churches rises from the fact that many Cistercian convents, especially the smaller ones, inherited an existing church or chapel, which needed adaptation and/or enlargement, and very often complete rebuilding. Such was the case when nuns of Marienkammer settled at Glaucha (G), and inherited the church of St George there. Gregory IX (1213) confirmed the grant to them of Glaucha, 'with all its appurtenances before the Cistercian nuns took over the church'.[17] At Bersenbrück (G), founded in 1231, the parish church of St Vincent was united with the nuns' church, so that between 1263 and 1287 a new church was created; the northern aisle being the parish church, the southern aisle the nuns choir, with a wall separating the two.[18]

At Rulle (G; about 1235), the nuns' church was situated in the southern aisle of the parish church of St Ulrich.[19] When Drolshagen nunnery (G; *c.* 1235) was founded, it was 'by the side' of the church of St Clement.[20] When nuns from Rathausen (Swz) settled a new convent at Ebersech in 1274, the bishop-elect of Constance permitted them to erect their cloister 'within the bounds of the church of Altshoven'.[21] When the nuns of Isenhagen (G; 1327) moved to Hankensbüttel, the bishop of Hildesheim approved the incorporation of the parish church there into the cloister.[22] In all these instances the fabric offered, not convention, dictated the architectural outcome.

The early churches inherited or built by the nuns were frequently later enlarged or rebuilt. This was true of Wintney (E), its early timber structure being replaced in stone by 1234,[23] as also of Marianowo (Pl), established in timber in 1248, but later transformed into a stone building with the help of Pomeranian knights.[24]

The nuns of Lilienthal (Lower Saxony; 1248), a few years after moving to their final site, proposed 'to build a church of stone to replace the present timber structure'. The papal legate, as was customary, granted a forty-day indulgence to those who 'lent helping hands' to the nuns in this enterprise. Another later deed, of 1287, couched in similar terms, may suggest an intention to replace or enlarge that stone church.[25] In 1281 the bishop of Paderborn granted a forty-day's indulgence to those who aided 'the work of carpentry' at Abbenrode nunnery (G), so timber was there still a useful commodity.[26]

Of the Cistercian sisters in Riga, Archbishop Albert of that city told in 1259 that they were based at St James' church, 'until they erect a church of chapel of their own'. This they did dedicated to St Mary Magdalene, and in 1262 the nuns also erected a precinct wall complete with loop-holes.[27]

Monasteries and abbey churches were not built overnight. Nuns had settled at Welver (G) in 1238, but it was only in 1267 that they could comment on their church as being 'newly built'; Benninghausen (G) had been in the Cistercian fold by 1240, but in 1262 the bishop of Paderborn had to grant a indulgence to those who gave 'helping hands' towards the completion of 'the poor monastery'.[28]

The emergence of a new church at Mariengarten, around 1290, is witnessed by its nuns then saying that whilst the dedication of the earlier church of Welderekeshusen (where they were located) had been on the eighth of September (the Nativity of Our Lady), they hoped that their new church could be consecrated around Christmas.[29]

The Early Cistercian Nuns, 1098–1350

The nuns of Termond had moved to Zwyveke (B) by 1234, but twenty pounds bequeathed to Zwyveke in a will of 1303 'for the construction of the church', shows that a new church or the enlargement of the old was under way.[30] Entries in a Polish chronicle suggest of the year 1389 that the church of Żarnowiec was renovated and dedicated, but also that the old church was pulled down.[31]

Timber played a significant role in the earlier nunnery churches. Alfonso VIII and his queen, Eleanor, allowed the nuns of Las Huelgas (1187) to 'freely take timber, for the construction of the monastery and its conventual buildings and granges', in all royal woodland.[32]

Fernand Ruderic (1191) gave Carrizo (Sp) its nuns the right to take 'all that stone which is in the valley of Roderico, and to take timber and all that is necessary for the work of the monastery, with rights in ingress and regress'.[33] The nuns of Catesby (E; 1229) had the right to take timber from the royal wood of Silverstone for the building of their church.[34] Bela IV of Hungary (1242/70) granted the nuns of Veszprémvölgy leave to take timber from the wood of Bokon 'for the reparation of their court or for building their church'.[35] Duke Bogislaw IV of Pomerania granted the nuns of Szczecin (Pl) in 1287, forty years after its foundation, the ability to take timber freely in the wood of Golnower 'for building their cloister'.[36]

The nunnery of Benninghausen (G) had been established by the 1220s, its new church was to be a stone edifice; so it was that in 1291 the Premonstratensian monks of Oelinghausen fraternally gave the nuns the right 'to break stone in their quarry' for the building of the nuns church.[37] In Spain at Ferreira de Pantón a fine-grained whitish granite was procured for some sculptured work, instead of the coarser type used for much of the construction.[38]

The building accounts of Maubuisson (F) for 1237 tell of the great quantities of timber employed, in addition to 800 pieces of cut stone, and make mention of 'the heating of the chapel' and 'the construction of the fountain'.[39] The architect was Richard de Tour. Construction started in May 1236, and by the end of November 1237 receipts totalled 5,122 pounds, expenses 4,912 pounds. Eight years were spent in building the church and cloister, as well as a suitable residence to receive the king and queen on their visits. The necessary lead, iron and timber, were bought up at the fair of Lendit.[40] Nuns from St Antoine in Paris formed the first community in 1242, and on 26 June 1244 the bishop of Paris consecrated the new church in the presence of the French king and queen. The nunnery was exempted by the pope from episcopal jurisdiction, it was to be 'a special daughter' of Cîteaux.[41]

On the north European Plain, the bedrock lay concealed at some depth by either glacial sands and gravels or fluvial clay. Stone was hard to come by, and recourse was had to the conversion of these materials into the use of brick, resulting in some fine architectural monuments.

Amongst medieval brick Cistercian nunneries, frequently with a striking brick cloister attached, were: in Holland: Loosduinen; in north Germany, Bergen, Börstel (Marienberg), Isenhagen, Neuendorf, Rühn, Wienhausen, Wanzka, and Zarrentin; in Poland, Chelmno, Marianowo, Trzebnica and Zarnowiec; in Sweden, Sko. The western portion of the nave of Parc-les-Dames (Vrouwenpark, Belgium),[42] and the nave of Maagdendaal (Belgium), were also of brick construction.[43] A brick-built convent was also to be found in Italy, at Sezzadio in the Piedmont (It).[44] The part played by red brick in the nunnery church of Goujon (Goion, F) has been linked to a lack of stone in the Garonne valley.[45]

The construction of a new church was by no means easily achieved, unless a generous founder paid the entire cost. The shortfall in finances encouraged many nunneries to obtain indulgences for those who in this respect 'lent helping hands' to them – in other words gave financial backing, as they sought to build or restore their churches and cloisters.

Very often, the need for cash did not cease with the completion of a building programme, and such indulgences were frequently issued to be effective on the anniversary of the day of dedication of a church or high altar, and/or on other stated feasts, to pilgrims visiting a nunnery and leaving their donation.

In 1251, the apostolic legate in Germany granted a forty-day indulgence to those who 'lent helping hands' towards the 'sumptuous works' of building the nuns of Rulle intended.[46] The same terminology of 'helping hands' was used by the archbishop of Cologne, the papal legate, and the bishop of Lüttich, to aid the construction of the nunnery church at Grafenthal (1252/55).[47] Countess Margaret of Flanders (1273) bequeathed 1,000 pounds worth of rents in divers places to Flines 'for the maintenance of its buildings'. Undoubtedly one prime purpose was the completion of the abbey church which was dedicated six years later.[48]

There are numerous examples of like indulgences, as for those granted to assist the construction of nunnery churches at Spermalie (B; 1257),[49] Rathausen (Swz; 1259),[50] Ilm (Stadtilm, G; 1267)[51] and Itzehoe (G; 1280),[52] or in retrospect to assist pay the costs already incurred. The archbishop of Trier awarded an indulgence of twenty days in 1234 to those who assisted the construction of the church at Bonneweg (L).

A further indulgence of one hundred days in favour of that nunnery was granted by Pope Alexander IV in 1258, and four years later the high altar was consecrated by the bishop of Chur, there being a vacancy in the see of Trier. In 1290 no less than twelve bishops jointly issued a forty days indulgence to those who financially aided necessary repairs at Bonneweg (L).[53] It seems that the nunnery was a building site for over half-a-century.

It appears that the nuns of Rinteln (G), established in New Rinteln in 1238, a little later embarked on new works, for the archbishop of Magdeburg (1270),[54] and the bishops of Halberstadt (1274), Minden (1277) and Osnabruck (1280), all granted forty-day indulgences to those who 'came with devotion' to the nunnery on certain feasts, and/or lent 'helping hands' to the convent. The lists of feasts, as given in 1274, included 'the first dedication' of the church, evidence that a new building programme was in progress. Indulgences granted in 1313 (by the bishop of Minden) and in 1315 (by the bishop of Paderborn), suggest the length of the building programme.[55]

Heiligkreuztal's (G) benefactors, those again who 'lent helping hands', were granted an indulgence by the bishop of 'Bosa' in 1293, and by the bishop of 'Recrensis', after he had consecrated in 1319 the high altar in honour of Our Lady, and three other altars – each dedicated to a group of saints.[56]

A further like indulgence granted at Avignon in 1332 by no less than fourteen bishops, suggests a continual building programme.[57]

Several indulgences, like those granted by the bishop of 'Bosa' in respect of Heiligkreuztal (1292), and by seventeen bishops (in the instance of Himmelspforten (G; 1289),[58] differentiated between 'criminal' (i.e. mortal) and venial sins; the former gaining a forty-day indulgence, but the latter a whole year. The bishop of Turin in 1280 granted a forty day indulgence to Brione (It) for its feast of dedication and its octave, as well as certain other feasts. Nuns settled at Bersenbrück in 1231, but it was to be over fifty years before their permanent church was dedicated in 1287, on 6 May and as the record notes, the feast of St John before the Latin Gate.[59]

The cartularies and registers of deeds of a number of nunneries record the details both of the dedication of their churches, and of subsidiary altars consecrated then or later. A few examples must suffice of what appears to have been in some instances, a seeming departure from Cistercian simplicity. When, on behalf of the archbishop of Spire, the bishop of 'Pruscie' on 15 September 1252 consecrated the church of Lichtental (G), only a few years after the nuns settled there, two altars were dedicated: one in honour of the Blessed Virgin Mary, the other of St Catherine the Virgin, and the Eleven Thousand Virgins. The next day two further altars were consecrated: one in honour of Saints John Baptist, Benedict and Bernard; the other of St John the Evangelist.[60]

The nuns' church at Rathausen (Swz) was consecrated in 1259, fourteen years after the foundation, by the bishop of Constance, the high altar was dedicated in honour of Our Lady, St Peter, St John the Evangelist and St Nicholas, and some dozen relics were conserved in the mensa, including a portion of 'the Cross of the Lord'.[61] There is reference (1282) to the 'altar of the holy cross there'.[62] Flines church (F) was consecrated in 1279 by the archbishop of Reims who dedicated the high altar to the Holy Trinity; the same day the bishop of Tournai consecrated eight secondary altars, and later three more. Those in its ambulatory were named in honour of SS Philip and John, Hubert, Andrew, Jerome and Anthony.[63]

Sonnefeld (G) had five subsidiary altars, dedicated to the Three Kings, St Barbara, StAndrew, St Nicholas, and the Eleven Thousand Knights.[64] Benninghausen (G; 1264), also had an altar dedicated to St Nicholas.[65]

The Cistercian nuns' church in Riga, Latvia, had perhaps seven altars in their church; but twelve dedications in all. These included those to Our Lady of Sorrows, St Bernard with St Anne and St Andrew, and St Prokup; its altar of the Holy Cross stood 'in the middle of the church'.[66] In 1359 Innocent VI granted a forty-days indulgence to those who supported the erection of a great new altar-piece and image of the Virgin Mary in the church, and who recited before it 'the angelic salutation' (perhaps the Hail Mary or the Angelus).[67] In 1271, Otto, a knight of Rambin, bewailing the fact that 'burnished iron and old stones were lacking', gave to the nuns of Szczecin (Steein, P), an annual grant of six measures of rye (to provide income) for the construction in their church of an altar dedicated to St Martin the Confessor, expecting a daily requiem there for his deceased family members.[68]

In 1289 a 'votive chapel' was added to the church of Heiligengraben in Brandenburg, in reparation for the profanation of a sacred host at nearby Techow.[69] In 1300 at Wolin nunnery in Pomerania a chantry chapel dedicated to St Mary Magdalene was endowed: specific votive or requiem Masses were said there daily, save on Sundays.[70] By 1330 the convent church of Voisins (F) was prolonged westwards by the addition of a chapel dedicated to St-Eloi.[71] At Mercoire (F) a chapel for strangers was added to the right of the choir, but separated from it by a grill.[72] At Riseberga Sw) was an altar, presumably a chapel, of St Olaf; in 1322, Catherine Björnsson bequeathed twenty marks towards its glazing.[73]

In 1288, eleven bishops resident in Rome and in 1289 the archbishop of Mainz, granted a forty-day indulgence to those who 'lent helping hands' to the nunnery church of St James at Waterler. By 1294 a new chapel of the Precious Blood had been erected there, and in 1300 comes reference to 'the abbess and convent of nuns of the church of the Precious Blood in Waterler'.[74]

The size of the nunnery churches varied, though the length of most ranged from thirty to fifty metres. The initial churches, be they of timber or stone, were perhaps often quite small: the early Romanesque church at Beuren (G) was but nine metres in length and six in breadth, but later was considerably extended.[75] At the lower end of scale were churches such as those at Chelmno (Pl) and Riseberga (Sw) – both twenty-seven metres in length;[76] at the upper point, churches like Mariaburghausen (G) – fifty metres long, and Sonnefeld (G) and L'Eau (F) – forty-seven metres in length. Roermond church (Ho) was much longer, fifty-eight metres.[77] La Cambre and La Ramée both touched fifty-five metres.[78]

Width depended on whether or not a church had aisles: churches with no aisles included Colonges and Fontes (F), but Bellecombe and Spermalie had two side aisles. Riseberga was eighteen metres broad, Frankenburg, fifteen, and Chelmno a little over nine metres. Interior height varied also: eighteen metres at Chelmno, fifteen metres at Riseberga, and thirteen metres at Heiligenthal (G).

A few churches were cruciform: as Marham in England, but Rosières had but one transept.[79] In England, excavation has shown the church of Ellerton (E) to have measured thirty-four by eight

Church and Cloister

metres, and to have been set within a precinct 120 by 150 metres.[80] In England and France, nunnery churches varied in length from 23 metres (76 ft) to 42 metres (139 ft), averaging about 32 metres (110 ft).

Three early medieval churches probably stand out amongst those monuments of the Cistercian nuns still standing. The most prominent is the church of Las Huelgas at Burgos, measuring no less than eighty-three metres in length and twenty-nine in breadth, its polygonal chevet akin to that of Maubuisson;[81] Porta Coeli's church (Cz) had a length of sixty-seven metres, a breadth of twenty-four, and surrounded by high walls and a moat, escaped destruction from both the Tartars (1241) and the Hungarians and Cumans (1253).[82]

An outstanding feature of the church of Porta Coeli, Tišnov (Cz), is the fine tympanum over the west doorway. This dates back to around 1240, although it has been subject to 'dubious restoration at a later date'. It portrays the image of Christ surrounded by a mandorla, which is supported by symbols depicting the four evangelists. At the sides, the Blessed Virgin Mary and St John Baptist look down upon the kneeling figures of the founders, Queen Constance and Margrave Přemysl.[83]

The abbey church of Trebznitz (Pl) also bears a tympanum over its west front. Dated to the 1220s, it shows King David seated and playing his harp, accompanied by his wife, Queen Bathsheba. Much smaller than Porta Coeli but still impressive, is the church of Trebznitz, originally some sixty-two by twenty-nine metres, but later lengthened with the addition of a prominent porch and the extension of an apse.[84]

Amongst numerous other notable nunnery churches from the early medieval period still in evidence are: in France: Vignogoul, with a thrice polygonal east end;[85] Bonlieu, of about 1215–20, also with an absidal east end; in Germany, Sonnenkamp, depicting stained glass windows dating from around 1250; in Holland: Roermond, with three naves, but subject to nineteenth-century restoration; in Italy, Conversano, a church of three naves with later Baroque adornment; in Portugal, Odivelas, absidal, Vallbona: dating from around 1200, and exhibiting 'all the simplicity and rigour of the Cistercians'.[86]

In Sweden, Vreta, a three-aisled church consecrated in 1289; in Switzerland, La-Maigrauge, with wooden elaborately carved choir stalls from the late fourteenth century;[87] and in Wales, Llanllugan, small, but with some medieval glass, including the image of an abbess; to name but a very few.[88]

In León, the church of Gradefes was 'one of the most original buildings of its time'; with its ambulatory of five bays. The decorated capitals include 'winged hybrids with human heads and serpentine' tails'. In France, Valbona has striking imagery of human faces and heraldic designs on columnar bosses,[89] whilst Cour-Notre-Dame and Mégemont, amongst others, possessed a rose window, so beloved of the Cistercians.[90]

The number of masons' marks can indicate a large work-force.[91] At Porta Coeli, in the Czech Republic, some forty have been identified, illustrative of a building period in the years 1232 to 1240.[92] Carrizo's church terminates in three apses, whilst Ferreira de Pantón's was, despite twelfth-century Cistercian simplicity, 'lavishly sculptured'. The pier capitals include one depicting no less than ten birds pecking at fruit.[93]

The 'master of works' at Carrizo in 1230 was a priest, Martin Gonzalez, who had been a pupil at the convent. He succeeded his brother in this role, and oversaw the completion of its church.[94] The rebuilding of the nuns church at Heiligkreuztal (G), consecrated in 1319, had as 'master of the new building', one Conrad, noted as being a 'mason or stone cutter'.[95]

In a Cistercian convent, provision had to be made presumably for separate worship facilities for the professed nuns and their helpers, the 'sisters' or *converses*. In several churches this was achieved by simply dividing the choir into two, as was commonly done in the male abbeys of the Order. Such a partition is to be found at Heiligenthal (Bavaria, G), Heiligkreuztal (G), Himmelkron (G), La Cambre (B), Frauenthal and Wurmsbach (Swz). At La Ramée (B; 1377) there were no less than three altars in the choir of the *conversa*, presumably the lay-sisters; they were dedicated to Our Lady, St Anne and St Barbara.[96]

At Las Huelgas (Sp) the nuns' choir was sited in the middle of the central nave, but separated off by a grille and a wall.[97] As one author, however, has observed, in the instance of Vignogoul nunnery (F), 'there is often no knowledge of where lay-sisters and lay-brothers were accommodated in a nunnery church'.[98] As for the laity, at Bersenbruck (G), a double-nave church, the northern aisle formed the parish church, the southern that of the nuns; the two

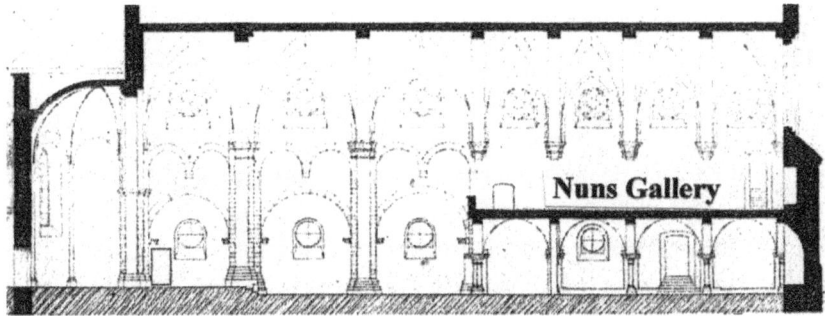

Fig. 3. St-Thomas an der Kyll Abbey Church, Rhineland: Longitudinal Section showing the Nuns' Gallery. (Eydoux, 1952; Copyright: Presses Universitaires de France; reproduced by permission).

being separated by a wall with barred windows.[99] The wall is no more, and the division is now marked only by a step, as the floor level of the nuns' church lay 1.4 metres above that of the parish church.[100] At Rulle (G) one nave was the domain of the nuns, the other of the parishioners and pilgrims.

One adaptation in nunnery churches, especially in Germanic lands, was for the laity (and, perhaps, the lay-brothers and the *converses*) to worship in the body of the church, whilst the nuns' choir was sited in a gallery or tribune extending from the west end over much of the nave, or less often sited in a transept – as at Bergen (G) and Halberstadt (G).[101] It was 'a church within a church'.[102]

The gallery was often a wooden structure supported on posts – as at Assen (Marienkamp; G), Ter Hunnepe (Marienhorst; Ho), and Loosduinen (Ho), or by stone vaults – like those at Chelmno (Pl), Hoven (Marienborn; G), St Thomas an der Kyll (G), and Wormeln (G).[103] Roermond (Ho) was founded primarily as a funerary monument for Count Gerard IV of Gelre and his wife; almost as if the nuns were purposely relegated to their west end gallery.[104] Excavation has proved the pillars of the nuns' gallery at Billigheim (G).[105] Some galleries, as at Isenhagen and Chelmno, were later additions to a church fabric towards the middle of the fourteenth century.[106] The erection of such galleries, and the removal of the nuns to them, freed up space, as at Loosduinen (B), for more burials in the church below.[107] At Vignogoul a triforium allowed of a private oratory.[108]

At Wanzka (G) the gallery occupied the whole length of the nave.[109] The church of Frauental (Würtemberg) was forty-three metres long, but the nuns' gallery occupied but twenty-three metres.[110] At Wienhausen (G), the upper-level choir had access for clergy via two polygonal staircases, so that the priests did not enter the cloister.[111] The nuns entered their gallery from the dorter or by means of a staircase from the cloister, as at Halberstadt (G) where the gallery was located in the south arm of the transept.[112] The nuns' gallery at Holy Cross, Rostock was demolished in 1865, but its entrance from the upper floor of the north wing of the cloister still exists.[113] The steps to the tribune at Roermond (Ho) are yet visible, whilst at Loosduinen (Ho) a tower built at the extreme west end served this purpose.[114]

It has been postulated that nuns galleries had a 'turn' or rotating cabinet, allowing them to witness the consecration and to receive Holy Communion, despite the high ledge or masonry wall which separated the gallery from the rest of the church.[115] The nuns' gallery at Brenkhausen (G) was demolished in the nineteenth century.[116]

Another feature of several Cistercian nuns churches are the tombs of founders and benefactors. Notable in this respect was Las Huelgas (Sp), which had some sixty carved and painted sarcophagi of royalty, including the tombs of twelve kings and queens (in their own right). In prime place are the caskets of Queen Leonora, the foundress, and her husband, Alfonso VIII (both dying in 1214). A common decorative feature is the triple-towered 'yellow castle', from the arms of Castile. The tomb of Berenguela (died 1279), daughter of Ferdinand III and herself a nun, includes the imagery of the Shepherds and the Magi.[117]

At Vallbona (Catalonia), where the church of around 1200 has 'all the simplicity and rigour of the Cistercians', are the tomb monuments of Violant of Hungary, second wife of James I el Conquistador (*ob.* 1275), and of her daughter, Sancha d'Aragon, lying either side of the quire[118] as well as several other fine sepulchral monuments, including that of Abbess Elisendis, who died in 1273.[119] At Clairefontaine (L), its founder, Henry V, count of Luxemburg, lies in his mausoleum erected in the sanctuary, together with his wife. He is depicted wearing a tunic, his hands clasped in prayer, and his sword partly obscures his shield.[120]

In Burgos Museum is now to be seen the sarcophagus of Urraca López de Haro (d. 1226), briefly Queen of León. She is dressed as a nun, and her tomb, formerly at Vileña nunnery close to Burgos, which she had founded came here after fire destroyed that monastery in 1970. The nuns church at Roermond (Vrouwemunster;

Ho) is the home, in the crossing, of the recently restored tombs of Count Gerard II of Guelders (*d.* 1229) and his wife, Margaret of Brabant (*d.* 1231), lying side by side.[121]

At Marienthal (Hesse) is the funerary monument of Count Otto I of Waldeck, buried there after his murder in 1305. It depicts Otto in armour, with shield and sword. At Odivelas, the tomb of the founder, King Dinis I (*d.* 1325) is to be found in a chapel of the apse, bearing his recumbent figure; also interred there is his daughter, Maria Alfonso (d. 1320).[122]

A very necessary adjunct in the churches was the provision of lighting, often provided for by rents from lands donated for the purpose, as at Heiligekreuztal (G), where in 1294 it received land to provide income to 'augment the lighting in the church'.[123] Borstel (G; 1274) had a property at Oldenlinghe, part of the income from which was allocated 'to lighting in the church by day, and in the dorter by night'.[124] On the entry there of his daughter, Gertrude, Duke Henry of Silesia (1224) made a gift of wax to Trzebnitz (Pl) 'to illuminate the church, and to have a light day and night before the altar of St Bartholomew'.[125] The nuns of Ołobok (P) in 1273 received lands to provide income 'to illuminate their church of Blessed Mary the Virgin'.[126]

A nun of Zyweke (B; 1343) was in a financial position to make provision for 'a good light to burn during the divine office and certain Masses'.[127] Especial respect was paid to the reserved Blessed Sacrament, by a light shining before it, as at Rinteln (G; 1351).[128] Rasse, Lord of Garre, 'in respect of his soul and for the redemption of his sins', gave a rent to Epinlieu (B; 1244) for the maintenance of two lamps, 'the one hanging before the Body of Christ, the other before the image of the Holy Virgin'.[129] The nuns of Oslavany (Cz; 1380) received a grant to sustain a light burning day and night 'before the cross of the Lord'.[130] Much earlier, in 1243, a land transaction had allowed them to purchase from the Franciscans of Prague, 'a gold chalice ornamented with fine gems, a *tabula* and two *ampulla* of crystal'.[131]

The daily life of the nuns followed that of their male counter-parts: 2 am Matins, perhaps then some rest; 6 am Prime, followed by the first Mass; Terce at 8.30 am, followed by the conventual Mass; Sext, at 11.15 followed by dinner. Glimpses of the divine office appear in monastic records: as the chanting of the Athanasian Creed on Sundays at Prime (in an unnamed nunnery noted by Caesarius of Heisterbach);[132] the singing of the Te Deum on Feasts of Twelve Lessons festivals at Medingen (G; 1334);[133] and 'the suffrages, matins, vespers, and the Salve Regina after Compline' at Zyveke (B; 1343).[134] Conrad of Massnu, noted of Szczecin (P) nunnery: 'the sounding of the organs, the canticles, hymns and prayers, day and night'.[135]

From 1218 the nuns kept the day of the Eleven Thousand Virgins as a Feast of Twelve Lessons.[136] From 1264, the nuns as well as the monks of the Order were daily to join in the suffrages for the Holy Father and the Holy Roman Church; a duty which was to last 'until the moment of the Resurrection of the Lord'.[137] As for extra-liturgical services, Herkenrode (B) possessed a monstrance dating from 1286;[138] Roermond (Ho; 1288) an image of Our Lady carried in procession on her feast-days.[139] As for the reception of the Holy Communion, the General Chapter ruled in 1260 that the nuns of the Order should receive the Blessed Sacrament at least seven times in the year, or even more often if the Visitor thought it expedient.[140]

Further insight into the liturgy is gained from the desire of benefactors to enhance the liturgy, or more commonly for funerary obsequies and annual obits. A benefactor in 1238 desired the celebration at Aywières (B) of a Mass of the Holy Trinity on Sundays, on Mondays for the souls in purgatory, on Tuesdays of St Mary Magdalene, on Wednesdays of St Gertrude, on Thursdays of the Holy Apostles, on Fridays of the Holy Cross, and on Saturdays of the Blessed Virgin Mary.[141]

Duke Barnim I (1252) gave an annuity of ten marks to the nuns of Szczecin (Pl) for prayers and Mass on the anniversary of his wife's death.[142] He also provided five marks on the occasion of her funeral for the construction of an altar there dedicated to St Katherine.[143] Reyner, a citizen of Magdeburg (1246) made a grant to the nuns of St Agnes there, which provided for 'the communion/common wine of the ladies' on the great festivals.[144]

At Catesby (E) was an altar of Edward the Confessor and an image of St Anne. When in 1267 William de Mauduit died, his body was buried at Westmnister Abbey – perhaps because he passed away during a pilgrimage to St Edward's altar there, but his heart was interred at Catesby. A grant of 1276 allowed a rental of 30d. each year to maintain the light before that image.[145]

When Bishop Conrad IV of Freising died in 1340 he bequeathed the princely sum of one hundred pounds to the nuns of Wald (G), expecting of them not only a weekly requiem with vigil, but also the chanting of the seven penitential psalms and the litany, and on Tuesday nights the singing of the Salve Regina.[146] There are many other such instances.

THE CLOISTERS

The original claustral buildings of early medieval Cistercian convents are often lacking, or in a bad state of preservation, but there are notable exceptions: not least at Las Huelgas (Sp) where two fine cloisters yet remain; the earliest in Romanesque style and dating from the late-twelfth century, the later a gothic edifice ranging in date from the thirteenth to the fifteenth centuries. Other well preserved cloisters are to be seen at Porta Coeli (Tišnov, Cz; thirteenth-century); Villamayor (Sp; where the pier capitals bear vegetative designs based on the local flora),[147] and vaulted in brick at Börstel (G), Heiligengrabe (G), Isenhagen, with a series of fine medieval consoles (G; dating from around 1350);[148] Neuendorf (G; the south aisle only surviving), and Żarnowiec (Pl; now restored).

A stunning display of foliage designs marks the capitals in the cloisters of both Las Huelgas (Sp) and San Andrés de Arroyo (Sp).[149] The cloister capitals of Celas (Pt) bear imagery of Christ, St Benedict and St Bernard.[150] Amongst the fine cloisters of Cistercian nuns that of Wienhausen (G) must take pride of place. Built in brick, there yet remain a series of early-fourteenth century wall paintings, amongst them those depicting Christ rising from the tomb, and a typical banner-holding Lamb of God.[151]

Off the cloister lay the necessary chambers for the life of the nuns: chapter-house, refectory, kitchen, etc., whilst steps led up to their dorter, as still to be seen at Fontaine-Guérard (F).[152] The claustral buildings at Grafenthal (G) took fifty years to complete (1248–98), and their erection was aided by grants of indulgence to donors by the archbishop of Cologne, and the bishops of Utrecht, Munster and Osnabruck.[153] Relatively little has been written regarding these domestic quarters of the nuns, but at Marham (E), whilst its church measured 58 by 17 metres, the refectory spanned 22 by 15 metres, and the guest-house, 43 by 11 metres.[154] Little is known of the provision made for the ancillary brothers and lay-sisters; but at Bijloke (B) the latter were accommodated in the west wing.[155]

The Early Cistercian Nuns, 1098–1350

There is scant record of nunnery buildings being used, as those of numerous male abbeys were, to safeguard the prized possessions of the laity. At Carrizo (Sp; 1269), however, the will of Teresa Morán reveals the safe deposit there of her objects of value, including 'cushions, gold rings, and sleeves embroidered with pearls'.[156] At Lübeck nunnery (G) faciliities in the cloister were said to be lacking in 1267, and a one hundred day indulgence was granted to those who aided the completion of the necessary works.[157]

CHAPTER-HOUSES

Several fine vaulted chapter-houses yet survive from Cistercian nunneries; notably those of Maubuisson (F) and Fontaine-Guérard ('one of the best examples of Normandy architecture from the early thirteenth-century'); Cañas (Sp; where the capital of the central pillar bears floral decoration);[158] Porta Coeli (Tišnov, Cz; where a stone lectern remains); Vallbona (Sp; its entrance a fine gothic portal), and Żarnowiec (Pl; of brick construction).[159] At Vallbona are to be seen several gravestones of abbesses buried in the chapter-house, as was their due; the ordinary nuns were interred in the cloisters.[160]

The imposing tomb of Blessed Urraca Diaz de Haro in the chapter-house at Cañas convent, abbess there for many years prior to her death in 1262, was opened in 1819 and her body found to be absolutely intact. Her sarcophagus shows her holding her pastoral staff, while the sides depict her funeral procession and her entry into heaven.[161] The vaulted chapter-house at Arroyo nunnery (Sp) contains the tombs of the first two abbesses, Mencia and Maria.[162]

DORTERS

The brick dorter at Bijloke (B) was built with money bequeathed by the nuns' confessor in 1316.[163] At an unknown date, Francis of Senzeille, monk of Jardinet (B), who acted as busar and provost of Marche-les-Dames for nineteen years, was praised for his care of the nunnery buildings, including 'the stable of the horses, the chamber of the guests above the postern gate, and the chamber of the abbess'.[164] The incorporated monastery of Veszprémvölgy (Hg), despite having considerable possessions, yet pleaded poverty in

1317 and bewailed the lack of noble support, which left it unable to restore its dormitory.[165] In 1349 not only the church, but also the dorter at Sonnefeld (G), were completed in stone.[166]

The General Chapter in the early-fourteenth century tried to prohibit nuns from sleeping in private rooms.[167] Archbishop Melton of York (1318) required on visitation at Swine (E) that the dormitory might be covered so that the nuns could use it without annoyance from storms, and that nuns were to sleep there not in different places.[168] Grants of rents and lands to provide the income for lighting dorters are on record for Börstel (G)[169] and Duissern (G).[170]

In 1287 the General Chapter prohibited individual nuns from having their own chambers, save those 'for whom the monastery was founded'. The Chapter of 1314 noted that a number of nuns now had their own chambers; these were to be 'irretrievably destroyed', and no new chambers were to be constructed. This ruling was modified in 1327, when a nun might have a separate chamber but it would be exceptional, and requiring the agreement of the General Chapter.[171]

INFIRMARIES

More is known regarding the infirmaries of nunneries and the care of the sick. As in male abbeys a suitable nun would be appointed to take charge, as the 'infirmary sister' at Nonenque (F; 1279),[172] and the 'mistress of the infirmary' at Neuwerk (Goslar, G; 1317).[173] The infirmary at Flines (B), as doubtless others, had its own chapel.[174] Lands and rents might be sought to assist in the expenses of the infirmaries. The work of the infirmary of La Ramée (B) was helped by a grant by the bishop of Liège of the tithes of Marilles and Piétremeaux, although the ownership of the former became a subject of dispute.[175]

The work of the infirmary at Aywières (B) was assisted when Alexander IV (1258) granted the nuns the profits of five churches, and directed the abbot of Aulne to see this happened. In 1294 Boniface VIII gave directions for the care of its sick members, and allowed Aywières to bury any dying there.[176] Adam, the provost of Neukloster (Sonnenkamp; G), assigned in 1260 the proceeds of two of its villages to the needs of its infirmary and 'to the restoration of the sick and the health of the weak'.[177]

A grant was made to Lilienthal (Lower Saxony; 1320) 'for the comfort of our sick',[178] whilst a lady of rank augmented the income for the infirmary at Börstel (G; 1274).[179] The bishop of Camin (1304) made a grant of three churches to Szczecin (P), and two churches to Ivenack (G) so that 'the sick nuns can be better provided for'.[180] Kunigunde Lengin (1330) gave during her life one silver mark yearly to the nuns of St Martin, Erfurt (G), after her death it was to be applied 'for the better service of those in the infirmary'.[181]

Holthausen (G; 1276) received a grant of ten measures of grain, 'specially for the infirmary'.[182] When a married couple gave Beuditz (G; 1297) a substantial annual rent of four silver marks, with hens and sheep, it was to claim the right of burial in the abbey church, the nuns promising that the income would be used to care for the sisters in the infirmary, and for 'the poor at the gate'.[183]

Count Thomas of Flanders and Hainaut (1240/41) gave Marquette (F) a large portion of woodland, the income deriving to be used to provide annually eight casks of wine, either for the infirmary or for a pittance.[184] A like grant to the nuns of St Agnes, Magdeburg (1271) allowed for a pittance for them and 'for the necessities of the sick nuns'.[185] The nuns of Acre received oil for the lamps in their infirmary from the church of Acre (Sy), and, in 1222, expressed the hope that the nuns of its daughter-house in Nicosia, Cyprus, might get their oil from the church of Nicosia.[186] Ichtershausen (G; 1195) received an annual rent worth six silver marks for 'lighting in the infirmary'.[187]

Archbishop Giffard on visitation at Swine (E; 1268) found that the sick nuns were badly provided for, despite Saer of Sutton earlier that century granting land for this purpose.[188] Visiting Sinningthwaite (E) in 1315 Archbishop Greenfield of York ordered better care of the sick, so far as the means of the house allowed.[189] Archbishop Zouche of York in 1346 said that the infirmary of Nun Appleton (E) was too limited in capacity, that certain chambers on the west part of the church beyond the parlour in which certain of the nuns, 'contrary to honesty of religion', were abiding, were to be pulled down so that the infirmary might be extended.[190]

Care sems to have been taken where infectious diseases were concerned. In 1287 the archbishop of York wrote to the Master of Sherburn Hospital near Durham, asking him to admit Basilia de Colum, one of the nuns of Handale (E), who was stricken with leprosy, and for fear of contagion could not dwell among healthy women.[191] There is a reference in 1293 in a deed of Arouca (Pt) referring to 'our infirmary grange': did that refer to a lay infirmary sited well away in order to avoid infection, as at the male abbeys of Neath and Tintern in Wales?[192] The deed more specifically mentions the 'the chaff house of our infirmary grange';[193] might that also suggest a grange sited, for health reasons, some way from the convent?

Gregory IX gave Cistercian nunneries the right to give burial to their benefactors,[194] Basedale (E) had a cemetery for the burial of 'nuns and sisters and our brethren who have taken our habit'.[195] Avise, mother of a fourteenth-century chaplain at Port Royal (F), gave its nuns ten pounds for the keeping of her anniversary, and for burial in their cloister.[196]

REFECTORIES: DIET

As for refectories, the south range at Bijloke, Ghent, built 1325–30, is the finest extant medieval Cistercian nunnery refectory in Europe. Its western end is 'a masterpiece of gothic brick architecture'.[197] At Mortain (F; 1232), the Visitor, Abbot Stephen Lexington of Savigny, ordered the refectory bell 'to be hung up high, according to the custom of the Order'.[198] Archbishop Greenfield of York (1311) was disturbed to learn that the nuns of Hampole (E) did not eat in common in their refectory, but separately in 'divers chambers and other places'. He ordered that they should have their meals together, unless one was ill or otherwise legitimately hindered.[199] A local knight in 1320 reconstructed the refectory and dorter of Itzehoe (G) as the nunnery was in debt.[200]

The rule of abstinence from flesh meat for nuns, save the weak and infirm, was an ancient one re-iterated by the General Chapter in 1283 and again in 1320, with the reminder that it was forbidden also to consume fatty products.[201] When, in 1285, the Chapter had agreed to the reception at nunneries of Franciscan guests for an overnight stay, it ruled that they were not to be served with meat, unless again weak or infirm.[202] Archbishop Sinningthwaite, on visitation at Sinningthwaite (E) in 1315, forbade its boy and girl boarders from eating meat in Advent and at Sexagesima, and in Lent, eggs and cheese, in the refectory; this was to be done in some other place on appropriate occasions.[203] Does this suggest a weakening of the practice of abstinence?

Bishop Hugh of Lincoln (1209-35) directed that at Nun Cotham (E) 'the nuns, chaplains, brothers and sisters, as well as any guests, will have the same type of bread to eat and the same drink', but special consideration should be given to the sick.[204] After their monastery was burnt to the ground, 'desolate and destroyed', until it could be restored, the nuns of Sonnefeld G) received permission from Rome to eat meat on three days of the week. The deed is undated, but perhaps refers to the time of Pope Urban VI (1378-89).[205]

Two early grants of flesh meat to Cistercian nunneries raises the question as to whether meat was eaten by others than the sick: possibly retainers, and as to how and by whom. Peter de Montfort (*d.* 1216) gave the nuns of Pinley (E) 'the tithes of all the food of his house; namely, bread, beer, fish and flesh, and what-ever was dressed in the kitchen'.[206]

William de Kahaynes, the son of its founder, made a like grant in the early-thirteenth century to the nuns of Tarrant (E), of the tithes of all salt meat killed in his household each year, as well as two barrels of ale at Christmas. It was perhaps Bishop le Poor of Salisbury, the reputed but not the true founder of Tarrant (E), who told the nuns, ' My dear sisters, ye shall not possess any beast, only a cat'. He also bade them that, when going to the house nearby of their real founder to collect the food they were due, 'to be glad in your heart if ye suffer insolence from Slurry, the cook's boy, who washeth dishes in the kitchen'. It would seem the good bishop had endured this himself.[207]

Some wealthy benefactors ensured that the nuns they favoured were well supplied with food. Jean, countess of Flanders, was a substantial benefactor of Aywières granting it lands for the maintenance of its chaplain, as well as pittances on certain days and a gift of 4,000 herrings in Advent and Lent. Other donors in the early and mid-thirteenth century made it grants of property to help sustain the relief of the poor 'at the gate'.[208]

Philip IV of France (1292, 1303) accorded the nuns of Gomerfontaine a tenth of 'the desserts of bread and wine at the royal table'.[209] Count Hugh of Chaumont gave the nuns of Gomerfontaine at its foundation (1207) a grant of one-tenth of the eels of his local fishponds at Gomerfontaine and at Lattainville as well as three 'muids' of wheat yearly from his mill at Gomerfontaine.[210]

His son, Count John, later gave a further 25 'muids' of wheat each year; and the first part of the wood of Crenne. Countess Matilda of Boulogne (1252) granted the nuns 500 herrings yearly, and in 1293 they received fishing rights on the local river.[211] Blanche of Castile (1247) bequeathed a substantial portion of the hearth-tax gained from Romorantin, so that the nuns might receive annually fifty pounds for purchasing wheat for making the community's bread.[212] Two brothers, 'known as cousins', gave Oberschönenfeld (1278) twenty Augsburg pounds for the formation of a grange at Zeyssenhoven, on condition that from the income derived from that property, two pounds were expended in Lent on herrings for the nuns, or other fish if herrings could not be obtained.[213]

PITTANCES

In practice, the abstemious diet the nuns might normally expect was tempered when an additional dish or accompaniment, like wine, was provided. These 'pittances' were normally provided from monies given to individual nunneries either in the lifetime of benefactors or bequeathed in their wills. Of course some convents fared in this respect better than others.

Few nunneries can have excelled Flines in this regard: its cartulary contains an undated list of 224 pittances enjoyed by its nuns, and also make mention of the nun pitancier, whose job it was to administer the system.[214] Some monetary gifts were very generous, as that of Mahaut of Bethune (1259) who bequeathed twenty pounds for a pittance for the nuns of Marquette (F).[215]

A widow gave forty pounds to Oberschönenfeld (G; 1340), one of the conditions being that three pounds was spent yearly to buy 'wine, fish and bread' for the nuns on her birthday.[216] Peter Martins (1322), cantor of nearby Coimbra cathedral, beqeathed fifty pounds to Celas (Pt) for a pittance: thirty five pounds destined for the abbess's' household, fifteen for the community refectory.[217] Guilhelme de Senmenat was the 'pitancier' for her fellow nuns at Vallbona (Sp) in 1264.

The nuns of Baindt (G) over its six hundred year history accrued over one hundred pittances of wine each year.[218] The nuns of Roermond (Ho) had each year 135 pittances of wine, in addition to several days of 'solemn service', and of 'wheaten bread' each Maundy Thursday.[219] Wald (G) had sixteen pittances recorded, or the money to cover their cost;[220] Notre-Dame-des-Prés (F) received twenty-two, ranging in value from twenty to sixty shillings, again to defray the cost.²²¹ Amongst the bequests made to Marche-les-Dames (B) by John of Chanoy and Joan, his wife, were four oboli for the recreation of the community on the day of his anniversary, inviting close blood relatives or friends'.²²²

For the nuns of Guldenberg (Mont-d'Or, B), Margaret of Constantinople, countess of Flanders and Hainaut gave £20 for pittances on the anniversary of her death.²²³ She also granted a rent to Val-St-Georges (B; 1252) to provide a pittance for its nuns, also on the anniversary of her death.²²⁴ Henry, duke of Silesia (1223) granted the nuns of Trebznitz (Pl) a lake and other properties to provide yearly two pittances for the nuns: one on the feast of St Bartholomew (the dedication of their church) and the other on the anniversary of his death.²²⁵

The abbot of Caesarea, on visitation at Selingenthal (G; 1285), ordered that from the profits of certain tithes the cellarer was to make provision for wine for the nuns at Christmas, Easter and Pentecost.²²⁶ A donor to Frankenhausen (G, 1296) requested a 'solemn service' on his anniversary, but it is not clear whether he meant a pittance or a liturgical obit. From the following year its nuns received a mark yearly for a pittance at CorpusChristi.²²⁷

Other nunneries to enjoy pittances of wine included Heiligkreuztal (G),²²⁸ Seligenthal (on 25th January), and Fontenelle (F; the latter on St Valentine's Day).²²⁹ Ludeman of Lichtenberg (1345) gave yearly a seemingly large measure of of white wine to Lichtenthal (G), where his four daughters were nuns, but it was to cease when all four had died.²³⁰ Margaret, lady of Woumen (1246), gave Zwyveke (B) an annuity of thirty shillings in Flanders money, payable each feast of St Remigius (1 October), for a pittance of wine for the community.²³¹ The necrology of Billigheim notes the obits of five donors who on the same day, 'in the advent of Our Lord', gave its nuns for this season five urns of wine.²³²

The provision of wine was not the only pittance. A grant to Neukloster (Sonnenkamp, G; 1279) included annual gifts of wheat, barley and oats, so that four times in the year, on the anniversaries of the grantor and his forebears, the nuns might have a 'special consolation in the refectory'.²³³ John of Luxembourg, King of Bohemia (*ob.* 1356) bequeathed an annual grant of six measures of razed spelt to Marche-les-Dames (B), a grain seen as a health food. (The nuns were later to receive much more).²³⁴ The nuns of

Coldstream (S) received a rent from a toft and croft in 'Dercester' 'to make a pittance for the nuns on the morrow of St Lawrence the Martyr', so on 11 August each year their spartan diet found a degree of luxury.[235]

Francis of Aische (1271) left Val-St Georges (B) a rent not only to provide an annual obit, but also for a pittance for its nuns of wine and fish on the vigil of St Gregory (11 March).[236] The nuns of Rathausen (Swz) received a pittance of 'wine, fish and white bread' on the anniversary of the death of their founder.[237] Interestingly, Caesarius of Heisterbach (d. c. 1240) told of fried eggs being distributed in an unnamed nunnery as a pittance, and of one nun being omitted in error![238]

These are but a few examples of pittances granted to Cistercian nuns. Mostly, but not entirely, they date from the second half of the thirteenth century. Unhappily for the nuns of Heiligkreuztal (G) it was reported in 1314 that they had not been served certain pittances of wine, and the father abbot of Salem was instructed to correct this shortcoming.[239]

BOOKS, MANUSCRIPTS, KALENDARS,
NECROLOGIES, SEALS, IMAGES, RELICS

Few manuscript works emanating from Cistercian nunneries, and dateable to the early medieval period are known. Even the catalogue of the library at the great Silesian abbey of Trzebnitz (Pl) yields only five or six such works – from the twelfth century – a Legend of St Bernard; from the thirteenth – a collection of the Epistles of St Paul with the Letter to the Hebrews; from the early fourteenth century, and all of course in Latin: a *Life of St Hedwig*, a psalter, and the *Oposcula* of the noted Francisan theologian, Richard of Mediavilla (d. 1308). The first is the foremost work, and includes the miracles attributed to St Hedwig, and the bull of her canonisation issued by Clement IV.[240]

The later library of Gravenhorst (G) contained but one thirteenth/fourteenth manuscript: a fragment of the *De diaetis particularibus* of the ninth-century Egyptian Jewish physician, Isaac Judaeus.[241] The libraries and choirs of most Cistercian nunneries will have contained all necessary liturgical works, and coming as many of them did from noble families the nuns will probably have taken an interest in spiritual and other literature. When Anrode (G) in 1287 founded the nunnery of Marksussra in Thuringia, four 'literate ladies' were amongst the ten sisters sent there.[242]

Kalendars were of significance as they guided the religious through the Church's year. A kalendar from Wintney (E) gives the date of dedication of the nuns' church, and is really the obit book of the convent. Attached is a detailed treatise on the *Rule of St Benedict* for religious sisters, written in both Latin and Middle English. Compiled perhaps not later than the early fourteenth century it lists over one hundred deceased sisters, including eleven former prioresses; occasionally noted as being of 'good' or 'pious' memory. It also notes the deaths of six monarchs, six bishops of Winchester and six abbots of Reading, as well as the death of Abbot Adam of Waverley – who perhaps had oversight of the house?[243]

A kalendar and obit book of the second half of the thirteenth century comes from Billigheim (Marienbrunn, G) nunnery. The kalendar gives 20 July as the feast of St Margaret, Virgin and Martyr; the obits include those of 'Henard, our father, sometime prior in Bronnbach' (*the nearby abbey of that name*: 3 January), *senex Alheidis conversae* (5 March), Reinbert (*conversus*, 21 April), Katherine, nun (20 May), and 'Gisela, our mother in *Coeli porta*. (25 December).[244] 'Our father' may suggest that he had perhaps been the nunnery's provisor or chaplain or confessor; 'our mother' may indicate that when Billigheim became Cistercian, nuns from Himmelspforten had settled there.

The nuns of Baudeloo and Billigheim were amongst those who observed the feast of St Thomas of Canterbury (29 December), and also that of the Crown of of Thorns (11 August).[245] Two sections of the cartulary of Fontenelle list benefactors who had requested that their obit be kept with the sum of money they had donated. Amongst them were a chaplain of the Steward of Flanders remembered on 9 August against a bequest of fifteen shillings, and on 22 November a Madame Yde de Boviler was commemorated having left twenty shillings.[246]

An outstanding extant manuscript is the necrology of Seligenthal (G). Originating perhaps in 1310 most of the entries relate to the later middle ages and to modern times. The listing of the dates for Easter Day suggests that some at least of the many entries were added in the seventeenth century: Easter came, the book reveals, in 1633 on 27 March. Apart from the lists of the deceased, the kalendar notes the feasts of the apostles, and there is a section relating to benefactors and their gifts.

In the fourteenth century prominence is given to the obits of members of the princely family of Bavaria: as Otto, 'the most serene king of Hungary and duke of Bavaria' (1313), and Otto, 'the illustrious duke of Bavaria' (1335). There is the occasional mention of a former abbess or nun, but also of laity who served the nunnery: such as in 1254 of Catherine Fraubergerin, 'our faithful waitress', and in 1259 the convent's doctor (John Raming) and apothecary (Philip Karthauser).[247]

Frequently surviving are graduals, containing the antiphons employed at the Eucharist. A gradual at Fürstenberg (G), dating from the first half of the thirteenth century, may have derived from Camp, whose abbot was its Visitor, as also a martyrology with later additions, including the procedure for visitation.[248] A Cistercian gradual at Seligenthal (G) of 1260 was the work of a nun, Elizabeth Hyttlin, precentrix there for thirty-five years.[249]

A Cistercian gradual dating from around 1240 can be ascribed to Burtscheid (G).[250] A notable gradual in the possession of Rulle (G) was commissioned or copied out by one of its nuns, Gisele von Kersenbrock, who died in 1300. It was decorated with exquisite miniatures and golden initials[251] Abbess Clare von Tigenscheyn (1347–8) had a gradual book decorated with eight gold patterned initial letters. The presence of kneeling Cistercian nuns in the initial letters and on the edges of the pages indicates Wonnental (G), whose Abbess Agnes (1311–26) is, in addition, pictured in one of the initials with St Agnes, her patron saint.[252]

An antiphonary of the thirteenth century belonging to Arouca (Pt) depicted St Bernard in the role of teacher; one of around 1300 emanating from Seligenthal featured both an image of St Bernard and of the nun who copied the manuscript.[253] An antiphonary of the fourteenth century belonging to Welver (G) contained a fine illustration of Gabriel and Mary within the intial letter for the feast of the Annunciation, whilst the initial letter for the feast of All Saints depicted a scene which included the wife of Emperor Diocletian, the Greek deity Artemis, and St Cyriacus, the hermit of Palestine.[254]

Where music was concerned the codex of Las Huelgas (Sp), dating back to the thirteenth/fourteenth centuries, would find few equals. It contains 185 pieces, including five *kyries*, nine settings for the *Agnus Dei*, and no less than fifty-eight motets.[255] Las Huelgas

(Sp) also acquired a lectionary of the second half of the 12th century.[256] Its thirteenth-century extant works include a *collectarium*, portions of the Scriptures, as well as a martyrology which includes the Rule of St Benedict and sermons of St Augustine, all preceded by a kalendar 'for the use of the Cistercian Order'.[257]

A few liturgical works survive from the nunnery of Arouca (Pt); amongst them is a thirteenth-century *collectarium*, inclusive of a kalendar and the Easter tables; the kalendar tells of 18 May as being the day of dedication of the nunnery church, whilst a collect entitled 'for the thirtieth of *Cisterciensi*, may reflect the remembrance of the year when Arouca entered the Cistercian fold.[258]

Together with the 'so-called gradual' of Lorvão (Pt), a very erudite and extremely detailed analysis of these works possessed by the nunneries of Iberia, suggests: firstly, that they were written perhaps at the turn of the twelfth century in a Castilian scriptorium by French clerics, who had been trained at Cîteaux and sent to Las Huelgas as chaplains and scribes; secondly, that 'the Cistercian use of the four manuscripts can be confirmed by comparing their conservative festal cycle with contemporaneous Cistercian kalendars, and thirdly, that their elaborate and colourful decoration was a departure from the Cistercian attitude to illuminated manuscripts at the time.[259]

Several late-thirteenth to early-fourteenth century antiphonals survive from Lichtenthal (G), incuding one with the propers 'of the saints', and another containing those 'of the times'. The nunnery also possessed a bible dating from around 1300, but incomplete in that it lacked the psalms.[260] Other aids to the liturgy known to be extant, included: a breviary transcribed by the nuns of Marquette (F) around 1257/58;[261] a diurnal compiled about 1300 at the male abbey of Altzelle but held by the nuns of Marienstern (G), from whose library a thirteenth-century psalter survives.[262] Little is known of the library of Isenhagen (G), but in 1253 the nunnery was bequeathed a missal.[263] Cañas (Sp) possessed, still extant, a Burgundian antiphonary dating from around 1200, as well as a Castilian missal of about 1270.[264]

Nor were the Scriptures neglected. A five-volume Bible was realised at Lichtental (about 1300),[265] whilst the Goslar Gospels 'reveal a lively artistic and spiritual life' at Neuwerk (Mariengarten; G) nunnery in that city, whether produced there or for the convent. The fine miniscules on gold demonstrate the transition from Romanesque to Gothic.[266] A nun of Rulle (G) was a scriptrix, Christina von Haltern. She died in 1280 but not before completing at least the first volume of an Old Testament in two volumes, and 'many other books'.[267] In 1342 Wanzka nunnery (G) bought a two-volume bible from Stolpe abbey.[268] Bersenbrück (G) possessed a manuscript dating from around 1300, and entitled 'Of the Apocalypse'.[269]

Other works included biographies. The *ex libris* shows a mid-thirteenth century Life of Ida de Léau (Ida of Nivelles) to have been owned by La Ramée (B).[270] In the time of Abbess Margaret (1302–17) a life of its foundress, Countess Agnes of Meissen, was written at Wienhausen (G).[271] The extensive collection from Marienthal (G) includes a *Rule of St Benedict* and a *Martyrology* in a mid-thirteenth century hand; it may have come from the Benedictine cloister of Posa.[272]

A copy of the 'Legenda Aura' of Jacobs von Voragine was bequeathed to the nunnery of Mariengarten (Erfurt) in 1316.[273] Nor must be forgotten the writings of the mystics, detailed before. Hildegarde von Hürnheim, born around 1255 and the daughter of a local lord, was sent for education at the age of seventeen to the convent at Zimmern. Its confessor, Rudolf, a monk of Kaishein, encouraged her to translate into Germany the *Secretum secretorum* of Philip of Tripoli; she finished it in 1282 but died the same year.[274]

Not least were the cartularies drawn up by, or for, the nunneries. The cartulary of La Cour-Notre-Dame at Michery (F), was drawn up in the late-fifteenth century on the orders of its father abbot of Cîteaux, concerned because the Hundred Years War threatened to overrun the region where the nunnery was located.[275] The charters it recites were kept in three chests.[276] The cartulary of Cotham (E) contains within seventy-one folios, 523 entries, comprehending papal bulls, charters, concords, enumeration of animal pastures and stock, as well as other deeds, though not in chronological order.[277]

The cartulary of Stixwould (E), comprising some 248 folios and enumerating some 560 twelfth and thirteenth century grants, with a further twenty-four charters written in a later hand, is clearly rebound with a leather cover, embossed with the Tudor rose surmounted by a crown. Each charter recorded is preceded by the name of the donor inscribed in red ink.[278] The collected charters of Sonnefeld (G) comprise 361 deeds ranging in date from 1252 to 1676.[279]

Care for documents was shown when the prioress of Cotham (E; 1300/1320) declined to send original deeds requested by the bishop of Lincoln, 'fearful that they or their seals might be damaged'. Instead she caused them to be copied for transmission into 'a little roll', authenticated by the seal of the deanery of Yarborough.[280] The nuns of Ivanics (Hg) in 1288, having lost their copy of a charter given them in 1246 by the bishop of Zagreb, asked his successor not only to confirm it, but also to 'renew and transcribe it'.[281]

Original charters were of extreme importance in defending challenges to a nunnery's possessions and privileges: as a 13th century deed issued to the nuns of Goslar (G) put it: 'so that things do not slip away in time, people should write them down for the eternity with witnesses'.[282] Bishop Gerard of Verden (1264) granted a charter to Medingen (G) so that 'by the evidence of this writing matters are not forgotten'.[283] A charter granted to Lichtental (G; 1340) by Wigand, an esquire of Barghusen, was 'committed to writing because the memory of men easily changes with the passage of time'.'[284]

Such words are commonplace in monastic charters. From the mid-13th century Latin script might be replaced in charters by the vernacular: Old French in documents of Clairefontaine (B) from around 1255.[285] Old German in the charters of Lichtental by 1288;[286] Grafenthal from 1323;[287] at Sonnefeld from the 1330's;[288] at Medingen from 1340;[289] at Gravenhorst from 1343;[290] at Frankenhausen (G) from 1349;[291] at Rinteln[292] and Sitzenroda (G) in the 1350's.[293]

The seals used by nunneries of the Order included all three main types known to the male abbeys: hand-and-staff, as at Ebersecken (Swz; 1288); an abbess seated with pastoral staff, as for Arouca (Pt; 1259); and an abbess standing holding her pastoral staff, as at Gnadenthal (G; 1305).

There was, however, a much wider variety of seal imagery tthan that associated with the seals of the male monasteries, particularly where the conventual/common seal of a house was concerned. That of Rostock (G) portrayed the Crucifixion with Our Lady and St John, as the convent was dedicated to the Holy Cross; that of Paradies nunnery, playing on its name, depicted Adam and Eve in the Garden of Eden; Eve eating of the forbidden fruit, the serpent rearing up from base. The provosts/procurators had their own independent seals (Chapter 3).[294]

As for imagery, Caesarius of Heisterbach (*d. c.* 1240) told of the nuns of Burscheid (G) possessing a picture about one and a half feet long, displaying the bust of 'the blessed pontiff Nicholas', who was depicted as having 'a bold brow, and the hair of his head and beard quite white'. The nunnery of Hoven (Marienborn, G), he reported, had an image of the martyred St Catherine 'decently sculptured in wood'.[295] As for stone sculptures, imagery of around 1275 on the sarcophagus of an abbess of Cañas (Sp) might be that of the father-abbot on visitation.[296]

The west front of Tišnov (Porta Coeli; Cz) church has a portrayal of Christ dating from 1240, depicting the Saviour surrounded by the founders of the nunnery.[297] The Dominican chronicler, Hermann von Lerbecke (*d.* 1410) noted in his day an early-fourteenth century funerary slab at Rinteln (G), which commemorated the burial there of several members of the nobility, and which expressed the hope that Christ would receive their souls.[298] The stone lectern survives in the chapter-house of Tišnov; a fourteenth-century image of Our Lady and her Child at Żarnowitz(Pl).[299]

A not infrequent imagery was that of Our Lord in His grave; the nunnery of Heiligengrabe (G) took its name from just such a shrine. The holy sepulchre at Heiligenkreuz (A) was well embedded in the floor. A wooden holy sepulchre at Maigrauge (Swz) dates from around 1330;[300] it is a movable shrine dedicated for use in the Easter liturgy.[301] At Chelmno (Pl) a fine wooden sculpture of Christ in the grave dates from around 1380.

Other wooden imagery of note included an oak lectern at Isenhagen (G) dating from 1247;[302] an early 14th-century meditation board at Holy Cross, Rostock (G), featuring the Crucifixion, with a sword piercing the heart of Mary;[303] and the rood cross of Maagdendaal (B; dated about 1260), which measured 4.57 x 2.72 metres, and which carried a figure worked from the wood of the stem of the cross.[304]

An early-thirteenth century oak cross covered with silver plate and part gilded survives from the nunnery of Paraclete-des-Champs (F), as does an early-fourteenth century silver reliquary. Both objects are now preserved at Amiens cathedral.[305] At Isenhagen (G) a two-tiered tabernacle on the high altar, dating from about 1300, reserved the Sacrament.[306]

The fragments of the retable, constructed in Maubuisson (F) around 1340, with sculptural reliefs, exhibit as their main motif the theme of the Eucharist.[307] Maubuisson also possesed 'a wooden statue of the Virgin, seated on a silver plate borne by four angels, she holding a fleur-de-lis', given by Queen Jean of France and Navarre (*ob.* 1371).

The nuns' choir at Wienhausen (G), built around 1330, is covered with paintings: the ceiling depicting scenes from the life and passion of Christ; the walls imagery from the Old Testament and the lives of the saints. Frescoes of similar date adorning the nuns' choir at Chelmno depict imagery based upon the Song of Songs and the Passion of Christ.[308] At Heiligenkreuztal (G) an early-fourteenth century painting depicts St Bernard giving a spade and a measuring rod to a kneeling nun.[309]

The nuns of Wienhausen by making and selling embroidery, and those of Wintney (E) by manufacturing vestments, gained some income.[310] A great deal of the tapestry and clothing emanating from Wienhausen dates from the fifteenth-century onwards, but one painting on parchment and ascribed to around 1320 depicts Christ with two angels. The nuns also possessed a coloured sculpture from around 1300 showing Our Lady enthroned.[311] The nuns of Heiligengrabe (G) prepared parchments.[312]

4

The Communities

THE NUNS AND THEIR PURPOSE

The foundation and later charters in favour of the many Cistercian female houses frequently spoke highly of the spiritual character of the nuns they housed. They were variously described as being the 'handmaids of Christ' (in Germany: Wienhausen, 1235;[1] Lübeck, 1246;[2] Saarn, 1251,[3] Himmelpforten, 1255;[4] Brenkenhausen, 1281;[5] Börstel, 1283;[6] Adersleben, 1300;[7] Wormeln, 1302;[8] Rinteln, 1310;[9] Isenhagen, 1330;[10] Medingen, 1331;[11] in Belgium: Groeninghe, 1286;[12] the 'maidens of Christ' (St. Katharine, Linz, A);[13] the 'poor in Christ' (Ichtershausen, G; 1195),[14] and as 'the servants of God' (Langendorf, 1246, G,[15] St Agnes, Magdeburg, 1270, G; where one provost saw himself as their 'servant'),[16] or 'of Our Lord Jesus Christ' (Börstel, 1253, G,[17] Szczecin, 1243, Pl ;[18] Ivanics, Croatia, 1246).[19]

Bishop Conrad of Osnabruck (1272) referred to 'the new plantation of the handmaids of Christ' at Gravenhorst,[20] as did the archbishop of Bremen (1249) of the nuns newly settled at Harvestehude, their convent name of Frauental (G) first appears in 1296.[21] The nuns of Gradefes (Sp) were viewed as 'serving God there by day and by night'.[22]

Many charters tell of their rule as being that of St Benedict.[23] A charter of Port Royal (F) refers to 'the female institution of the Cistercian Order, observing the Rule of St Benedict',[24]

A benefactor, Count Otto of Tecklenburg (1258), saw the nuns of Gravenhorst as 'devotedly serving God and the Blessed Mary Ever-a-Virgin day and night';[25] those of Lilienthal (North Rhine-Westphalia, 1259) as displaying 'the devotion and poverty of the handmaids of Christ'.[26] Vitslav II, prince of Rügen (1276), saw the life of the Cistercian nuns at Ivenack as one of 'true and continuous prayer'.

Gregory IX, requesting the incorporation of the former 'maison-Dieu', now the abbey of L'Amour-Dieu (F), saw its nuns as 'being desirous of serving the Lord, under the habit of your Order'.[27] With laudatory sentiments such as these, the presence of Cistercian nuns in any locality must have been viewed as having the potential to impart a goodly and godly influence. The offices they held paralleled those within a male community: so, in 1271, a deed names for Valledemaria (Sp) its prioress, infirmarian, sacristan, cellarer, and cantor.[28]

THE CONVERSAE

Within any communiy there would usually be found a number of female *conversae* (or 'sisters' as distinct from the 'nuns'), but they too were enclosed, wore white veils not black, and performed mundane tasks.[29] The deaths of several of the lay sisters of Żarnowitz (Pl), probably from the thirteenth century, are on record in the obit book of nearby Oliwa Abbey, as: 'Barbara, sister and *conversa*', Hedwig, 'sister and *conversa*', and Catherine, 'sister and *conversa*'.[30] The professed nuns were listed as 'sisters'.

The visitation records of the abbots of Kaisheim suggest that, at the close of the thirteenth century, the nunneries of Pielenhofen, Seligental and Zimmern, had five to ten of these sisters, as opposed to perhaps twenty male brothers and some sixty or more nuns.[31] In Bavaria, at Himmelkron church is to be seen the wall separating the church of the sisters from the choir of the nuns, whilst a portion of it still remains at Heiligental.[32]

At Eschenbach (Swz) the sisters worked in the kitchen, gardens, pantry, infirmary and gate-house,[33] but the episcopal rules drawn up in the early-thirteenth century for Nun Cotham (E) forbade even them to live on the abbey's granges, whether to see to the raising of animals or for any other reason'.[34] After the death of its provost, John of Rottorf, the nuns of Rinteln (G; 1345) were each to receive an equal annual payment from the proceeds of his properties, but a *converse* sister was only to be given half the amount a nun received.[35] This notion of nuns having a limited amount of 'pocket money' is noted later, but was certainly a feature of St Antoine, Paris, by the later thirteenth century.[36]

The Communities

A benefactor of Cotham (E), Rohais of Roxton, confirmed the grant of land made by husband to that nunnery 'when he gave their two daughters in religion'. She added to this grant, becoming herself a lay-sister of the convent so that she could be buried there at her death.[37] Somewhat unusually, Mabel of Thorn in granting land in Killingholme to Cotham, perhaps at the close of the twelfth century, remarked that she was a sister of the house, and would return there 'either in life or in death'.[38] The lowly status of the 'sisters' was perhaps reflected in the case of a sister of Parc-aux-Bois (F), Agnes de Chempieng. In 1329 she was described as a *conversa* of the abbey, but the next year as 'a familiar and servant'.[39]

APPAREL

The most significant item of a nun's clothing was her veil, and an early distinction between the professed choir nuns and the lay sisters, the *conversae*, lay in the colour of the veil: that of the former was black, of the latter white. This difference was reiterated in the 1257 codification of Cistercian statutes,[40] but it occasionally led to resentment.

On visitation at Sinningthwaite (E) in 1315, Archbishop Greenfield of York directed that the lay sisters should not wear the black veil, and the prioress was not to place sisters above nuns.[41] Archbishop Giffard at Swine (E) in 1268 had found many discords between the nuns and the sisters; the latter counted themselves equal to the nuns and maintained they too could wear the black veil.[42] In 1328 the archbishop of Cologne reminded the nuns of Welver of their privilege of wearing the black veil.[43]

Although symbolic of their religious profession, the veil was not always treated with the respect it was due. It was said of the nuns at Molèze (F, 1232), that they had 'thrown off their white veils, and grown their hair long'; this must be a reference to the *conversae*. The sisters at Pons (F) and its daughter-house of Lamanarre had done the same. The General Chapter ordered the disobedient sisters to conform, or else leave the Order.[44] By 1272 the Chapter heard that some rebel sisters at Frauenthal (Swz) had cast off both habit and veil. Unless they ceased their disobedience in this and other matters, the Chapter ordered that they be 'cut off and separated from the unity of the Order'.[45]

When nuns had been apostate and wandered away, or had committed other major transgression, they forfeited their veil, until (in the case of the diocese of York) the archbishop saw fit for it to be restored. This was the lot of two nuns of Swine at a time of discord in that nunnery: Archbishop Le Romeyn ordered in 1289 that the veil be restored to Elizabeth St Quintin, and in 1291 to Elizabeth de Arrains; their penance ended.[46]

As for the rest of their habit, the codification of statutes in 1237 and 1257 both stressed the need for uniformity; variations had occurred perhaps because nuns had dressed differently before their admission into the Order.[47] They might henceforth wear 'cowl without cloak', or 'cloak without cowl; the former was their dress in choir, the latter their everyday attire.[48]

In 1243 the General Chapter required simplicity: the nuns' cowls and sleeves were not to be too long nor too ample, nor were they to drag along the ground. Cloaks were not to be made of rabbit fur nor of hare skin.[49] During work a black scapular was always to be worn; it was the equivalent of an apron to-day.[50] Whilst visiting Hampole (E; 1314), Archbishop Melton of York directed that four scapulars be provided for the nuns who waited on the convent at meal-times.[51]

The codifications of statutes makes no mention as to the early colour of the nuns' habits, save for the veil. There are indications that white would become the norm. In 1218 the bishop of Pavia placed 'nuns in white habit' in a monastery outside the walls of that city.[52] In 1230 the monks of Montier-la-Celle complained to Gregory IX of women living in a farm-house at Chichery who wore white habits, professing to be Cistercian, but wandered about;[53] that community later was Notre-Dame-des-Prés (F). Ten years before they were incorporated into the Order (1234), the 'daughters of God' at St Loup (F) began to wear white habits.[54]

Other early groups of women also wore white, as a sign of a life of penance and piety, and of the religious life.[55] The indicative name of a former Savigniac nunnery, now Cistercian, was L'Abbaye-Blanche (F). By 1240, in England, there was reference to the 'white sisters of Worcester', and by 1291 to the 'White Ladies of Aston'.[56] In Wales, the Celtic poet Dafydd ap Gwilym (fl. 1340–70) referred to the Cistercian nunnery at Llanlllugan 'where the chalk-white ones are', whilst Huw Cae Llwyd (fl. 1431–1504) spoke of a 'white maiden' at the convent of Llanllŷr.[57]

The Communities

The fact is that the 'white', deriving from undyed wool, was more often 'grey', and particularly in central Europe, and from the late-twelfth century through to the early-fourteenth, there are numerous references to Cistercian nunneries as being 'of the grey Order', and in this respect they did not differ from their male counter-parts.[58] The *Chronicle of Pforta* said of the Cistercians in general that 'their habits are grey, and so from the beginning they have been called Greys'.[59] Change did come, and the Dominican, Hermann von Lerbeck (*c*. 1345–91) chronicled of the nuns of Rinteln (G) that 'at first their habit was grey according to the Cistercian Order, but afterwards was white'.

He attributed this to a vision of twelve carpenters dressed in white experienced by Count Adolph IV of Schouwenburg, when he resettled the nuns from Stadthagen in Rinteln.[60] Not long before his death, Frederick Barbarossa (1188) told how he had replaced Benedictine nuns at Woltingrode (G), so that he could 'gather there nuns of the grey Order'.[61] Seven sisters of 'the grey order' came from the Cistercian nunnery of SS James and Burchard at Halberstadt in 1229 to found Helfta (G).[62]

The 'grey ladies by the walls of Nordhausen' (1237), were never incorporated, but were accounted Cistercian and came under the authority of the archbishop of Mainz.[63] Count Otto of Tedlenburg, founding Himmelpforten in 1250, called it 'a cloister of ladies of the grey Order'.[64] The nuns of Brasso (H) were referred to as 'grey nuns, otherwise Cistercian nuns'.[65] The nuns of Waterler (Wasserleben; G), noted as being Cistercian in 1302, 1306 and 1318, were also said in 1324 to be 'of the grey Order', so the terms were synonymous.[66]

When the Benedictine nuns of Arouca (Pt; 1224) became Cistercian under the auspices of Princess Matalda of Portugal and with the backing of Honorius III, it was noted that they were 'of black habit, but changed their habit under the observances and direction' of the Cistercian Order. No mention was made of the colour of their new habits, whether grey or white.[67] White habits were adopted at St Loup (F) soon after 1234, and had been employed by the sisters of Notre-Dame-du-Plan (1200) before the nuns were moved by the bishop of Marseille to St-Pons-de-Gémenos.[68]

The ascription of 'grey nuns' or 'of the grey Order', was also used in respect of Plötzky (G; 1230),[69] Tišnov (Porta Coeli, Cz; 1238),[70] Wormeln (G; 1246, and 1282)[71], Frauensee (G; 1266),[72] Rinteln

(G, 1268),[73] and Szczecin (Stettin, P, in 1306),[74] and of the nuns of Marienborn (G) as late as 1330.[75]

On his election as the first provost of Mendigen (G; 1241), Nicholas was clothed in 'a grey cowl'.[76] At Zarrentin (G; 1320) it was the custom to provide the male *conversi* and the familiars with grey tunics and togas. One of its familiars was noted in 1320 as wearing 'a well-fastened grey tunic'.[77] The parish priest of Walbertsweiler, of the patronage of Wald (G; 1318), had amongst his entitlement from the nunnery, a yearly grant of a 'tunic of grey cloth', every second year an outer garment of the same material, in adddition to a black fur coat and black fur hood.[78]

All the evidence is that grey (perhaps off-white) was in the Germanic lands the common colour of Cistercian habit, at least in the earlier part of the thirteenth century. The usage of white as well as grey cloth may be indicated in the generous grant of grey or white cloth made to the poor at Pforta (G: 1350), even to those 'confined and hidden in prison'.[79] As for the nuns' cloaks, Archbishop Melton on visitation at Hampole (E; 1314), told those nuns wearing black cloaks that they were to use cloaks of russet colour, 'according to the old fashion of the house, and the institutes of the Order'.[80] Honorius III (1224) permitted the nuns of Neuwerk (Goslar; G) to wear linen clothing next their skin.[81] At Pinley (E; 1294) the bishop of Worcester allowed the nuns to use ungirded linen rochets.[82] A quite separate Order of 'Grey Sisters', non-Cistercian, evolved in Belgium from about the mid-fourteenth century.[83]

Clothing cost a convent money, unless made within the nunnery, and that expenditure might be met by grants made by relatives, or by specified rents received. Renaud de Hamel (1261) donated an annual rent of ten Paris shillings to Blendecques (F) 'to pay for the habits needed by his sister, Liesse, over the course of her life-time'.[84] From 1261 the religious of St Antoine-des-Champs (F) received rents worth eight pounds, so that they could line their cloaks with fur.[85]

The demise of a chamber in Bersenbrück (G; 1273) provided income for 'the clothing of the ladies',[86] whilst certain rents due to Lilienthal (1324) provided for newer clothing for its religious.[87] A will of 1350 provided each nun of Sko (Sw) with a cape trimmed with marten fur.[88] Gravenhorst (G; 1362) received a bequest of ten Osnabruck marks, intended for the office of its wardrobe and the betterment of the garments of its nuns.[89] There was discontent at

Rinteln (G; 1315) because its provost had failed to apply a rent set aside for the repair of the nuns' habits.[90]

There were difficulties at two poorer English nunneries. On visitation at Swine (1268), Archbishop Giffard of York noted that unless they could beg from relatives or friends, its nuns might not be adequately clothed. Money donated for this purpose had not been properly used: its nuns received only one pair of shoes a year, and had scarcely received a single tunic in three years, and a single cloak in twenty.[91]

The limited resources of Sinningthwaite meant, as Archbishop Melton pointed out in 1319, that its nuns were dependent on the good offices of their relatives and friends for clothing; those, he said, who had no relatives and friends were suffering from the cold, and should be provided with such clothes as the house could afford.[92] Poverty indeed!

As the years passed by, some English nuns fancied an elaboration of their vesture, and had to be curbed by successive archbishops of York.[93] Archbishop Newark (1298) ordered the nuns of Swine not to wear 'large collars, barred girdles, or laced shoes'.[94] The nuns paid little attention for in 1318 Archbishop Melton threatened them with 'the greater excommunication' if they wore 'super-tunics, barred girdles, in one combination of garment, outwardly or inwardly cut, or ornamented in a curious fashion'.[95] Visiting Hampole in 1314 he had ordered its prioress and sub-prioress to correct and even chastise those nuns using 'new fashioned narrow-cut tunics and rochets'. All the nuns were to use 'uncut garments of the old fashion, long time observed in this house'.[96] At Keldholm that year, he directed its nuns 'to avoid secular finery and singularity of dress, and to wear nothing but such as befits religion'.[97]

RECRUITMENT

In the early medieval period, a number of Cistercian nunneries admitted only girls of noble blood, as at Las Huelgas (Sp),[98] Gravenhorst (G; *fd.* 1256)[99] Himmelkron (G; 1280), and Riga (by 1200);[100] the latter founded specifically for ladies of the upper class.[101]

Pope John XXII (1316–34) requested the admission of some noble girls at Dalheim (G).[102] Salenques (F) was founded and well-endowed in 1353 by Gaston III and his mother, Eleanor de

Comminges, specifically for the daughters of the noble families of Foix.[103] Graurheindorf (G; fd. 1149) was at first reserved for members of noble families, but later ladies of the upper middle classes were admitted.[104] Adelaide, mother of Duke Matthew of Lorraine, entered Tart in 1148, but transferred to Étanche, on its foundation by her son.[105]

In 1287, one noble man, Albrecht of Ebeleben, referred to his having placed four 'educated ladies of laudable character' in the nunnery at Anrode (G), the implication is that they were of noble birth.[106] Żarnowitz (Pl) recruited from the pious female members of neighbouring knightly families.[107] Other nunneries primarily intended for members of noble families included Chumbd, Rhineland;[108] and Ilm, Thuringia.[109] The fourth abbess of Valduc (B) was the youngest daughter of its founder, Duke Henry II of Brabant.[110]

Two of the daughters of Count Gottfried of Löwenstein were Cistercian nuns: the one was Mechtild (*ob.* 1266) professed at Gnadenthal (G); the other became abbess of Lichtenstern.[111] Bohas, marshal of Moravia, in 1287, gave one and a half villages to Oslavany (Cz) nunnery, where his 'most dear daughter', had made her vow.[112] Two of the nuns of Szczecin (P) in 1306, Beatrice and Mechtild, were grand-daughters of Duchess Mechtild of Szczecin (Stettin).[113] Count Nicholas of Schwerin granted a vill to Zarrentin (G) in 1282, his niece, Margaret, having 'assumed the religious habit there'.[114]

Nunneries which encouraged the admission of the offspring of other than noble families included Heiligkreuztal (G), which became Cistercian in 1231 under the influence of Cardinal Conrad von Urach, and 'for that reason it always flourished'.[115] Very soon after its foundation (1231) Himmelstadt (G) opened its doors to ladies not of the nobility; the first abbess coming from the common people took office in 1352; Holthausen (G) also sought vocations outside the nobility.[116]

Convents in an urban setting, like the Paris nunneries, attracted many from the daughters of the townspeople. Throughout the thirteenth century St-Antoine, as well as Notre-Dame-des-Pré and Clairmarais, had many recruits not only the families of nobles and knights, but also of the bourgeoisie.[117] Medingen (G) attracted many recruits from the patrician families of Lüneburg.[118] Nevertheless, it is unlikely that many Cistercian nuns derived from the poorest classes of society, though they may have formed the majority of the *conversae* sisters. Exceptional vocations included that of a young Jewess named Rachel, who after baptism and being named Catherine, entered the religious life at Parc-les-Dames (F; 1223).[119]

The acceptance in numerous cases of only girls of noble birth may have been partly because of family ties, and because of the dowry a nun was expected to bring to help sustain the economic life of the community. Did not the restriction on entry to ladies from families of substance limit the Holy Spirit's choice in guiding females to a religious vocation? If the grants by her family of lands or rents or money on the entry of a young lady were not voluntary but unwritten or unspoken conditions of admission, in the view of some English bishops the procedure amounted to simony. Bishop Hugh of Lincoln (1209–35) told the nuns of Cotham that 'since the sin of simony has led many into error and ruin, for the sake of their souls' health they are forbidden ever to receive man or woman for money or any temporal possession'.[120] Archbishop Greenfield of York (1304–15) also repeatedly forbade the practice.[121]

When the mother of Archbishop Edmund Rich of Canterbury (1233–40) left money to him to procure his two sisters admission into a convent of high standing, the archbishop considered such a dowry as bordering on simony, and searched for a convent which would receive his sisters with nothing but their piety to recommend them. He took them to Catesby where they received a warm welcome; one, Margaret, succeeding the prioress in 1245.[122]

Despite such misgivings the grants made on the entry of a family member were many. They included monetary gifts, as when one Ermengarde (1182) in her will 1182 gave a dowry of five hundred shillings to Nonenque (F) for the entrance of her daughter, Sibilia, as a nun. Blessed Ida of Nivelles, becoming in 1216 a postulant at Kerkom, the first site of La Ramée (B), brought with her a dowry of forty pounds of silver.[123] The lands or money brought with them by young girls desirous of entering Itzenhoe amounted, in the year 1369 alone, to 105 marks.[124]

That such sums were expected is evidenced from the acknowledgement by Bernard de Bailleul, lord of Ledrenghiem, in 1240 that he owed Marquette (F) 450 Flanders pounds, a debt occasioned by the entry of his sister, Matilda, into the community. It was to be paid off yearly by £30 arising from his property at Damme near Bruges.[125] In 1246 John of Mandre was obliged to pay yearly 100 shillings for his sister, Isabella, a nun at he same convent.[126] An entry payment on profession also seems to have been expected at

Benninghausen (G).¹²⁷ Frederick Wlpic, a knight, granted property to Ivenack, where his daughter, Elizabeth, was a nun.¹²⁸

Count Guy of Flanders (1283) and Hainaut made several donations to Flines (F), including an annual rent one hundred pounds, 'for the needs and necessities of his dear daughter, Sister Jeanne, nun of Flines'.¹²⁹ Mary, daughter of Countess Jean of Flanders (1245), was also a nun there.¹³⁰ The life pension of a fourteenth-century Gevelsberg nun derived from a property that nunnery held in the Schilder-gasse, Cologne.¹³¹ Henry of Homen, knight, made an annual gift of two pounds to Grafenthal (G; 268) on the reception of his daughter, Jutta, as a nun there.¹³²

Port Royal received many grants, sometimes of income, as when it was made a gift of no less than five thousand pounds on the entry of a nun who later became abbess; this money supported the building of the refectory. Amongst the largesse in lands it received were vineyards given 1228 by Odilo of Sèvres for the soul of her late husband; a daughter was a nun there. Others entered their noviciate 'with all their earthly goods'.¹³³ At Voisons some rents granted were valid only during the lifetime of the nun concerned.

Amongst early grants made to Obazine (F) was that of lands by Gerald Fulk of Turenne in 1168, when his daughter Plazense became a nun there,¹³⁴ whilst Peter and William Arnold gave Obazine (in 1170) a meadow on the occasion of their mother taking the habit there.¹³⁵ Nonenque (F) benefited in this way: Raymond of Montdidier (1195) gave it two fields on the profession of his daughter, Ruda.¹³⁶ Somewhat later (and before 1267) Sicard Alaman gave Nonenque the village of Vaissa Rabia on the admission of his daughter, Aiceline.¹³⁷

Roger Potelles and his wife Gelvide donated land at Potelles to Fontenelle (F; 1250) on behalf of their daughter, Elekin, described in the charter as a future choir nun. In 1281 Jean, lord of Velu, gave land to Notre-Dame des Près (F), but stipulated that the revenue arising was only to be used for the necessities of his daughter, Isabelle, already a nun.¹³⁸ When, in 1291, his daughter, Alheyde, became a nun of Stepnitz (Marienfliess, G), Zabel von Plaue, a knight, gave the convent four holdings in Blefendorf.¹³⁹ Peregrin of Alspach in 1301 gave to Heiligkreuztal (G) a vineyard on the reception of his niece into the convent, 'to hold it for her life'.¹⁴⁰

Count Henry of Osterfeld (1293) gave Beuditz (G) rents and a wood on the profession there of his two daughters.¹⁴¹ Jean, lord of

Velu (1281), gave land to Notre-Dame des Près (F), but stipulated that the revenue arising was only to be used for the necessities of his daughter, Isabelle, already a nun.[142] Medingen (G; 1343) used alms given by parents and friends of its nuns to purchase the tithes of Almstorf, in order 'to better sustain itself.[143] Other entry dowries included twenty-three grants to Stixwould (E) of holdings such as tithes and mills,[144] while one nun alone brought three farms to Gudhem (Sw).[145]

Bogislaw IV, duke of Pomerania (1298), augmented the possessions of Wolin (Pl) when his daughter, Jutte, became a nun there.[146] Blanche of Paciac (1277) gave four hundred Paris pounds in rents to Saint-Antoine-des-Champs before becoming a nun there herself, and 'after she took the veil, gave an additional one thousand five hundred *livres tournois* over the course of some years for the purchase of rural lands, including virtually an entire grange at Beaumont-sur-Oise. The abbot of Cîteaux himself, as father-abbot, recorded this contract'.[147] These are but a few of numerous instances.

The potential exclusivity of the membership of Cistercian nunneries was reinforced when such major grants were made on the entry of would-be nuns. This was common practice in the Scandinavian nunneries. When Catherine Mattsdotter entered the novitiate at Gudhem (Sw) in 1292 she brought with her three large farms. When Margarethe Pik some years later became a nun at Gudhem her father gave the nunnery land he owned in Halland.[148] When Margrave Rudolf I gave Lichtenthal (G) the village of Geroldsau in full possession, the charter gives a picture of the settlement with its 'waterfalls, water, paths and bridges'.[149]

While such gifts may call into questions the motives of some entrants, numerous vocations (especially in Belgium – where many nuns came from the merchant class[150] – and other areas affected by the 'religious women' movement) were genuine calls from God, the nuns entering religious life of their own choice. Of those Cistercian convents, Jacques de Vitry said: "Virgins throng there, widows hasten there, and married women with their husbands' consent".[151] Not for nothing did four nunneries in Germany and one in Bohemia bear the official Latin name of *Porta coeli* ('the gate of heaven'). Archbishop Melton of York (1318), however, stipulated on visitation at Nun Appleton (E), that no more than two of three members of the same family were to be received as nuns there, 'for fear of discord arising'.[152] Adilheid, the mother of Abbot Rhydigier of Oliwa (1291–1310), became a nun of Żarnowiec, a nunnery much under the support of the male abbey.[153]

The 1257 codification of the statutes of the Order made no mention of the minimum age at which Cistercian nuns might make their profession, having served a year's novitiate, as emphasised in 1241.[154] Very often, girls entered the convent as boarder-pupils at a very early age, with a view to profession at a later date. The determination of age appears to have varied from region to region. Stephen Lexington, as abbot of Savigny, enjoined twelve years old as the age at which girls could be received (with a view to later becoming nuns), and stipulated eighteen as the age when the novitiate could be entered.[155]

He did allow a minimum age of eight for entry at Saint-Antoine-des-Champs.[156] In Belgium, Ida de Léau (d. 1260) entered La Ramée at the age of thirteen; Bl. Ida of Nivelles became a postulant at its first site, Kerkom, at the age of sixteen. Bl. Beatrice of Nazareth was professed at Florival at the age of fifteen, and then she was sent to La Ramée to learn the art of transcribing books.[157] The General Chapter ruled in 1206 that young boys were not to be admitted,[158] but in England there were breaches of this rule at Esholt and Heynings.[159]

Those entering at a very young age were presumably given educational opportunities, like St Mechtilde of Hackeborn who was said to have entered Rossdorf (the precursor of Helfta, G) at the age of seven, and St Gertrude at Helfta when only four years old![160] At Sinningthwaite (E; 1319) Archbishop Melton ruled that girls over twelve were not to be retained unless special permission granted.[161]

COMMUNITY SIZE

Economic considerations limited the number of nuns in any particular monastery, accounting for the wide disparity between houses in this respect. A further factor was the rule of strict enclosure, which meant that nuns were not supposed to leave their convent in order to beg.[162] From time to time the General Chapter of the Order provided guidance in this respect, as did pontiffs, bishops and father-abbots.

The Communities

The Chapter ruled in 1218 that Visitors, normally the father-abbots, were to fix the number of nuns which convents could sustain, according to their resources; this ruling was repeated in 1219, and had to be re-iterated even eighty years and an hundred years later – in 1298 and 1326. Abbesses and prioresses who exceeded the stated limits were to be deposed.[163] After the ruling regarding numbers was reiterated in 1242, the General Chapter – as so often, modified it the following year, to the intent that if convents wished to increase their numbers, and could do so without incurring penury, then they might do so if their father-abbot was agreeable to the move.[164]

When eventually, in 1287, the General Chapter passed a series of regulations regarding its nuns, these included the fixing of a minimum age of ten years old for admission or maintenance of a girl into a convent with due regard being given to the potential of those offered or given. Any nun who, having served her year of probation, did not wish to continue, was not to be retained.[165]

Innocent IV (1245/46) ruled in bulls in favour of Flines (F), of Groeninghe B), Tišnov (Porta Coeli; Cz), and Zwyveke (B), that convents were to retain any kind of property given on the profession of nuns, should those sisters return to the world;[166] Urban IV (1262) used like terminology in a bull in favour of Maubuisson (F);[167] Alexander VI (1256) in respect of Lichtenthal (G), he adding the saving clause 'except feudal things';[168] and by Clement V (1312) in favour of Flines (F).[169]

When Cecilia, a nun of Welver (G; 1347), left that nunnery she renounced any claim to the money given when she entered.[170] When Catherine Sant Liter entered Valldemaria (Sp) in 1349, the nunnery 'received all her property'.[171]

In determining admissions, diocesan bishops who had visitatorial authority might intervene. In the diocese of York, archbishops in 1281, 1290 and 1346, directed that no novices be received at Nun Appleton, without their consent. The reason for this, as given in 1346, was lest the nuns overstep the means of their house. Archbishop Melton in 1318 directed that no more than two or three nuns from one family be admitted at Nun Appleton without his special licence for fear of discord arising.[172] In 1312 Archbishop Greenfield of York was displeased to hear that, although Hampole was burdened with debt, it had received two little girls, one the niece of the prioress and the other a niece of the abbot of Roche that after a time they might be admitted as nuns; he forbade their profession until he determined otherwise.[173]

Abbesses might be selective or reluctant when admission was sought. In 1264 Innocent IV had to intervene when the abbess of La Ramée (B) refused to admit Catherine, daughter of Henry d'Incourt, a familiar of the abbot of St Laurence, Liège. When one day a new-born child was found left outside that abbey's gate the abbess declined to receive her.[174] In 1297 the General Chapter ordered the abbess of Consolation (F), to admit a girl that a cardinal had pleaded for unsuccessfully several times.[175]

In 1308 the archbishop of Magdeburg, acting on papal authority, required the nuns of Marienkammer (G) to receive within thirty days into their community one Elizabeth, the daughter of Heino Japel, giving her a place in choir and chapter, in dorter and refectory.[176] At least one patron felt he had a role to play. Richard de Lestre, founder of Sewardsley (E) in the twelfth century, notified the bishop of Lincoln that he had granted lands to the nuns 'they promising in return to use his counsel in the reception of nuns and to admit none except through him'.[177] At least one bishop of Worcester, Adam de Orleton (1329), expected his permission to be sought before the nuns of Whiston could admit another to their house.[178]

The blessing of nuns, at their profession after a year's novitiate,[179] was to be the duty of the father-abbot or Visitor of a house, or by any other abbot given the authority to do so.[180] When the abbess of Marquette (F) contravened this rule in 1243, she was excluded from her abbatial stall in choir for forty days.[181] Innocent III (1199) had ruled that the ordination of chaplains and the blessing of newly-professed nuns belonged to the local bishop; this in a letter to the bishop of Hildesheim.[182] Where, as in most English cases, the local bishop exercised visitatorial control, he or his delegate would perform the ceremony.

For this purpose, successive bishops of of Worcester assigned others for this task: as the Benedictine Prior of Worcester Cathedral (1318), or its sub-prior (as Nicholas Moryce in 1339 and 1344), commissioned to receive the professions of the nuns of Whistones in his diocese.[183] In 1318 the General Chapter said that as a monk or nun at his or her profession had 'put on the new man' [Ephesians 4, v. 24], he or she that day should receive Holy Communion at a special Eucharist'.[184]

The Communities

Profession involved stability: Alexander IV ruled (1256, in the case of Lichtenthal G) that no nun, having been professed, might transfer to another convent, even if elected abbess elsewhere, save with the permission of her father-abbot and her abbess.[185] The pontiff that year also reminded the nuns of Clairefontaine (B) they could not leave their abbey withthout the leave of their abbess.[186] Much earlier, Alexander III (1159–81) had prohibited, in the instance of Nun Cotham (E), 'any brother or sister, having made their profession, from leaving without permission of the master and chapter, unless wishing to transfer to a stricter Order'.[187]

There are but few references to the name a nun took at her profession, but in 1243 the rules were amended, and repeated in 1244, to say that the name with which the bishop blessed a nun ought to be stated by the abbess, who should be present when her nuns were blessed.[188] It would appear that some nuns, certainly for legal purposes, adhered to their maiden names. Certainly Sister Margaret of Benninghausen (G; 1330) was the former Claritia von Elner, and still used the latter name for legal purposes.[189]

THE EVIDENCE OF NECROLOGIES

Cistercian necrologies are a source of much information.[190] They tell of the passing of monks, nuns, benefactors, and family members, as well as grants given and prayers afforded. The necrology of Marche-les-Dames (B) listed over five hundred relatives of the community granted an annual *obit*.[191] Billigheim remembered 'Hernand, our dearly beloved father, once prior in Bronnbach'.[192] The nuns of Soleilmont prayed for Hubert, 'worthy abbot of Florennes', to name but a few, and more than one of its benefactors desired 'an annual *obit* for his father and mother, brothers and sisters'.[193] This was a frequent request.

Not surprisingly the necrologies tell that more nuns died in winter than in the summer months.[194] The necrology of Notre-Dame-des-Prés (F) dates at latest from the early-fourteenth century. It lists sixty-six religious of noble birth, and ninety-nine of patrician birth, reflecting its urban location close to Douai.[195]

The necrology of Seligenthal (G), originating perhaps in 1310, tells of the death in 1313 of 'Otto, the most serene king of Hungary, and duke of Bavaria', and in 1335 of the passing of 'Otto, the illustrious duke of Bavaria'. It also notes the obits of those who served the nunnery, as in 1254 that of Catherine Fraubergerin, 'our faithful waitress', and in 1259 of the convenr's doctor (John Raming) and apothecary (Philip Karthasuser).[196] The nuns of Wald remembered King Richard I of England 'on the third feria after the octave of Easter'.[197] The necrologies also tell of financial gifts to a nunnery.

COMMUNITY SIZE

Economic considerations limited the number of nuns in any particular monastery, accounting for the wide disparity between houses in this respect. A further factor was the rule of strict enclosure, which meant that nuns were not supposed to leave their convent in order to beg.[198] From time to time the General Chapter of the Order provided guidance in this respect, as did pontiffs, bishops and father-abbots. The General Chapter ruled in 1218 that Visitors, normally the father-abbots, were to fix the number of nuns which convents could sustain, according to their resources; this ruling was repeated in 1219, and had to be re-iterated even eighty years and an hundred years later – in 1298 and 1326. Abbesses and prioresses who exceeded the stated limits were to be deposed.[199]

After the ruling regarding numbers was reiterated in 1242, the General Chapter – as so often, modified it the following year, to the intent that if convents wished to increase their numbers, and could do so without incurring penury, then they might do so if their father-abbot was agreeable to the move.[200] Innocent IV (1250), in the instance of the newly-founded Lichtenthal (G), had decreed that the nunnery was not to be compelled to admit more nuns and *conversae* than its resources would allow.[201]

The same concern was expressed by Stephen Lexington in his visitation of French nunneries in the 1230s.[202] The maximum numbers might, therefore, fluctuate slightly from year to year. In 1259 the Chapter said that convents should have no more than seventy religious, five familiars, forty *conversi* and the necessary number of chaplains.[203] It is unlikely that the larger nunneries adhered to this ruling.

More realistically, Clement IV in 1268 fixed the number of personnel in nunneries as one hundred religious, eighteen *conversi* and *conversae*, and two chaplains. For the right to have a confessor, a community should have at least twenty-five nuns.[204]

The visitation records of the abbots of Kaisheim suggest that, at the close of the thirteenth century, the nunneries of Pielenhofen, Seligental and Zimmern, had sixty or more nuns, perhaps twenty male lay brothers, and five to ten lay sisters.[205] Abbess Constance of Cour-Notre-Dame (F) recorded in 1285 that she had to maintain 'nearly fifty nuns, lay sisters, and dependents, including eighteen orphans, plus servants, and horses and oxen, all needing to be fed'. A monastery servant at the time added that the poverty of the nuns had forced them 'to beg in public'.[206]

Papal prescriptions regarding individual communities came from Innocent IV (1245) who fixed the number of nuns at Vignogoul (F) at forty;[207] from Urban IV (1262) who determined the number of personnel at Maubuisson (F) at 140: one hundred nuns, the remainder – clergy, male *conversi* and female *converses*, Clement IV (1268) reducing this to one hundred and twenty.[208] He fixed the number of nuns at La Cour-Notre-Dame (F) at forty, but only thirty were there in 1285.[209]

The ruling of Clement IV was immediately heeded by Abbot Philip of Clairvaux who, in 1270, fixed the maximum numbers at Flines (F) to be one hundred nuns, eighteen *conversi* and *conversae*, one secular chaplain and one monk confessor.[210] Las Huelgas followed suit in the 1270s, with a limit of one hundred choir nuns and forty *conversae* being felt desirable.[211] Subsequent abbots of Clairvaux showed equal solicitude for their many daughter-houses. So that it did not exceed its resources, Abbot Matthew in 1320 fixed the number of personnel at Fervaques (F) at fifty choir nuns, ten *conversae* sisters, and twenty others: *conversi* and chaplains; in all eighty persons.[212] In 1330, either he or his successor Abbot John IV, fixed the maximum numbers at Parc-aux-Bois (F) at fifty: thirty-eight professed nuns and novices; seven *converses* and five *conversi*.[213]

Stephen Lexington, as abbot of Savigny, showed similar thoughtfulness. He fixed a quota at Moncey (F; 1231) of thirty nuns, six *conversae*, four priests and two *conversi*: a seemingly small number in view of the tasks the latter might have to perform. At Mortain (F; 1231) he permitted a total of fifty nuns, and at Port Royal (F; 1233) of sixty.[214] A visitation at Frauensee (G; 1233), led by the prior of Walkenried, fixed the maximum number of nuns ('young and old'), juniors and *conversae* there at sixty-six, on account of insufficient local resources to maintain more.[215]

Reform by local abbots of the convent of (Marien) Benden (G; 1277) limited its number of nuns to thirteen with an abbess.[216] Other father-abbots who found it necessary to restrict numbers included: the abbot of Léoncel (1263), in respect of Vernaison (F): thirty nuns;[217] the Benedictine abbot of Fulda (1319), regarding the nuns of Allendorf (G) who lived a Cistercian life under his supervision: forty-five nuns,[218] and and the abbot of Arnsburg (1327), for Patershausen (G): fifty nuns.[219] Contrariwise, the restriction of a maximum of fifty nuns at Lilienthal (G; 1333) was lifted by the cardinal bishop of Albano for the well-being of that nunnery.[220]

In England, where most Cistercian nunneries were under episcopal control, relevant diocesan bishops were to the forefront regarding their care. At the close of the twelfth century the bishop of Lincoln decided, as it was not a wealthy house, that Nun Cotham should have no more than thirty nuns, with twelve lay brethren for outdoor works, two chaplains, besides the master, attached to the house. There was mention also of its lay sisters.[221]

In 1267 Archbishop Giffard of York instructed Hampole to receive no one as nun or sister without his special leave, as the number then in the house exceeded its means. In 1308 Archbishop Greenfield regarding Hampole repeated that no one was to be admitted to the habit of nun, sister or *conversus*, without his special licence.[222] Archbishop Melton stipulated the same at Sinningthwaite in 1319.[223] On account of it being heavily in debt, in 1318 he instructed Esholt not to receive any more nuns, sisters or brothers *conversi* without his leave.[224]

At its foundation the archbishop of Cologne fixed the number of nuns at Dûssern (G; 1237) at twenty-five 'unless licence is given for more if the resources of the convent allow it'.[225] In 1308 the archbishop of Mainz limited the community of Georgenberg (G) to a total of thirty-six,[226] the same number as was permitted at Harvestehude (G; Frauental, Hamburg).[227]

Special considerations might come into play. Vauxbons (F; 1216), an incorporated filiation of Tart, having ceded much of its territory to the canons of Saint-Mamonès, was therefore obliged to limit its numbers to the abbess and twelve nuns, a chaplain, two male *conversi* and two female *converses*.[228] Ten years after its own

The Communities

foundation, Beuren (G) in 1260 had sufficient nuns to send ten to settle, with the support of the duke of Brunswick, a new convent at Teistungenburg. The archbishop of Mainz commented in 1265 that the reason for this was that 'on account of poverty Beuren could not sustain many people'.[229]

A portion of church land at Teistungenburg was granted for the site by Günzel of Bodenstein, and later (1279) Günther of Hardenberg resigned to the nuns the third portion he owned of the tithes of Teistungenburg. The provost of Beuren for a time continued to handle the affairs of Teistungenburg, but by 1268 Teistungenburg had its own provost and difficulties arose between him and the mother house.[230]

A few nunneries had, at their zenith, very large communities: as San Arevalo-Lugaraja in Castile with two hundred personnel, and Vallbona in Catalonia with one hundred and fifty.[231] Houses having one hundred nuns included Wechterswinkel (G; 1231)[232] and Coyroux (F; 1300 – surprising given its restricted site).[233] In Bavaria at Seligenthal (1288) were eighty-eight nuns and *conversae* sisters, as well as twenty male *conversi*.[234]

The numbers of personnel at Aywières (B) were fixed in 1250 according to its revenues: seventy religious and five familiars, whilst forty or so male *conversi* tended its estates.[235]. In 1354 the provost, prioress and convent of Holy Cross, Rostock (G), agreed that they could sustain no more than sixty nuns,[236] whilst at Wanzka (G) the number of nuns was limited in 1341 to a maximum of fifty.[237] There were fifty nuns, apart from *conversae* at Grafenthal (G) in 1280, a number attributed to the generosity of the counts of Gueldre and the dukes of Clèves in their territorial support of the nunnery.[238]

Many convents could only support considerably smaller communities. Around 1280 the number of 'ladies' (nuns and sisters presumably) was fixed at forty at Roermond in Holland, and in Germany thirty at Fürstenberg, twenty-eight at Düsseren, and twenty at Sterkrade and Schledenhorst.[239] In 1250, thirty years after its foundation, a deed of Rifreddo (It) listed but twenty named nuns; in 1261 eighteen nuns formed the 'major part' of its community, and twenty were again listed in a deed of 1292.[240]

The numbers at Doornzele (B) were fixed in 1234 as twenty nuns.[241] Bouchet (F) had sixteen nuns in 1239, but twenty-six in 1250.[242] Valsauve (F) had an authorised limit of twenty nuns in

1187, but only eight were there in 1354. Waterler receievd a dispensation in 1333 permitting it to have less than the fifty nuns it was supposed to have.²⁴³

Contrariwise, Nonenque (F) with twenty nuns in 1279, had eighty in 1346.²⁴⁴ Himmelthron (G; 1343/48) accommodated fourteen nuns at its foundation²⁴⁵ and when Ichtershausen founded Neuwerk (Goslar, G; 1186) the initial community consisted of thirteen of its nuns: a typical Cistercian arrangement reminiscent of Christ and the twelve apostles.²⁴⁶ In Germany also, Gravenhorst had perhaps a community of only around eight to ten nuns, and Holthausen of perhaps about ten to twelve.²⁴⁷ Several English and Welsh communities were small in size, like Greenfield, Lincolnshire, with but twelve nuns in 1377; though admittedly this was after the Black Death had ravaged the population.²⁴⁸

ENCLOSURE

The General Chapter took a far reaching step in 1213 when it said of those monasteries already incorporated that the nuns must not leave their enclosure without permission from their father-abbot.²⁴⁹ It was a restriction repeated in 1220 and 1225, and firmly maintained in the statute codifications of 1237 and 1257,²⁵⁰ and may have owed much to a precept of Lucius III in 1184 to the nuns of Mortain, forbidding them to leave the cloister without leave of the prioress, and also by his teaching in his bull that year, *Prudentibus Virginitibus*.²⁵¹ Other religious houses wishing to be 'admitted to the unity of the Order' were to adopt strict enclosure;²⁵² any nunneries which would not obey this requirement were to be 'eliminated' from 'the care of the Order'.²⁵³

It was this insistence on strict enclosure that was cited when in 1220 the General Chapter ruled against the absorption of houses of other Orders,²⁵⁴ and, when noting that certain 'dispersed nuns' were associated with the Knights of Calatrava, ordered that they be 'brought together as one and enclosed in a suitable place at least two or three days' journey from Calatrava.²⁵⁵ The nuns of Le Betton (F; 1213) had been immediately unhappy at the new rules, but were bidden by the Chapter to be obedient to their abbess in all things, warning them that if rebellious they might be expelled from the Order.²⁵⁶ Exceptionally, Constance of Conangell, a nun of Valledemaria (Sp), was permitted in 1329 to live at Grions, thirty-five kilometres distant, because she suffered from leprosy.[257]

The General Chapter, in 1225, enquired of the countess of Flanders as to whether the endowment of a nunnery she wished to found would be sufficient – as the nuns would be unable to go out to beg;[258] nor could they any longer move freely amongst family and friends.[259] A ruling was also made that year, repeating that if an incorporated house had not conformed to strict enclosure within four years, then it was to be cut off 'from the body of the Order'.[260] In 1298 the Chapter, noting that some abbesses and nuns were breaking enclosure, reminded them of their strict enclosure and the prohibition of any others entering their cloisters,[261] whilst the rule of enclosure was also reinforced that year in a bull issued by Boniface VIII.[262]

Repeatedly, when a request was made for a particular nunnery to be incorporated the rule of enclosure was enforced: this happened in the instances of Amboise (F, 1213),[263] Heiligenkreuztal (G; 1231/33);[264] Wauthier-Braine (B; (1233),[265] and Rifreddo (It),[266] amongst others. A decision on the incorporation of Berg, requested by the archbishop of Cologne (1219), was deferred until his wishes regarding its nuns' enclosure became known.[267] Bishop Hugh of Lincoln (1209–35) stipulated that the nuns of Cotham were not to go out at all, unless given permission by the master and the prioress, and in case of great and obvious necessity.[268]

It was not only diocesan bishops and the General Chapter that insisted on strict enclosure so, too, in 1250 did the counts of Oldenburg, Otto and John. They prescribed in the case of Börstel (G) that for security, 'all the doors of the cloister, through which it is possible for seculars to pass, be closed: one key to be held by the abbess, another by the prioress, and the other by the provost'.[269]

The nuns of the Order had to speak to all visitors through 'the opening specially prepared', and no-one was to enter the cloister except the father-abbot.[270] This opening was later described as having to be a 'strongly and closely made' iron or timber barred grill.[271] From 1237 this stipulation was mitigated, in that more open conversation could be held in a place appointed by the Visitor with 'good and honest persons', and (later on) with relatives. For others, the grill was still to be used.[272]

At Swine (E) food for the canons, the *conversi* and the *converses*, was passed through two windows. In 1268 the archbishop of York noted that these were not properly kept by the nuns called 'janitrices', so that unwarranted conversations between the different sections of the community took place.[273]

Such strict enclosure had practical effects, for presumably the nuns could no longer go out to work in the fields. In the twelfth century there is evidence that they did so: as at Montreuil-les-Dames (F) where Herman of Laon noted them as preparing and tilling the land just as did their male counter-parts,[274] and (even later) as at La Ramée (B) whose nuns, including St Ida, rested in the fields of its Kerkom Grange after harvest. The sisters went to Kerkom for eight days.[275] Bouton points out that much depends on what was meant by 'enclosure', the meaning of which in the twelfth century was still quite broad, and might, he postulated, have extended to adjacent fields'.[276]

When Aywières (B) was incorporated (by 1211) Abbot Arnald of Cîteaux referred to the necessary 'perpetual enclosure', and that the nuns were never to go out without permission.[277] Later, around 1240/50, John Godard, the first abbot of Newenham wrote a treatise for the abbess of Tarrant (E), and included the admonition: 'You should not see seculars, nor should you be seen by them, you are not to go out into the fields with sickles for harvesting, since dangers abound'.[278] As the nuns proper were limited in what they could do, it begs the question: Did the insistence on strict enclosure negate one of the very fundamentals of the Cistercian vocation: living by the labours of one's own hands?

The other consequence lay in the ability to collect alms. Many of the smaller nunneries of Champagne spent money on the poor, the sick, the leprous and the needy, leaving little for themselves, and in the later thirteenth century did send out some nuns to beg.[279] Stephen Lexington, urged the nuns of his filiation in the 1230s only to receive as guests 'the manifestly sick and truly poor'.[280] In 1275 the bishop of Lausanne told local clergy to look favourably on nuns of Fraubrunnen who came seeking alms from the faithful.[281] A grant made to Kapellendorf nunnery (G; 1252) included provision for alms to be given to the poor.[282]

In 1301 the nuns of Brione (It) complained that their father abbot from Locedio had, following the constitutions of the Order, imposed strict enclosure upon them. This, they said, prevented them from receiving 'the alms of the faithful', which were necessary to sustain themselves as they were in a state of 'grave poverty', and were 'making their cloister'. Boniface VIII delegated the prior of Santi Apostoli to enquire into the mater, and he passed on this duty to a canon of Turin.[283]

Exceptions were made, though only with the leave of the father-abbot if it were practicable to obtain it. An abbess might go out on business, but with an escort of two sisters;[284] a sister-cellarer also – with an escort of one.[285] Such excursions were to be 'made rarely and for sufficient cause'.[286] When, in 1276, negotiations were necessary regarding Gravenhorst's patronage of its local church at Riessenbeck (G), the abbess, the prioress and one other nun, travelled to Kloster Levern, as the convent's representatives.[287]

The biography of Ida of Nivelles, then a nun of La Ramée (B), tells how she 'and a certain nun were travelling together and stopped off at Liège on business'; they stayed the night in a private house, but did not omit to say their office.[288] The nuns of Whiston (E; 1283), however, when bidden by the archbishop of York to attend his visitation at Worcester Cathedral, absented themselves sending their chaplain to represent them, for they wrote 'it is not proper for women to mingle with a company of men'.[289] The nuns of Lübeck were, in 1267, permitted to go out to raise alms, as they were said to be in poverty, yet in 1268 they bought a vill for 224 marks.[290]

The life of Arnulf of Villers tells how Mother Lucy, the prioress of Épinlieu (B), travelled with two other nuns to Villers, and having acomplished her business at its gate-house, spent the night in the nearby village in the home of 'two devout women'.[291] The will of Agnes, a widow of Kutná Hora, was sealed in 1336 by the abbot of Sedlec and the abbess of Frauental (Cz); did this involve travel on her part?[292] In 1311 Abbess Mettha of Cedynia (Pl), accompanied by her convent's chaplain, went to visit the bishop of Kamień asking for financial help in order to sustain the nunnery.[293] In 1342 Abbess Judith of Veszprémvölgy (H) personally visited the Queen of Hungary in order to successfully plead for the restoration of certain tithes.[294]

A notable nun was Jeanne of Valois, sister of King Philip VI of France and mother-in-law of King Edward III of England, her daughter being Queen Philippa. Her husband, Count William le Bon of Hainault, having died, she took the veil at Fontenelle (F) in 1337, but came out in 1341 to travel to Ghent where she successfully pressed for a treaty between English and French troops. Dying in 1342, she was buried in a magnificent tomb in the choir at

Fontenelle.[295] Another abbess whose duties perhaps took her afield was the superior of Frauental (Pohled, Cz; *fd.* 1265) who had the privilege of crowning the queen of Bohemia.[296]

Nuns were not to be sent to site where a monastery was still in the process of construction.[297] In 1232 the abbots of Cambron and Loos were bidden to visit the convent of Fontenelle and enjoin its abbess that the nuns who had been sent to a monastery under construction were to be recalled without delay, and to desist from that building project. Despite this, the new monastery – L'-Olive, previously a hermitage – was incorporated into the Order in 1233.[298]

When nuns did have to travel it was not to be in fine carriages, but in carts with a complete covering of green or black cloth; the contrary practice by some had come to the ears of the General Chapter (1240). The following year the Chapter reiterated this ruling, adding severe penalties for abbesses who disobeyed.[299] In the mid-thirteenth century the General Chapter issued a series of statutes which made some nuns (many of noble blood) chafe at the restrictions placed upon them. In 1241 the General Chapter ordered that nuns who committed grave faults should be subject to imprisonment – just like male monks and for the same deeds.[300]

In 1242 the Chapter stipulated that nuns who would not live by the rules of the Order should be expelled; that in normal circumstances nuns should only speak to Visitor through the grille; that the number of nuns officially fixed was not to be exceeded; that nuns should use the name given them by the father-abbot at their blessing, and that enquiry should be made as to the lifestyle of their chaplains and *conversi*.[301] In doing this the Chapter further said that whilst individual nuns should be sent to other houses,[302] expelled if they did not wish to conform, yet entire convents and male abbeys could not be removed from the Order without leave of the Chapter.[303] By 1257 it was also stipulated that abbesses, nuns and *conversae* should confess their faults 'on their hands and knees'.[304]

VISITATION

Cistercian nuns had in a very few instances a semi-legislative local grouping of their own (below), but never a General Chapter of their own. Cistercian abbesses were debarred from attendance at the annual Chapter of the male houses held yearly, usually in mid-September and mostly at Cîteaux. The usages prescribed for the nuns in 1237 said that: 'Because the abbesses do not have a general chapter, faults are to be acknowledged to the Visitor'[305] It seems that some abbesses had attempted to attend the General Chapter of the male abbeys, for that same year it ruled that abbesses were not to attend, and those who did were 'from the day of leaving their house until the day of their return to wholly abstain from wine'.[306]

The authority of an abbess over the affairs of her convent's daughter-houses was also very limited. The Chapter of 1228 ruled that where a mother-house had daughter nunneries, the inspection of these was to be made by the father-abbot. Of Argensolles (F; 1225) it was decreed that the same customs and constitutions might apply in its daughter-houses as at Argensolles itself, but the abbess of Argensolles was not to deprive any of the daughter-abbesses without the counsel and assent of the abbot of Clairvaux, nor was she empowered to institute new abbesses.[307]

When Hedersleben (G; 1253) was settled by nuns from Helfta, the mother-abbess could visit it in a spirit of love and correct anything amiss, but she was not to presume to vary the rules of the Order. In 1221 a dispute between Walberberg and Hoven (G) nunneries was caused by the abbess of Hoven claiming the right of visitation of Walberberg. The abbots of Himmerod and Heisterbach concluded that both abbeys were of equal status and daughters of St Thomas-an-der Kyll, of which the abbot of Himmerod was Visitor.[308]

Each officially recognised nunnery was made subject to a father-abbot or Visitor. It was his duty to care for both the spiritual and economic well-being of the convents placed under his watch – this being exercised in theory at least, by the making of a formal annual visitation. The Visitor, procurator and chaplain at Sonnefeld (G) were all monks of Langheim.[309] The nuns of Mègemont (F) said of the abbot of Montpeyroux (1282) that he was 'our father, on whom the abbess and the monastery depend spiritually'.[310] When the nuns of Marienborn (Hesse, 1316) sold a substantial property for 260 marks, their father-abbot of Arnsburg issued his own confirmatory charter.[311]

An abbot might delegate his duty of visitation. At monasteries such as Camp, with twenty-four dependent nunneries, this was a practical necessity.[312] The abbot of Pforta (1210) found himself unable to visit Trzebnica (Pl) because of wars and long distance, so the nearby abbot of Lubiąż fulfilled his duty.[313] The nunnery of Conversano (It), said in 1271 to be 'united and incorporated' as a daughter of Cîteaux was again, for reasons of geographical location, visited by the abbot of Daphni, Greece, en route to and from General Chapter, but perhaps only spasmodically – as in 1272 and 1283.[314] The abbot of Lucelle (1266) was released, on account of the distance away and the expense, from oversight of the Swiss convents of Rathausen and Mariazell (either Kalchrain or Wurmsbach).[315]

The priory of nuns in Nicosia, Cyprus, was far distant from its mother-house of Saint-Mary-Magdalene de Acre in Syria. In 1222, therefore, the abbess in Acre with the support of the archbishop of Nicosia and the abbot of Belmont, Lebanon, agreed that the house in Nicosia be raised to the status of an abbey, but 'because no one already there is suitable to cope with the violence and other upsets', a nun of Acre should be elected as the first abbess and be sent to rule in Nicosia.[316]

Another problem for Cîteaux came in 1238 when Belmont abbey, Lebanon, claimed the oversight of the nunnery of St Mary Magdalene at 'Achon', undoubtedly Acre. The local abbots of Jubin and St Sergius were told to investigate, and send their findings 'in writing under their seals'. The matter was brought to a swift conclusion at the following year's Chapter when 'Acon' was made a 'special filiation' of Cîteaux, and the abbot of Belmont was told not to raise the matter again.[317]

Amongst numerous other abbeys, Cîteaux received the oversight of nunneries afar as far field as Boitzenburg (Marienpforte) in Brandenburg, and Poszony in Slovakia;[318] Nazareth in Zeeland, and Val-St-Bernard in Brabant,[319] but in this latter case the duty of care seems to have been delegated to the abbot of nearby St Bernard-sur-l'Escaut.[320] In Holland, Cîteaux had the paternity of Binderen and Ter Beek, but the actual oversight perhaps lay with Villers.[321] When Hemelsdaele (B) was built in 1240 and put under the authority of Clairvaux, visitation was delegated to the abbot of the Dunes.[322]

Clairvaux also had a number of other nunneries in Belgium amongst its filiations including La Paix-Dieu, Ter Hagen, Vivegnis,[323] and Doornzele.[324] It delegated the paternity of the latter house to Baudeloo (1235), and the oversight of Groeninge to the abbot of the Dunes (1260s).[325]

The Visitor also exercised a watchful eye over the temporal well-being of his nunneries, and no major transaction would be made without his approval. Abbot Walter of Villers authorised the nuns of Aywières (B) to transfer to a more suitable site; and Abbot William (1230) approved a rent granted by La Ramée (B).[326] When in 1264 the nuns of Feldbach (Swz) reached an agreement with Eberhard, a knight of Stekborn, regarding three vineyards, it was sealed by the abbess, Julita, but also by Abbot Eberhard of Salem.[327] The seal of the abbot of Aulne ('our Visitor'), as well as that of the abbess, was appended in 1271 to an agreement made by Val-St-Georges (B).[328]

In the absence of its Visitor's seal (the abbot of Strata Florida), the seals of the abbots of Strata Marcella and Valle Crucis (W; 1284) were appended to Llanllŷr's receipt for war damage compensation.[329] When in 1319 the nuns of Fraubrunnen (Swz) sold certain lands it was 'by licence of Volric, abbot of Aurora [Frienisberg], our Visitor'.[330] The nuns of Porta Coeli (Cz) were affronted in 1287 when their father-abbot of Velehrad disposed of some of their temporalities. The General Chapter required the abbot of Morimond to investigate.[331]

The initial choice of a father-abbot to supervise a particular nunnery might, at a later date, be changed in favour of the abbot of another male house. Bonlieu (F) was founded in 1199 under the oversight of Mazan, but from 1216 the paternity was transferred to La Bénissons-Dieu.[332] When Billigheim (Marienbrunn, G; 1239) was incorporated it was placed under the oversight of Ebrach, but later of Schöntal.[333]

The nunnery of La Bussiêre (F) was founded in 1188/89 as a collaborative effort of the monks of Noirlac and the nuns of L'Éclache. One of the founding deeds, now seen as a later forgery, gave the abbot of Noirlac 'the same power over Bussière as the abbot of Bellaigue had over L'Éclache and the abbot of Cîteaux had over Tart'.

For reasons unknown, the abbot of Clairvaux in 1228 withdrew from the abbot of Noirlac all vistatorial powers in respect of La Bussière, and the abbot of Cîteaux also forbade the mother-abbess of L'Êclache from visiting the nunnery. A decade later relations were restored, and the nuns of Bussière acknowledged the abbot of Noirlac as their rightful and historic Visitor.[334]

In northern Italy, Rifreddo had been founded with the abbot of Staffarda heading the list of witnesses to its foundation charter, but later relations between Staffarda and Rifreddo, were to take a turn for the worse. Pope Nicholas III, in 1279, therefore appointed the abbot of Lucedio as Rifreddo's Visitor, 'because of the many and diverse questions' between the two houses'. In 1284, the nuns rebuffed a projected visitation by the abbot of Staffarda, but by 1292 matters seem to have mended.[335]

Some convents knew a peaceful change of paternity, as Wechterswinkel (G); initially under the oversight of Ebrach (1134) this passed to Bildhausen (1156) which lay very much closer;[336] for a like reason the initial oversight of Trzebnitz, Silesia, exercised by Pforta in Germany, passed over to the abbots of Lubiąż much nearer at hand.[337]

The right of visitation of a particular convent was jealously guarded. So much so, that in 1252 the General Chapter noted that there was contention between 'persons of the Order' regarding the paternity of nunneries, and insisted that who-ever had exercised paternity for ten years should be the *de facto* Visitor.[338] The Chapter further decreed, the next year, that the name of a Visitor, and by what authority he performed a visitation of a male or female monastery, should be stated in the charter of visitation.[339]

Even Cîteaux had to fight off claims to the oversight of Beauvoir (F) from Lorroy (1239),[340] and of Port Royal from Vaux-de-Cernay (1257),[341] and Clairvaux (1235) from Aulne (B) as regarding Aywières and, later, Valloires (1238; F) and La Cambre (1240; B).[342] When the abbots of Lucelle in Alsace and St Urban in Switzerland were in 1235 at variance regarding the paternity of Olsberg nunnery (Swz), the abbots of Tennenbach, Pairis and Wettingen, were commissioned to bring about a peaceful solution.[343]

The abbeys of Mazan and of Silvanès were in disagreement in 1254 over the paternity of Nonenque (F).[344] Nonenque tried, unsuccessfully, to leave the Order in 1293 and the abbess was deposed for rebellion. The abbot of Silvanès, confirmed as the nunnery's Visitor,[345] inspected Nonenque, in 1303, urged its nuns to a better keeping of enclosure, humility, obedience, silence and of attendance at the daily chapter. He also gave instructions which helped the convent climb out of debt.[346]

In parts of France and Germany, as also in much of England, the local diocesan bishop exercised the visitatorial powers. Around 1175 Bival (F; founded by 1154) was removed from the oversight of Beaubec and placed under that of the archbishop of Rouen. It continued to maintain all Cistercian observances, and this juridical position applied also to its four daughter-houses: Bondeville, Saint-Saëns, Neufchâtel and Yvetot.[347] Allegedly the abbots of Beaubec had exceeded their visitatorial power.[348] Bishop of Conrad of Hildesheim (G; 1233) claimed the right of oversight of Wienhausen whether 'in temporalities or of spiritualities'. A successor, Bishop Otto (1331) reminded the nuns of Wöltingrode that he had both temporal and spiritual jurisdiction over them.[349]

The archbishops of York and the bishops of Lincoln held regular visitations of the Cistercian priories of nuns in their dioceses, probably because they had not been fully incorporated into the Order. Archbishop Le Romeyn of York ordered visitations at Swine nunnery, in 1287, 1290, and 1294: he may have held the first two himself, but that of 1294 was committed to William de Blyth, sub-dean of York. The visitation of 1287 was to be 'without verbal inquisition'; given the rebellion of some nuns there a little later, it might have been best otherwise.[350] In that year he committed the visitation of Cistercian Kirklees to the Augustinian prior of St Oswald's, York.[351]

Innocent IV did make moves to place all communities of nuns under the control of neighbouring abbots; in this respect, in 1252, when St Felix de Monceau (F) was elevated to abbey status he transferred its obedience from the local bishop to the abbot of Valmagne.[352] When, however, the nuns of Sinningthwaite (E; 1276) contested the right of the archbishop of York to hold visitations there it was seemingly unsuccessful.[353]

The record of visitations in English episcopal registers tell of the procedures followed. Before the visitation proceeded, a sermon would be preached to the community. Bishop Giffard of Worcester at Pinley convent in 1284 spoke on the text 'Hearken, O daughter, and consider, and incline thy ear' (A. V., Ps. 45, v. 10), and in 1290 on 'thy name is as ointment poured forth' (A. V., Song of Solomon, 1, v. 3).[354] In 1284, at the nunneries of Cook Hill and Whistones, he preached on the text: 'Hast thou daughters? Have a care of their body' (Eccles. 7, v. 24).[355]

At Swine (in 1268) the archbishop of York heard that its chaplains and *conversi* had so misused the convent's funds that the nuns were short of food, and (in 1290) certain rebellious nuns there had to be transferred to another house.[356] At Nun Appleton (in 1281) he reproved the nuns for holding private property.[357]

The bishop of Lincoln visiting Heynings in 1347 was not happy with breaches of the rule of silence, lack of care in reciting the divine office, the visits of friends, and the admission of children and seculars to the cloister and dormitory'.[358] It is important to remember that visitation charters generally outlined only points for improvement, and rarely uttered praise for all that was good in a convent's life.

The demands made by a father-abbot, particularly at a time of visitation, could lead to resentment on the part of a community. The statutes of the General Chapter loom large in some years with the record of disobedience and obstruction on the part of some communities, or at least a proportion of their members. Such disturbances must, however, be placed in context, and seen against a background of perhaps hundreds of other convents where peace and holiness reigned.

In 1243 the Chapter had to remind abbesses in general not to be 'impudent and irreverent' when their Visitor came.[359] That same year it drew attention to the need for reform at Droiteval and Les Îles (F); Tarrant (E), and Rottermünster (G), and ordered special visitations.[360] The resentment was such that at Parc-aux-Dames (F) in 1243, when the Visitor read out the rules imposed the previous year, the nuns 'shouted, stamped and walked out' of the chapter-house. They menaced and argued with the Visitors, saying that they had no mandate to excommunicate them, and then defiantly proceeded to chant Sext 'in a high voice'.[361] That same year, at Lieu-Notre-Dame (F) the door was not opened although the Visitor knocked three or four times; eventually the lay person placed as door-keeper sent him away.[362]

The prioress of Moncey (F) was deposed in 1243 because, the Chapter noted, she had many times been disobedient and had excluded with force the Visitors sent to her abbey. The sub-prioress and the portress, who had joined in her rebellion, were also dismissed from office.[363] Four years later those who had been excommunicated there were allowed to be reconciled and absolved, so long as they humble promised obedience to the dictates of the Order.[364]

The abbess of Heilig-kreuz, Meissen (G; 1243), who also 'did not wish' to receive her Visitor, was excommunicated, deposed and ordered to be sent to another house. The nearby abbot of Buch was further to punish nuns who had been party to her misdemeanour, but to reconcile and absolve those penitent, but for a further four years at least the nuns did not conform.

The repeated censures by the General Chapter had little effect for in 1253 the nuns of Heiligkreuz were still in a state of rebellion.[365] In 1244 the convents of Voisins (F) and Mariensee (Lower Saxony, G) were excluded from the Order 'until such time as they were obedient to its institutes'.[366] The difficulties of the period led to a bull of Innocent IV in 1256 giving authority to the Cistercian Order to cut off 'from the unity of the Order', rebellious and disobedient nuns.[367]

Abbesses and nuns were also noted as rebelling at Blendecques and at Woestine (F), one of its daughter-houses (1244).[368] The lack of conformity at Blendecques was to last for several years. In 1246 the Chapter authorised the abbot of Clairvaux to employ such papal and secular help as he thought fit to end the rebellion. It also ordered that religious from Blendeques were not to be received in any house of the Order, although penitent nuns could be reconciled and absolved.

The next year the Chapter referring to the 'grave contumacy' at Blendecques ordered its sentence of excommunication to be repeated each Sunday publicly in all monasteries of the Order within the archdiocese of Reims. In 1248, 1249 and 1250, this instruction was repeated.[369]

Problems surfaced again at Blendecques thirty years on when it was reported its abbess had many faults, including blessing her own nuns and allowing secular priests to hear their confessions. She had been deposed by the abbot of Clairvaux, but continued in her obstinacy. Secular aid was to be sought if necessary to remove her and regain the abbey seal.[370]

There were to be later protests and rebellions as at Colonge (F; 1250), Königsbrück (F; 1260),[371] and Düsseren (G; 1269).[372] It was said at the General Chapter in 1250 that Colonge had been for some while without an abbess, and that the prioress had refused to deliver up the abbey seal. The nuns joined with her in rebellion and they refused to hold an election. Another nun of the house was intruded, unconstitutionally as superior, and she had refused admission to the father-abbot of Theulay. The intruding abbess and offending nuns were excommunicated by the General Chapter, and the next year it ordered that the sentence of excommunication regarding Colonge was to be publicly read if possible in the synod of Langres; if not, then at least elsewhere in that episcopal area.[373]

In 1277 the General Chapter noted the need for the reform of a number of nunneries and asked the abbots of Cîteaux and Clairvaux to organise it.[374] In 1268 the General Chapter heard of the 'excesses' of some of the nuns of Fraubrunnen (Swz), and of their total disobedience to their father-abbot of Frienisberg, but when it sent Visitors there they were repulsed 'with swords and cudgels', and the rebels had expelled the faithful nuns. The needs of these the Chapter said were to be met in other houses of the Order whilst the rebellion lasted, and the abbots of Hautcrêt and St Urban were deputed to overcome the disobedience using secular force if necessary. In 1270 it was reported that the abbess of Fraubrunnen had been deposed and a new abbess installed.[375]

There were other forms of discontent. During a rebellion against the abbess at Étanche (F; 1272), the General Chapter ordered its chaplains and *conversi* to have no dealings whatsoever with the disaffected nuns, not even to speak to them whether 'by word or by sign'.[376] Of Droiteval (F), it was said in 1291, that some nuns had not been professed 'according to the institutes of the Order'; if they were not willing to be so professed, they were to be made to leave.[377] In some nunneries matters were to worsen: in 1355 it was reported at the General Chapter that in some nunneries very unseemly spectacles took place on the feast of the Holy Innocents (28 December) and at other festivals. Father abbots were told to be vigilant in this matter, whilst any nuns who so persisted were to be publicly excommunicated.[378]

Occasionally a Visitor might be overbearing, as an abbot of Villelongue (1225) who, at the convent of Garriga (F; Cevennes), excommunicated the nuns, took their keys and tore up their charters.[379] An abbot of Ihlo, Frisia (G; 1239) allegedly visited an unnamed nunnery, and 'violently introduced a certain matron' there – presumably as abbess.[380] The abbot of Eldena, on visitation at Bergen (G) in 1338, faced disobedience from the nuns who wished to change their cloister rules. Both sides referred the matter to the bishop of Roskild, and the outcome is unknown.[381]

The Communities

LOCAL CHAPTERS

Two small groupings of Cistercian nunneries did have their own chapter, but any statutes they promulgated had to lie within the framework of the decisions of the male General Chapter held at Cîteaux.[382] By the late-twelfth century eighteen abbesses constituted the General Chapter held each Michaelmas at Tart, under the joint presidency of the abbot of Cîteaux (or his delegate) and the abbess of Tart.[383] Tart's seniority derived from its foundation (around 1120) by St Stephen Harding. The abbess had limited authority in her 'congregation', and the statutes of her Chapter dealt with such matters as abstinence, absenteeism and dress.[384] In France, the abbess of St-Antoine-des-Champs was also the head of a mini-congregation.[385]

The records of five of Tart's general chapters are extant.[386] The Chapter of 1242 ordered a visitation of a priory at 'Areloch', set up irregularly by Molèze convent, Burgundy, and where allegedly the nuns ate meat.[387] The following year the rule regarding abstinence from flesh meat was restated, and now also simplicity in clothing was enjoined. Cowls and sleeves were not to be too long nor too ample, nor were they to drag along the ground; cloaks were not to be made of fur nor of rabbit or hare skin. Those who disregarded these injunctions were to be deprived of wine for as long as they did so.

In 1268 the abbess of Montarlot, who had not attended Chapter for three years and on this occasion had not even sent a representative, was ordered not to occupy her abbatial stall until she had presented herself at Tart, and to fast on bread and water on Fridays. The abbess of Ounans who had sent an 'insufficient excuse' for non-attendance by the hands of a 'rough and rude' servant was to live on bread and water until she too came to Tart. The same Chapter reiterated the rule against eating meat outside the infirmary. If an abbess did so she was to be deposed; if a nun or *conversae* she was to abstain from wine on all Fridays, and take the lowest place in the community for a year.

In 1272, when the abbot of La Bussière and the prior of Cîteaux took the place of the abbot of Cîteaux, the abbesses of Montarlot, Droiteval and Benoîtvaux were absent, and each was requested to pay 20 *sous* to Tart to help cover the expenses of the Chapter. In 1290 the abbess of Tart was urged to visit all her filiations, and given full powers of correcting abuses and disciplining the blameworthy. In 1302 it was prescribed that if an abbess could not attend Chapter she must be represented by her prioress or another of her nuns, and not by servants.

In Spain the primacy of Las Huelgas owed much to its foundation by Alfonso VIII (1187),[388] to the papal bull (1188) which placed it 'under the protection of blessed Peter and mine own', and to having (like Tart) the abbot of Cîteaux as its Visitor.[389] Abbot William of Cîteaux (1188), in line with the wishes of Alfonso VIII, declared Las Huelgas to be the mother of all Cistercian nunneries in Castile.[390] This led the way for the Chapter established in 1189, and held yearly at Las Huelgas at Martinmas (11 November) for the nunneries of Castile and León. At first it was composed of eight abbesses,[391] but their number grew to fourteen.[392]

The chapter meetings took place in the chapter-room at Las Huelgas, and there the abbesses were to show the same reverence and submission to the abbess of Las Huelgas as abbots did to the abbot of Cîteaux. The abbesses of Perales, Gradefes, Canas and San Andrés were to be effectively the first four abbesses with the right to visit Las Huelgas each year, just as the four proto-abbots visited Cîteaux.

If the abbess of Tulebras consented to be under the authority of Las Huelgas, she would rank first. Each abbess could be accompanied to Chapter by six persons of either sex; 'she would be the seventh'.[393] Abbot Guy of Cîteaux visiting Burgos in 1199 made attendance at the Las Huelgas Chapter obligatory for the abbesses of the filiation,[394] as some of the abbesses (like those of Tulebras and its daughter-house of Perales) were reluctant to attend.[395] The abbess of Perales only came into line after a visit from the abbot of Cîteaux.

The intention of holding this annual Chapter was to allow the abbesses to discuss how they might live more uprightly and in a more religious way. They might invite one or two wise neighbouring abbots to instruct them in the observances of the Order.[396] The third abbess of Las Huelgas (1210) overstepped the mark when she, and perhaps other Spanish abbesses, blessed her own nuns, heard confessions and preached publicly. Innocent III forbade these practices for, he said, 'the Lord had commended the keys of the kingdom not to the Blessed Virgin Mary, but to the apostles'.[397] A similar tendency towards independence may have caused Abbot

The Communities

Guy of Cîteaux (1191–1202) to reminded the nuns of Tart that their convent was 'the peculiar daughter of Cîteaux'.[398]

DISAFFECTED NUNS : THE ENGLISH NUNNERIES

Like modern newspapers, visitation charters and the statutes of the General Chapter mostly give the bad news, rarely the good. The few examples, therefore, of nuns who strayed from Cistercian life in its fulness must not be allowed to detract from those sisters who lived lives of humility and gained holiness. There were, though, some incidents in English nunneries, mostly those in Yorkshire, which caused concern to the Visitors and disruption within the communities.

When Archbishop Giffard of York visited Swine in 1268 he found a breakdown in relations between rebellious nuns unwilling to accept correction and an overbearing prioress. More than that, silence was not well observed in church, cloister, refectory nor dormitory.[399] Archbishop Le Romeyn in 1290, sought the names of rebellious nuns at Swine. A new abbess was elected there, and he ordered that the rebels be sent to the Cistercian nunnery of Rosedale, but one was moved to Nunburnholme, a Benedictine house, and was to be escorted there by a brother of the house and with the aid of a horse.

For the good of Swine, a further nun was sent away in 1293, this time to the Cistercian convent of Wykeham. So that Wykeham was not over-burdened, the archbishop ordered that a worthy nun of Wykeham be sent to Swine, for as long as the other's banishment lasted. This reflected the limited resources of the smaller Yorkshire nunneries.[400]

Maud, daughter of Roger de Hunmanby, a nun of Ellerton, had been excommunicated by 1274, perhaps on account of apostasy; she was clearly wandering abroad as Archbishop Giffard of York notified her excommunication to the justices of the King's Bench, asking them to shun and repel her by every legitimate means, until she came to him to seek absolution.[401]

The nunnery of Keldholme suffered intermittently in the late-thirteenth and early-fourteenth centuries from nuns who were of poor faith or of a cantankerous nature.[402] Two had apostasised but were to be readmitted and undergo salutary penance: Maud de Tiverington in 1287 and Cristiana de Styvelington in 1299. In 1308 six nuns of Keldholme refused obedience to the new prioress, Emma de York, who after four months resigned; the archbishop then appointing Joan de Pickering, but a number of nuns and laity protested. The archbishop sentenced one lay-man to perform public penance, and sent one of the refractory nuns to do penance at Handale, another to Swine, another to Nun Appleton, and another to Wallingwells.

Yet another nun a few months later, Emma de Newcastle, was adjudged guilty of conduct contrary to the honesty of her rule, and the archbishop directed that she be sent for a time to Esholt, there to do penance and rank last in quire, cloister, refectory and dormitory. At the same time another nun of Keldholme, Maud Bigot, was sent to Nunkeeling under the same conditions.

Similar problems of disobedience at Keldholme resurfaced a few years later, when in 1314 the archbishop had to forbid the keeping of young dogs in the conventual buildings.[403] The following year he forbade the presence of puppies in the church or choir at Rosedale.[404] In 1310 a nun of Swine was found to have had sexual relations with two monks of Meaux.[405] All these disobedient sisters must have been a burden and an embarrassment to their communities. Further afield, there was discord at Heiligkreuztal (G) after the election of a new abbess in 1311, when certain of the nuns laid 'violent hands' upon her.[406]

THE ABBESSES

The superior of a recognised and incorporated Cistercian community of nuns was the abbess, with her second-in-command being the prioress. In numerous instances, as in England and, where a convent was not fully part of the Order and perhaps subject to episcopal visitation, the superior bore the lesser title of prioress. The customs of the Order, as translated by a thirteenth-century Cistercian chaplain, 'poor Martin', have an abbess as occupying the first place on the south side of the quire, intoning the Te Deum at Matins on feast-days, imparting a blessing to the readers of the lessons, sprinkling the nuns with holy water after Compline, and enjoining faults in the daily chapter meeting. She also named who should be the prioress, sub-prioress and precentrix, she ate in the guest-house, and she might carry her pastoral staff, but only in the procession at the blessing of nuns.[407]

Within their respective domains, some abbesses came to have considerable authority. The abbess of Marham (E) had the privilege of proving the wills of those who died within the precincts or the jurisdiction of the house. This was disputed in 1401, but confirmed to the nunnery by the bishop of Norwich.[408] The abbess of Las Huelgas exercised seignorial rights over sixty-four villages, and had the rights of 'high' and 'low ' justice.[409] All her villages were exempt from episcopal control; she appointed the clergy and acted through ecclesiastical judges appointed by her, and might even convoke a synod.[410]

The blessing of a new abbess was the prerogative of the diocesan bishop or his delegate, as when the first Cistercian abbess of Fontaine-Guérard (F), Ada, was blessed in 1253 by the archbishop of Rouen at his manor of Déville.[411] On such profession the abbess took an oath of obedience to the bishop, so far as the constitutions of the Order would allow. As others, both Margaret, abbess of L'Eau (F; 1250-6) and her successors, making her profession of obedience to the bishop of Chartres, and to his successors, included the clause 'salvo ordine meo' ['saving my Order'].[412] So, too, did Abbesses Eustachie (1261) and Elisabeth [1295] of Parc-aux-Bois (F), and Abbess Héceline of Fervaques (F; 1295), at their blessing by the bishop of Noyon.[413] The English prioresses, certainly at a later date, did not normally include this clause.[414]

A Cistercian abbess paralleled the privileges of her counter-part in a male monastery, save that she did not celebrate the Eucharist nor hear confessions. From 1251 onwards, she must have achieved thirty years of age before being elected to her office. Some abbesses had previously been too young and immature: a point emphasised by a countess of Flanders (1245) who successfully sought the Chapter's agreement that her daughter (Margaret of Constantinople) was not to be compelled to become an abbess before her thirtieth birthday.[415]

Most papal confirmatory bulls assured the nuns of a Cistercian convent of their right to elect whom they wished as their superior. In England the nuns of Tarrant had been assured by King Henry III [1252] of the right of free election of their abbess 'as fully as obtains in the Cistercian Order'.[416] In practice this was not always the case. A founder might nominate a close relative as the first abbess; his descendants and other later patrons might make their wishes known, as might a diocesan bishop in the case of prioresses of houses where he had authority.

When in 1261 a new prioress of Sewardsley (E), Florence, was admitted by the bishop, it was with the approval of the then patron, Sir Robert de Paveley.[417] When, in 1303, the prioress of Esholt (E), Juliana de la Wodehall, wished to resign, the archbishop of York asked her to carry on until he could visit the house or discuss the matter with Simon le Ward, its patron.[418] The nunneries where a founder's daughter occupied the position of first abbess included Vauxbons (F; 1181),[419] Arroyo (Sp; 1186),[420] Bon Répos (F; 1204),[421] Differdange (L; 1235),[422] and St. Bernard-by-Horn (A; 1269),[423] to name but a few. Mothers, aunts and nieces of founders might, as described in Chapter 1, also assume the role. The question arises, what formation did they have, if any?

Not only were many nuns of noble blood, but there was for long a continuing attachment to the founding family. The first two abbesses of Valduc were daughters of its founder, Duke Henry of Lorraine and Brabant, the Blesseds Alice and Marguerite.[424] In France, four of the abbesses of Mollégès were nieces, several times removed of its founder, and a similar nepotism existed at Notre-Dame-de-Sion (Mont-Sion). Two members of the De Roquefort family were abbesses there, and in 1287 they held the posts of prioress, sub-prioress and precentor.[425] In Belgium, the second abbess of Florival, Alice de Mombecq (1247–62) was a cousin of Abbess Gentla her predecessor. Alice's husband had died in Palestine in 1220.

The third abbess of Florival came from the noble family of Bierbais (1262–72). Its fourth abbess, Hildegarde de Sombreffe, resigned in 1272 'out of devotion and humility' and handed the reins to her niece, Marie Hosdin, whose life was marked by many miracles and who died in 1313. Her successor, Ida de Waltain, also resigned in 1327 out of humility, and handed on the office to her cousin.[426] These two resignations may have been influenced by difficulties experienced with the dukes requiring exactions. Helwide, abbess of Nivelles in 1216, was the daughter of Gérard of Jauche, who gave the founding site for La Ramée.[427]

In Baden the first abbesses of Lichtenthal derived mostly from the families of the margraves: Adelheid (1263–95), daughter of Margrave Rudolf I; Elizabeth (1310–20): widow of Margrave Rudolf

The Communities

II; Adelheid (1336–8), widow of Margrave Frederick II, and Agnes, Margravine of Baden (1338–61). The three daughters of the second Adelheid also entered the community.[428] Can all these elections of Cistercian abbesses have been entirely free and without constraint?

In some English nunneries a small body of the nuns appear to have been the nominators of a new abbess, the whole community then acquiescing in their choice. In 1308 the bishop-elect of Worcester gave Lucy de Solers, the sub-prioress of Whistones, permission for the election of a new prioress, Agnes de Bromwych having died.

The sub-prioress sent the bishop-elect a full description of what then happened: On the vigil of the apostles Peter and Paul [28 June] she and all the nuns assembled in their chapter-house and appointed the following Monday to be the day of the election. On that Monday all those who should not be there were told to leave the chapter-house, and after they had heard 'the Word of God expounded, and had devoutly invoked the Holy Spirit', and two [presumably experienced] nuns of the convent had instructed the others in the form of election, all present then unanimously, 'as if inspired by the Holy Ghost', chose Alice de Flagge 'a woman of discreet life and morals, of lawful age, professed in the nunnery, born of lawful matrimony, prudent in spiritual and temporal matters'.

Alice, with a modesty befitting her virtues, could not be persuaded to agree to the election, but 'weeping, resisting as much as she could, and expostulating in a high voice as is the custom', was carried to the church as the *Te Deum* was sung, and there Brother William de Grimesleye, a monk of Worcester, proclaimed her election. She ruled the house for twenty years. In 1349 when another prioress had to be found, the community petitioned the then bishop that the choice might lie from within the convent, and the bishop as patron chose Agnes de Monynton.[429]

On 28 September 1306 the archbishop of York confirmed the election of Margery de Claworthe as prioress of Kirklees, She was a nun of the house, and the electors were two of the nuns, Alice of Swillingtoun and Alice de Screvyn, acting on behalf of the community. The archdeacon's official was directed to 'assign her a stall in the choir and a place in the chapter'. Her rule was short-lived; in January 1308 another superior took her place.

Margery had been either deposed or had resigned, and she was now commanded to show humble reverence to her successor.[430] When, in 1271, a vacancy occurred at Cotham (E) after the celebration of a Mass of the Holy Spirit and the chanting of the *Veni Creator* in the church, the inquisitors: the master, two 'con-canons', and four nuns, entered the chapter-house, scrutinised the possibilities, and on behalf of the convent elected Lucy of Mablethorpe as prioress.[431]

The General Chapter (1249) ruled that a nun who ceased to be an abbess was to remain in her nunnery, if that could be 'without scandal', otherwise, she was to revert to another convent her cost being met.[432] General Chapter (1294) reminded abbots and abbesses who resigned or who were deposed, not to take goods away to the monastery to which they transferred.[433]

Some superiors governed their houses well for a number of years, before gracefully retiring. The archbishop of York directed in 1320 that Joanna de Anlaghby who had been prioress of Swine since 1290, though possibly with a short break, and had resigned on account of old age and had laudably performed her duty, was to have due provision made for her.[434] Elizabeth de Holbeck, prioress of Nun Appleton (E), resigned in 1320 owing to old age and bodily weakness; she had, the archbishop wrote, laboured with efficacy while her strength lasted.[435]

Where abbesses served for a lengthy period, the consequence might well be a high degree of stability and prosperity for their house; as for Gravenhorst (G), whose first abbess ruled for forty-two years, though her community was small in numbers.[436]

Superiors who retired might be accorded special privileges: By this time it was customary for retiring abbesses to be awarded a pension and a chamber of their own. Unfortunately, the Chapter noted in 1323 that some nuns assumed the office of abbess too quickly, and then resigned after a short while in order to have a pension and their own chamber. The Chapter ruled that those who withdrew from their position were to have neither pension nor chamber. It is not spelt out but abbesses who had served say ten years would have not been so penalised.[437] As for perquisities, the abbess of Nonenque came to have a summer residence in the medieval fort of St Jean d'Alcas.[438]

At Catesby (E; 1291) the prioress, Biblisia, was admitted by the bishop of Lincoln; when her brief rule ended the nuns elected the cellaress, Joan of Northampton, as prioress, but as he had not given permission the bishop declared the election null, only shortly afterwards to confirm her on account of her merits.[439]

The Communities

At Greenfield in 1303 the bishop of Lincoln ordered Cecily de Parys, prioress of Greenfield, to resign as she had been absent for two years and that the nunnery was in danger of serious loss.[440] In 1294 the archbishop of York commissioned the chancellor of the diocese and another cleric to receive the resignation of a prioress of Sinningthwaite and to confirm the election of her successor.[441]

There were some unsatisfactory superiors. When Catherine, the former abbess of 'Fenesia' wandered off in 1298, the Chapter gave her six weeks to return to the house of her original profession in order to be professed 'according to the statute of the Order'.[442] Others were deposed on orders where the Yorkshire nunneries were concerned from the archbishop: – like Joan de Percy of Basedale (E) in 1307 on account of her notorious misdeeds and wasting of the goods of the house. She left taking some of the nuns with her; eventually she returned but the next year the archbishop sent her to Sinningthwaite on account of her being disobedient at Basedale. Alas! in 1343 the archbishop had to order an inquiry into the demerits of Prioress Katherine Mowbray of Basedale, and if necessary she too was to be deposed.[443]

There were superiors with discontented factions within their community. At Bottenbroich (G: 1294) some of the nuns forcibly expelled their abbess. The General Chapter ordered that those nuns and their adherents should receive her back 'and obey her humbly and devotedly'.[444] At Nonenque (F; 1299/1300) a nun, Ransa, and 'her adherents' were opposed to Abbess Ermengarde (1299/1300). By 1301 one Elys was abbess, though Ransa seems to have held that position in 1320.[445]

There were superiors who accumulated a private income. Abbess Guimar Gil of Arouca (Pt; d. 1286) left a will which suggests that she was a wealthy woman in her own right, Based on the income deriving from her properties at Colimbrie and the Three Towers, which she seems to have still owned personally, she made provision for an altar of the Holy Trinity to be erected in the nunnery church, to be served by a stipendiary resident chaplain, and there she was to be buried.

She left income for the nuns to receive two pittances; one on Trinity Sunday, the other at Christmas. Her monetary bequests favoured amongst others a former abbess, local Dominican and Franciscan friars, and the monastery's confessor, and to one Gerald Martin who had been of service no less that twenty pounds. After her death her properties appear to have become possessions of the nunnery, and one Peter Miguéis was appointed to handle the affairs arising from the will.[446]

THE CLAUSTRAL OFFICERS

A nunnery had officers equivalent to those in a male house. A deed of Carrizo (Sp; 1212) was confirmed by thirteen named nuns, including the abbess, prioress, cellarer, porter, precentor, sacrist, sub-prioress, sub-cellarer and sub-cantrix.[447] Between 1230 and 1340 the names are known at Trebznica (Pl) of seven prioresses, seven sub-prioresses, four 'keepers', one cellarer, and three sacristans.[448]

A list of the officials of the nunnery at Rathausen (Swz; 1282) included not only the sub-prioress, the porter and the cellarer, but also of 'Beta custode'.[449] At Veszprémvölgy (H), in 1318, Afra was prioress, Judith was cantrix, and Clara, custos.[450] On a deed issued at Conversano (It) in 1349, the abbess, prioress, sub-prioress and cantrix, all inscribed the sign of the cross against their names.[451] Deeds relating to San Clemente (Seville, Sp; 1316, 1347) give similar listings.[452]

Their duties were analogous to those of the monastic officers in the male abbeys, and are outlined in a French modification of the rules of the Order.[453] Amongst the duties specified were those of the sacristan, whose responsibility it was to attend to the clock, to arouse the sisters for matins and lauds, and to ensure in the early hours the lighting of the dorter steps, the church and the cloister. The nun appointed as guest-mistress might talk to her *conversa* attendant, and to the guests 'who ate or slept in the hospice'.

The portress, wearing her scapular, was after Lauds to take up her position at the gate, where in her room she was to keep bread for alms and for passers-by. For the poor waiting at the gate her assistant was to receive left-overs, and the portions of recently deceased nuns from the kitchen. The duties of the infirmarian encompassed not only bringing their food from the kitchen and the refectory, but also washing each Saturday the feet of those who wished, as well as their clothes. A nun, Maria Aires, was the porter at Arouca (Pt) in 1319.[454]

Officers mentioned in deeds of Duisseren (G; 1338) included the bursar and the infirmarian;[455] in a deed of Nonenque (F; 1279) were included its infirmarian sister and its pitancier sister;[456] a deed of Leyme (1351) referred to nuns holding the positions of porter, sacristan and hospitaller.[457] A 'master of the scholars' was noted at Rinteln (G; 1345).[458] A listing of the community at Frauensee (G; 1228] included a keeper (cellarer) and a custodian (*circatrix*).[459] A deed of Neuwerk (Goslar, G; 1317) mentions the provost, cellarer, the 'keeper', the chamberlain and the 'mistress of the infirmary'.[460]

It was such nuns holding responsible positions that Archbishop Wickwane of York had in mind when he ruled in 1281 that all the prioress of Nun Appleton (E) received in money or kind for the use of the monastery, she was not to receive alone, but in the presence of two or three of the older and wiser of the nuns. At the end of the year she was to reckon up before the seniors, chosen for that purpose, the receipts and expenditure of the house.[461]

The keeping of accounts was clearly essential: on visitation at Cotham (E) Bishop Hugh of Lincoln (probably Hugh of Wells, 1210–35) required that 'all rents, stock and produce shall be written down each year, and the record kept by the prioress, sub-prioress, and four of the most prudent nuns chosen by the whole chapter, or the better part of it'. The master and proctors were to hand over to these six all the monies of the house, wherever it came from, and when it has been counted in their presence they were to spend it on the business of the house, 'as much and as often was necessary'.

The remainder was to be kept under the seal of the master, and each month these six were to hear the detailed accounts of the house. The common seal of Cotham (E) was, Bishop Hugh directed, to be in the custody of the master, the prioress, and a discreet nun chosen by the whole community. It was to be kept under 'a triple lock' so that nothing could be signed without the knowledge of the chapter or the better part of it.[462]

By 1294 the priory of 'St Vincent' had acquired over twenty years some 500 pounds, and the abbots of Fontfroide and Santes Creus were bidden to advise the nuns to handle the money cautiously.[463]

VISIONARIES AND MYSTICS

Secluded in a number of Cistercian convents were many holy women, who more than outbalanced sisters of less virtue. One such was Margaret Rich, a sister of St Edmund Rich, and prioress of Catesby (E; 1245–57). The contemporary chronicler, Matthew Paris (d. 1259), wrote of her as 'a woman of great holiness, through whose distinguished merits miracles have been made gloriously manifest'. Her brother had bequeathed her in 1240 a pall and a silver tablet bearing an image of Our Lord which he always carried with him, miracles became also associated with these. She was sometimes termed St Margaret of Catesby.[464]

Most is known of the Cistercian mystics of Flanders and Belgium, sometimes from their own writings (like the autobiography of Beatrice of Nazareth; d. 1268), or from biographies written by those who knew them well (as by Abbot Philip of Clairvaux concerning Elizabeth of Spalbeek).[465] It was not easy to be a mystic; it could cause embarrassment and persecution, sometimes within one's own convent.[466]

Beatrice's diary-notes were kept so secret by her that not even her two blood sisters in the same community knew of them. It may be that because of concern for orthodoxy that her vernacular autobiography, composed about 1275, was destroyed by the abbess and chaplains of Nazareth, and only the Latin translation retained.[467] Beatrice, born in 1200, had been schooled first by beguines and then at the nunneries of La Ramée and Florival, but soon after moved to Maagdendaal where she took her vows at the age of sixteen. In 1235 Nazareth was formed and two years later Beatrice became its prioress, an office she held until her death in 1268.[468]

Beatrice of Nazareth constantly dwelt on the Passion and (about 1250) wrote her treatise on the *Seven Degrees (or Manners) of Love*.[469] This work, written in Middle Dutch prose, commences with the words: 'There are seven manners of love that come from the Most High and return to the Highest', and influenced in part the writings of Marguerite Porete (who later died in 1310 at the stake as a relapsed heretic). Where Beatrice wrote 'There are seven manners of love that come from the Most High and return to the Highest', Margaret in her *Mirror of Simple Souls* paraphrased: 'There are seven states of the soul by which one climbs from the valley to the summit of the mountain, which is so isolated that one sees nothing there but God'.[470]

Cistercian visionaries also included St Lutgard of Aywières (d. 1246) who fasted rigorously and had visions of the sacred wounds of Jesus, successfully exorcised a troubled nun, and saw Our Lord pointing to His pierced side. Lutgard was given to prolonged fasts 'on behalf of the Church', and may have experienced the stigmata. Poorly educated, she did not write a single line and was blind for the last ten years of her life. Her life was written by a contemporary, Thomas de Cantimpré.[471]

Ida de Léau entered La Ramée at the age of thirteen and triumphed over temptations; given to charity she was devoted to the Eucharist and Our Lady and she desired to communicate each Sunday.[472] Ida of Argensolles was originally a Benedictine nun and prioress of St Leonard's, Liège, but became the first abbess of Cistercian Argensolles (1222). Dying four years later she was reputedly illiterate, and yet having a perfect understanding of theological works including those of St Augustine on the Trinity, and she was also a clairvoyant.[473]

Ida of Nivelles at Ramée (d. 1231) left no work of her own composition, but the gift of clairvoyance enabled her to tell others of their standing with God, and one Christmas Day at Mass she saw in the priest's uplifted hands not the host but the Infant Jesus. Her mystical life was grounded in sublime experiences of the Blessed Trinity, and on her death-bed she uttered the words: 'The Holy Trinity is thundering to descend'. Her biographer, probably Godwin, a cantor at Villers, said of Ida that 'her soul was imprinted by the glue of the most ardent love for the Holy Trinity, so that it made her spirit one with the spirit of the Lord'. One sister of La Ramée who was given to blasphemy knew peace after the prayers of Ida, who died in 1231, after sixteen years and nine months of profession.

Ida, entered the nunnery at Kerkom at the age of sixteen, had difficulty at first in that most the nuns spoke Dutch, a language with which she was unfamiliar. She came to be much sought after for spiritual advice, and conveyed her wisdom to the novices. Devoted to the frequent reception of Holy Communion, she had a special insight into spiritual suffering, backed by her own mystical experiences. She knew the gift of tears, and popularly was to bear the name of Ida the Compassionate.[474]

Adeline de Mombecq, mother of the second abbess of Florival, and seemingly in its community, one day at Matins had a vision of the devil, but also of a good angel.[475] Abbot Walter of Villers told how a monk sent to a Cistercian nunnery observed that a certain nun seemed to be living close to God. He sought her prayers that he might during solemn matins have the gift of tears, and this grace was granted him.[476]

The mother of St Ascelina, born in 1121, was a relative of St Bernard, and Ascelina had a vision in which he announced his death. She was a Benedictine nun of Poulangy (F), who became prioress of Lieu les-Dames near the abbey of Boulancourt, and although never a Cistercian she appears to have been close to the monks of Clairvaux. It was Goswin, a monk of Clairvaux who died in 1203, who wrote her life and spoke of her holiness and miracles; she having died in 1195. Goswin told of her devotion to the recitation nightly of the entire psalter, whilst Caesarius of Heisterbach wrote of the vision she experienced of a former prior of Clairvaux suffering in purgatory.[477]

Caesarius also told of Elizabeth of Hoven (Ho), who persecuted by a demon fell backwards down the dorter stairs, and Christine of Volmunsteine who in her nunnery at Bergen (G) in ecstasy experienced paradise. The nunnery of Hoven was under the oversight of Heisterbach, and so Caesarius also told of its Abbess Gertrude, whose sight was restored during a vision of St Linthild; and of Abbess Sophia, a disciplinarian, whose small beer once turned into wine.[478]

The Cistercian nuns of Helfta (G) produced several important texts in the late thirteenth century, including *The Flowing Lights of the Godhead* by Mechtild of Magdeburg; she had written the first six volumes in the Magdeburg beguine community, and added a seventh after entering Helfta. It was 'a mystical text focusing on Eucharistic piety and the cult of the Sacred Heart'. Another sister in the community was Mechtild of Hackeborn (d. 1298/99) who gave an account of her spiritual life, *The Book of Special Grace*. The community pressed both mystics to describe their visions in writing, overseen by Dominican and Franciscan theologians.

Gertrude of Helfta (d. 1302) wrote of devotion to Our Lady, emphasising her pregnancy, and asserting that Our Lady had asked her recite the Ave Maria forty-five times a day during the octave of the feast of the Annunciation. Visual representations might take the form of small figures of Christ and John the Baptist in front of their mothers' bodies, in allusion to spiritual pregnancy.[479] Her major work was *The Herald of Divine Love*, in which she asserted that she bore the stigmata interiorly not visibly, and encouraged meditation before a crucifix. She had been a child oblate at Helfta when only four years old, possibly because her parents had died.[480]

The Communities

The hermit writer, Richard Rolle (*ob.* 1349), spent his last years and was buried at Hampole nunnery (E).[481]

THE MALE COMMUNITY

The rule of strict enclosure meant that male folk had to do a great deal in the work of a Cistercian nunnery, meaning convents became effectively double-communities (albeit men and women living quite separately), with a parallel household of clerks, chaplains and male *conversi* (lay-brothers) to attend not only to the nuns' spiritual needs but also to the necessary manual work and external business.

When, for example, Heiligenthal (Bavaria; 1234) was founded, the abbey of Bildhausen supplied its provost, chaplain, and *conversi*,[482] despite the request previously made by the General Chapter (1222) to Honorius III that the male abbeys should not be forced to send monks to help their nuns with their temporal affairs, as this was 'to the prejudice of the Order and danger to their souls'.[483] The necrology of Gnadenthal (G) enumerates thirty-eight male *conversi* as serving its nuns between 1253 and 1370;[484] whilst the obit list of Sonnefeld convent (G) reveals thirty-three male *conversi* as assisting its nuns between 12373 and 1390, including a shoemaker, a baker, a brewer, procurators, and waiters.[485]

Although their paths in work and worship were treaded separately, the very presence of brothers and nuns within the same precinct, and the profession of obedience made by the male members to the abbess or prioress, did give some convents the appearance of being a double community. A concord witnessed at Cotham (E; 1258) was made in the presence of not only the nuns, but also of 'the canons, brothers A. and J., and the servants'. An undated agreement made by Cotham was 'between the brothers and sisters of Cotham and their man Gelewin'.[486]

A grant of land to Cotham (undated) was made to 'the canons, nuns, brothers and sisters'.[487] All this was perhaps exceptional, but it lifted the *conversi* of that nunnery from being lowly adjuncts to equal partners. Certainly in death they were equal. A reference in 1232 to the newly-founded Haste nunnery, later at Rulle (G), refers to the presence within its precincts of 'nuns, monks, *conversi* and others, servants and maids'.[488] Basedale (E) had a cemetery for 'the nuns and sisters, and our brethren who have taken our habit'.[489]

The terminology employed in some charters suggest that the 'brothers' were no mere servants of a women's community, but true sharers in it. Not only were charters addressed to 'the nuns and brothers' at Ichtershausen (G; 1221, 1231), but also petitions to Ludovic, Landgrave of Thuringia (1225, 1228) came from 'the provost, nuns and brothers' of that nunnery.[490] Five of the male *conversi* of Wald nunnery (G; 1333) were described as being 'prebendaries and *conversi* there'.[491]

When Sonnenkamp (Neukloster, G; 1233) made a grant of spiritual fraternity, the witnesses to the deed were the provost, the prioress, two other nuns, and four or more 'brothers' of the nunnery.[492] A necrology of Flines (F) dating from the thirteenth century yields the names not only of twenty-six female *conversae* but also of twenty-nine male *conversi*, as well as of six female and two males 'familiars', suggesting the value that convent placed on their former membership of its community.[493]

The Provosts

The business affairs of most Cistercian nunneries were handled, hopefully in co-operation with the superior, by a male procurator. Indeed, from 1218, it became a condition of incorporation into the Order of a female community that a procurator be appointed to attend to its temporal affairs. He was to be chosen by the community, agreed by the father immediate, and installed by the abbess.[494] As soon as they had settled at Old Medingen (1241), its nuns elected one Nicholas, who had been brought up with the prayers of his aunt at Dambeke, as their provost, investing him with a grey cowl.[495]

Free election of their procurator was assured by the papal bulls addressed to numerous communities, but in 1321 the General Chapter found it necessary to remind communities that their procurators should be chosen only with the approval of their father-abbot, who could reject any already in post if need be.[496]

Unknown concerns in the case of Beuren (G) meant that in 1238 the heirs of the founder, the lord Rudolf, called in the abbots of Reifenstein (Cistercian), Gerode (Benedictine), and Reinhusen (Benedictine) to secure the peaceful election of a provost for that nunnery.[497] In 1354 the nuns of Bersenbrück (G) promised that after the death or resignation of their provost, Albert of Luneburg, that they might not choose another, save with the agreement of the abbot of Camp, their Visitor.[498]

Interference from external sources made it necessary for the nuns of Cotham (E, 1265) to petition the bishop of Lincoln for the right to make a free choice of its master 'as it has always done'. The procurators it appointed included a canon of Thornton and of Stixwould and the vicar of nearby Barton, but occasionally they proved less than satisfactory.[499] The names of many provosts are on record, and some could be long-serving, as at Neuwerk (Goslar; G): John, 1250–68; Heinrich, 1272–81; Albrecht, 1273–93, and Dietrich, 1296–1311.[500]

In north England, the archbishops of York frequently thought it best to impose a procurator, and very often these were drawn from outside the ranks of the Cistercian Order. In 1268 Archbishop Giffard of York appointed a monk of Whitby, William de Bardenay, as 'guardian' of Handale and Basedale nunneries.[501] Richard, vicar of Wath, was named as 'keeper' for Hampole in 1280, and Roger, vicar of Arksey, in 1308. In 1314 its nuns were urged to work with their keeper to strive to be relieved of their debts.[502]

When in 1287, the nunnery of Swine (E) was in a state of 'depression and poverty, want and ruin', Archbishop Le Romeyn appointed as 'master of the house of the poor women of Swine', a canon of Premonstratensian Croxton, Robert of Spalding. He required the prioress, her nuns, and 'the canons and brethren' of Swine to show him obedience. Three years later the archbishop praised Robert for his 'industrious and commendable work' at the nunnery.[503]

In 1318 Archbishop Melton commissioned Thomas de Mydelsburg, rector of Loftus, to administer the temporal goods of Handale, to receive the accounts of the servants, and to substitute more capable ones for those who were useless.[504] Stixwould (E) operated under the leadership of a prioress and a 'master', who might be a religious or a secular cleric.[505]

The General Chapter ruled in 1267 that 'provisors' who were sometimes termed 'provosts or priors' should be known as 'procurators'.[506] Hitherto, and indeed still thereafter as noted above, the office of procurator went by different names in many of the nunneries: as 'provisor' (as at Lilienthal, Lower Saxony; 1300, 1322),[507] 'provost' (as at Waterler [Wasserleben] G; 1311/1312): in the latter year he was named as 'John, by the grace of God, provost');[508] 'prior' (as at Saarn, G; 1225, 1262);[509] but sometimes as 'master', as at Coldstream, S;[510] Cotham, E;[511] Feldbach, Swz; 1255;[512] and Flines (F; 1281);[513] 'guardian' (as at Basedale and Handale, E; 1267/1268),[514] or 'keeper' (as at Duissern, G; 1256,[515] and Wald, G; 1333).[516]

A reference to this officer at Heiligen Kreuz (Gotha, G; 1347) terms him 'provost and head'.[517] One deed relating to Lilienthal (Lower Saxony, 1272) refers in the plural to its 'procurators'.[518] Surprisingly, in 1317, Waterler (Wasserleben, G) had both a provost, Jordan, and a provisor, Walter.[519] A deed relating to Wormeln (G; 1299) still referred to 'provost or provisors' there.[520] The term 'procurator' was employed at Parc-aux-Bois (F; 1257) in respect of Brother Renerus,[521] and at Las Huelgas (Sp; 1307] in reference to Peter Martinez.[522] At Himmelspforten (G; 1338) Brother Henry of Nürnberg was 'governor and procurator', and Gottfried von Karsbach acted as its notary.[523] A male provost of Wienhausen (G) is depicted in a medieval painting.[524]

Who were the procurators, for rarely is their provenance known? The father-abbot of a male abbey which had complete oversight of a fully incorporated nunnery, very probably endeavoured to supply a monk or *conversus* with suitable talent to fulfil the role. This was certainly the case at Wald (G; 1233) where John de Rhierach, a monk of the mother-house of Salem was procurator,[525] and at St Bernard-by-Horn (Swz; 1276) where a *conversus* of Zwettl occupied the position.[526]

A *conversus of* Rifreddo (It; 1231), John Tenca, in selling land 'in the name of the prioress', was described as '*conversus* and minister' [agent], whilst the same year, Peter Cafer, was described as its 'prior, and minister'.[527] Another *conversus* whilst on the business of the convent, Enrico, found himself lodged for a time in 1284 in prison at Borgo Sal Dalmazzo, but the matter was cleared up.[528] The procurator of Sonnefeld (G; 1302–5), Gotfride, was a *conversus*; he may have held this post since 1276.[529] In these latter cases, the *conversi* named may well have been senior lay-brothers already on the staff of the convents, rather than imports from a male abbey.

At Catesby (E) apart from the 'master' there appear to have been other clerics named 'canons', another hint of a semi-double community. The names of a succession of 'masters' of Catesby are on record: John (1286) was already resident and a 'canon' of Catesby; but Robert of Waddington, appointed master by the bishop of Lincoln in 1293 was an Augustinian canon of Canon Ashby, and the following year he was succeeded by another canon

The Communities

of Ashby, William de Grutterworth. Richard of Staverdon, canon of Catesby, was appointed master in 1316, in succession to Roger of Daventry.

The master had the rule of the house, admitting the canons as well in spiritualities as in temporalities. In 1310 when large supplies of victuals by way of loan were exacted from the heads of religious houses for the expedition of Edward II into Scotland, the master of Catesby was named in the list of Northamptonshire houses - he was its business manager.[530]

By the mid-thirteenth century, with perhaps a decline in numbers of monks and *conversi*, some provosts were lay-men. In 1261, if not by 1250, the 'procurator' of Rifreddo (It) was Ruffino di Giglio, 'judge of Pineroli'. In 1262 the nuns' procurator was the abbot of San Pietro in Ciel d'Oro, and in 1291 James Grenona of Gambasca. In 1292 different laymen there acted as procurators for specific cases.[531]

Known procurators of Arouca (Pt) were all laymen, including: Domingos Migueis (1287), Luke Rodrigues (1293), and Girald Vicente (1326), and the same was true at Celas, like Gonçalc (1292).[532] Arouca also appointed other procurators, as and when the need arose, as in 1287 Alfonso Lopes, a notary of Porto.[533] One John Diaz, a favourite of the deceased abbess of Cañas (Sp), Teresa Yvannes (who died by 1298) was described as her 'servant and merchant'. He took advantage of the vacancy after her death to use her seal to make forged receipts for 'fictitious payments of feudal rents'. There is no suggestion that he was a cleric.[534]

A *conversus*, by the name of Christian, still occupied the role of procurator at Belfays (F) in 1329,[535] but in 1347 the provost of Mariengarten (Lower Saxony) was seemingly Henry de Grone, a married man with three sons.[536] When their former provost, John of Rottorf, died, the nuns of Rinteln (G; 1345) each received an equal annual payment from the proceeds of his properties, but a *conversa* sister was awarded half the amount a nun received.[537]

Little is known of the life-style of the procurators. Clearly, they had their board and lodging in quarters removed from those of the nuns, and their own domestic arrangements. A lay benefactor made provision for a chaplain to live within the precincts of Waterler (Wasserleben; 1327) and to have a place at the provost's table.[538] At Medingen (1344) the chaplains and boy pupils ate at the provost's table.[539]

At Nun Appleton (E; 1306), the 'keeper' was to have his meals in the chamber assigned him, but if the prioress was entertaining guests in her chamber, for the sake of company he might join them.[540] It was a matter of concern for Archbishop Giffard of York (1268) that at Swine 'the canons and [male] *conversi*, under pretence of taking care of the external property of the house wasted it, which, if it were carefully looked after, would suffice for the maintenance of all. The nuns were only receiving bread, cheese and ale, and on two days in the week they only had water. The canons, however, and their accomplices were having plenty and were daintily provided for'.[541]

An early grant of land at Burgh was made to the nunnery of Cotham (E), the income gained was to provide three loaves for the master, and one for everyone else, at Candlemas.[542]

The procurators exercised considerable authority over the temporal well-being of a nunnery and its economic activity. It was in this vein that the abbess of Lilienthal (Lower Saxony; 1260) notified the dean of Bremen that their 'provost or provisor', Werner – perhaps newly appointed, would act on behalf of the nunnery in all causes and litigation.[543] There are many instances of a provost taking the lead in such business matters: as when Herbord, the provost of Mariengarten (Lower Saxony; 1282), surrendered its church of Elkershausen into the hands of another monastery – there was no mention of the abbess in the deed.[544]

Henry, the provost of Stepnitz (Marienfliess, Brandenburg; 1300), took the leading role when that nunnery bought for thirty-five marks the entire village of Quaslin.[545] Henry, the provost of Seligenthal (G) was the only monastic witness to a grant for his nunnery in 1336.[546] The provost of Tišnov (Cz; 1278) was authorised by the bishop of Olomuch to proceed with the appointment of a new priest to the vacant parish of St Peter, Brno.[547]

Duke Albert of Brunswick (1278) granting the tithes of Niendorf to Medingen nunnery (G) addressed his charter to 'the provost and the nuns'.[548] A long-serving provost perhaps brought stability to a convent's economic affairs: for instance, Hermann was provost of Rulle by 1269 and until at least 1277; one John was provost of Bersenbrück by 1285 until certainly 1300.[549]

Provosts frequently took precedence of an abbess or prioress on the charters recording business transactions. When in 1253 Gunzelin, Graf von Schwerin, confirmed several grants made to

Zarrentin (G), the charter referred to its 'provost, abbess and convent' in that order;[550] like terminology was employed on a sale made to Kapellendorf nunnery (G; 1271).[551] In the preamble of a charter granted by the nuns of Sczcecin (P) in 1280, the name of the provost, Wolter, comes before that of the abbess, Gertrude.[552]

When in 1251 a leading citizen of Mülhausen imparted a house in that city to Beuren (G), the charter was addressed to 'the provost and his college'.[553] When, in 1254, the nunnery of Neukloster (G) was incorporated into the Order, the charter was granted to 'A. the provost and A. the prioress' in that order.[554] When Teistuntenburg (G) in 1297 made a grant of spiritual fraternity, the deed was sent under the names (in that order) of Albert the provost, Bertrad, abbess, and Isentrude, prioress, in that sequence.[555]

A deed, however, issued by the abbess of Börstel (G; 1274) had its provost's name in second place.[556] A charter of Wienhausen (G; 1255) commenced: 'Elizabeth, abbess, Matthias, provost, and all the convent'.[557] It was, however, Adam, the provost of Neukloster (G), who in 1260 assigned the proceeds of two of its villages to the work of its infirmary.[558] Wolfram, the provost of Ichtershausen (G; 1190) listed its 'extraordinary treasure of relics'.[559] At Waterler, in 1309, Abbess Sophia and the provost, John, jointly issued a deed.[560]

Procurators/provosts had their own seal independent of that of the nuns: that of the provost of Allendorf (G; 1300–44) bearing the imagery of the Blessed Virgin and her Child,[561] as did that of a provost of Frauensee (around 1320).[562] The seal of Hermann, provost of Waterler (G; 1327), depicted him standing at an altar in eucharistic vestments and elevating the host;[563] that of Adam, provost of Sonnenkamp (G; 1238) depicted a priest holding a book in his left hand, a palm in his right.[564] The seal of a provost of Beuren (G; 1236) had a priest standing at an altar and holding a chalice.[565]

The seals of two early-fourteenth-century provosts of Wormeln (G) included a catherine-wheel; why is unknown, but frescoes remain in its church of St Margaret and of St Katherine, although the church was reputedly dedicated to SS Simon and Jude.[566] The seal of the provost of Mariengarten (Erfurt; G) depicted the nuns' patron, St Martin, mitred and holding a book in his right hand, his pastoral staff in his left hand.[567] The seal of the provost of Frankenberg (Georgenberg, G), despite its dedication to St George, showed the Blessed Virgin Mary and her Child.[568] The seal of the provost of

Berka (G) by 1348 depicted Christ crucified flanked by two kneeling saints, and in base the provost in prayer.[569]

The arrangement whereby a procurator had such a great significance in the life of a nunnery, could clearly lead to difficulties if his decisions conflicted with the wishes of his nuns. This happened when the abbess of Rinteln (G; 1315) referred to discord between her community and the provost, as while a rent had been set aside for the repair of their clothing, the provost failed to apply it for that purpose.[570]

When Chumbd (G) was founded, the archbishop of Mainz (1196) in his confirmatory charter stipulated that 'its *conversi*, sisters and the provost' should promise obedience to the abbbess 'without murmuring'. He also emphasised that 'in selling or buying things, or in the reception of sisters and *conversi*', the provost should not act without the consent and advice of the abbess and her community.[571]

The procurator of Conversano (It; 1315) was obliged to regularly present his accounts in the presence of the abbey's two chaplains.[572] Contrariwise, when in 1287, the nunnery of Swine (E) was in a state of 'depression and poverty, want and ruin', Archbishop Le Romeyn required the prioress, her nuns, and 'the canons and brethren' of Swine to show obedience to their provost.[573]

Did all Cistercian nunneries have a provost? A pact of Carrizo (Sp; 1214) with a widow, Elvire, has ten witnesses but no mention of a provost under that title.[574] Other of its deeds have its chaplains as witnesses,[575] but also lack the name of a provost, though one Martin Dominic may have been its 'prior' in 1224.[576]

A deed issued by the abbess of Las Huelgas (Sp; 1225) was witnessed by three of its clerks, three of its 'brothers', the 'chico' and the 'alcade' [governor], but in these abbeys the procurator/provost seems to have played a less prominent role than elsewhere.[577] Bernstein (G) certainly did have provosts, and the names of some are known: Herad in 1295, Heinrich in 1303, and Dietrich in 1389.[578]

The Male Conversi (Lay-Brothers)

The demands of strict enclosure meant that the agricultural work on the lands of Cistercian nunneries had to be performed by servants, tenants and lay-brothers who lived and dressed as their equivalents, the *conversi* of the male monasteries of the Order. Despite the

The Communities

misgivings of the General Chapter (1222; supra), it is very probable that a male house taking a nunnery under its wing would provide some of its *conversi* to assist its nuns.

This was certainly the case after La Cambre had been established (1201) on a site given by the duke of Brabant, Henry I, and placed under the oversight of Villers, which provided chaplain, confessor and some *conversi*,[579] when Bildhausen supplied brothers on the foundation of Heiligenthal (Bavaria; 1234),[580] and when Staffarda (1249) was required by Innocent IV to provide the nuns of Rifreddo (It) 'with two suitable lay-brothers' as their business agents.[581]

It has been suggested that Thoronet (F) had so many vocations in the early-thirteenth century, that it assured the nunneries of Alamanarre, Gémenos and Sion a supply of the necessary helpers.[582] Lay servants might well live at home, as did the ploughman of St-Lawrence nunnery (Magdeburg; G; 1351), residing with his wife at a house in Grünen Street, a name which still survives.[583]

As that century the numbers of *conversi* vocations declined, it became the norm for the convents to seek their own lay brothers, and the detailed instructions for their probation and their profession are witness to that. Some of these, coming from the world, might prove difficult, and so General Chapter (1254) required them to serve a six month period of probation in lay clothes, before commencing their year-long noviciate.[584]

Very little is known of the quarters the male *conversi* occupied at a Cistercian nunnery, nor where or how they worshipped. Certainly their contact with most of the enclosed nuns would have been minimal, and physically they would have been separated. Their number at Las Huelgas (Sp) was probably quite large, and accommodated in its 'house of the *conversi*', for the building of which Alfonso VII (1203) gave 2,500 gold pieces.[585] It is not clear whether Gazal, who in 1214 promised in the chapter-house of Casbas (Aragon) to be 'faithful, good, and obedient', was a professed *conversus*, or a familiar.[586]

The charter of incorporation of Trebnitz (Pl, 1218) told its *conversi* to promise stability before the abbess in chapter, and to make their profession to her. Its clerics were to also make their profession before the abbess, and making the sign of the cross, to place their deed on the altar.[587] The practice was spelt out when in 1254 the General Chapter ordained that all lay personnel, be they clerks, chaplains or *conversi*, were after their year's noviciate, to prostrate themselves in the chapter-house of the nuns, to promise unquestioning obedience and to renounce private property.

That done, the candidate on bended knee, placed his hands on the Book of the 'Rule' laid on the knees of the seated abbess, and said: 'I promise you good obedience unto death'. The abbess was to reply, 'God give you eternal life', all the nuns assenting saying 'Amen'. He then kissed the book and departed.[588] When, in 1292, Brother Vioto of Chieri, was admitted as a *conversus* at Rifreddo (It), he promised 'stability, conversion and obedience, clasping his hands in the hands of the abbess'.[589]

In 1281 the General Chapter told the *conversi* that they must conform both in profession and habit,[590] and in 1296 reminded chaplains, familiars, clerics and *conversi* of nuns that they were not to wear the habit until they had served their novitiate and been professed, and taken the vows of obedience, chastity, continence and voluntary poverty, just as the monks did.[591]

What was the situation of these *conversi* vis-a-vis their counterparts in the male abbeys. In 1229 the General Chapter ruled that they were to be counted equal with those in the male monasteries. That year, following successful petitions from the nunneries of Trebznitz (Pl; 1218)[592] and Argensolles (F; 1224),[593] the Chapter stipulated that *conversi* visiting a male abbey, and if properly attired 'in hair style [tonsure], beard and habit', were to be admitted to the quire and refectory of its *conversi*.[594]

Trebznitz also made provision for visiting *conversi* and clerics coming to its monastery. If properly habited, they were to be admitted to church, chapter and refectory, they were to be fed and their other needs met, and 'a suitable place' was to be provided from them, separate from any lay guests.[595] Like privileges were granted to the *conversi* of Flines (F; 1250), at the request of the countess of Flanders.[596] The General Chapter (1281) further provided that any *conversi* who were sent from a nunnery to a male abbey on account of their faults, were to be admitted to its 'company of *conversi*', providing that they were properly habited.[597]

These would-be helpers came from varying backgrounds and walks of life. Barthélémy, a rich citizen of Tirlemont, assisted the erection of three nunneries in Belgium: Florival, Val-des-Vierges and Nazareth. His four daughters became Cistercian nuns, and a few years after the death of his wife he took the habit of a *conversus* in the monasteries he had assisted. He died at Nazareth about 1250, aged ninety-seven years. One of his sons, Wichert, imitated his example, and followed him in each of the three foundations.[598] In 1268 another father took the habit of a *conversus*, and thus joined his daughter among the nuns of Val-des-Vignes (F).[599] Blood brothers and cousins might enter, as two nephews of William de Octon at Wykeham (E),[600] and Gerard and Tylmann at Duissern (G; 1314).[601]

There were other instances of founders of nunneries, perhaps of lower social status, becoming *conversi* in the abbeys they had helped to established: this was true of Renier de Dive (1215) who gave a new site at Dive to the nuns of Parc-les-Dames (F), and of a vassal of Arnoul IV of Diest (1235) who founded Val-Saint-Bernard (St-Bernards Daal, B) on land granted by his lord.[602] One deed of Waterler, in 1311, referred to its 'lower class *conversi*'; another *conversus* there, whose name is known, was Conrad, in 1342.[603]

It seems that in 1320 Swine (E) was unwilling to receive two would-be *conversi*, Symon Chapeleyne and Geoffrey Palmer, but Archbishop Melton told the nuns there to receive them as 'your brothers and *conversi*'.[604] At Heiligkreuztal (G; 1349) one Heinrich Rapp came as a *conversus*; he was a servant at the Premonstratensian Marchtal abbey, but its provost and convent gave him leave 'to enter the religious habit at Heiligkreuztal, and there to serve God for the rest of his life'.[605]

Married couples might enter, like Peter Salvat and his wife Egilabelle (1239), who gave themselves 'body and soul' as *conversi* of Vernaison (F).[606] When *conversi* were professed, they might well bring into the nunnery's possession property they owned: this was true at Welver (G; 1255) when three of the nunnery's brothers: Christian, Theoderic and Godfried, gave over to the convent three areas of arable land and three of woodland: Bredenlo, Stemme and Horst.[607] Indeed, such grants of part at least of their patrimony was a frequent occurrence on the profession of German nuns' *conversi*.[608]

The male *conversi* were the mainstay of a nunnery's economy, managing its granges and, as it seems their numbers were never great in some houses, presumably they supervised the hired labour. The variety of their tasks is on record at Himmelspforten (G; 1262), where the brothers included a skinner, a baker, a shepherd, and a vine-dresser.[609] The brothers of Sonnefeld (G; 1302) included Frederick, its cobbler, and Bertold, its fisherman.[610] Brother Bruno, a *conversus* of Duissern (G; 1320–5) was keeper of its Lützerat grange.[611]

In 1306 a nun named Gertrude was cellarer of Helfta (G), but a Brother Tylo was its weaver.[612] How far did the *conversi* retain property and finances of their own? One, 'H. named Schmid', a brother of Oberschönenfeld (G; 1262), gave its nuns twelve pounds on condition that each autumn, and from the revenue of its property at Merierhof in Mesishoven, one pound was expended on behalf of its sick sisters.[613] Rinteln (G; 1336) granted one of its brothers, John of Hemerighe, property including half-a-mill, presumably as a reward for good service.[614] Such *conversi* who remained in the fourteenth century may well have had a far higher status than their fellows of a century before.

As has been noted, several brothers came to occupy the position of procurator of a nunnery. Yet others, with business acumen, might serve their monastery in different ways. They might be witnesses to charters, as Peter of Auriac and Bernard Rotguer at Nonenque (F; 1170).[615] In a business transaction of 1233, Brother William of Brione (It) was described as being 'a *conversus* and agent' of that nunnery.[616] Another brother of Brione, Boniface Valdamar, was described in 1273 as being 'a *conversus* and zealous'.[617]

Abbess Isabella of Note-Dame-des-Prés (1251) issued a charter to John, one of her *conversi*, authorising him to swear on her behalf to an agreement between the nunnery and the canons of St-Pierre regarding lands in the suburbs of Troyes.[618] Pope Honorius III (1222), the nuns of Trebnitz (Pl) now fully Cistercian, directed the abbot of Lubiąż to provide some of his conversi to assist in their well-being.[619] After the absorption of Rifreddo (It) into the Order, Innocent IV in 1249 requested its Visitor, the abbot of Staffarda, to send two of his *conversi*, 'discernng and wise', to the convent to carry out negotiations on the nuns' behalf'.[620]

Three *conversi* of Himmelspforten (G; 1291) were its agents in purchasing land from Graf Conrad von Hildberg.[621] Burcard, '*conversus*-monk' of Lichtenthal (G; 1305), handled a transaction for its nuns before the consuls of Spire.[622] Another, Cunrad of Argentina, did likewise with Ludeman of Lichtenberg (1345).[623] Alred von Eldingen, who entered the cloister at Isenhagen (G) in the early-thirteenth century, proved to be a skilful negotiator, but also showed great enthusiasm in religious matters, so much so that visions and wonders were attributed to him.[624]

Less happily, some of the *conversi* and familiars of Benninghausen nunnery (G; 1320) slew Regenhard von Zelynchusen, one of three brothers.[625] Robert of Weston, a *conversus* of Catesby (E), was noted in 1307 as having some ten years before thrown off his habit, and was now living with a woman in London.[626]

Chaplains and Confessors

The spiritual needs of the nuns, in particular the daily Mass, were provided by resident 'clerks' or 'chaplains', called 'canons' at Catesby (E), who were recruited mostly from the secular clergy and – after serving a year's novitiate in the nunnery – assumed a habit of cloak and scapular and made their profession before the abbess.[627] At first (1218) before the altar in the church,[628] later (by 1254) in the chapter-house, promising (like the *conversi*) 'good obedience until death'.[629]

The chaplain, who might be a religious or a secular priest, was to be chosen by the nuns,[630] but from 1288 their appointment became subject to the approval of the father-abbot.[631] Nunneries might present clerics on their staff who were in minor orders to the diocesan for ordination. Cotham (E) presented to the bishop of Lincoln 'A. our clerk' (1275) to be made subdeacon, and also for ordination Ralf of Barton (1279), 'acolyte and our clerk',[632] In 1296 the Chapter reminded chaplains, familiars, clerics and *conversi* of nuns that they were not to wear the habit until they had served their novitiate and been professed, and taken the vows of 'obedience, chastity, continence and voluntary poverty', just as the monks did.[633]

The abbot of Sylvanes on visitation at Nonenque (F; 1303) ruled that the chaplains of the nunnery might eat in the hospice, but were always to wear their scapular, whether within or without the nunnery, even when at a distance on a journey;[634] then in 1320 the General Chapter had again to be remind chaplains that they must wear the habit of the Order.[635] Accommodated within the precincts, but very separately from the nuns, chaplains were permitted to meet and talk with friends and others of the laity in a room set apart.[636]

The chaplains were bound to celebrate Mass in the Cistercian rite,[637] and were to be honourably received if visiting an abbey of the Order: worshipping in the church – perhaps in the retro-choir, and accommodated separately from seculars.[638] Not all chaplains appear to have been fully appreciative of the norms of the Order: the General Chapter (1258) instructed Visitors to 'correct and reprove' those chaplains who did not wish to celebrate Mass 'according to the manner and custom of the Order'.[639] In 1256 the Chapter ordained that chaplains of nuns of the Order, wishing to stay at houses of the Order and away from company, should be given privacy and be properly cared for.[640]

Small convents would perhaps have had no more than one or two chaplains, but in 1310 Clement V referred to there being two confessors and no less than twenty chaplains to serve the needs of the nuns at Las Huelgas (Sp) and, presumably, the associated Hospital de Rey next door.[641] Nonenque had at least three chaplains and four male *conversi* in 1301.[642] Gradefes (Sp) had perhaps four or five chaplains at any one time, occasionally they may also have served nearby parishes.[643]

The names of eight late-twelfth to mid-thirteenth century chaplains of Coldstream are on record,[644] as is that of Gerhard of Amelineburen, chaplain of Bersenbrück (1285).[645] Individual chaplains of note included a thirteenth-century cleric, 'poor Martin', who translated the Rule of St Benedict and the Usages of the Order into French.[646] Walter, Cotham's chaplain (E; 1234), acted for the nunnery at a concord made in the royal court at Lincoln regarding pasture rights.[647]

When Cook Hill (E) was stricken by poverty and perhaps mismanagement, the bishop of Worcester (1285) required that Thomas, the chaplain, was to have full charge of its temporal affairs.[648] A few perhaps did not live up to the standards required, and unfortunately for Reiner, chaplain of Kirklees (E; 1275), when adjudged guilty in a dispute regarding an heifer, he was described in court as 'a little idle man'.[649] One chaplain at Bouchet, Just de Visan, later became abbot of Aiguebelle (F; 1289–95).[650]

Nunneries needed to support their chaplains. Count Baldwin of Namur (1237) bequeathed an annual rent of ten pounds to Val-St-Georges (B) for that purpose.[651] A rent from land given to Duissern (G; 1275) paid for a chaplain there.[652] In 1327 a lay benefactor made provision for a chaplain to live within the precincts of Waterler (Wasserleben; G), and to have a place at the provost's table; or else to be provided for in his chamber.[653]

Additional chaplains might be employed as chantry priests, as when a knight, Girard of Chartres (1261), gave lands to L'Eau (F) for its nuns to maintain by its income a chaplain to celebrate Mass daily for the repose of his soul and those of his kinsfolk. The chaplain, who might be a religious or a secular priest, was to be chosen by the nuns.[654] Godfrey, lord of Dave (c. 1300), in founding a chantry altar at Val-St-Georges (Salzinnes, Namur), made provision for a chaplain to serve it.[655] A rent of twelve Paris pounds was gifted to Épinlieu (B; 1244) for the support of a chaplain, but it may have been for chantry purposes.[656] The two chaplains at St Agnes, Magdeburg (G; 1271) were also supported by chantry obligations.[657]

Stephen Lexington, when abbot of Savigny (1230) assumed three resident monks in the nunneries of his congregation: one was to act as chaplain, another as vice-cellarer, whilst the third was to look after the gate-house, granary and bake-house. At meals one of them was to read from a book at the beginning and end of each repast. Monks staying in a nunnery did so in their own house, but had to rise when the bell for vigils sounded from the nuns' church, and then recite the hours in their oratory.[658] In those nunneries within the Savigniac family all clerks and *conversi* employed on a convent's business were to keep and render faithful accounts to the prioress and her council.[659]

The chaplains did not at first hear the nuns' confessions; this was done either by the father-abbot or experienced monks delegated by him.[660] The Order, taking strict enclosure into account, stipulated that confessions were to be heard through 'a window suitably prepared',[661] save in the cases of the gravely ill and except to the Visitor – to whom it was possible to speak more openly in the chapter-house.[662] The General Chapter in 1233 provided that the Visitor of an abbey, usually the father-abbot, should choose 'suitable and prudent men' as nuns' confessors.[663]

The *Chronicle of Villers* envisaged that those senior monks sent out to hear confessions would be ones zealous for the Order, 'shining in word and by example'.[664] Abbot Walter, however, found this a heavy burden for his house, as their absence deprived the younger monks of a sage and stabilising influence.[665]

Villers provided confessors for fourteen convents, half of them in the province of Brabant, four of which had been founded under its aegis.[666] The monks of St-Bernard-sur-l'Escaut served eight convents as their confessors.[667] Clement IV (1267), noting that the 'enclosed nuns' of Flines had no resident confessor, ordered the abbot of Loos to appoint one.[668] The pontiff further provided, in 1268, that for the right to have a resident confessor, a community should have at least twenty-five nuns.[669]

The General Chapter in 1237, reiterated that nuns of incorporated houses might only have their confessions heard by the father-abbot or one appointed by him.[670] Such a person should be the Chapter (1263) later insisted a member of the Order, but then two years later permitted father-abbots to appoint chaplains of a nunnery to hear confessions, providing they were of 'praiseworthy and virtuous life'.[671]

In 1320 the General Chapter allowed nunneries having twenty members or more to retain a confessor, but one to be appointed by their father-abbot or Visitor. As well as hearing confessions, he would also say Masses as did the other chaplains. The convent was to provide their permanent confessor with food and clothing, but some nunneries were slow to do this, and in 1332 had to be reminded of their duty.[672]

Aulne provided confessors and provosts for the nuns of Herkenrode (B);[673] Hardehausen for the convent at Wormeln (G);[674] Salem for the nuns of Wald (G);[675] Salzedas for Arouca (Pt).[676] The monks of Kołbacz (Pl; 1283), going to hear the confessions of the nuns of Szczecin (Pl), journeyed 'by water or on horseback, by boat or riding', and the sisters were reminded to pay their expenses'.[677]

In 1276 Archbishop Giffard of York wrote to the Cistercian nunneries in his diocese that the Friars Minor were to hear their confessions, as had been the custom, in spite of the inhibition of the abbots of the Order who possessed no jurisdiction, ordinary or delegated, over the nuns.[678] He may have been referring to the decision of General Chapter the previous year that nuns of the Order were to have nothing to do with the Franciscans, some of whose members who had captured in Toledo and badly beaten up the abbot of Matallana. It was a time there of hostility between the two Orders.[679]

Matters seemingly improved, as a statute of 1285 presumed that sometimes convents would have Franciscan guests – they might be fed for one day only, but they were not to be offered meat, unless weak or infirm.[680] In 1314 the then archbishop appointed a Franciscan, William de Calverleye, as confessor at Hampole (E).[681] In 1318 at Sinningthwaite (E) archbishop Greenfield forbade the friars to enter the cloister proper, but to hear confessions in the church.[682] The General Chapter enjoined in 1334 that when Franciscans celebrated Mass and preached the Word of God they could be cared

The Communities

for, but only in the guest hospice; they were not to talk to nuns in the cloister or chambers or other private places.[683]

In the later thirteenth century, Helfta (G) employed local Dominican friars to hear its nuns' confessions.[684] In 1309 the archbishop of York appointed the vicar of Huddersfield as confessor for the nuns of Kirklees (E).[685] The abbot of Loroux (1321), coming to General Chapter, reported that the nuns of Bonlieu (Maine, F) had rejected his authority, and refused to receive the appointed confessor.[686]

Extant records reveal something of the finances of confessors. The monk-confessor and the chaplain at Zwyveke (B; 1303) both received fifteen shillings under the will of Michael van der Strate.[687] The brick dorter at Bijloke (B) was built with money bequeathed by the nuns' confessor in 1316.[688] The obit book of Wintney (E) records the death on 'the Ides 'of January' in an unnamed year of 'Geoffrey Gabriel, our confessor'.[689]

SPIRITUAL FRATERNITY

Close and helpful relations with male and female houses of the Cistercian and other orders, as well as with benefactors, might be well be achieved by entering into spiritual fraternity with them: a mutual sharing in the Eucharist, offices and prayers, of both communities. Some examples are noted elsewhere in this chapter. At Baindt (G), each June 22nd were commemorated all those deceased 'who have held fraternity with us';[690] the necrology of the nuns of St Servaas, Utrecht, gives two lists of those in fraternity: the second being of donors to the cost of windows in the refectory.[691]

The necrology of Seligenthal (Bavaria) appends the names of twenty clerics and over fifty laity in fraternity, as well as the Cistercian monks of Kaisheim; surprisingly there is no mention of those of Raitenhaslach, with which it had close associations.[692] The nuns of Günterstal (G) were in fraternity with the Cistercian monks of Tennenbach, as arranged by its abbot, Burchard Iselin (*ob.?* 1452), and those of Welver (G; 1269) with the monks of Camp.[693]

The nuns of Lilienthal (G) entered into fraternity with the male abbey of Cistercian Loccum in 1284; whilst those of Waterler in 1311 entered into fraternity with the Congregation of St Catherine the Virgin, Wolmirstedt, and in 1312 with the Confraternity of Priests in

Brunswick.⁶⁹⁴ The nuns of Marche-les-Dames (B) enjoyed fraternity with the Crucifers (the Crutched Friars) and canons of the Holy Cross at nearby Huy, listing in total 114 of them.⁶⁹⁵ The nuns of Ichtershausen (G; by 1291) enjoyed fraternity with the religious of St Peter's abbey in Erfurt.⁶⁹⁶ Later, in 1446, the nuns of Wintney (E) admitted Bishop William of Winchester into fraternity.⁶⁹⁷

OTHER RESIDENTS, AND GUESTS

Enclosure meant not only keeping nuns in, but also keeping out any unwanted persons, who might be a distraction for the contemplative life. Many nunneries came to have guest hospices, and found the need to board servants and familiars, to receive pilgrims, relatives and overnight travellers, and to educate young boys and girls presumably for a fee. The consequence was that the General Chapter and Visitors from time to time issued injunctions to control the reception of guests.

The potential dangers were recognised by Bishop Hugh of Lincoln (1209–35) who said that 'because the frequenting of the house by seculars upsets the quiet of the religious house', only overnight stays by travellers were to be permitted at Nun Cotham (E).⁶⁹⁸ Likewise, Alexander IV (1257) forbade noblewomen to stay for more than a brief period at Roskilde nunnery (D), as this was contrary to the rules of the Order, involved the nuns in additional expenses, and was detrimental to their spiritual life.⁶⁹⁹ On visitation at Nun Appleton (E; 1346), Archbishop Zouch of York noted 'the guests who flocked there, were to be admitted to the hostelry constructed especially for that purpose'.⁷⁰⁰ The poor were not forgotten: several donors in the early and mid-thirteenth century made grants of property to Aywières (B) so that the income arising could help sustain the relief of the poor 'at the gate'.⁷⁰¹

Foundresses of consequence might reside, seasonally or permanently, within the precincts of a convent. In 1242 Margaret of Constantinople, its foundress, stipulated that the house she had built within their precincts of Flines (F) was to pass to the nuns the day after her death.⁷⁰² Countess Jean of Flanders built a house for herself within the precincts of Marquette (F), which she and her husband had founded; there she died in 1244, clothed in the habit of a novice, and in the presence of her second husband, Thomas

The Communities

of Savoy, and the entire community. She was buried in the nuns' cemetery, and by her wish the house passed to the nuns.[703]

Another resident at Marquette in 1268 was Sybil, lady of Cysoing who, noting that she had built dwellings and houses within the precincts there, gave them to the abbey excepting the house she dwelt in, and that after her death she left it for the use of her daughters if they were still unmarried, but if they were both married that house too was to pass to the abbey.[704]

Within the enclosure at Groeninge (B; fd. 1285, the nuns having moved from Marke), Princess Beatrice of Courtrai, its foundress, had her own residence and chapel. The nuns of Groeninge were soon in dispute with the chapter of Courtrai, regarding the offerings from her chapel. The countess had constructed for her own use a house with this chapel built within the nunnery's precincts. She intended to stay there with her family for part of each year. A compromise was reached: all oblations made in the chapel were to belong to the nuns, save on Christmas Day, Easter Day and Whitsunday, when they were to pertain to the chapter of Courtrai. The agreement was made in the presence of the countess.[705] Dying in 1288 her body was interred like that of her husband at Marquette nunnery, but her heart at Groeninge.[706]

Cotham (E; 1246) granted to Agnes, a local lady, and her two daughters, Cecily and Letty, food and clothing, so long as they served the convent; the probability is that they were resident servants.[707] A benefactor of Duissern (G; 1249) having died, his widow was permitted, on payment and with the consent of the father-abbot of Camp, to sleep in the nuns' dorter and to eat in a chamber appointed, it having a window by means of which she could converse.[708]

In 1281 the General Chapter agreed that two sisters who lived in the abbey of 'St Hilary near Hyllerdam' might do so sharing in its goods, this was the custom as their forebears were benefactors of the monastery.[709] On account of the goodwill they had showed its nuns, Fraubrunnen (Swz) in 1310 promised to Nicholas called 'Klueli' and Berchta his wife, a 'prebend' in our monastery, and the assurance of being clothed in Cistercian habit at the approach of death, if not before. Essentially, they became resident 'familiars'.[710]

When a local priest, Martin Dominic, was received at Carrizo (Sp; 1230) as a 'familiar', he gave all his possessions to the nunnery. He had, in 1224, already been a witness to a deed issued by the convent.⁷¹¹ At Zarrentin (G), in 1320, lived a couple who served the convent, and had 'a house or good chamber' within the precincts. The husband, Heinrich, appears to have been a familiar and was clothed with 'a well-fastened grey tunic'. After, Grete, his wife died, he was to 'render obedience to the abbess' and be tonsured – presumably becoming one of the male *conversi*.⁷¹²

Taken in at Duissern (G; 1338), with the abbot of Camp's blessing, was one Gernand, to be a 'confrater and familiar'. In return for a payment of forty marks, he received a prebend in bread and beer and everything else that was necessary. That same year a prebend in like terms was also accorded to one 'Henry, called Hirnen'.⁷¹³ Bishop Siegfried of Hildesheim (1280–1310) forbade married people from living within the precincts at Wöltingrode (G).⁷¹⁴

EDUCATION

There is plenty of evidence of schools being conducted by Cistercian nuns, with resident boarders, teaching a variety of subjects such as grammar and logic, arithmetic and music, geometry and astronomy.⁷¹⁵ This was evidenced when Michael van der Strate (1303) left two shillings to each scholar in the school at Zwyveke nunnery (B) on the day of his death,⁷¹⁶ and by the mention at Rinteln (G, 1315) of the 'rector of the scholars', and of the 'master of the scholars' (1345).⁷¹⁷ In 1298 Cunegund, daughter of the count of Rietburg was a pupil of the nuns of Bennighausen (G).⁷¹⁸

In the late-thirteenth century a school was established at Las Huelgas (Sp) for forty girls of noble birth, with a view to attracting vocations, but the bishop of Cammin (1306), on account of difficulties experienced, forbade the nuns of Wolin (Pl) to receive secular girls unless adequate funding came with them.⁷¹⁹ In the 1260s two under-age girls were sent by their father, a Parisian goldsmith, to Port Royal for their upbringing; there will have been others.⁷²⁰

Martin Gonzalez, later to be ordained and 'master of the works' at Carrizo (Sp) in 1230, gained his early education at the convent before proceeding to the cathedral school in León.⁷²¹ It has been pointed out that the Cistercian nuns of Riga, Latvia, had as a specific feature the education of ten to thirteen-years old girls from the Livonian nobility, some whom were later professed there as nuns. (Later, in 1468, having acquired relatively cheaply a valuable manor, its nuns took in the grantor's daughter, promising her education, maintenance, and her own room).[722] At least one deed pertaining to Arouca nunnery (Pt; 1329) implies that girls were educated there under a secular tutor, Rui Gonçalves.[723]

A chapel was founded in 1287 at a site near the village of Techow, where a stolen consecrated host had been retrieved. In 1317, Otto V, margrave of Brandenburg, founded there the nunnery of Heiligengrabe (G) which ran a school and became a pilgrimage centre.[724] John XXII (1316–34) permitted the nuns of Coyroux (F) to receive a number of young lady pupils; they included Alpassia de Molseone in 1328 and Géraud du Fay from Limoges in 1329. A little later, the knight Hugh Gautier obtained the concession for his daughter, Bertrade, and Peter Gros for his daughter, Guillelme.[725] A school was also attached to the cloister at Frankenhausen (G).[726]

The rules of enclosure also forbade boys being educated, it was seen as a 'grave scandal';[727] though there were breaches of this rule in England at Esholt (1318) and Heynings (1347).[728] In 1313 Archbishop Melton of York visiting Hampole ordered that no boys over the age of five were to be permitted in the house, as he found had been the practice.

Archbishop Greenfield visiting Sinningthwaite in 1315 seems to have accepted the presence of boys and girls, but forbade them to eat flesh meat in Advent or Sexagesima, or during Lent eggs or cheese, in the refectory. At those seasons when they ought to eat such things they should be assigned other places in which to eat them. At Rosedale nunnery that year, he stipulated that no boy nor girl was to sleep in the dorter. Four years later (1319) at Sinningthwaite Archbishop Melton ruled that girls over twelve were not to be retained unless special permission was granted.[729]

The nuns of Medingen (G; 1344) admitted two seemingly teenage boys, Siegfried and Nicholas, the sons of Nicholas Hoyken, 'our spiritual friend'. They were accorded food at the provost's table, as given to the chaplains, and quarters where they were to remain to be diligently governed and educated. Each year they were each to receive two tunics, one grey and one coloured. If they misbehaved, the provost was to 'correct' them.[730]

There is only occasional mention of young people being wards of a nunnery, like John Attelkirke (1299) who had been a ward of the nuns of Cotham (E), but then refused to marry as the nuns wished.[731] Alfonso VIII (1185) gave to the nuns of Gradefes (Sp) an *infantaticum* he had in Villacreces; was this an orphanage?[732] An agreement made (by 1205) by Robert of Croxton with the nuns of Cotham (E) saw the convent in return for a gift of property taking in his two elder daughters until they were old enough to be professed, and later a third daughter. He promised to provide sufficient clothing for the girls before and after profession. It is not certain that this agreement was fully consummated.[733]

TRAVELLERS

Passing travellers, especially members of religious Orders, might expect hospitality. Travelling monks and *conversi* from the male abbeys of Herrevad (Sweden), Tvis and Øm (Denmark), breaking their journey stayed one night in 1241 at the nunnery of Vrouwemunster (Roermond, Holland). They were later severely censured by the General Chapter, since after supper they went to a tavern in Roermond and spent part of the night there.[734]

The General Chapter (1294) reminded those concerned that all abbots and personnel of the Order, if staying in a nunnery hospice, were not to eat at the same table as the sisters.[735] That the reception of such guests became a problem for some convents was emphasised when the General Chapter (1296) realised that some members of the Order were placing a burden on poorer nunneries by calling in for meals. It prohibited this practice, unless the monks concerned had leave of the father-abbot.[736] At Vallbona (Sp), two nuns in 1264 were named as 'hospitaler' or 'hosteler': Anglesis de Bellvis and Raymundede Tion.[737]

Archbishop Greenfield of York (1315), on visitation at Sinningthwaite (E), directed that mendicant friars were not to enter the cloister but be received outside it, perhaps in the hall of the guesthouse or some other place appointed.[738] Other travellers visiting a Cistercian nunnery included: Brother Andrew de Claringyano, procurator of the Order of the Hospital of Jerusalem. At Rinteln (G; 1312), whilst on 'the business of a Crusade', he took the opportunity to enlist its nuns into spiritual fraternity with his Order.[739] St Elizabeth of Hungary especially looked towards the nunnery church of St Catharine, Eisenach (G): it was there that after their birth each of her children was offered to God before the altar.[740]

The Communities

Whilst visiting the nuns of Bouchet (F) in 1230, Blessed Bertrand de Garrigue, a Dominican and one of the first companions of St Dominic, was taken ill and died there. In 1253 his body was exhumed from the nuns' cemetery, and reinterred in the church. For pilgrims visiting his tomb, a door was opened on to the public way, but in 1306, concerned that the number of pilgrims was to the detriment of the nuns' solitude, the father abbot of Aiguebelle ordered that the door be walled up, but this was not done immediately.[741]

Caesar of Heisterbach maintained close links with the Rhineland nunnery at Hoven, while a Premonstratensian monk of Steinfeld, St Herman Joseph, made several stays there, acted as spiritual director to one of its nuns, a mystic named Elizabeth, and may have been their chaplain; he died there and was buried there in 1241, but later the canons of Steinfeld reclaimed his remains.[742]

OTHER VISITORS

Nunneries might well be the host of important meetings or other occasions, as at Las Huelgas (Sp), although the bull in its favour of Clement III (1188) stated that 'no seculars could treat of worldly matters there'.[743] Three Spanish sovereigns [Alfonso X, Alfonso XI, and John II] were crowned there, and its church also saw in 1269 the marriage of Fernando de la Cerda with Blanche, daughter of St Louis.[744] In 1198 the election of Philip de Souabe as King of Germany was entered upon at Ichtershausen (G), where also in 1204 Philip received the homage of Landgrave Herman I of Thuringia.[745]

Guests might be generous donors: visiting Baindt (G) in 1241 King Conrad IV granted the nunnery many privileges and took it under his protection.[746] Bruce, King of the Scots, is said to have stayed at Douglas nunnery whilst on an expedition to the Isle of Man in 1313.[747] There are numerous charters issued by Cistercian nunneries which contain the laity amongst their witnesses, whilst the archbishop of Cologne took the trouble to point out in 1221 that at the consecration of the cemetery at the new cloister of Saarn nunnery (G), 'he had made it possible for certain men and women to be present at the gifting of the Buchel woods to the cloister'.[748]

Episcopal and other visitations reveal something of the difficulties which might ensue from the presence of the laity in any number. Archbishop Wickwane of York (1281) ordered that at Nun

Appleton (E) the refectory and cloister were to be better guarded from strangers than was wont, lest the good fame of the nuns should vanish hereafter more than it had already done.

Archbishop Zouch (1346) found that at Nun Appleton the doors of the church, cloister and parlour, had for long time past been negligently guarded. This was to be corrected, and no secular woman was to spend the night in the dorter. He also said that the guests who flocked to the house were to be admitted to the hostelry constructed for that purpose.[749] At Nun Cotham (E) the early-thirteenth century episcopal injunctions forbade a nun to talk alone with a stranger; visits to friends were only to be allowed under special licence and in case of real necessity.[750]

On visitation at Sinningthwaite (E), Archbishop Greenfield (1315) had to forbid William Tymberland, or any other man, from sleeping in the wool-house under the nuns' dorter. Archbishop Melton (1319) forbade frequent comings and goings in the cloister there, as by servants bringing their food through the cloister; food was to be delivered in outside places appointed for the purpose.[751]

In 1315 Archbishop Greenfield drew attention to the fact that three of the nuns of Kirklees were consorting too much with laymen within the nunnery, 'from which there is suspicion of sin and great scandal arises'. This, he directed, was to cease. He also ordered that Joan of Wakefield was to live in common with her fellow nuns there, and not to inhabit a separate chamber.[752] That same year, he instructed Esholt to remove within six days all the secular women boarders over the age of twelve years.[753]

Bishop Gynwell of Lincoln in 1347 visiting Heynings (E) drew attention to matters needing reformation: 'the divine office was not carefully attended nor was silence well kept; friends visited, children and seculars were admitted to the cloister and dormitory'. Poverty made the nuns of Heynings take in lady boarders as well as girls for education.[754] Bishop Thoresby of Worcester ordered the removal of certain ladies from Pinley (E) in 1350, through whose presence its nuns were being defamed.[755]

Even at the prestigious abbey of Trebznitz [Pl; 1252], one abbess was sentenced to spend forty days in choir outside her own abbess's stall, because she had brought noble ladies and other friends into the convent to eat meat and spend the night. An abbess of 'Coeli Vallis' (1252), its location uncertain, was deposed after she had hid a fugitive Friar Minor in her nunnery for eight months. Certain

The Communities

layfolk had put him in fetters, but once released from his chains his affairs with the nuns were an occasion of scandal.[756]

PILGRIMS

Pilgrims might be attracted to a nunnery church possessing relics. This was especially true of Flines (F) to which its founder, Margaret of Constantinople accorded a piece of the True Cross, a thorn from the Crown of Thorns, and teeth of SS Peter and Paul. Flines also possessed eighty-four heads from the remains of the 11,000 virgins martyred at Cologne. By the mid-fourteenth century it was an important place of pilgrimage.[757]

Herkenrode (B) also possessed several relics of the Eleven Thousand Virgins.[758] In 1190 the archbishop of Mainz ruled that the relics on the altar of St George at Ichtershausen (G) were never to be moved elsewhere, but in 1197 the bishop of Hevelberg, acting for the archbishop, consecrated a chapel in Kerspleben at the request of the provost of Ichtershausen. Its altar contained the relics of more than thirty-five saints.[759] Prominent amongst its relics were those of St Godehard of Hildesheim (*d.* 1038).[760]

5

The Economy

THE WORK FORCE

Despite the nuns themselves being unable by reason of enclosure to participate fully in the economy of their houses,[1] that mostly depending on a male labour force, their agricultural concerns and other sources of income were much the same as those of the male monasteries, albeit usually on a smaller scale. Their work-force were the male *conversi* and hired labour, the former often acting in a supervisory role under the guidance of the procurator. The nuns themselves did not mostly have the one-to-one contact with their helpers an employees, but they were involved behind closed walls on matters of economic importance to their convents.

Much land was leased out and worked by tenants but, as a papal bull of 1226 in favour of Aywières (B; 1226) stipulated, no sale or demising of lands or benefices should take place without the concurrence of a majority of the chapter of a convent.[2] A rent roll of about 1340 pertaining to Catesby (E) lists some one hundred and fifty tenants on its lands, many holding one virgate – equivalent perhaps to around thirty acres.[3]

Lands worked directly under the supervision of the *conversi* would have found a labour force in the serfdom of the period, though Flines (F; 1252) was noted as granting freedom to a dozen or so serfs and their offspring.[4] At its foundation (around 1160) the whole vill of Coton was given to Cotham (E) with the men belonging to it.[5] The nunnery received several later such grants of men 'with all their offspring and chattels', like William of Limber,[6] Ernald of Killingholme,[7] Bartholomew of Silvedune (*c.* 1230),[8] and Turgis of Keelby,[9] as well as others in the early thirteenth century.

The 'colonists' of Bersenbrück (1273) in at least two localities were 'in servitude'.[10] In his great charter in favour of Las Huelgas

(Sp; 1187), Alfonso VIII insisted that whatever field labour the inhabitants of Bienvivre and Pampliga had done for the king, they were now to perform for the nuns.[11] The nuns of Parc-aux-Dames (F) were fortunate in that a benefactor arranged in 1239 for them to receive, yearly presumably, ten thousand herring and three containers of butter from the Cistercian monks of Cercamp.[12]

CHARTERS, AND BENEFACTIONS

The nuns had the same need for charters as their male counterparts. More than one charter granted to Neuwerk (Goslar, G) emphasised the need for a written and witnessed record 'so that things do not slip away in time', and because of the hostility of 'malicious men'.[13] By 1355 it had amassed 235 individual properties and sixteen sets of tithes.[14] A charter granted to Lichtenthal (Bremen, G; 1340) was 'committed to writing because the memory of men easily changes with the passage of time'.[15]

The cartulary of Rifreddo (It) records some forty deeds relating to grants of land and other transactions in the first ten years (1220–30) of the nunnery's life, but it also tells of problems with its near neighbours, the canons of Revello.[16] The nuns of Cour-Notre-Dame (F) were also assiduous in recording over 280 grants made to them into their cartulary.[17] The thirty evidences recorded in 1337 in a dispute between the nuns of Heiligkreuztal (G) and one Ulrich Oswald, were contained in 'divers pieces of parchment, whether great or small, contained in one roll'.[18]

Thirteenth-century charters were mostly written in Latin, but in the fourteenth a change might take place. The charters of Frankenhausen (G) switch to the vernacular from 1349; those of Sonnefeld (G) are mostly in German from 1330.[19] The National Archives of Portugal contain no less than 1125 charters and deeds relating to Arouca nunnery (Pt).[20]

The convent of Val-Saint-Georges (B) had its deeds of benefactions from the dukes of Brabant and the counts of Flanders and Namur, and confirmatory charters from the bishops of Cambrai and Liège, as well as bulls of protection (including tithe exemption rights) from three popes.[21] Confirmatory charters could be very important in upholding a nunnery's rights following the death of a major patron or other benefactor: as when Bishop Peter of Camin in 1297 confirmed all the grants made to Wolin (Pl) by its 'pious founder', Bogislaw, and previously confirmed by his predecessor, Bishop Herman.[22] Honorius III, in 1225, had to request the archbishop of Tarragona, to protect the nuns of Casbas (Sp) from their 'malefactors'.[23]

Those monetary grants and annuities revealed in the necrology of Port-Royal (F), perhaps only a fraction of what it received ultimately, amounted in total to over 900 Paris pounds, over 900 Tournai pounds, and a further unspecified 140 pounds, including gifts from French queens. Its thirteenth abbess, Agnès de Trier (*ob. c.* 1348) raised a thousand pounds for the restoration of the monastery, cloister, and houses.[24]

The several benefactors of Maubuisson (F) gave to the convent by direct gift, or in rents, or in bequests, a known total of around 4,000 pounds; again perhaps a fraction of its actual receipts.[25] Frauenthal [Harvestehude, G] had grants yearly, not entirely free, of some thirty measures of rye, six of wheat, as well as eight quarters of butter.[26]

Innocent IV (1243) took Maubuisson (F) under his protection and exempted it from the payment of new tithes, as also Flines (F; 1243), whilst Alexander III (1162) exempted Nonenque (F) from the payment of 'any tithes or first fruits'.[27] This was in accord with common Cistercian privileges. Louis IX of France freed Maubuisson from all secular taxes and levies, and Philip VI (1328) from providing provisions for the army.[28]

The labourers of the nuns of Roskilde (D; 1268) were also exempted from military service and other payments.[29] The Cistercian nuns of England were not always exempt from royal taxation: when a fifteenth was demanded by Edward I (1299), the nuns of Cotham were bidden to enter into negotiations as to how much they should pay.[30]

The assent of spouse and children to a grant was also important to avoid future claims by family members on a property. Otto, knight of Medinge (G; 1237/41), making a grant to the newly-founded nunnery there, did so 'with the consent of my wife and my sons and my brothers and others of my legitimate heirs'.[31] When Henry von Barmestede (1234) gave his foundation charter to Uetersen (G), it was with the approval of his wife Adelheid, and his sons, Henry and Godescale.[32] A grant to Beuditz (G; 1267) was with the assent of the donor's seven sons and two daughters![33]

Ave, the widow of Hélin de Pitei, granting land at Vieux-Walève to Clairefontaine (B; 1284), did so with the consent of her children.[34] When his daughter, Ermentrud, became a nun of Bersenbrück (G; 1297), her father, with the agreement of his wife and his son, gave a property at Andervanne 'into the hands of the provost for the use of the monastery'.[35] When Theodoric of Belgart in 1284 gave the nearby vill of Rogzon to the nuns of Koszalin (P), it was 'with the consent of his son, John'.[36]

The feelings an heir might have were clear when Count Guy of Flanders (1282) arbitrated when the heir of Robert, a clerk of Douai, wished to reclaim property given to Flines (F) by his father.[37] Alas! The nuns of Ołobok (Pl; 1292) forged a document purporting to give them the ownership of certain lands in order to avoid any claims by heirs.[38] The Benedictine nuns of Shaftesbury (E; c. 1278) complained when Queen Eleanor of England removed land at Gussage (Dorset) from their ownership and gave it to the Cistercian nuns at Tarrant.[39]

To avoid any doubt, the bounds of the lands of Barria in Navarre were officially established in 1237.[40] In the demise to Caldern (G; 1290) by the Teutonic Knights of Marburg of property at Brüngershausen, the possibility of the nuns being unable to maintain their rent payment because of 'hostility, sterility, and tempest' was alluded to.[41]

Charters can assist in compiling lists of the superiors of a convent over the years. Thus we learn in 1265 of the death of Elizabeth, the fourth abbess of Wienhausen (G), and also that in 1267 Sonnencamp (Neukloster, G) was led by a prioress, not an abbess. The papal bull of Clement IV noting this, also told of a Cistercian nunnery as being a place for 'laity fleeing from the world', but also reminded them of their need for strict enclosure.[42] The cartulary of Maubuisson (F) lists the dates of death and the names of the abbesses leading the house between 1275 and 1482.[43]

BENEFACTORS AND THEIR MOTIVES

The motives of benefactors in granting lands and privileges were much the same as those expressed by founders. Common-place and foremost was the hope of an eternal reward. Phraseology such as: 'for the remedy of my soul', or 'for the remission of my

The Economy

sins', and/or in the expectation of burial there, occurred in all the ten major grants of property made to Gradefes (Sp; between 1183 and 1215.[44]

One of those grants was made, the donor stated, 'for the love of God, and for the remedy of my soul and for my wife and all my forebears'.[45] Another benefactor of that monastery gave it all her property, save one portion reserved for her son, wishing to be buried there at her death.[46] Archbishop Conrad of Cologne (1258) granted pilgrims to the new abbey church at Grafenthal (G) an indulgence, mindful of the fact that he himself 'would stand before the judgement seat'.[47]

Like wording was used by Bishop Dietricht of Naumburg (1264) in a grant favouring Grimma (Marienthron, G),[48] and by Archbishop John of Rïga (1299) in issuing an indulgence in favour of Medingen (G).[49] Two brothers of Brakel making a grant to Wormeln (G; 1299) did so 'for the salvation of their souls',[50] whilst a beguine, Kunigunde of Mengeringhausen (1309), made a grant to its nuns 'on account of the Blessed Virgin Mary our patron, and of the salvation of her parents'.[51] A donor to Sonnefeld (G) made her grant in 1305 'at the point of death'.[52]

Rudolf, count of the New Castle and lord of Nidowa, granted Fraubrunnen (1327; Swz) freedom from taxes and other charges in return for 'prayers in life and death'.[53] The notary of Rifreddo (It; 1257), Manuel, gave that nunnery a vineyard 'for the remedy of his soul', and because he had chosen to be buried there.[54] Two lords of Putliz made a grant to Marienfliess (G; 1295) also 'for the remedy of their souls'.[55] Waterler (G; 1300) received a grant from a donor who made it 'in the hope of an eternal return'.[56]

Bartholomew, a novice of Holy Cross abbey in Coimbra (Pt), granted to Celas nunnery a property 'in the valley of Paíncą, on condition that the abbess gave annually to his nephew, Andrew Anes, a measure of wheat and two 'puzais' of wine.[57] Otto, a knight of Rambin, made in 1271 an annual grant to the nuns of Szczecin (Pl), with the consent of his sons, of six measures of wheat in return for a daily Mass 'when there is opportunity' at its altar of St Martin the Confessor for his soul and those of his departed family.[58] After his father, Barnim I, died in 1278, his son, Bogislaw IV, now duke of Pomerania, made a full confirmatory charter to the nuns of Szczecin (1278) as well as making further grants in memory of his father. The nunnery came to own two churches and other grants of tithe, several mills, seven villages and one hundred *mansos* in Szczecin itself.[59]

Many other such grants were made in the expectation of spiritual services provided. A benefactor of Frauensee (G; 1305) expected the yearly recitation of the psalter by the community for his spiritual welfare.[60] Michael van der Strate (1303) bequeathed one hundred shillings of rent to Zwyveke (B) for Masses there for his intention, twenty shillings for candles burning during these Masses, and fifty-seven shillings sixpence for the celebration of his anniversary.[61] Ponce of Costa Pelata (1233/38], proposing to go on pilgrimage to Compostella, and in return for spiritual fraternity granted him by the nuns of Brione (It), gave the convent property at Costa; should he die on the journey the nuns were to pay his wife 11 *sestaria* annually, and she to hold the lands for life.[62]

Swine (E), in return for a grant of marshland and the advowson of a church, promised to maintain a chaplain and clerk, vestments and all necessaries for a service in the chapel of St George at Ganstead for his soul and the souls of his family members.[63] Queen Katarina of Sweden, the wife of King Erik Erikson, was buried at Gudhem (Sw, 1250), and bequeathed it extensive estates in Denmark which she had inherited. Her aunt was prioress there at the time.[64]

Bequests in wills were obviouly advantageous, as when in around 1289 a burgher of Lübeck left 20 marks to the Cistercian nuns of that city, though only five marks each to other German convents of the Order: Itzehoe, 'Rane', 'Rene', Reinbek, Rostock, and Zarrentin.[65] Unhappily for the nuns of Rifreddo (It; 1258), the receipt of fifty pounds bequeathed them under the will of Leone, marchioness of Ceve, was long delayed.[66]

The exclusivity of the membership of Cistercian nunneries was reinforced by the practice of women bringing gifts upon their entry as novices, or such gifts being made by their parents or other relations. This was common practice in the Scandinavian nunneries. Several of that convent's donors mention in their charters that their daughters were amongst the nuns of Gudhem.[67] When Catherine Mattsdotter entered the novitiate at Gudhem (Sw) in 1292 she brought with her three large farms. When Margarethe Pik some years later became a nun at Gudhem her father gave the nunnery land he owned in Halland.[68]

Innocent IV (1246) in a bull directed to Zwyveke (B) authorised that convent to retain properties given on the profession of nuns,

The Economy

should those sisters return to the world;[69] Urban IV (1262) used like terminology in a bull in favour of Maubuisson (F).[70] When Cecilia, a nun of Welver (G; 1347), left that nunnery she renounced any claim to the money given when she entered.[71]

Bogislaw IV (1299) granted Wolin (Pl) the village of Curnow in recognisance of the fact that his daughter, Jutta, had become a nun there. He had founded the convent in 1288, and the deed was dated at Wolin itself.[72] He seems that summer to have stayed at Wolin for several days during which he made further grants to the convent.[73] In 1302, he further gave Wolin 'the land of Bucow with its fisheries and pastures and woods'.[74] Later Jutta was to become abbess of Krummin on the island of Usedom. Krummin (G; 1323) also benefited from grants made by Prince Warcislaw IV of Greifswald, Jutta's brother.[75]

Count Henry of Osterfeld in 1293 gave an annual rent of a talent and twelve shillings to Beuditz nunnery (G), on the profession there of his daughters, Gertrude and Elizabeth.[76] On the entry of his daughter, Gertrude, into the nunnery at Trzebnitz (Pl), Duke Henry of Silesia (1224) granted further properties to the convent and confirmed those made by others. He also made gifts of malt (*melte*) for 'the drink of the ladies', and of wax to illuminate the church and to have a light day and night before the altar of St Bartholomew.[77]

Börstel (G; 1319) received a substantial property from Everhard of Recklinghausen with the wish expressed not only for obit Masses, but also that on his anniversary a pittance be provided for the nuns, and a payment of one penny made to the provost, the chaplain, the precentrix and the 'keeper'; a recital of this grant in 1343 states rather larger payments.[78]

The well-being of Spermalie (B), Cistercian from 1228, was assured when a rich heiress, Jean de Merris, entered as a nun.[79] Later, when Adeline uten Thune (abbess by 1315) entered Spermalie, her family gave a rent to the convent.[80] Benefactions were received at Lilienthal from a number of local men whose daughters or other relatives were received there.[81] At Coyroux (F), its Ramière Grange developed from property brought with them when four relatives entered its community after the deaths of their respective fathers.[82]

Family consent was always important. With the entry of Kunigunde, daughter of Balberts of Mulhausen, to Beuren (G; 1260), as a nun a holding she possessed passed to the convent, with the consent of her four brothers.[83] Agnes, a widow of Wizenburg, with the approbation of her son, granted property at Minderlachen to Lichtenthal (Bremen, G; 1273) on her two daughters becoming nuns there.[84] A knight of Forst, Rikolf (1232), gave a farm and a mill to Burtscheid (G) because his three daughters were professed there.[85] When later (1245) a lady of rank became a nun there, rents and part of the income from a malt-mill in the suburbs of Aachen passed to Burtscheid.[86]

On the entry of Isabel, the sister of Thibaud l'Auneau, as a nun of L'Eau (F; 1260), her brother granted its nuns an annual rent of two measures of wheat; as did William of Chartres, lord of Ver (1271) when his sister, Petronilla, also became a nun of L'Eau,[87] and Robert de Chartres, lord of Ver (1301), when his two daughters, Lucette and Jean, entered the convent.[88] Two 'measures' seems to have been the accepted custom for when the three daughters of Nicholas of Chaulnay were professed at L'Eau (1288) the nunnery received an annual rent of six measures.[89]

THE ESTATES

The prosperity of a community depended in large measure on the endowments and benefactions it received from founders and other patrons. The consequence was that while a number of nunneries became quite wealthy, there were others which frequently had to plead poverty. The charters of confirmation a convent might seek in order to preserve its lands and rights, are one of the chiefest sources in revealing the extent of a nunnery's possessions. In 1232, Theodoric, the provost of Mariengarten (G; Lower Saxony), submitted to the duke of Brunswick a lengthy account of the possessions of his nunnery, and received in return a detailed confirmatory charter.[90]

Throughout the thirteenth and fourteenth centuries, Heiligkreuztal (G) built up its possessions of lands, mills, vineyards, meadows – one of which was 'sited by the stone cross'.[91] In 1327 the nunnery received a gift of a vineyard in Überlingen, but from 1295 onwards the majority of its transactions were fairly expensive purchases, including in 1335 the payment of sixty-eight Constance pounds to Salem abbey for one of its granges.[92]

The Economy

Shortly before her death, Countess Jean of Flanders (1236) listed some twenty-seven major grants of lands, including rights of justice, tithes and other rights, which had been granted to Marquette (F) founded only ten years before.[93] In 1252 Archbishop Willibrand of Magdeburg granted a confirmatory charter to Marienkammner (G; Saxony-Anhalt) listing its possessions: the church of St George, Gloucha; a court; five villages with agricultural land and some properties in six other villages.[94]

A a charter from the archbishop of Bremen (1299) showed Lilienthal (G; Lower Saxony) to have lands, houses, and/or tithes, in nearly sixty localities. Founded in 1232, it built up its estates well into the fourteenth century.[95] A grant to Welver (G; 1269) of property at Schnehausen encompassed 'pastures, fields, broom land, waters and fisheries', but in 1263 it had paid for some other land, 'fertile and unfertile; cultivated and uncultivated'.[96] These are but a few examples of many.

An initial grant was frequently followed, as at Lilienthal and perhaps for decades, by gifts or purchases of other estates. A few instances must suffice. In Poland, the nunnery of Owińska at its foundation received generous grants in 1252 from its founders, Przemysl I of Greater Poland, and his brother, Boleslaw, but also two other villages deliberately for the 'enlargement' of its lands.[97] In southern France, the nunnery of Nonenque (founded in 1148) was elevated from the status of priory to that of abbey in 1232, having become economically self-sufficient with an estate of 10,000 hectares.[98]

Count Otto II of Ravensberg, and his wife, Sophia, in giving the site and lands for the foundation of Bersenbrück (G; 1231), also gave the rents of twenty-four properties, and by 1238 stretching through to 1271, the nunnery headed by Provost Werner and Abbess Clemence, bought up much more, spending over six hundred marks on twelve substantial properties.[99] Within a few years of nuns settling at Marquette (F), that nunnery between 1228 and 1231 received eight grants or sales of lands, seven grants of tithe, and six grants of rents – including some in kind, like wheat, oats and capons.[100]

Countess Blanche, founding Argensolles on a grange of Hautvillers, gave the nuns also 1,000 arpents of woodland, as well as rents and tolls from the fair towns. Her son, Count Thibaut IV in 1229 gave several mills; his grant forged a link for the nuns with the towns of Épernay and Vertus where the mills were situated.

During the 1250s and 1260s the nuns consolidated their properties in three main areas: at Argensolles itself, in pasture rights outside of Épernay, and in banal rights over mills and ovens in the surrounding territories.[101]

Within three years of the foundation of Parc-aux-Dames (1205), Bishop Stephen of Noyon confirmed twenty-three grants made to it, including tithes and rents in kind.[102] Between 1248 and 1350 Heiligenthal (G; Bavaria) received nearly fifty major grants of lands and woods, but also of rents, some in kind.[103] Within ten years of its foundation in 1256, Gravenhorst (G) received twenty-five substantial grants from counts, bishops and others, but thereafter purchases were made rather than grants received.[104]

In 1266 Teistungenburg (G), newly-founded, extended its local territory by buying local lands from the Teutonic Knights who were desirous of increasing their funds 'for the legitimate business of the Holy Land'.[105] Fifty years later it extended its local demesne by buying up four holdings at Teistungenburg for seventy-eight marks.[106]

In Luxemburg, Bonneweg, founded perhaps in 1234, had received over seventy major grants before 1300; though initially it was much poorer, a grant of tithes being made in 1243 on account of its 'poverty'.[107] With royal backing of the dowager Queen Elizabeth of Bohemia, Staré-Brno (Cz) within seven years of its foundation in 1330, possessed no less than twenty-five villages.[108] The initial benefaction of Trebnitz (Pl; 1203) by Duke Henry of Silesia included in excess of twenty grants of villages and tithes.[109]

Other nunneries with fairly substantial estates came to include: Anrode (G): 4,500 morgen of land, twenty-two farms, two mills and four woods;[110] Aywières (B): nearly 2,000 hectares of land;[111] Frankenhausen (G) owned four villages, and lesser properties in thirty other localities;[112] Bergen (G): holdings in twenty-three villages as well the possession of three churches;[113]

Beuren had: greater or lesser properties in some seventy localities by 1221;[114] Frauensee (G): an estate of some thirty square kilometres around the abbey;[115] Herkenrode (B): 3,000 hectares of land on which it had sixteen dispersed granges;[116] Ivenack (G): the patronage of five churches, as well as important properties in fourteen localities.[117]

Mariengarten (Friedland, Lower Saxony; G): possessed ten villages and twenty hamlets, given by the Brandenburg nobility;[118]

Mariengarten (Erfurt, G): fourteen villages and lands in eleven other localities;[119] Stepnitz (Marienfliess): 600 *mansos* in the locality, given at its foundation in 1248 by its founder, Duke Barnim I of Pomerania, who confirmed the nuns ownership of a further five hundred *mansos* given by other benefactors;[120] and Val-St-Georges (B): fifteen major properties as well as the tithes of six parishes.[121]

The Parisian nunnery of St Antoine very carefully enlarged its estates, by grants and by purchase of land, so that it built up important granges, such as those at Aulnay (a substantial source of grain), Montreuil (significant for wine production); Champagnes (for both); frequently this was done by buying up or being granted territory adjacent to an initial holding – a significant feature on the estates also of Notre-Dame-des-Prés in the region of Troyes.[122]

All these were outshone by the acquisitions of the greater convents, notably Las Huelgas (Castille, Sp.). Its abbess exercised seignorial rights over fifty-four villages, and had the rights of 'high' and 'low' justice.[123] All her villages were exempt from episcopal control; she appointed the clergy and acted through ecclesiastical judges appointed by her, and might even convoke a synod.[124] She, or the 'infanta' nominated the 'governors, judges, notaries and physicians' in each village'.[125]

The charter granted the nunnery by Alfonso VIII of Castille (1187) was generous and wide-ranging. The nuns had: the right over the bath-house in Burgos, and 'if new bath houses are made anywhere in my kingdom, those establishments will belong to the nuns'. The nuns might build a mill at Monio, and were granted enclosed woodland at Estepar. Whatever field labour the inhabitants of Bienvivre and Pampliga had done for the king, they were now to perform for the nuns.[126]

By no means were all the grants to the nunneries free gifts; as they expanded their possessions quite considerable sums of money might be expended by the more prosperous convents. In 1220 Marienkammer (Saxony-Anhalt, G; 1220) bought for ninety-five marks a mill at Ammendorf on the river Elster with the island and lake and a willow bed there.[127] Later (1234) it bought for sixty silver marks mills and other properties from the abbey of Sittenbach.[128] Bersenbrück (G; 1257) bought for 250 marks a major property in Hast.[129]

Fraubrunnen (Swz; 1258) paid seventy-two marks of silver for a holding at Cheminaton with the patronage of the church there, and in 1262 sixty marks for land sold it by Count Rudolph of

Tierstein.[130] Seligenthal (G; 1275) bought the village of Mostenin from the local Teutonic Knights for seventy-five pounds;[131] in 1297 it bought goods in Hökchen for forty Ratisbon pounds from the dukes of Bavaria, Otto and Stephen.[132]

Casbas (Sp), founded by Oria, countess of Pallars, her action being confirmed by King Alfonso II, had a long list of properties listed in a confirmatory charter, but felt the need to enlarge its possessions by purchase. At an unknown date it bought the mill in Casbas for three hundred *sueldos*, and in 1187 a mill and vineyard adjoining the monastery for a further three hundred *sueldos*. Later, in 1286, it expanded its home base by paying thirty-five *sueldos* for land on the borders of Casbas.[133]

The profession of Betengar as a nun in 1190, saw her parents grant Casbas the vill of Lavata, 'with all its lands, pastures, and vineyards'. It also prospered when in 1289 Don Arnal and his wife entered the monastery to be professed, presumably as a *conversus* and a *conversa*, giving the nuns their property at Foces.[134]

Three brothersof Bergen (G), one a knight, gaveMarienborn (Hesse) a rent of twelve measures of rye on the profession of their sister, Gertrude, at the monastery in 1275; Heinrich Müller in 1289 gave the same nunnery a holding and mill nearby the abbey 'for the sustenance of his sister professed there'.[135]

Wormeln (G; 1276) bought for 150 marks several holdings at Warburg together with a meadow and a fish-pond, though it also received outright gifts that year, including a pasture and fish-pond at Wormeln itself.[136] The nuns of Rathausen (Swz; 1277), established now for some thirty years, were able to buy a property at Vozingen for 75 silver marks on buying property at Greislau (1251), and 32 silver marks for a mill 'situated within the precincts' (1269).[137]

Tišnov (Porta Coeli, Cz; 1281) spent 130 'marks of pure silver' on the purchase of the village of Augezd;[138] Oslavany (Cz) spent in 1269 thirty-four silver marks in purchasing substantial property at Studyň.[139] The marquess of Brandenburg sold for sixty marks the village of Breitenfeld to Techow (Heiligengrabe, G; 1306),[140] whilst that year Waterler (G) paid 'thirty-six marks of pure silver' for two holdings in Romsleben.[141]

Bergen (G);1306) paid out seven hundred marks in Slav money for the village of Bartholomew, a novice of Holy Cross abbey in Coimbra (Pt), granted to Celas nunnery a property 'in the valley Oldenkamp.[142]

The Economy

In modern equivalent many of these monetary payments amounted to thousands of pounds sterling. A pound sterling in the year 1300 would now be worth at the very least £700, making the purchase by Techow of Breitenfeld no less than £28,000 in modern equivalent. Payment could take the form of an annual acknowledgement in kind. Granted a building plot locally, Gradefes (Sp; 1182/1183) was expected to render yearly fixed amounts of wheat and wine;[143] Frauensee (G; 1220/1227) granted four villages by Count Ludwig IV of Thuringia yielded him every year specified quantities of cheese and fish.[144]

Numerous nunneries ran into financial difficulties sooner or later, and by some the pleading of poverty is a constant theme. Nuns had hardly settled at Haste (G) when in 1232 King Henry VII referred to the 'deficiency and poverty' of the convent. The nuns moved to Rulle in 1246, by which time they could afford to buy a major property at Vorenholte for one hundred marks.[145]

Only forty years after its foundation, Val-St-Georges (B; 1245) was excused by Innocent IV from accepting any new nuns on account of its 'grave poverty', and forbade anyone from pressurising the convent into so doing.[146] Was it poverty, or the need to rationalise their estates, or to raise income for some special purpose, that led the nuns of Woltingërode (G; 1266), Goslar (Neuwerk, 1268), and Wienhausen (1276), to sell property that brought them in thirty Brunswick marks, 150 marks, and fifty silver marks, respectively?[147]

Innocent IV (1245) referring to the 'grave poverty' of Marquette; excused its nuns from accepting more religious.[148] Bishop Herman of Cammin (1284) was active in making grants to the nunnery of Koszalin (Pl), especially as 'with a deficiency of timber and of pastures' it would be difficult for it to survive, despite one hundred and thirty acts recorded in its cartulary during the first twenty years of its existence (1226–46).[149]

Compared to the male abbeys of the realm, the income of most English convents was at best moderate. The English *Taxatio Ecclesiastica* (1291) reveals the income from its estates of Nun Appleton as being £37 each year, together with a further £10 from tithes and other spiritual income.[150] In modern equivalent, this figure equates to at least £28,000. Tarrant was more wealthy, with only £7–16–8 accorded it in spiritualities but £118 in temporalities, giving (in modern terms) an income of not less than £95,000 per annum.[151]

Surprisingly, if the figures are correct, Ellerton had temporal income of £67, and spiritual income of £53.¹⁵² Humble Llanllŷr in Wales possessed a temporal income of only £7–10–0; its spiritualities are not on record, but was this an acccurate record?¹⁵³ Catesby (E; 1301) pleaded 'poverty and necessity' when seeking confirmation of its possession of Yardley church.¹⁵⁴

Alleged poverty was frequently claimed by several of the smaller English nunneries. The convent of Cook Hill, Worcestershire, despite its foundation by a countess of Warwick, was said to be suffering when, in 1276, the king granted six oaks on account of the nuns' poverty, and in 1279 when certain tithes were awarded it 'for the relief of the nuns'. In 1313 and again in 1402 the nuns were exempted from the payment of a tenth to the Crown 'because its rents were poor and weak'. The poverty was undoubtedly due to a slender endowment, but perhaps not helped by mismanagement of its affairs; for that reason in 1285 the bishop of Worcester required that Thomas the chaplain was to have full charge of their temporal affairs.¹⁵⁵

The prior of Worcester referred in 1308 to 'the extreme poverty of the nuns of Whistones'. In 1275 Bishop Giffard had backed the claim of its nuns to be unable to pay their taxes; in 1284 he aided them financially, and in his will bequeathed them £5 and vestments for the high altar. The nunnery's meagre income came about despite the fifty-five acres with which the convent was endowed at its foundation (before 1255) by Walter de Cantilupe. In 1301 the bishop of Worcester granted the nuns twelve acres of land and a wood in Northwick, and further lands were received there in the early fourteenth century.¹⁵⁶

In 1308, whilst petitioning permission to elect a new prioress, the nuns of Whistones mentioned 'the smallness of their possessions, which compelled them formerly to beg'. In 1319 the bishop of Worcester referred to the 'poor religious' in his diocese, amongst them the Cistercian nuns of Cook Hill and Pinley, and sought their exemption from payment of a tenth towards a collection for the Holy Land.¹⁵⁷

Nuns, like the monks of the Order, might seek to rationalise their estates by making exchanges of territory with other bodies or individuals. Within ten years of its foundation, Rifreddo (It; 1224, 1230) made exchanges of lands and woodland to help it build up its home estate.¹⁵⁸ In Portugal, King Dinis (1290) exchanged a ten-

The Economy

ement held in Lisbon by Celas nunnery, in return for half of other holdings there.[159]

Other instances included Bersenbrück [G; 1235], wishing to acquire a property close to the abbey, obtained it in exchange for two houses in Hesle and Hone,[160] and later exchanged fields in Antum (1295) with the church there.[161] Bergen (G) (1242) exchanged the village of Ztarcowe for that called Lubanovitz;[162] Marquette (F;l 1260) made an exchange of lands at Wachtebeke with St Peter's Abbey, Ghent,[163] whilst Langendorf (G; 1300) exchanged its 'court' in Weissenfels for that in the city belonging to the abbey of St Clare.[164] Beuditz (G; 1334) gave property at Burcwerbin for holdings at Vparz.[165]

At the close of the thirteenth century, Plötzky (G), located not far from the right bank of the river Elbe, exchanged its possessions across the river to make its home estate more compact.[166] Duisseren (G; 1343) exchanged a piece of arable land for another similar piece at Steyntbrynken.[167] Cotham (E) made small exchanges of lands at Habrough and Burgh.[168] Catesby (E; 1287) consolidated at least one of its properties by enclosing the land, and obtaining the quitclaim from a layman of his property within the enclosure.[169]

In Moravia, the nuns of Oslovany in 1259 exchanged their vill of Řeznwice for that of Maŝowice.[170] In Pomerania the sisters of Szczecin (Stettin) in 1280 exchanged their property at Pomelle for one at Razow, with Wetzelo, a burgess of Stettin.[171]

ESTATE BOUNDARIES, AND PROPERTY DISPUTES

Disputes might be avoided if boundaries were firmly established. It was to prevent false claims that when Duke Henry of Silesia (1203) issued a detailed charter granting many villages and lands to Trebnitz (Pl), he caused the bounds of its possessions to be spelt out in detail by reference to rivers and streams, to other markers as piles of stones especially erected, to certain marked trees and to firmly fixed boundary stones engraved with his own name.[172]

Patrick, earl of Dunbar (1273), gave to Coldstream (S) the land of Hersil, 'as he had perambulated it'.[173] When he granted the nunnery 'all the grazing' at Selbuchlethe, he spelt out the limits of that privilege: 'from the head of Wlveshope outside of the wood across as far as the valley descending between Farniley and Strikesley, descending upon the rivulet of Crumbesyde, and so ascending by that rivulet between Crumbesyde and Senedewde'.[174]

When the bounds of certain lands of Nonenque (F; 1280) were verified note was made of the boundary stones, and of limits proceeding along 'an old road' and from 'bole to bole'.[175] A boundary accord reached by the abbess of Conversano (It; 1292) was 'sworn on the holy gospels'.[176] Sancho IV (1292) confirmed the partition made of 'la Torre de Guadiamar' between San Clemente of Seville and the cathedral chapter of Seville.[177]

A determination of the boundaries of the lands of Żarnowiec (Pl; 1324) saw them marked by 'stones, trees and cairns'.[178] A further and very detailed listing of its bounds in 1342 went: 'by the marks of trees and cairns all the way to the oak and stone standing by the way between Gelanschin and Sobencziz … to the great oak marked and the bank around'[179]

King Dinis ordered an inquiry into the demarcation of his property of Bobão from an hereditament of Lorvão (Pt; 1279), whilst in 1322 the limits of the nunnery's possessions at Esgueira were also in dispute.[180] A demarcation of certain lands of Arouca nunnery (Pt) was made in 1330 at the request of neighbouring parties; and the next year, at the command of King Alfonso IV, as to where they abutted upon the lands of the Hospitallers.[181]

Disputes there were. Alix, widow of Siger of Courtrai (1233), sought a payment of fifty pounds within forty days from Marquette (F) in respect of lands and rents her late husband had sold the nunnery, asserting that they were part of her dowry.[182] Jacques of Bondues, a knight, sold to Marquette the mill and pond of Marcq-en-Baroeul, but within a year of the sale another knight, Henry of Breucq, laid claim to the property. Countess Margaret of Flanders (1251) ruled against him, after his claim was rejected by a jury of twelve.[183]

Duissern (G) was involved in more than one dispute. Winmar, son of Meinolf of Duisburg (1257) was aggrieved because lands he thought were his had come into the ownership of the nuns through his sister, Salmena.[184] Later, Duissern (1303) was involved in a case necessitating lengthy proceedings in the church of St Salvator in Duisburg when fifteen witnesses gave evidence.[185] Yet another dispute involving Duissern (1336) was amicably resolved.[186] In 1337 a compromise was reached regarding the 'metes, circumferences and limits' of certain lands of Mariasaal (Cz).[187]

The Economy

Nonenque (F) endured a series of intermittent disputes: as those with the abbey of Lodève (1177) regarding the tithes of Saint-Beaulize, and with Vabres abbey (1243) concerning the tithes of Ste Marie de Combabrias. The convent reached agreement with the inhabitants of La Roquetreboulon (1255), some of whom had invaded the nunnery's pastures, and with the Knights Templar of Sainte-Eulalie regarding conflicting pasture rights and other matters.[188]

Gregory IX (1228) appointed Galfridus, a canon of Turin, to bring to an end injuries suffered by Brione (It) from citizens of Turin.[189] Not long after its foundation, the nuns of Lichtental (G; 1251) had a disagreement with the inhabitants of Rietbur over the reparation of their village chapel and cemetery.[190]

With the course of time, land holdings of the nuns might be encroached upon by local landowners. Tišnov (Porta Coeli, Cz; 1264) had occasion to complain to King Přemysl of Bohemia when a certain knight had violently wrested the village of Luka from its possession; the monarch ordered its return.[191] In 1291 Pope Nicholas IV ordered the return to Porta Coeli (Cz) of lands withdrawn from its ownership; a demand repeated by Boniface VIII in 1295 and again in 1298, mentioning its 'tithes, lands and rents'.[192] Local warfare might well be damaging: The properties of Porta Coeli had also suffered in 1255 at the hands of 'the Turks, Hungarians and Cumans'.[193] The nuns of Coldstream (S) lost their holdings in Northumberland during the Scottish wars of King Edward I, and in 1305 sought their return.[194]

In 1300 a retired abbot of Sittenbach arbitrated in a dispute concerning Helfta (G): a knight claimed the tithes of half a holding, and it was ruled that the convent were to give him two marks in recompense.[195] A dispute between the nuns of Boitzenburg (Marienpforte; G) and a local knight, Dietrich von Kerlow, and his four sons, regarding the siting of a chapel there, necessitated a bull from John XXII (1328).[196] Dissension between the nuns of Żarnowitz (Pl; 1334) and a knight called Boczey regarding Lake Zarnowitz, had to be settled by Jordan, 'commendator' (probably of the Teutonic Knights) in Gdańsk.[197]

Regrettably, there were also contentions between some nunneries and other religious houses, even of the Cistercian Order. The latter are noted in the statutes of the General Chapter, but often without the subject matter being disclosed. Such disputes included those between the abbot of Matallana and the abbess of Las Huelgas

(Sp) in 1259, who the same year was also at variance with the abbot of Veruela. The nunnery of Cambron (Aragon, Sp), of which Veruela had oversight, was also in dispute with it. In 1260 the abbots of La Oliva and Piedra were delegated to investigate, but in 1271 there were further difficulties and the solution was committed to the abbots of Morimond (living far distant) and of Berdoues. The former at least presumably delegated his task.[198]

Disputes between nunneries included the quarrels between the abbesses of Katherinental and Seligental (G) in 1255, and between Port-Royal and Le Trésor (F) in 1258.[199] The Chapter of 1279 was concerned at 'the considerable labours and expenses' that a disagreement between the abbey of Grandpré (B) and the nunnery of 'Valle Beatae Maria' (perhaps Burvenich, G) had brought about, and attempted to find a solution.[200]

More is known of some other contentions within the Order. When disagreement arose between Gradefes (1236) and the male monastery of Valediós regarding mutual land boundaries in Nava de Juan Diaz, the arbitrators appointed by General Chapter were the abbots of Carracedo, Moreruela and Sandoval.[201] The fact that it had been founded under the auspices of Staffarda, did not prevent Rifreddo (1236) being at variance with that male abbey regarding the ownership of a certain farm and wood.[202]

The abbots of Grand-pré and of St Bernard (perhaps St-Bernard-op-Scheldt) were made arbitrators in 1291 by the General Chapter in a tithe dispute between the convents of Zwyveke and of Nieuwenbosch (Heusden; B) regarding tithes in the parish of Heusden. It was decided that Nieuwenbosch should pay annually to Zwyveke sixteen pounds and ten shillings of Paris money, whilst Zwyveke was to renounce to Nieuwenbosch the ancient tithes (prior to the day of the agreement) at Heusden.[203]

As for friction between a Cistercian nunnery and a monastery of another Order, one such controversy arose from the proximity of certain granges of La Ramée, Belgium, with those of the Premonstratensian abbey of Averbode. The latter complained in 1230 saying that this was contrary to the agreement made previously between the two Orders – perhaps the 'peace' of 1142. The abbots of Aulne and Villers were bidden to enquire into the matter.[204] The dean of St Aubain at Namur (B; 1232) arbitrated in a dispute between Val-St-Georges and Géronsart priory regarding the ownership of certain lands.[205]

The Economy

A problem arose in 1293 when the abbey of Celle built an 'overmill' in Grimma, which lessened the water-supply to the cloister and lands of Grimma (Nimbschen/Marienthron, G) nunnery; on arbitration by the abbots of Georgental and Dobrilugk the monastery of Celle paid the nuns forty marks of silver in compensation.[206] It took ten years to settle a disagreement between Leyme and the Augustinian priory at Escarmeil (1298), following a partial exchange made of lands and rights.[207]

A considerable amount of time and energy was spent on an unusual case: the settling of differences between the nuns of Heiligkreuztal (G; 1323) and the hospital for the poor at Esslingen. The issue centred on a red horse, valued at ten pounds, belonging to the hospital but accommodated at the nunnery. Burchard, a *conversus* of the nunnery, reached an agreement with the hospital, but it was then said that he did not have a mandate from the abbess and the convent to achieve this. A commission of enquiry, headed by the dean of Esslingen, listened to twenty lay witnesses giving evidence on ten articles of difference.[208]

CRIMINAL JURISDICTION

Through their provost or other official appointed, the nunneries would hold manorial courts; as at Nun Cotham (E) where the provost/master had 'a free court from three weeks to three weeks' in Keelley and Cuxwold,[209] These would be chiefly concerned with estates matters, as the admission of tenants to property. They might also take cognisance of petty offences, but very few Cistercian nunneries were able to exercise 'high justice', for offences like murder, wounding and theft, crimes which could carry the death penalty.

Those convents which did have that right included: Heiligkreuztal (G), Las Huelgas (Sp), Marienstern (Saxony), Marienthal (Haute Alsace), Rottenmünster (G) and Trebnica (Pl), whilst with a grant to Ivenack (G; 1276) of Niendorp by Vitslav II, prince of Rugen, went 'all law, whether greater or lesser'.[210] Vitslav III accorded the nuns of Ryd (D) the right of justice on its lands, 'whether greater or lesser, and the deed mentions 'death or hand mutilation'.[211]

Duke Barnim I of Pomerania gave the village of Stöwen to the nuns of Szczecin (Pl; 1251) 'with all rights of justice'.[212] With a grant to Heiligengrabe (Brandenburg; 1320) of the village of Kemnitz was included 'all law and justice',[213] and rights of justice also pertained on the lands of Ichtershausen (G; 1305).[214].

Mostly, the grant of lands to a convent was accompanied by a specific exclusion retaining 'high justice' in the hands of the grantor. Blanche of Castile (1247) in bequeathing lands to Lieu-Notre-Dame-lez-Romorantin (F), gave the nuns 'all right and lordship excepting only the high justice which I retain for myself and my heirs'.[215] In granting Baeruel to Flines, Countess Margaret of Flanders (1245) reserved to herself 'the four high justices and homages'.[216]

In founding Himmelkron (G; 1280), Count Otto III of Borderland also reserved to himself the 'high justice'.[217] The nuns of Zwyveke (B; 1248) surrendered all their rights of justice in the village of Appels, to Robert, advocate of Arras, but he returned the rights of 'medium' and 'low' justice to the convent. His deed states that 'high' justice meant cognisance of 'abduction, murder, arson, hanging and brigandage'.[218]

King Wenceslas in a grant of rights of justice to Marienthal (Cz., 1238) excluded oversight of penalties for 'robbery, murder, wounding and violent assault'.[219] An agreement between Leyme (D; 1351) and the count of Turenne affirmed that 'low' and 'medium' justice belonged to the nunnery, but 'high justice' to the count'. The concord provided that agreed that no execution of high justice was to be made at Leyme, between 'the crosses or oratory which mark the limits of the precincts', without the consent of the abbess.[220] 'High justice' was also excluded when Déodat de Caylus (1246) granted the chateau of La Peyre-sur-Sorgue to Nonenque (F) with 'all civil and criminal jurisdiction' except cases which deserved capital punishment,[221] and when the village of Höffstedten was granted to Sonnefeld (G; 1288).[222]

In Poland, the abbess of Ołobok (1253), through her judge, had the right in her villages following Polish law and custom, to try cases by 'the duel with staffs, ordeal by iron (i.e. fire), ordeal by water' and similar means.[223] Otto, count of Bentheim and Heilwig, his wife, granted to Rulle (G; 1254) the court of Garthusen with the power of justice vulgarly called 'holtgraschap: judicial authority over forest and commons'.[224] The same power was given to the nuns of Rulle (1259) by Herman Uncus and Ludwig Uncus in the march of Rulle.[225]

The Economy

Count Albert von Gleichen (1274) ruled that where criminal proceedings had taken place in Anrode (Thuringia) nunnery's court, he personally or through a judge should give judgement.[226] The lord of Ver, Robert of Chartres (1294), made amends to the nuns of L'Eau (F) for offending their rights of justice by taking two men from within their precincts and imprisoning them at Loché.[227]

ISOLATION/COMMUNICATIONS

The contemplative life demanded a degree of isolation, nor did some convents wish strangers to stray too close to their properties. Evrard of Chartres (1241) gave to the nuns of recently founded L'Eau (F) 'the way next to the convent' for their 'peace and quiet', with the right to obstruct the way and turn it to their own use.[228] Added seclusion was afforded when the nuns of L'Eau (1257) paid seventy Chartres shillings to buy up land located outside the abbey gate.[229]

Count Heinrich of Gleichenstein (1294) gave to the nuns of Anrode (Thuringia), 'for their greater peace', the common way adjoining the convent so that it should no longer be a public thoroughfare.[230] The nuns of Mariengarten (Saxony) were given leave by the duke of Brunswick (1314) to close to the public the way which abutted on the upper part of their home grange, so long as they provided a similar way across their fields.[231]

The ability to have ingress and egress for their vehicles was a necessity for each nunnery. In this connexion, Eustace of Coton (12th C.) gave Cotham (E) the use of a road leading from the nunnery's great gate westward to the 'common road'. It passed between his two tofts, and was to be wide enough for two wagons to pass.[232] The abbey of St Peter, Ghent (1262) gave Marquette (F) the use, though not exclusively, of a road between Saffelaere and Wachtebeke, at the request of Countess Margaret of Flanders.[233]

Barnim I, Duke of Pomerania, insisted in 1278 – not long before his death, that the common way from the city of Szczecin to the mill of the nuns of Szczecin (Pl) was a free way for those coming and going, it was not to be impeded, and that any hindrances were to be removed.[234] Marienkammer (G; 1299) allowed a new way to be made over its land, as the public road between St Maurice's Gate at Halle to the village of Glaucha where the nunnery was situated was subject to flooding both in summer and in winter, in return for a site on common land where the nunnery might build a windmill. Indeed, one translation of *glaucha* is 'swampy land'.[235]

A bridge built at Carrizo (Sp; 1198) was partly funded by Alfonso IX.[236] Adersleben (1285) was given leave by Count Otto of Ascaria to build a bridge across 'the Boda',[237] whilst tenants of San Clemente, Seville (1316), had the duty of constructing a bridge over a local river bed.[238] When Margrave Rudolf I gave Lichtental the village of Geroldsau in full possession, the charter gives a picture of the settlement with its 'waterfalls, water, paths and bridges'.[239]

Letters written by the abbess of Flines (F; 1259] were carried to Lille by Ansiel, its 'messenger'.[240]

ARABLE FARMING AND FOOD SUPPLY

A pre-requisite to agriculture on monastic estates might be the improvement of the land. In the thirteenth century it was not only great abbeys like Ter Duinen which assisted the reclamation of marshland in Flanders, but Cistercian nunneries such as Flines. The new site at Flines to which nuns moved in 1253 was very marshy, so the nuns caused a twenty-foot canal with enclosing bank to be built to take the waters of the plain and divert them into the river Scarpe;[241] the convent also caused the river Rache to be canalised in order to drain that valley.[242]

The nuns of Zwijveke participated in dyking the Escaut.[243] Groeninghe and Marquette also undertook drainage works, as did those of Lieu-Notre-Dame in the Sologne marshes; they also received much waste land which needed reclamation.[244] Sparsely populated lands in Poland were actively filled by colonists from the west; those of Żarnowiec nunnery (1257) were exempted from paying tolls by Duke Swantopolk.[245] Other nunneries, like Marienstern (G), were also prominent during the Germanic process of colonising the east.[246]

Nuns' granges might be well organised, like those of Tart (F): on four it practised mixed farming, at Beauvoir – arable, at Battalut – arable and viticulture, while Hautserre was near a vast forest where its herds were pastured.[247]

William of Coton demised all his land there to Cotham (E) in 1237 for eight harvests on a share-cropping basis. The convent was

The Economy

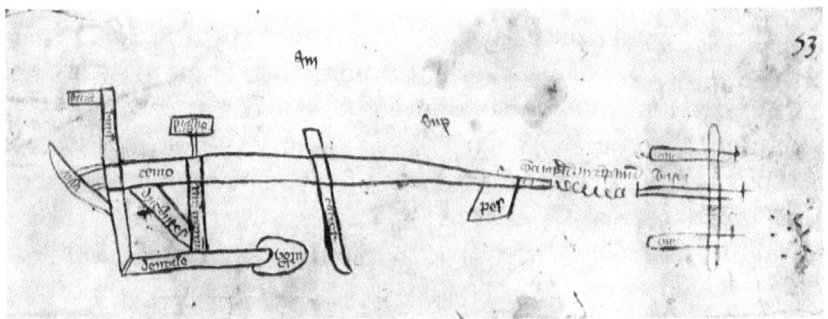

Fig. 4. Cartulary of Nun Cotham Nunnery, England: a medieval plough. (Bodleian Library, Oxford, MS Top. Lincs. d. 1, fol. 53r, detail).

to till, harrow and manure the land, and William would sow half of it and mow it.[248] For manure in those days Cotham used 'rich mud from the stream'.[249]

Its founder granted Parc-aux-Bois (F; 1202) the right to 'assart and bring into cultivation' the land he gave the nuns,[250] but most of a nunnery's income stemmed from the rents – in cash or kind, paid by its many tenants. The forty-four demised properties of Teistungenberg (G; 1268) included around 370 hectares of arable land and thirty of meadow.[251]

Returns from tenants on the lands of Rifreddo (It) included not only cash payments, but also rents in kind – like pork, grain, chestnuts, oats, eggs and wine, and labour services – such as haymaking and the gathering of acorns and chestnuts.[252] The nunnery bought a chestnut wood in 1256, and received further chesnut rights locally in 1272.[253] A list of the days work expected by Cotham (E) of ten tenants mostly ranged from one day to three, but six days in the autumn by William the skinner.[254]

Improvements by tenants of their holdings might be looked for: a tenant of Lilienthal (G; 1294) was obliged on the property demised to him to erect a house and 'wort' and barn to the value of five marks within one year.[255]

Bersenbrück (G; 1247) was granted by Countess Sophia of Ravensberg a property which brought in fixed amounts of wheat, barley and oats, 'by the measure of Damme'.[256] A tenant of Rulle (G; 1272) was to pay annually three weights of wheat, two of malt and an urn of butter.[257] One village of twenty-eight and a half fields belonging to Wolin (Pl) brought in an annual rent of 38 *guldens* and twelve farthings, and in kind of four measures of rye and oats, as well as sixteen roasted cocks.[258]

On leasing out a property at Altenpark in perpetuity, Seligenthal (G; 1336) was to receive yearly fixed amounts of grain (corn and oats), eggs, four cheeses, six chickens and three 'fat geese', as well as a monetary rent.[259] All such dues added greatly to a nunnery's food supply. Conversely, Wormeln (G; 1301) receiving a lease of land in Welda from the chapter of Paderborn was required to pay an annual rent of both cash and fixed amounts of agricultural produce – including rye, wheat and barley.[260] This giving an indication of crops produced.

The dietary needs of nuns could also be assisted by direct grants from other sources. St Louis IX gave the nuns of Le Lys (F) from his granaries at Melun and Sens certain rents of wheat, but in time the lessees tried to pay the nuns in cash. As the price of grain rose they were at a disadvantage, and in 1311 Philip IV confirmed that the rents were to be paid in kind.[261]

In Spain King Ferdinand IV (1299) granted the nuns of Gaudalajrara tributes of wheat from churches in that deanery.[262] Peter de Montfort (d. 1216) gave the nuns of Pinley (E) the tithe of all the victuals of his house, viz. bread, beer, fish and flesh, and whatever was dressed in his kitchen. In 1277 this grant was changed into a definite yearly supply of wheat and barley.[263] Philip IV of France (1292, 1303) accorded the nuns of Gomerfontaine a tenth of 'the desserts of bread and wine at the royal table'.[264]

THE MILLING INDUSTRY

The possession of mills was essential to any medieval community, not only for food supply but also for financial gain, when others used the mills to grind their own corn. There was a further advantage: a supply of fish from the mill-pond. At its foundation (1252) Ivenack (G) received the local mill-pond with the leat;[265] Wormeln (G; 1277) received from Duke Otto of Everstein a mill 'before the gate of Volkmarsen'.[266] Frequently monastic mills were demised to lay tenants who paid rent in either cash or kind or both.

The *Rule of St Benedict* dictated that workshops and water-driven mills were to be within the precincts (the 'outer court'), this was the case at at least six of the Cistercian nunneries of the Low Countries, including Herkenrode, and Valduc,[267] whilst Bersenbrück (G; 1293) erected a mill within its curtilage.[268] Mills figure prominently in the confirmatory charter granted by Henry II of England, Duke of Normandy (1154–84), to Bival (F).[269] Arnold of Gymmich and Jutta his wife gave a water-mill to Burtscheid (G; 1231), but expected the nuns to keep the obits of their family members.[270]

Kirklees (E; 1240) demised the moiety of a mill newly-built at Heton, but reserved the right to grind corn there.[271] Milling rights were important to the nuns of Parc-aux-Dames (F), and it had a stone bridge for access to its mill at Arnold.[272] The grant of numerous other mills finds place in this book.

Within two or three decades of its foundation, Mariengarten (Lower Saxony) in 1268 accumulated a mill at Marzhausen and three mills at Witzenhausen, but at a cost of sixty-one marks. Other mills were to follow.[273] The importance of the possession of mills was exemplified when Gravenhorst (G; 1279) bought a mill from Count Otto of Tecklenburg for sixty-one marks,[274] and when Börstel (G; 1311) purchased a mill at Grafeld for sixty marks.[275] These figures, in modern equivalent, suggest a purchasing price of around £30,000 or more, but the potential value was greater.

Barnim I (1271) gave the nuns of Szczecin (Pl) a mill of four wheels sited on the river Vuelsam at Bierroden.[276] L'Eau (F; 1274) entered into an agreement with a local gentleman, Geoffrey of Meslay, to share the mill of two wheels at La Fosse.[277] At a time when it suffered economically, King Ladislas IV (1275) gave Veszprémvölgy (Hg) a mill in Gerzom, 'to help the nuns better perform divine worship'.[278] In demising two mills close to Goslar, Neuwerk (G; 1293) expected three measures of malt weekly, as well as other payments.[279]

Nunneries with lands in exposed situations, open to strong winds, such as coastal sites and hill-tops, might utilise such renewable energy. Nunneries noted as building wind-mills included: Parc-aux-Bois (1214), with leave of its founder;[280] Zwyveke (B; 1241), with permission on the land of Robert, advocate of Arras;[281] and Marienkammer (G; 1299) in a land exchange deal.[282] Marquette (F; 1227) inherited a wind-mill when founded on land acquired from Loos abbey.[283] Groeninghe (B) owned a wind-mill at its first site of Marcke.[284]

Gravenhorst (G; 1294) bought for seventeen marks the local wind-mill at Riesenbeck, with 'the ways leading to it'.[285] Other nunneries possessing wind-mills included: Flines (F; 1289), a wind-mill at Hali;[286] Dusseren (G) in Duisburg (1312),[287] Whiston (E; close to the city of Worcester),²⁸⁸ and Neukloster (Sonnenkamp; G; 1318), near Dessin, east of Schwerin.²⁸⁹ Countess Margaret of Flanders (1261) bought for the convent of Flines (F) a wind-mill close to the leper-house of Lille.²⁹⁰ The windmill of the nuns of Koszalin (Pl) close to the Baltic coast still stands to-day.

VITICULTURE

Apart from water, the common drink of nuns in northern Europe was apparently beer, with imported wine on special occasions. Further south on the continent many nunneries acquired vineyards of their own, for not only was wine a safe drink and often featuring amongst the pittances nuns received (See Chapter 3), but it was also a necessary adjunct of divine worship, and in the instance of some convents an important item of their trade.

Wine was also obtained by the gift of benefactors, usually on an annual basis. Archbishop Reinhard of Würzburg (1183) made an annual grant to Wechterswinkel (G) of two casks of wine.²⁹¹ An early grant to Gomerfontaine (F; *fd*. 1207) was of a ton of wine yearly from the vineyards of Mareuil.²⁹² The founding count and countess of Chartres granted L'Eau (F; 1228) an annual payment of three measures of wine from one of their properties.²⁹³ Duke Reinold of Geldern (1343) granted the nuns of Gräfenthal (G; 1342) a yearly gift of two *fothers* of wine out of his toll at Lobith.²⁹⁴

There are frequent references in the charters of the acquisition of vineyards, some by purchase. Gradefes (Sp) acquired, mostly by purchase, nine vineyards between 1186 and 1220.²⁹⁵ Carrizo (Sp; 1217) was made a grant of a portion of a vineyard by Bernard and Marie Petri, their daughter being one of its nuns.²⁹⁶ One of the first recorded grants to Beuditz (G, 1244) was of a vineyard at Lobdeburg.²⁹⁷ The nuns of Feldbach (Swz), installed at a beguinage in 1253, immediately acquired several vineyards.²⁹⁸

L'Eau nunnery (F) also made several purchases of vineyards, as in the parishes of Challoel (in 1254 for one hundred Chartres pounds), and of Luisant (the same year for twenty pounds).²⁹⁹ In 1285 L'Eau bought up a further vineyard at Luisant, but also the same year received yet more from Jehane, countess of Chartes, as a gift.³⁰⁰ Those of Notre-Dame-des-Prés in the region of Troyes were extensive; in 1282 alone they spent over sixty French pounds in the acquisition of further vineyards.[301]

An early grant to Lichtental (G; 1253), by a knight, Drucher and his wife, was of the court in which they resided, together with its orchard and a vineyard.[302] Ichtershausen (G; 1247) was granted a vineyard at Kerspleben,[303] and Beuren (G; 1261) received a small vineyard in Urleben.[304] Kapellendorf (G; 1263) bought up a vineyard 'under Kirchberch' for twenty-two silver marks.[305] The nuns of Billigheim (G; 1335) received the gift of a vineyard in Weissenhulde, 'next to a vineyard of the cloister', thus extending their property.[306]

The location of Lys nunnery by the river Seine allowed its nuns to transport their wine for sale in Paris, and its timber rights (noted later) facilitated the manufacture of the requisite barrels and vessels.[307] The nuns of Val-des-Vignes accumulated a substantial holding of vineyards, especially at Ailleville, paying for this over twenty years (1257–77) 543 French pounds. A grant of a vineyard, valued at ten pounds, in 1268, was to mark the entry into the nunnery of the donor's niece, but also of his becoming a *conversus* there.[308]

Fraubrunnen (Swz) built up a sizeable number of vineyards by the mid-fourteenth century, receiving protection in 1287 in respect of certain vineyards from Herman de Bello, and exchanging a vineyard at Bahn in 1348 for one at Kapff, and paying ten marks for other viticulture rights in 1344.[309] In 1329 Saalburg nunnery (G) received three vineyards from the three brothers of the Herbsleben family as dowry for their three sisters who had become nuns.[310]

Himmelspforten (G) between 1270 and 1316 received by purchase, bequest or gift, fourteen areas of vineyard totalling well some sixty *yokes*. The names of the localities of some suggest their situation on hill slopes: Berg Hurrich, Bittenberg, Rossberg and Ziegenberg.[311] Its stock-book tells that Engenthal (Hesse, 1344) had interests in some twenty vineyards, some of which yielded rents in kind, and several were on life tenancies; on the death of the tenant returnable to the monastery.[312] The three granges of La-Cour-Notre-Dame (F), had both wine-presses and forges.[313]

When Himmelspforten was granted a vineyard in the 1320s by a widow of Würzburg, the latter renounced any claim to it 'with mouth, hand and blade', perhaps referring to renunciation both 'by word, oath and written deed'.[314] San Clemente (Seville, Sp; 1309] demised a piece of a vineyard for three years, on condition that the tenant was to give one-third of its produce in the first year to the nuns, but one-half in the next two years; he was to keep the vineyard in good condition, and replant as necessary.[315] The nuns of Carrizo (Sp; 1228) granted Suero Petri and his wife, 'all our vineyard in San Martino del Camino, for the good service you have shown us'.[316]

OLIVE GROVES

These featured prominently amongst the possessions of Conversano (It; 1294),[317] as well as vineyards.[318] Las Huelgas (Sp) received several olive groves in the first half of the thirteenth century.[319] Olive groves, as at Colimbrie and Coimbra, featured in 1292 amongst the possessions of Arouca (Pt).[320] In Portugal also, by the will of Martin Pais (1277), a canon of Coimbra, a vineyard and an olive grove were to revert to Celas nunnery on the death of one Marina Fernandes.[321] Celas nunnery (Pt) was granted an olive grove in 1285 at Mainça.[322] San Clemente (Seville; 1307) demised an olive grove for an annual rental of one thousand *maravedis*.[323]

PASTORALISM

Despite the rare occasions on which they ate meat, the early Cistercian nuns, through the labours of their *conversi* and servants, engaged in the raising of animals, thus providing flesh for the sick, hides for the tanning of leather, cheese for food, and wool for trade.

Where transhumance was required, the right of free passage was of great importance. In these respects, so far as Las Huelgas (Sp; 1187) was concerned, Alfonso VIII provided that its animals might have pasture where-ever the king's animals have pasture; its shepherds' huts were to have the same protection as those of the king's shepherds; and its animals were to be free of tax 'going up or coming down from mountain pastures'.[324]

The nuns in Castile of Cañas also practised transhumance with their flocks, and their engagement in pastoralism was shown when they converted a corn mill into a fulling mill in 1272.[325] La Vassin (Puy-de-Dôme) had a grange, Riom-ès-Montagnes, which specialised in cheese-making; its name implying transhumance;[326] the movement of animals up to, and down from, summer mountain pastures, a practice also known on some of the granges of Coyroux.[327]

Actual numbers of animals are hard to come by for this period, but at Nonenque (F; 1303) the stock included 435 sheep, 103 pigs, 118 oxen and 31 cows, as well as many goats,[328] and forty horses.[329] At one locality alone, Wangenier, the nuns of Soleilmont (B; 1284) were granted common of pasture for 120 sheep, four horses and four cows.[330] Bequests made in wills might assist a nunnery's economy, as when William de Paveley left two oxen to Sewardsley (E; 1240) as well as his complete suit of armour.[331]

The cartulary of Cotham (E) shows the importance of sheep-rearing and wool production in its economy. In 1271, Hugh of Griseby, its shepherd, received from the master, in the presence of the prioress and convent, 1048 ewes and 300 lambs to take under his care; in 1276, he sheared 1201 ewes belonging to the nunnery and 339 lambs of his own stock.[332] Its pastures and rights of common of pasture, were located, by the late twelfth century, chiefly at Cadeby, Coton, Cuxwold and Grimesthorp.[333] It had pasture for forty sheep and grazing for draught animals in 1233 in Habrough salt marsh,[334] whilst 350 of its sheep grazed at Swallow.[335]

Amongst other such instances, Belfays (F; 1176) early received a grant of pasture at Choiseul for its 'oxen, cows, sheep, goats, pigs, horses and other animals'.[336] By 1236 Kirklees (E) had received several grants of common of pasture, as in the vill of Cullingworth, for their beasts of burden, their pigs and cows and oxen, as well as for 400 sheep.[337] King Louis gave Maubuisson (F, 1245) the right to pasture 300 pigs in his forests of Resty and of Guise.[338] In one locality alone, Thornidicke, Coldstream (S) had 'the whole common grazing for forty mares and their followers, until the said attain the age of three years'.

Nearly all the Cistercian convents in Flanders and Hainault received donations of 'pastureland and prairie' and became wool-producers.[339] Flines enjoyed common of pasture in the vast marsh of Flines.[340]

The thirteen Cistercian nunneries of Yorkshire (E) contributed a total of thirty-six sacks of wool to the export trade by the thirteenth century – wool to Flanders and later to Italy, whilst the Lincolnshire nunneries provided on average at least thirteen sacks. In 1309 Archbishop Greenfield of York granted leave to Hampole to sell wool at 12 marks per sack.[341]

In Lincolnshire (E), Stixwould nunnery alone produced fifteen sacks, and its export trade was facilitated by docking facilities at Washingborough on the river Witham, and ease of access to the port of Boston.[342] Count William of Albemarle (*d.* 1179) gave half-an-acre of land at Paull on the Humber estuary to Cotham [E], with permission for the nuns own ships to freely land and depart from the earl's havens free of toll at Paull and Hedon.[343] Both Henry III (1170/71) and King John (1199/1200) had granted Cotham freedom from all 'tolls, passage and pontage'.[344] Merchants sold wool on behalf of Cotham (1268/79) at St Ives' Fair, valued at twenty marks, but were slow to render the money so raised.[345]

In Scotland, pastoralism formed an important sector of the economy of Coldstream nunnery, fortified by expansive pasture rights, and with the ability of the nuns to export its wool through the port of Berwick.[346]

Skins were also obtained from rabbits: Henry III gave to Tarrant in 1252 the right of warren on all its lands in Dorset (where the convent was sited), and in Wiltshire and Sussex.[347] As for horses, in order to resolve in part a dispute in 1323 between the nuns of Heiligkreuztal (G) and the 'hospital of the poor' in Esselingen, the convent conceded to the hospital 'a horse coloured chestnut, worth ten Halle pounds, which carried wood to Grüningen'.[348]

The *Wikipedia* plan of Wormeln (G) shows that it had a substantial dove-cot.

THE FISHERIES

Given their abstinence from flesh meat, a goodly supply of fish was important to Cistercian nuns. Fish featured prominently in their diet, especially in Lent, and was a frequent component of pittances (Chapter 2). Nunneries obtained fisheries or fishing rights in adjacent rivers and lakes, and also had recourse to fish found in their mill-ponds, as at Neukloster (Sonnenkamp, G; 1280),[349] and St Agnes, Magdeburg, G; 1245). Queen Blanche of Castile (1247) bequeathed to the nuns of Lieu-Notre-Dame-lez-Romorantin (F) many rights, including possession of 'two ponds next to the abbey which I have acquired for them, so that the nuns may use the water of those ponds according to their own needs, increasing or decreasing the size of those ponds as necessary'.[350]

The Economy

As the nuns prepared to move from Haste to Rulle (G, 1244), the overflowing of their fishpond at Rulle led to discontent on the part of a local man and his mother. When ten years later the nuns of Rulle wished to enlarge the fish-pond, the possibility of local flooding and silt deposits was envisaged.[351] At its foundation, Soleilmont (B; 1237) received a fish-pond from the Countess of Flanders sited close to the abbey. The inhabitants of Gilly (1285) later withdrew the pretensions they had towards it.[352]

Fisheries might be obtained as a gift or by purchase. An archbishop of Bremen gave Lilienthal (G) (1264) its grange or 'court' at Ottersted, complete with chapel, fields and fisheries.[353] Count Otto III of Geldern (1283) sold to Gravenhorst (G), for thirty-two Osnabruck marks, a house in Dankelscheid with a fishery in the river Ems pertaining to it. The same nunnery received a grant from Count Everhard of Mark (1287) of two fish-ponds in Ibbenbüren.[354]

Mariengarten (G; Erfurt) bought up a fishery as well as an orchard in Wendehausen,[355] whilst Neukloster (G) was given the right to take forty eels from a lake in Plawe.[356] Duke Otto of the Slavs and Demmin (1301) confirmed all the properties of Ivenack (G), including 'all the islands between Ivenack and Bosepol and the adjacent fisheries'.[357] Himmelspforten (G, 1302) acquired the whole of the fish-ponds at Zum Spiche in Himmelstadt, which it had only partly owned before.[358] Zehdenick (G) had a 'fish-master' to oversee the fishing in its lakes.[359]

Riverine fisheries were owned by Lilienthal: 'Gravenware' and 'Seware' in the Elbe in Hamburg,[360] whilst Count Otto II of Ravensberg with his wife gave the new foundation at Bersenbrück (G; 1242) 'the fishery in our lordship in Ems, to have it without perturbation'.[361] Very early, Ichtershausen (G; 1157) received a fishery in the river Gera 'between Rudisleben and the bridge of Ichtershausen'.[362] The nuns of Rottenmünster (G) had by 1328 fishing rights in the river Neckar nearby, and a century later were on record of enjoying pittances of carp caught by local boat men.[363]

The newly installed nuns at San Clemente, Seville (Sp; 1284) received by royal command the fishing canals in the marshland around Trebujena, on condition that the fishers of Seville could also freely fish there.[364] Later, in 1314, they were in contention with local lay-folk over the possession of the canals of Tarfia with their fishing potential; two decades later their rightful possession was confirmed. In 1347, in granting lay-folk permission to fish in the canals, the convent imposed a number of conditions, including the duty of maintaining the canals and the fishing tackle, of rendering half of their catch to the convent, and likewise half of any profits from the sale of fish in Lebrija.[365]

In Poland the nuns of Szczecin, fishing in the Oder, were not allowed until 1280 to use seine nets, but their boats also caught herrings near Baltic coast, where they were free fom tolls for their 'boats and goods, brothers and servants'.[366] The fishermen of Koszalin, were allowed to fish in local lakes owned by the bishop of Camin, using small nets called 'stokenettes', and especially for herrings in the adjacent Baltic with one net.[367] The nuns of Wolin were privileged – they had three 'great nets' in their freshwater fisheries.[368]

Żarnowiec was another boat-owning fishing house,[369] to which nunnery Duke Bogislaw IV of Pomerania (1291) gave 'the right of fishing in the river leading to the sea, and in the sea with one boat freely to take herrings or sturgeon [rumbos] or other fish'.[370] Sonnenkamp (G) also enjoyed fishing rights in the Baltic, as at Malpersdorf and Braunshaupten,[371] but like many other religious houses profited from its situation on the post-glacial North European plain with its numerous lakes. It had four lakes at one vill, Plowe, where it caught eels in abundance.[372]

The beaver was a valuable and protected animal, and in the thirteenth century was particularly sought after in Poland in the middle and upper reaches of the rivers Warta and Vistula, and their tributaries. Owinska nunnery had the right to hunt and take beavers in the Warta;[373] Trzebnitz also had the monopoly of beaver trapping on its local waters, and the skins were probably sold in the local towns.[374] Przemysla II, duke of Greater Poland (1292), granted the newly-founded Ołobok convent part of 'the water of Prosna with the beavers, for the work of the vestments of the monastery', in addition to a gift of ten vills and their men.[375]

As for annual gifts of fish (see also Chapter 2), Count Hugh of Chaumont (1207) gave the nuns of Gomerfontaine (F) at its foundation a grant of one-tenth of the eels of his local fishponds at Gomerfontaine and at Lattainville.[376] Countess Matilda of Boulogne (1252) granted the nuns of Gomerfontaine 500 herrings yearly, and in 1293 they received fishing rights on the local river.[377]

Jean, countess of Flanders and Hainaut (1224), granted Aywières (B) an annual gift of four thousand dried herrings each St Andrew's

The Economy

Day (just in time for the Advent diet!) from Mardyck, near Dunkirk. With her husband, Count Fernand, she gave from 1228 a grant to Marquette (F) each St Martin's Day (11 November) of a rent of five thousand eels taken from their eel-traps between Bergues and Dunkirk, and one load of herrings (equivalent to 10,000 herrings).[378]

Twelve cartloads of fish formed part of the annual grant of food given to the nuns of Seligenthal (G; 1255) by Countess Kunigund of Grunenpach,[379] whilst Vitslaz II, prince of Rügen (1265) granted one *last* annually to Sonnencamp (G) of herrings in his city of Stralsund.[380] Gudhem (Sw) had the duty of rendering yearly thirty salmon to its king, in commutation of its obligation to quarter royal troops, whilst the nuns of Nonneseter (N) had a share in the salmon fishery of Døvil on the river Drammen, as well as on the river Os near Lyse.[381]

WOODLAND, AND TIMBER

As for all medieval communities the access to timber by nunneries was vital: for the construction of buildings of all kinds, vehicles and agricultural equipment, as well as for fuel. Further, woodland and forest provided pannage for pigs. Alfonso VIII (1187) hinted at these varied usages when he stipulated that the nuns of Las Huelgas (Sp) 'may cut wood, beams, and other building materials for the needs of construction of the monastery, its conventual buildings, and its granges in all woods and places where those materials are cut for purposes of the king's construction'.[382]

Countess Isabel of Chartres (1247) was generous in her will towards the nuns of Lieu-Notre-Dame-lez-Romorantin (F; 1247), but in granting them forest land retained for herself a portion of woodland delineated by stakes. In Brioud wood its nuns could take dead wood and branches for fuel, and green wood for construction purposes. In Romorantin wood they might pasture one hundred pigs.[383] The nuns of Val-des-Vignes had the right 'to gather daily a two-horse cartload of dry wood for heating and cooking' from the woods of Boccicaut.[384]' A neigbouring landowner gave to Marienborn (Hesse; 1283) a significant grant of land, in return for 'twenty-five loads of timber each year to burn'.[385]

St Louis (1245) gave Maubuisson (F) the right to pasture three hundred pigs in the forests of Resty and of Guise. It was an abbey where forest rights were significant, not only by other royal grants but also by purchase by the nuns themselves, paying in one instance to increase its forest holding at Bonfosse in 1250, no less than six hundred French pounds.[386] St Louis in 1246, before his departure on crusade, granted the nuns of Voisins a daily wagon load of dead timber from the royal forest.[387]

The building accounts of 1237 for Maubuisson show the importance of constructional timber: wood was bought for the rafters and roof beams of the dorter and the chapel, no less than 44,000 flooring boards were employed, as well as 1,000 panels of beech wood.[388] The nunnery of Le Lys (F) was fortunate in this respect by a grant from Louis IX in 1248 of two hundred *arpents* of wood in the royal forest of Byers. The section had been marked for 'perpetual ownership for the nuns to do whatever they want', such as taking timber 'for constructing and repairing buildings within the enclosure of the abbey, and at its granges outside the abbey and its two mills'.[389]

The nuns of Sczcecin (P) in 1280–1 were given by Bogislaw IV, duke of Pomerania, the right to take timber in the marsh by the river Oder and in the thickets close to Ukermunde, as well as wood elsewhere' for consummation, the repair of buildings, and the use of the church'.[390]

Establishing nuns at Salzinnes (B; Val-Saint-Georges), Count Philip I of Namur (1196, 1218), gave eighteen *bonniers* of local woodland to the convent: in the first grant adding the right to take 'dead wood' at Salzinnes, and in the second allowing the woodland to be converted into arable or pasture.[391] Countess Marie of Flanders (1202/303) gave its nuns land and woodland at Mont-Sainte-Geniève so that they might build a grange there.[392] The nuns of Szczecin (Pl), founded around 1243, were forty years later in receipt of grants of timber for the completion and maintenance of the convent.[393]

A wood at Krahn-berge granted by the count of Schwarzburg was amongst the initial gifts made to Gotha (G; 1263), whilst two years later the count of Thuringia gave it the wood of Gross-berlach.[394] Bishop Godfrey of Cambrai (1230/31) made gifts of forest land to newly-founded Zwyveke (B), but later (1245) it was in a position to buy for 157 pounds from Robert, advocate of Arras, a wood called La Warande, encompassing eight *bonniers* and three hundred *verges*.[395]

The Economy

Anrode (G; 1288) bought a wood at Ammern called Schern.[396] Amongst other purchases were those by Kapellendorf (G; 1272) which bought for eighty marks 200 *acker* of the wood called Bivank/Bivanch, and added to this a further 200 *acker* for 55 marks in 1288.[397] Countess Jean of Flanders gave Epinlieu (B; 1226) six *bonniers* of land and wood at Ammewinsart 'in perpetuity and free from all charge',[398] whilst Margaret, countess of Flanders, confirmed the gift by the lord of Sens to Épinlieu (1246) of thirty-six *bonniers* of 'great wood' situated between Herchies and Chièrres.[399]

Count Lothar gave Hoven (Marienborn, Westphalia; 1212) the right to cut coppice wood in the woods of Hizbrucht.[400] Empress Matilda gave Bondeville (F) thirty acres of woodland in the forest of Roumare.[401] Ludwig IV, Landgrave of Thuringia, made a substantial grant to Ichtershausen (G; 1221) of one hundred *Jock Acker* in the wood by the river Godeniz stretching up to the mountain called Bolschele.[402] These are but a few of many examples.

WILLOWS/PEAT MOSS

Willows could be important in the making of baskets, fences, fish traps and furniture, as well as in the preparation of drugs, and the attraction of bees. Himmelspforten (G; 1232) was granted a willow-bed by Fulda abbey,[403] whilst Aderslebel (G; 1275) bought for three marks a willow bed between Gundesleves and Adesleve.[404] Beuren (G), in 1289, bought up properties which included willow beds, paying twelve marks for each holding,[405]

Archbishop Eric of Magdeburg leased to Beuditz (G, 1289) for four marks yearly an island 'beyond Sala' and sited opposite the nunnery, with its willows 'standing and growing', as well as a mill there. It received further grants of willow beds in 1315.[406] Bonneweg (L, 1296) had access to willows at Livingen in Luxembourg.[407] In 1266 the count of Kevenberg restored to Ichtershausen (G) fishing and willow rights, which presumably had been misappropriated.[408]

An early grant of peat moss at Markle and Wyden was made to the nuns of Haddington (S).[409]

The Early Cistercian Nuns, 1098–1350

SALT EXTRACTION

Salt was a much sought-after commodity in the Middle Ages. Primarily employed in preserving food, especially meat, to be eaten over the winter months, it also enhanced the taste of food, was vital to health, and might be employed in the tanning of leather, the curing of skins, the making of cheese, and the packing of fish in transit.

Often hard to come by, it was an important commodity in trade. Rock salt was rarely quarried or mined, but salt was chiefly obtained by the evaporation of sea water trapped at high tide in salt pans (partly by the natural air, partly by artificial heat), or of naturally occurring brine in springs and underground water – usually in Triassic strata, using boilers of one kind or another.[410]

The Order stipulated in the late-twelfth century that Cistercian houses which had salt-pans in towns might sell only enough to meet the production costs, but this restriction did not apply in the case of salt pans located near the coast.[411]

One of the major continental sources of salt was the Lüneburg salt-field, where there was a growing Cistercian presence from at least 1230 onwards. It contained two principal ducal salt-works: 'Wechpanne' and 'Gungpanne' – the latter, divided into two, formed 'Gungpanne' and 'Guncpanne'. Each was separated into sections called 'houses', probably the individual underground pits and workings, and monastic rights were spelt out very precisely in the relevant charters.[412]

Grants of salt rights in the Lüneburg salt field to Medingen (G) find constant mention in its charters from 1280 and for much of the ensuing fourteenth century. They included gifts or purchases of salt or ability to take salt in the 'houses' of Hanringe (1280), Thitmeringe (1281), Beringe (1281), Everinge (1281), Beringe (1287), Velinge (1287), Loteringe (1288), Muntzinge (1291) Erderinghe (1295) and Udinghe (1296).[413] A typical transaction was that of 1281 when Medingen purchased for thirty-four marks from Scharnebeck abbey half a 'measure' of salt in the 'house' of Beringhe in the Lüneburg salt-field, 'which is called guncpanne and sited at the left side'.[414]

Other German nunneries with interests there included: Harvesthude – which enjoyed salt rights in Lüneburg partly by gift from the endowment of a daughter of Johann von Wenden (1332), and

The Economy

by purchase from a citizen of Hamburg (1333): 2½ *chor* in all;[415] Lübeck (1284) and Mariensee (1289);[416] Neukloster (Sonnenkamp; 1315, 1328): rights in the salt pan called Wechpanne, including salt from 'the house of Eynghe' and from 'the house of Eminghe'.[417] Wienhausen ws given a salt-pan at Luneburg by Otto das Kind, nephew of Herzog Otto des Kindes.[418] Salt production and the associated trade, contributed to the prosperity of Frankenhausen nunnery.[419]

In the salt-field of Halle, Glaucha (Marienkammer) was favoured by the archbishop and chapter of Magdeburg; the former granting the nunnery (in 1308) twenty *sartagines* of salt there;[420] the latter, taking into account problems being suffered by the nuns, sold them :for 150 marks of silver eight *sartagines* in the salt spring called Ducischeborn, together with other properties and rights.[421]

The nuns of Bergen (G; 1267) were given an annual grant of one *last* of salt from a salt-house next to Marlow demised to a citizen of Rostock,[422] and (in 1289) another annual *last* from Sulta-iuxta-Marlow.[423] The nuns were able, by 1289, to demise part of their salt interests.[424] The nuns of Rühn (G; 1289), obtaining salt from 'Salta', sold it on to the abbey at Dargun further east.[425] In 1307 Wormeln bought up for three marks salt interests at Salzkotten.[426]

Cyriacus Kalf gave to St Agnes, Magdeburg (G; 1334/37), salt rights at Elmen (sixteen kilometres from that city) as both his sisters and two daughters were nuns there: a salt-pan and an eighth part of another in the 'new spring' at Elmen.[427] In France, L'Étanche had access to salt at Vic by gift of the duke of Lorraine, with free passage bringing the salt to the nunnery.[428] Benningshausen (G; 1325) received a rent arising from a salt-house at Westerenkoten.[429]

In Poland, Count Boleslas V of Sandomierz (in 1263) granted the convent of Ołobok salt rights in Bochna, his daughter was a nun of the house.[430] Trebnitz (1214) received a tax free salt plant at Kolobrzeg on the Baltic coast, for the production of salt which was then transported to the convent free of toll, presumably on the river Oder.[431] Bishop Hermann of Kamień (1267) permitted the nuns of Żarnowiec (Pl) to bring in yearly one ship laden with salt for the convent.[432]

In Spain, Alfonso VIII early gave to Las Hulegas, 'a salt works at Atiencia that should produce a cartload of salt to be taken each day for the monastery; if those works do not provide sufficient salt, the deficiency should be made up from my other saltworks at

Atencia'.[433] Ferdinand III (1228) granted Las Huelgas one hundred measures of salt from his salt-pans at Añana, fifty for the abbey and fifty for the hospital;[434] four years later it received a annual further grant of twenty *kaficios* of salt as a rent in kind from Atienza, and yet further gifts were to follow.[435] Alfonso X (1266) granted the nuns of St Clement (then at Cordoba) 'all the salt necessary for their upkeep'.[436] In the Lincolnshire Fenland of England nunneries with salt interests included Stamford (late 12th C).[437]

METALLURGY

As for metallurgy, Tišnov nunnery (Cz) was early granted the tithes of the silver and other metals mined in the hills near Zuberstein,[438] whilst King Adolf (1296) granted Grimma (G) the tenth of metals mined in hill region of Bergwerkzehten in Meissen.[439] Duke Swantopolk, in 1257, gave the right to the nuns of Żarnowiec (Pl), to search for minerals, 'under the earth or above the earth', mentioning gold, silver, iron, lead, and salt.[440]

TRADE

Nunneries might sell some of the produce their *conversi* and servants raised, perhaps aided by the possession of town houses, freedom of tolls in passage, and a visible presence at markets and fairs. The archbishop of Mainz (1196) freed the nuns of Ichtershausen from tolls on their goods going to and from the market in Erfurt.[441] King Rudolph I of Germany in 1281 confirmed the grant of King Henry VII to the nuns of Billigheim (G) of freedom of taxes and tolls on their goods in Heilbronn, suggesting that its *hof* there had a trading aspect.[442]

In England Catesby was one of the wealthier nunneries, and had from the mid-thirteenth century royal licence to hold a weekly Monday market within their manor of Catesby, and a three days' fair over the festival of St Edward the Confessor; the influence of Margaret Rich, the prioress, daughter of the archbishop of Canterbury, may be seen in these grants.[443] It was also granted, around 1247, 'free entry and exit' at the local Warwick Market by Countess Margaret of Warwick.[444]

The Economy

Bival (F; 1151/54) was early granted by the Empress Matilda freedom from all tolls and passage throughout Normandy.[445] Gautier, lord of Avesnos (1241), gave Marquette (F; 1241) immunity from way-leave 'which ought to be paid for crossing his land'.[446] Countess Joan of Flanders, and Robert, advocate of Arras, both afforded Zwyveke (B; (1243) freedom from all tolls and exactions, and this was emphasised by Innocent IV.[447] There were many like grants (see above). In Portugal, Lorvão nunnery, in 1318, had at Almoster, 'a hostel for the poor'.[448]

The various charters assisting Cistercian trade show the possession by some convents of their own boats, the very important toll-free privileges, and the commodities carried, amongst which wine had a significant role. In northern Poland, the convent at Żarnowiec which was free of toll in Gdańsk, imported salt, fish and textiles, and sold what was surplus.[449] Its boats were also free of toll at Kolberg on the Baltic (1267).[450] The nuns of Sczcecin (1278/1280) were free of toll throughout Pomerania on their goods, and for the fish their boats brought in.[451]

In Flanders and the Low Countries several charters also enumerate goods carried. Marquette (1233) gained from Countess Jean of Flanders freedom from all tolls on the passage and handling of goods. This exemption was confirmed by Louis IX (1255);[452] Innocent IV (1245/46) confirmed the freedom from toll of Flines (F) and of Val-St-George's (B) on 'grain, wine, wool, timber, stone, and other necessaries',[453] whilst Alexander IV (1254) exempted the nuns of Aywières from taxes on imported goods, including wine, wool, iron and stone.[454]

The river Rhine was an important artery of Cistercian trade. The archbishop of Trier (1329), as adminstrator of the see of Mainz, gave Anrode freedom from toll at Bingen and Mainz and at three Rhine ports for wine, grain and other goods.[455] Ludwig IV, Emperor of the Romans (1332), exempted Lichtental 'from all tolls on one boat ascending and descending the Rhine with wine, merchandise, or other goods whatsoever'.[456]

Count Thomas I of Savoy gave Brione (It; 1198) freedom from all tolls for its persons, animals and goods.[457] Frauenroth (G; 1247) was granted freedom from toll in Henneberg, presumably in its market.[458] St Louis (1265) gave to Fontaine-Guérard (F) freedom of tolls 'by land and water of that which was necessary for the nuns'.[459] These are but a few of many examples.

URBAN PROPERTY

The possession of houses, and sometimes substantial 'courts' in towns and cities, facilitated monastic trade, where demised to tenants became a potentially substantial source of income, and might also be a convenient place of refuge when troubled caused nuns to leave a countryside convent.

Not surprisingly, given their location, Port Royal (c. 1260) possessed at least twenty-three properties in Paris, yielding it an annual return of two hundred *livres*, whilst St Antoine (c. 1300) gained some 600 *livres* in cash from more than 130 houses in Paris, most of them situated near its eastern border or in the Latin Quarter. Several were bequests by clerics, desirous of prayers for their souls; others from artisans and guild members; sometimes the donor staying in the property until his or her death.

One grant to St Antoine, by Bishop Peter of Paris in 1213, had been purchased by him for seventy French pounds.[460] Widows also favoured the nunnery with rights to urban prperty, as Girendis, who in 1261 gave a Parisian house to St Antoine, to fund a distribution of food to the poor.[461] Goion (Goujon) in southern France founded the bastide of St-Sauvy.[462]

Cologne, conveniently sited by the river Rhine, contained the town houses of eight nunneries (Benden, Bottenbroich, Burbach, Dalheim, Gevelsberg, Hoven, Roermond and Walberberg). Several owed multiple holdings in the city, the most being owned by (Marien) Benden (fifty properties) and Burbach (thirty-five).[463] Hoven early had property there: a papal privilege to its nuns in 1191 mentions 'the houses and rents you have in Cologne'.[464] Certain houses were meant for exclusive use by the nunneries, perhaps like 'the stone house' Walberberg possessed there, but Dalheim and Gevelsberg seem after a time to have sold theirs.[465]

Benden acquired properties 'of interest' (i.e: paying rent in cash or kind) by 1235, and ultimately owned at least two dozen. Its first principal house lay behind St Maurice's church, in what is now Taubengasse, but later its headquarters was to be a new house close to the river Rhine and in the cathedral, favouring its wine trade and giving greater security.[466]

Burbach, which acquired property in Cologne by 1233, owned by 1243 sales-booths in the Unter Hutmacher district of Cologne, and eventually accumulated over sixty rent-paying properties.

The Economy

These included houses in the Altermarkt, Buttermarkt, Heumarkt, Marsplatz, and Neumarkt. Its early medieval headquarters gave way in the 17th century to a substantial dwelling surrounded by a precinct wall, more centrally placed.[467]

Dalheim had by 1259 a house in the Tranksgasse, Cologne, where the nuns may have experienced difficulties around 1271. By 1293 they too possessed a house by the river Rhine, but no more is heard of Dalheim in Cologne after 1347.[468] Gevelsberg had a property in Cologne by 1247, which attracted some attention in 1271, but the nuns sold it to St Gereon abbey in 1343, the community being 'in need and depressed'.[469]

Hoven (Marieborn) also acquired around twenty-four properties in Cologne, some inherited from the Benedictines of St Thomas. The principal house lay close to the Neumarkt, and was 'sited between the stall-holders'. Another property, held by 1231 in the parish of St Columb, provided 'leibzen' for three Hoven nuns.[470]

The prinicipal house of Roermond by 1247 lay in St Maximilian Place, not far from the river Rhine, thus facilitating its wine interests. It had a gateway entrance, and consisted of two houses 'covered by one roof". Its business was handled by *conversi*, of whom Wolter was one in 1316.[471]

The nuns of Walberberg had interests in Cologne, probably by 1204 and certainly by 1231. They had over forty rent-paying properties in the city with a concentration in the St Severin quarter, not too far from the Rhine. Several houses were granted in return for the keeping of obits; one had a stable, one possessed a vineyard; one stood in theAltermarkt, another in Thurnmarkt.[472]

At least ten of Walberberg's nuns derived from the Overstolz family of Cologne, which also yielded two nuns to Burbach. Benden and Burbach each had at least two vocations from the Hardevust family of the city.[473]

Elsewhere in Germany the nuns of Marienkammer (1231) were bequeathed a *terna* and part of the hawker's storage building which lay next to the merchant's house in Halle.[474] Neuwerk (Goslar) was granted in 1246 places in the market square of Nordhausen;[475] Frauensee (1246) and Ichtershausen (1247, 1249) both had property in Erfurt;[476] Lilienthal received two houses in Hamburg in 1234, as well as holdings in Bremen (1241, 1259) close by the convent;[477] Gotha (1263–5) was given at least two properties in that city.[478]

Oberschönenfeld (1260) acquired a substantial house in Augsburg which possessed a large cauldron, and also an enclosed space in which game could be confined.[479] Rulle (1290) obtained for purchase [17 marks and 6 shillings] two houses in Redlinger Street, Osnabruck.[480] Gnadenthal (Hesse, 1304) sold rents it possessed in Frankfürt.[481]

Neuwerk had a bath-house at 'Penestical Place' in Goslar which it demised in 1275 to John Ritter, junior, for term of his life only.[482] He was obliged to pay the nuns one silver mark annually, and to maintain the building in good repair, as also the 'pans, vat, and cauldron'.[483] The 'family' of the convent, be they clerics or lay-men, were to be received there benignly, free of charge, and amicably treated. 'Out of friendship' the convent granted Ritter six wagon loads of timber annually towards the fuel needed.

Within its *gaverium* at Harlebeke (B), eighty-eight rents were received by Marquette (1245; F), six of these tenants being women. In most cases there was both a cash payment and a return in kind; the cash annual payments varied from 6s 6d. to 78s, and the kind rent was usually two capons, sometimes more, sometimes less. The rents were due at All Saints (1 November). If a tenant died, or indeed entered religion, his/her heir was to pay 'relief', in cash the equivalent of one year's rent, and double the number of capons expected annually.[484]

A confirmatory charter from the duke of Brabant in 1298 showed La Ramée to have had a house in each of seven towns: Louvain, Brussels, Antwerp, Bois-le-Duc, Tirlemont, Nivelles and Léau.[485] Voisins, by 1275, had accumulated houses and urban rents in Orléans and elsewhere to the value of 17½ pounds, together with nearly four hundred sacks of grain annually, but not all were free gifts, the nuns did spend quite a large amount in securing this income in cash and kind.[486] In 1238 Brione (It) had a house in Turin where its merchants traded;

The bishop of Würzburg (1297) granted the nuns of Himmelspforten the right to transport their goods to the town of Würzburg, to store them there, and to trade with them as they wished.[487] Later (by 1347), Himmelspforten bought for 122 'Heller' pounds three more properties in Würzburg, including a house by the gate called 'Hangerburgehr', and a house 'in which is a common kitchen'.[488]

St Martin's, Erfurt (1304), was at variance with the Cistercian nuns of Ober Weimar regarding the ownership of a property in

The Economy

Drat Street, Erfurt, to which both laid claim. Two leading citizens of Erfurt arbitrated in the dispute, which saw St Martin's yield the property to Ober Weimar in return for a payment of fifty pounds.[489] This amount paid emphasises the usefulness of town houses to the nuns. Himmelpforten (G; 1270) was granted a house in Bremen, but its purpose is unknown.[490]

Most nunneries probably held urban property on a greater or a lesser scale, as in Spain, where the trade of Carrizo (1199) was assisted by the ownership of a ware-house in the city of Léon,[491] whilst the nuns of St Clement in Cordoba (1272) bought a house with a corn loft in that ciy for 140 *maravedies*, not long before they migrated to Seville.[492] In England, enquiries were held in 1312 and 1352 as to the potential damage done to the king (because of reduced taxes perhaps) if three messuages in the city of York were granted to Appleton.[493]

In Poland, Szczecin held one hundred 'mansos' in that city;[494] whilst Koszalin (1281) was granted six 'mansos' in 'the Castle Field by Koszalin'.[495] In Scotland, Coldstream had annual rents from at least six properties situated at Crossgate, Soutergate and Uddingate and 'in the street of the shoemakers'. in the border town of Berwick-upon-Tweed; 'twenty shillings of silver' was a common payment expected.[496]

In France, Louis IX when confirming the possessions of Maubuisson requested that the nuns limited their ownership of houses to one or two in each village and town, possibly because of resentment from the local populace.[497] A fourteenth-century doorway at its principal house in Paris has the arms of the abbey sculpted on the lintel.[498] Flines (1288) had 'a house of refuge' in Douai which became an important trading asset. The property was exempted from any duties on its vehicles and boats carrying its goods, as were any of its men coming to or going from Douai for selling or buying in the name of the nuns.[499]

By 1300 Clairmarais drew up a rental list detailing its seventy separate urban properties.[500] L'Eau (1362) sought leave to construct a chapel in its house by the bridge of Pontceau at Chartres.[501] In Belgium, a detailed listing of the properties of Salzinnes, made around 1305, shows that nunnery to have had some thirty holdings or rents in neighbouring Namur.[502]

APPROPRIATED CHURCHES, AND TITHES

The possession of churches, and thereby the right to the greater or rectorial tithes and to appoint the parish priest, could be a lucrative source of goods and income. It was the mainstay of some of the less well-endowed convents, and it was not unusual for churches and tithes to be granted to a nunnery on account of its poverty.

Between 1306 and 1309 Börstel (G) received three churches, the bishop of Osnabruck referring to 'the evident necessity and need' of the nuns'.[503] The Grand Master of the Teutonic Knights took pity in 1345 on the poor nuns of Toruň (Pl), granting them a school and a church with its tithes.[504] In 1360, Gudhem (Sw) was granted the parish church of Gudhem, as well as those of Ugglum and Tunhem, because these churches were said to be too poor to be able to support their own priests.[505]

The number of churches a convent might hold varied considerably; some were fortunate as La Cambre (B) with its nineteen benefices.[506] In Germany several convents were well provided for, as Stepenitz (Marienfliess): the patronage of ten mother churches and four daughter churches, and Beuren with ten churches.

Hedersleben, however, had but two churches and Glaucha but some nunneries, like Keldholme (E), had none at all.[507] In Czechoslovakia, Alexander IV (1255) confirmed Porta Coeli (Cz) in its patronage of three churches granted them by King Wenceslas, including St Peter's, Brno. Its possession of the latter was to be challenged but upheld.[508] In total, Porta Coeli held ten churches, as well as thirty villages.[509] Possession of a church meant the acquisition of it greater tithes, and the right of appointing the parish priest. In 1332 Porta Coeli presented Hermann, a scholar and perhaps versed in medicine, to be provost of St Peter's, Brno, following the death of Sebastian, the previous provost.[510]

Oslavany (Cz; 1261) held St James's church in Brno, there,[511] but later the respective limits and rights of the two churches were subject to arbitration.[512] Another of Oslavany's ten churches was that of 'All Saints, without the gate of Brno'.[513] In 1289 Ernest of Rudikow restored to Oslavany the patronage of the church of Rudikow, which seemingly he had wrongly appropriated.[514] Porta Coeli, in 1248, had been engaged in a tithe dispute with the Teutonic Knights of Austerlitz.[515]

The Economy

Bishop Hermann of Camiń promised in 1278 the church of Koszalin (P) to the Cistercian nuns of that place, as and when the then rector died. In passing he noted that (as in all Cistercian houses) the 'rule of Blessed Benedict' was followed.[516]

In southern France, Nonenque had possession of four parishes, whereas the male abbey of Silvanès had only one.[517] In Portugal, Lorvão nunnery had the patronage of at least five churches: Cantanhede (St Peter), Couto de Tio, Covilhã (St Andrew), Rio de Asnos, and Treixeda,[518]

In England, Nun Appleton possessed four, if not five churches; that at Coddenham in Suffolk was given by Eustace de Mersc for the nuns of Appleton to found a convent there, but so far as is known that was never done.[519] Marham acquired the advowson and/or the appropriation of five churches, but its income remained rather limited: Carleton St Peter, 1274; Stow Bedon, 1290; Hackford, 1327; Rockland St Peter, 1349; Rockland All Saints, 1350.[520] Lavington church had early been granted to Stixwould (Lincs.) by one Ralf fitzGilbert, but around 1208 his grandson, Hugh fitzRalf, sought unsuccessfully at law to reclaim it.[521] Alice Constable, daughter of the founder of Legbourne, also failed to obtain the return to herself of the advowson of Saltfleetby church.[522]

The importance attached to the acquisition of tithes, whether by the patronage of churches or partial tithes elsewhere was shown by the contrary claims in regard of such possession, and by the means used to achieve them. A number of tithes were purchased, as by Rulle (G; 1233) which paid twenty-eight marks for tithes arising from just four properties in Ludinchausen,[523] whilst Lilienthal (G; 1277) paid no less than 150 Bremen marks for certain tithes.[524] Under the leadership of its new provost, John, Bersenbrück negotiated for and bought up tithes, paying for instance in 1288 twenty-one marks for the commutation of tithes in Dersburg.[525]

The small convent in Wales at Llanllugan, located in a pastoral setting, received tithes of oatmeal, wool and lambs.[526]

Medingen (G; 1333) was able to purchase the tithes of Bardowick, and the patronage of the church there, because the Benedictine nuns of Kemnade found it difficult to collect the tithes on account of 'the distance and dangers of the journey'.[527] Conversely, Archbishop Gerhard II of Bremen when founding Lilienthal (1231) awarded its nuns certain tithes in Norderland; there was difficulty for the convent in obtaining these, so an agreement was reached in 1278 whereby Norden abbey accepted the tithes (four urns of butter and four cheeses) paying the sisters of Lilienthal yearly eighteen new shillings.[528]

The ownership of a church did involve the nunnery concerned with the duty of keeping its chancel in good repair. In a move not entirely approved of locally, Cotham (E; *c.* 1280) cut ash trees in the churchyard of its church at Cuxwold to repair its chancel, whilst the parishioners did the same in order to restore the nave.[529]

The other, and principal duty, was to appoint a parish priest, and make provision for his maintenance. In this respect, the bishop of Naumburg enjoined the nuns of Langendorf (G; 1281) to present to the parish of Upper Greislau a priest of good character and faithful to his vocation, who would be completely devoted to the cure of souls.[530] The provost of the nuns of Börstel (G) had to provide the priest's stipend for its three parishes: at Menslage, thirty shillings; at Berge, only eighteen shillings, but at Herzlake, no less than four pounds yearly, a princely sum in those days.[531]

Bishop Conrad of Osnabruck (1272) required the nuns of Gravenhorst to pay the local parish priest three marks yearly: eighteen shillings in the octave of the Epiphany and eighteen shillings in the octave of Pentecost, and that without delay.[532] Also that year Gravenhorst made a payment of one hundred marks to the diocese of Osnabruck for parochial lands and rights lost in the years since its foundation in 1256.[533] Granted the churches of Teistungenberg and Wehnde (1294), the archbishop of Mainz ordered that the nuns of Teistungenberg were to give the vicars instituted 'a proper portion of the fruits'.[534]

When the nuns of Rulle (G; 1247) were in controversy with the priest of Rulle, twelve arbitrators, both clerical and lay, decided that the priest was to receive two houses, one in Rulle, one in Espelo, and every year: fourteen measures of grain from the nuns' granary: six being of wheat, four of barley and four of oats; he was to be able to maintain a horse, and to receive a stipend of twenty shillings, plus one mark on the feast of St Thomas (21 December) – just in time for Christmas![535]

The parish priest of Walbertsweiler, of the patronage of Wald (1318), was entitled to a daily allowance from the nunnery of a half-measure of local wine, two loaves of white bread and two of rye bread. He also received regular clothing (Chapter 3), the lesser tithes, Mass and mortuary fees, and other profits of the parish.[536]

The Economy

Wheresoever sited, the establishment of a Cistercian nunnery – given its tithe-free privileges on lands they brought into cultivation, might affect the income of the local clergy. It was to compensate the parish priest of Löningen for this, that the nuns of Börstel, settling at their first site of Menslage, were required to pay him five shillings annually and fixed amounts of malt, rye and barley 'by the measure of that place'.[537]

When, about 1227, the nuns of Battant commenced the building of their new church, the archbishop of Besançon intervened to make sure that the rights of the nearby collegiate church of St Mary Magdalene were not affected.[538] When the nuns of Flines (1234) first settled at Orchies, they were required to pay thirty-three shillings, four pence, to the parish priest each Christmas, on account of diminution of his income by their coming.[539] When, in 1237, the nunnery of L'Amour-Dieu was incorporated the chapter of Soissons drew up a deed to preserve the parochial rights.[540]

6

Epilogue: The Fourteenth Century

So far as Cistercian nuns were concerned, the fourteenth century was to involve at least some of their convents in considerable change. Isolated problems in the keeping of the conventual life, the failings of perhaps a minority of the religious, proclamations of poverty, and a growing financial independence of some sisters, were all factors which perhaps made the female sector of the Order somewhat different from its inception two centuries before.

There is no evidence, however, of any decline in the numbers of religious, nor of any widespread lack of spiritual formation and development. What did grievously affect the life of some nunneries were the armed conflicts in various parts of the continent, especially the ravages occasioned by the Hundred Years War (1337–1453). Numerous communities had to migrate to the safety of their town house, or set up completely anew in a neighbouring town or city. In the decade of the 1330s the nuns of Valldemaria (Sp) knew problems with some of it neighbours and the local clergy issued a statement designed at protecting them.[1]

Something of the problems emerge from the statutes of the annual General Chapter, and from the visitation charters extant for some English convents. The Chapter (1314) heard that many individual chambers were being erected in convents, which obviously affected the keeping of the common life. It ordered that no new chambers were to be constructed, and if it was possible all such existing chambers were to be destroyed.[2]

The Chapter (1320) further referred to the 'many excesses and disobediences' of the nuns, especially by breaking enclosure and going out. It stipulated those nuns who acted in these ways were to be imprisoned.[3] As for enclosure, Archbishop Melton of York, holding a visitation at Nun Appleton (E; 1318), straitly enjoined that its nuns were not to leave their monastery by reason of any vows of pilgrimage which any of them might have taken. If any had taken such vows, then such a one was to say as many psalters as it would have taken days to perform the pilgrimage, so rashly vowed.[4] Archbishop Greenfield, on visitation at Rosedale and Sinningthwaite in 1315, simply said that leave granted for nuns to be absent should not exceed fifteen days.[5]

The Chapter (1321) later noted that some nuns like to go their own way; it commanded that those who persisted were to have their habits removed.[6] That year, the abbot of Loroux coming to Chapter reported that the nuns of Bonlieu (Maine, F) had rejected his authority, and refused to receive the appointed confessor.[7] By 1334 there appears to have been a break-down of discipline at Anrode, Thuringia, and an abandonment there of the habit.[8]

In a few nunneries matters were to worsen: it was reported at the General Chapter in 1355 that in some convents very unseemly spectacles took place on the feast of the Holy Innocents (28 December), and at other festivals. Father abbots were told to be vigilant in this matter, whilst any nuns who so persisted were to be publicly excommunicated.[9] Two nuns of Whiston (E; 1307) were professed despite stipulating that they would not refrain from eating meat.[10]

In 1340 the nuns of Gudhem (Sw) moved site without the permission of the father-abbot of Varnhem; the abbot of Cîteaux appointed the abbots of Alvastra and Varnhem to investigate. If the reasons for the move were valid no action was necessary, but the nuns were to be reminded to acknowledge the rights of the father-abbot and to warn them of the consequences of placing themselves under the jurisdiction of the local bishop. The abbot of Julita complained in 1356 that the nuns of Sko (Sw) did not obey him, an episcopal visitation was ordered by the Holy See, and the outcome is not known.[11]

YORKSHIRE VISITATION CHARTERS

In the English diocese of York the duty of visitation lay firmly in the hands of the archbishops or their delegates, and their injunctions also show isolated cases of nuns 'going their own way'. At Nun Appleton (1308) the archbishop directed that Maud de Bossall be sent away to Basedale nunnery as she had for many years been disobedient, setting a bad example to the other nuns. A year later she was allowed to return on his instructions, and in 1309 he ordered the re-admission of Maud de Ripon, a nun who had incurred excommunication on account of apostasy. In 1346 Archbishop William le Zouche directed that if one of Nun Appleton's nuns, Katherine de Hugate, who had retired from the house in a state of pregnancy, returned, then she was to be severely punished, but that if Margaret, another nun, returned she was not to be taken back for she had become pregnant more than once.[12] To Sinningthwaite in 1343 Archbishop Zouche wrote concerning Margaret de Fonten, a nun there, who had left the house and become pregnant, but as she had only done so once, her penance was mitigated and he directed that she was not to be locked up, but not allowed to go out of the church and cloister.[13]

At Kirklees (1306) the archbishop directed the nuns to receive back as a nun or sister or as a servant Alice Ragged, a member of the community who had wandered off long before and put off her religious habit. If Kirklees was unwilling, the archbishop would send her to another convent, but Kirklees would be responsible for the cost of her maintenance there. Nine years later she had improper sexual relations with a lay-man.[14] Another nun of Kirklees (1313), Elizabeth de Hopton, who had apostasised and 'rashly changed her habit', was given two weeks by the archbishop to return to the convent.[15] Later on, the then archbishop required Kirklees (1337) to receive back another apostate nun, Margaret de Burton, who was to 'devoutly prostrate herself before the gates', on seeking admission, and to be disciplined.[16']

Archbishop Melton, concerned about the state of affairs at Swine (1318), ordered an enquiry and consequently enjoined that all the nuns, unless lawfully prevented, should attend attend matins and the canonical hours, to be said with note. He insisted that the dormitory might be covered so that the nuns could use it without annoyance from storms, and that nuns were to sleep there not in different places. Other roofs needed repair also. The prioress was to make both old and young nuns keep to the cloister at due times, and especially the young ones who had not yet completed their novitiate. No brothers or guests were to be received within the inner door.[17]

As their numbers dwindled in England, there could be problems with a few of the lay-brethren. One of the *conversi* of Catesby, Robert of Weston, left in 1307 to live with a woman in London.[18]

Adam, a *conversus* at Rosedale (1326), knelt with tears in his eyes before its community and confessed his offences against the nuns; at his request they released him from his vows.[19] William Bomour, a *conversus* of Swine (1335), was sent to live for a time with the monks at Sawley, on account of his excesses, but Swine had to pay his costs there.[20]

PRIVATE INCOME, AND POCKET MONEY

The founding constitutions of Nun Appleton (E) reminded its nuns that they might not hold anything of their own, whether goods or money by way of contract.[21] There is plenty of evidence, however, certainly on the continent, that from the second half of the thirteenth century, at least some nuns had access to money of their own and, indeed, were in a position to administer personal property. On the anniversary of the death of Countess Beatrix of Dreux and Montfort, March 7th, each nun of Port Royal (F) received forty Paris shillings.[22]

At St Antoine (Paris) no less than thirty grants of private income were received from relatives by members of the community between 1281 and 1302. They included five *livres* each year for life to Joan, daughter of Henry, lord of Trainel, and seventy-five shillings per annum to Regine, daughter of a citizen. The gifts were often stated as being 'for her necessities', and after the recipient's death either ceased or passed to the convent.[23]

At Maubuisson (F), at an unknown date, Sister Lucia who, as sacristan had one hundred pounds for the use of the church, left ten pounds to be distributed amongst the nuns.[24] Thielmans, a citizen of Luxembourg, paid each St Stephen's Day five shillings in local currency to his sister, Margaret, a nun of Clairefontaine (B; 1323).[25] Not all the nuns of Clairfontaine were so fortunate so, some time after 1302, Abbess Gila purchased rents to be distributed to nine members of the community who did not have a private income.[26]

A priest in 1296 left six silver Brunswick marks to Neuwerk (Goslar) to be distributed on the keeping of his obit: 'half a silver Goslar mark for us in the cloister; one shilling to the provost; and to our scholars and priests two shillings in Goslar money'.[27] The question arises: if the nuns were strictly enclosed, how did they employ their money?

Epilogue: The Fourteenth Century

A nun of Beaupré (B), Ida van Idegem, had the resources to enable her to donate a rent of six shillings and four capons to her convent. After her death the money was to be used to provide an obit Mass for herself, while the rent of capons was to revert to a fellow nun Elizabeth van Geraardsbergan.[28]

Adelheid of Camenz, a nun of Marienthal (Oslavany, Cz; 1336), was able to provide from her own income financial assistance for the nunnery infirmary; 'this with the knowledge and consent of the abbess'.[29] Albert of Oberfeld granted his daughter, Kunigunde, a nun of Frauenroth (G: 1284), a yearly income of 10 shillings and a portion of corn from his property in Machtolshausen.[30]

A rent of forty shillings of Paris money arising from two houses in Courtrai, given in favour of Catherine Lours, a nun of Groeninge (B; 1315), was to be received by her for her life-time, but after her death it was to pass to the nunnery.[31] When in 1340 Gillette de Galende entered La Cour-Notre-Dame de Michery (F) her sister Marie assigned her an annual rent of 100 shillings 'out of love and great affection'.[32]

In 1326 the nuns at Sko (Sw) received one mark in the will of a noblewoman, Ingegerd, whilst Abbess Katherine was given a ring. Ingegerd's sister and daughter, both nuns in the nunnery (since 1318) received ten marks each and gifts of superior clothing. A will of 1350 provided the abbess with a carriage, complete with harness; and a rug lined with the fur of a bear; each nun received several gifts including a cape trimmed with marten and a book; whilst an eiderdown and pillow with bolster were to be given to the sick nuns.[33] When in 1341 the daughter of Saint Birgitta took the veil at Riseberga (Sw), her father gave the nunnery a village, a house and a mill, but stipulated that from the income so received his daughter was to receive seven marks annually during her life.[34]

In the will of Kristine Blaafod (1308), probably because two of its nuns were related to her, Roskilde nunnery (D) received ten marks, and the two relatives four marks each for their own use.[35] Michael van der Strate left thirteen shillings to each nun of Zwijveke (B; 1303),[36] whilst also as a result of a bequest Waterler (Harz, G; 1306) received not only fixed amounts of beer and ground wheat annually, but the abbess received a one-off payment of one shilling and each chaplain of the convent, six pence; whilst the residue was to be divided amongst the nuns.[37]

Margaret of Arras (around 1320) left to 'all the nuns of Flines (F), the children, the *conversae* and the *conversi*, each and everyone, five Paris shillings; to the two monk confessors, ten shillings each, and to the clerk and all the chaplains, five shillings each'.[38] When their former provost, John of Rottorf, died, the nuns of Rinteln (Lower Saxony; 1345) were each to receive an equal annual payment from the proceeds of his properties, but a *converse* sister was only to be given half the amount a nun received.[39]

As the fourteenth century progressed, at the nunnery of Zwijeke (B) individual nuns were entrusted with the administration of income which either came with them when they had been professed or was bequeathed to them thereafter. In 1309 the convent permitted its sister, Margaret, full administration of the lands and revenues left to it by her father, Wautier Lonijs.

Much later, in 1333 when she was perhaps advancing in years, Margaret granted rents to her abbey for the keeping of the anniversary of her parents, and a pittance of wine on her father's anniversary; she accorded to the convent's wardrobe fifty shillings annually; to the sacristan, twenty shillings; to 'the ladies of the infirmary', ten shillings for buying cherries; and for annual charity at the gate, ten shillings.[40]

Another nun of Zwijveke, Elizabeth van der Heiden (1335), was able to provide a rent of thirty-three Paris shillings annually to be used by the cellarer to provide each nun in the refectory with an egg, 'each day from Rogation-tide until Shrove Tuesday' – at least forty weeks of the year. This was in addition to the two eggs each nun received by custom. Elizabeth also provided for each nun to receive annually a pair of stockings, and – perhaps because of advancing years – a pittance of wine on her anniversary and those of her parents. Because of this largess, the abbess granted Sister Elizabeth, for the rest of her life the profit of the rent.[41]

Two nuns of Zwyveke (1337) were able likewise to provide money for the cellarer, and of their bounty each nun was to receive on the Sunday before Lent ('the Sunday of the great carnival'), a 'quarteron' to be used during Lent. Further, the abbess allowed these two nuns to appropriate during their life-time the revenues they had received.[42] Lastly, in 1343, another nun of Zwyveke, administered rents left to her nunnery by her deceased mother, sister and brother. She made provision for their obits, but also for the nuns to receive fish on all the Sundays of Lent, as well as white

Epilogue: The Fourteenth Century

bread on Good Friday. She assigned fifty shillings to be distributed amongst the nuns of the feast of St Catherine, and for a 'a good light' to burn during the divine office and certain Masses.[43]

In Portugal in 1338 Maria Peres, a nun of Arouca, sold to her subprioress, Guiomar Mendes, for 145 pounds, all her property in Burgos; perhaps on admission, but certainly benefiting her convent.[44] Earlier, in 1280, a nun of Arouca, had been able to issue a charter of direction in family affairs, with the approval of her abbess.[45] In 1320, another nun of Arouca, Berengária Fernandes, with her sister, Maria Fernades, a nun of Corvão, was in dispute with their brother, Martins, regarding their family farm at Vila Nova.[46]

Enclosure therefore did not always mean being completely cut off from worldly affairs: Darguslawa, cantrix of Bergen nunnery (G; 1328), gave her assent to a family territorial agreement with one Ludolf Gerst from which she was to receive an annual payment of four marks. The first witness to the concord was 'our provisor, John of Hagen, of the Cistercian Order'.[47] A nun of Arouca, Mary Michael, was able to demise part of a house she owned in Sanctarena to lay tenants; on her death the property was to pass to the convent.[48]

A *conversa* there, Mary Colaça (1289), with the agreement of her abbess and community, was similarly able to demise a property she owned in Molares to layfolk for an annual monetary rent, but on her death it was to pass to her nunnery.[49] When, in 1304, Bishop Conrad of Ratisbon, granted the wood of Koenigsholz to Seligenthal (G), in exchange for other properties, it was at the request not only of the abbess, but also 'especially' of Sister Elizabeth, one of the nuns and formerly one of the household of the dukes of Bavaria.[50]

POVERTY

Despite the thirteenth century benefactions accorded it by the counts of Tecklenberg and Ravensberg, the nuns of Gravenhorst (G) were described in 1317 as being 'in urgent necessity and vehement poverty', and sited 'in the middle of a perverse people who oppressed them'.[51] The nuns of the neighbouring convents of Benninghausen and Welver complained in 1301 of 'necessity and hunger'.[52] Between 1306 and 1309, Börstel (G) received three churches, the bishop of Osnabrück referring to 'the evident necessity and need' of the nuns'.⁵³ Between 1345 and 1348 three parish churches, Malsch, Pforzheim and Eberstein, were 'united and incorporated' with Lichtenthal (G), in order to support the convent. It had eighty nuns, but was 'daily troubled by the hospitality expected by nobles and others'.⁵⁴

The very limited resources of Ellerton in Yorkshire were not helped when in 1347 Scottish troops entered Swaledale, and carried away seven of the nunnery's charters.⁵⁵ Clement V (1309–10) had occasion to request senior clerics to 're-establish the free enjoyment of its goods' by Clairefontaine (B); a few years later the abbot of Cîteaux foresaw the need to disperse its nuns if this could not be done.⁵⁶ By 1362 the nunnery at Groeninge (B) was in a state of ruin, and so Count Louis de Mal authorised the abbess to collect alms throughout Flanders for its reconstruction.⁵⁷

Several of the English nunneries had occasion to complain in times of financial stringency. During a time of severe famine in England, Wintney (1316) was in a bad way economically, and some of the nuns were dispersed because no proper provision could be made for their food.⁵⁸ Whilst petitioning their diocesan bishop for authority to elect a new prioress, the nuns of Whistones (1308) mentioned 'the smallness of their posssessions, which compelled them formerly to beg'.

A bishop of Worcester (1319) referred to the 'poor religious' in his diocese, amongst them the Cistercian nuns of Cook Hill and Pinley, and sought their exemption from payment of a tenth towards a collection for the Holy Land.⁵⁹ Agnes of Swystane, a nun of Kirkleees, was dwelling in 1323 at Hampole nunnery 'for the relief of her house'.⁶⁰

To relieve its poverty, the bishops of Lincoln granted indulgences in 1300 and 1319 to those who came to the help of the nuns of Sewardsley, and in 1366 permitted them to beg for alms. The poverty of the house may have accounted for one nun, Joan de Fynemore, leaving it in 1300 and abandoning the religious life and her habit.⁶¹ The nuns of Fosse in Lincolnshire claimed in 1341 that their endowment was so slender that they could not support themselves without the alms of the faithful.⁶² The endowment of Heynings it was claimed in 1348 was very meagre on account of the death of its founder, Rayner de Evermue, before its completion; in 1331 the nuns were referred to as 'impoverished by divers misfortunes'.⁶³

Epilogue: The Fourteenth Century

The reasons adduced by Bishop Adam of Worcester (1331) when granting the nuns of Cook Hill (E) the church of Bishampton are worth spelling out in detail. The bishop wrote that he 'would be held guilty were he to fail to provide for those devoted to the worship of God, so that poverty forced them to desert their monasteries and to engage in secular activities for the support of their everyday life. He understands that they are oppressed by such a burden of poverty because of the sterility of their lands, the destruction of woods, the murrain of animals, and the withdrawal of alms which they were wont to receive from certain great men, as well as other hazards of the times'.[64]

THE EFFECTS OF CONFLICT: THE MIGRATION TO THE TOWNS

The Hundred Years' War, more local conflicts and other factors led to the General Chapter (1348) noting that a number of nunneries were gravely affected by the 'desolation and destruction of the times', and it requested the commissaries of the Chapter to do what they could to help and assist them.[65] Many nunneries sought an urban location for protection, but some were closed down and their site and property united to a male house.

The archbishop of Mainz had restricted in 1303 the number of nuns at Teistungenburg (G) to a maximum of forty, as the convent had been subject to 'plunder, pillage and fire by bad men and could no longer maintain sixty nuns as formerly'.[66] The small nunnery at Gravenhorst (G) was pillaged around 1317 during one of the 'quarrels of Tecklenburg', John II subsequently granting its nuns a bull of protection.[67]

War between Flemings and the Dutch ravaged the monastery of Bethlehem at Damme, so that in 1327 Count William IV of Holland and Zeeland, intervened to fix the total numbers there as not to exceed thirty in all, including nuns, male *conversi* and pupils.[68] Helfta nunnery (G) had been pillaged in 1284 by the troops of Gerard of Mansfeld, and was later burnt in 1342 by the forces of Albert of Brunswick. The nuns then founded New-Helfta, close to the walls of Eisleben.[69]

In Scotland, Haddington was badly burnt in 1356 during conflict between English and Scottish forces, and two years later was threatened by a disastrous flood, but it recovered to have twenty-four nuns in 1461.⁷⁰ In Wales, the small nunnery of Llanllŷr (1284) received financial compensation for damage incurred during the Edwardian Conquest of the Principality.⁷¹

During the Hundred Years War at Fervaques (F; 1339) English troops quartered themselves at the nunnery.⁷² All the nuns of Mollégès (1346) removed to live in the former hospital of Notre-Dame-de-Beaulieu, granted to their mother-house, Saint Pons, a century before.⁷³ By 1370 the buildings of Beaulieu (Ariège) had been burnt, the nuns dispersed to other convents, and the goods given in part to Boulbonne.⁷⁴ The Abbaye-dux-Bois, Oise, was burnt by the English in 1370, but the nuns did not immediately move,⁷⁵ whilst the abbess and some of the nuns of St Antoine, Paris, found themselves in prison.⁷⁶

The General Chapter thought the situation of Les Îles (F; 1399) precarious and its resources insufficient; it tried to suppress the nunnery, send the religious to other houses, and give its goods to Pontigny abbey, but the nuns resisted and the measures were never executed. Les Iles survived until the French Revolution.⁷⁷ Belfays with only two nuns left and the buildings dilapidated, transferred to Morimond in 1393, becoming a grange of that house. The two remaining nuns were given a pension allowing them to be admitted to another nunnery.⁷⁸

Voisins (1358) was burnt during the Hundred Years War, and pillaged by English troops in 1420.⁷⁹ Belmont (F) was also pillaged during the War,⁸⁰ as was Valbaion – which the General Chapter closed in 1393, ceding its possessions to Auberive.⁸¹ Benoîtevaux (Champagne) was united to Clairvaux in 1397,⁸² whilst the nuns of Les Rosiers were replaced by monks of Clairvaux in 1389.⁸³

The convent of Consolation was united to the male abbey of Élan in 1399;⁸⁴ and after devastation the convent of Saint-Jacques, Champagne-Ardenne, was suppressed in 1408 and became a grange of Jouy.⁸⁵ Montarlot, Franche-Comté, became a priory of Bellevaux in 1391.⁸⁶ Valnègre, central Pyrenees, passed to Boulbonne in 1432, as did Marenx in 1442.⁸⁷ Other nunneries destroyed or badly affected by the Hundred Years War included: Fontenelle, Pas-de-Calais;⁸⁸ Vignogoul;⁸⁹ Woestyne, Pas-de-Calais, burnt in 1328;⁹⁰ Gomerfontaine, Picardy, ruined in 1434;⁹¹ and Le-Bosquet, completely ruined and suppressed in 1413.⁹²

In northern Germany several monasteries, like Jüterbog, were badly damaged during the Thirty Years War.⁹³ In Bohemia the

Epilogue: The Fourteenth Century

prestigious nunnery of Pohled was secularised after being sacked and pillaged in 1424 by the Hussites.[94] In Moravia, hardly had the church of Porta Coeli been consecrated that it was devastated by the Tartars in 1241, and again in 1425 by the Hussites.[95] Local affrays saw the nuns of Maubuisson transfer into Paris in 1356.[96] The nuns of L'Eule (F) found it necessary to remove to Perpignan in 1362.[97]

Devastated by local wars, the nuns of Bouchet (F) in 1375 removed to a new monastery on land they owned in Bollène.[98] The nuns of Groeninghe (B) (1385), after several incursions from brigands, were moved from their rural location to just outside the walls of Courtrai 'for the protection of religious women'.[99] In Navarre, the pre-eminent abbey of Tulebras was badly damaged in wars in the fourteenth century between the kingdoms of Navarre and Castile, but it survived.[100]

Later still, for one reason or another, a number of French Cistercian convents transferred into towns and cities, like Notre-Dame-aux-Bois, Picardy, whose nuns transferred into Paris in 1564;[101] Battant moving into Besançon in 1595, and Ounans into Dôle in 1595 – where later it took in the nuns of Corcelles (1609) and Colonge (1622).[102] The first Cistercian nunnery, Tart, moved into Dijon in 1623.[103]

The nuns of Notre-Dame des Olives, took refuge in Narbonne in 1574, those of Vernaison in Valence in 1614, those of Bussière in Bourges in 1625;[104] and those of Rieunette in Carcassone in 1652.[105] In 1673 the nuns of Derses (Limousin) united with the Bernardines of Tulle, a town which also received the nuns of Coyroux.[106] The nuns of Le-Vivier, Pas-de-Calais, moved into nearby Arras in 1649, those of Épagne (1642) and of Villancourt (1652) into Abbeville,[107] and those of Montreuil into Laon in 1657.[108] The nuns of Le-Paraclet, Picardy, transferred into Amiens during the seventeenth century.[109]

The nuns of Rupertsberg, Rhineland, found a home in Cologne in 1631 after their convent had been destroyed by the Swedes.[110] Cambrón, Aragon, transferred in 1563 for reasons of security to the abbey of St Lucia, Saragossa.[111] For the like reason, the nuns of Sant Felix de Cadins, Catalonia, transferred to be close to Gerona in 1492, it having been affected during a French invasion.[112]

In Belgium, Bruges received within its walls the nuns of Spermalie ('New Jerusalem') after its devastation by the Gueux in 1577, and later those of Hemelsdaele in 1671.[113] Ghent took in the nuns of Doornzele, Oosteeklo, and of Ter Hagen in the 1580s; the latter seeking a new home on account of marine inundations.[114] The nuns of Nieuw-Mariëndael, Brabant, founded only in 1338, returned to their mother-house of Mariëndaal less than fifty years later, after its 'liquidation'.[115] In the late-sixteenth century the nuns of Perales, Spain, moved into Valladolid.[116]

CONCLUSION

Occasionally a Cistercian convent might pass into the hands of another Order, as when the nuns of La Peyrouse (Levretes; 1254) seceded to become regular canonesses. The nunnery of Rute in Spain, emerging from a hermitage in 1162, was but an ephemeral Cistercian convent, passing into the possession of monks twenty years later.[117] The nuns of Pozsony, Slovakia, incorporated in 1235, were said in 1297 to have neglected their possessions for some twenty years and often to have been absent from the convent; so King Andrew III of Hungary gave everything to sisters of the Order of St Clare.[118]

The nuns of St-Felix-de-Monceau (F; 1332) ceased to be Cistercian, 'presumably disaffected with the increasingly hostile attitude of the General Chapter to the Order's women'.[119] Not all was gloom; King John of Bohemia requested burial at Clairefontaine (B; 1340), and for his annual obit left it a yearly rent of fifty pounds.[120] Cistercian Langendorf passed to the Benedictine Order about 1385,[121] as did Chelmno, Poland, in around 1430,[122] and Żarnowiec (Pl) in 1589.[123] In the fifteenth century also, Marienfloss (1415), Lorraine, became a charter-house; its Cistercian religious moving to Freistroff.[124] Kirschgarten, founded outside the walls of Worms in 1226, passed to canons regular in 1443.[125]

Tilgenkloster (Münster), Cistercian from the time of its foundation about 1180, became Benedictine in 1468.[126] The bishop of Würzburg (1485) absorbed the nunnery of Ramsen (Ramosa) and its land into his estates; the Order protested but to no effect.[127] Ivanics, Croatia, was accepted by the Friars Minor in 1508, but for fear of the Turks they fled in 1537.[128]

There were yet to come the widespread closure of nunneries due to the Reformation, the French Revolution, and the policies of Joseph II in Austria and Germany. Few Cistercian convents escaped unscathed from their foundation down to present times, but not all

Epilogue: The Fourteenth Century

was lost. There are those nunneries which have had an unbroken Cistercian history of some eight hundred years, like Las Huelgas and Vallbona in Spain, as also Lorvão in Portugal. Other convents have known privations, as the nuns of Tisnov, Moravia, who under the Communist régime were directed to field and other labour in lay attire. Thankfully, the female monasteries of the Order are yet to be found in several regions of the modern world, not least at Holy Cross Abbey, Whitland, in my native Wales.

Notes

Notes to Chapter 1

1. *LCC* 1, *passim*.
2. Kratzke, 'North of Germany', 2005, p. 135.
3. Brewer, J. S (ed.), *Giraldus Cambrensis, Opera*, London, 1869. 4, p. 153.
4. *Statuta* 3, pp. 442–3 [1336/8].
5. *TBC*, *passim*.
6. *UKL*, p. 117 [107].
7. *PDC*, pp. 176–7 [108], *Cf.* pp. 182–3 [112].
8. Freeman, 'Ælred of Rievaulx's Pastoral Care', 2001, pp. 13–26.
9. Jamroziak, *Cistercian Order*, 2013, p. 125.
10. Berman, *Medieval Women and Monasticism*, 2002, p. 95.
11. Berman, *Cistercian Evolution*, 1999, p. 42.
12. *DSHG* 3, p. 656.
13. E. Connor, 'Las Huelgas and Tart'. In: J. A. Nichols and L. T. Shank, *Hidden Springs*, 1995, p. 40; L. Lekai, *The Cistercians*, Kent State UP, 1977, p. 347; Bouton, J. de la Croix., 'Les abbesses cisterciennes'. In: *Les Religieuses dans le cloître et dans le monde*, Acts of the International Colloquium of CERCOM; University of Saint-Etienne, 1994, p. 187; Campion, 'Cîteaux, Our Mother', 1999, pp. 488–9.
14. King, *Cîteaux and her Elder Daughters*, 1954, p. 338; *Monastic* Matrix on-line.
15. J. de la Croix Bouton, 'The Nuns of Cîteaux', 1995, pp. 14–15; G. C. Carville, 'Cistercian Nuns in Medieval Ireland'. In: Nichols and Shank, *Hidden Springs*, p. 64.
16. Peugniez, *L'Europe cistercienne*, 2012, p. 346.
17. Campion, 'Cîteaux, Our Mother', 1999, pp. 485–6.
18. France, 'Iconography of Bernard of Clairvaux', 2005, p. 2.
19. *Ibid.* p. 3.
20. Thompson, 'Problems of the Cistercian Nuns', 1978, pp. 229–30.
21. Berman, *White Nuns*, 6.
22. *Ibid.* p. 230.
23. K. Berthier, 'Notre-Dame de Tart'. In: Barrière, *Cîteaux et les femmes*, 2001, p. 123; L. Veyssière, 'Cîteaux et Tart', *Ibid.* p. 189.
24. Quoted in Berman, *White Nuns*, p. 12.
25. Ganck, 'Integration of Nuns', 1984, p. 240; Thompson, 'Problems of the Cistercian Nuns', 1978, p. 230; Venarde, *Women's Monasticism*, 1996, pp. 73–4, 84, 159–60.
26. Richard, 'L'Établissement', 1953, p. 98.
27. Campion, 'Cîteaux, Our Mother', 1999, pp. 490–1; Jamroziak, *Cistercian Order*, 2013, pp. 126, 128.

28. Richard, 'L'Établissement', 1953, p, 99.
29. Richard, 'L'Établissement', 1953, pp. 99–100; *DHGE* 7, p. 123. (Chazeaux in the later Middle Ages was a Benedictine house).
30. Wieland, 'Wechterswinkel', 1899, *passim*.
31. Williams, *Cistercians in the Early Middle Ages*, 1998, p. 21.
32. Bonis, A. and Wabont, M., 'Cisterciens et Cisterciennes en France du Nord-Ouesy'. In: Barrière, *Cîteaux et les femmes*, 2001, p. 155.
33. Barrière, *Cartulaire D'Obazine*, University of Clermont-Ferrand 2, 1989, pp. 11–12.
34. Campion, 'Cîteaux, Our Mother', 1999, p. 496.
35. *Ibid*. pp. 495–6.
36. Barrière, *Cartulaire D'Obazine* 2, 1989, pp. 11–12.
37. Berman, *Women and Monasticism*, 2002, pp. 77, 79–80.
38. Barrière, B., 'Coyroux, Doublet Fēminin de L'Abbaye d'Obazine'. 1994, pp. 131–2.
39. Information on-line; Cowan, *Medieval Religious Houses*, 1976, pp 145–8; Jamieson, 'St Mary, Haddington', 1952, pp. 1–3.
40. Burton, *Yorkshire Nunneries*, 1979, pp. 5–8.
41. France, *Cistercians in Scandinavia*, 1992, p. 175.
42. Peugniez, *L'Europe cistercienne*, 2012, p. 884.
43. Alvergnat, 2017, p. 196.
44. Connor, 'The Royal Abbey', 1988, p. 128.
45. *Ibid*. p. 131.
46. *Ibid*. pp. 128–9, 140–1.
47. *Ibid*. pp. 130–1, 133; *DHGE* 25, pp. 73–5.
48. Connor, 'The Royal Abbey', 1988, p. 131.
49. *Ibid*. pp. 128–9, 140–1; *DHGE* 25, pp. 74–5; Escrivá, *Las Huelgas*, 1944, p. 42, for a reproduction of the charter, and pp. 363–6 for a full transcription.
50. D'Emilio, 'Las Huelgas', 2005, p. 216; *DHGE* 25, pp. 74–5.
51. Connor, 'The Royal Abbey', 1988, p. 132.
52. Peugniez, *L'Europe cistercienne*, 2012, p. 812.
53. Connor, 'The Royal Abbey', 1988, pp. 129–30.
54. Peugniez, *L'Europe cistercienne*, 2012, p. 822.
55. D'Emilio, 'Las Huelgas', pp. 195–6, 202–3.
56. Connor, 'The Royal Abbey', 1988, pp. 13–39.
57. Gayoso, 'The Lady of Las Huelgas', 2000, pp. 102–3; Connor, 'The Royal Abbey', 1988, pp. 129–30.
58. *Statuta* 2, pp. 338–9.
59. D'Emilio, 'Las Huelgas', 2005, pp. 211–13.
60. Alvergnat, 2017, p. 204.
61. Gayoso, 'The Lady of Las Huelgas', pp. 91–116; *DHGE* 25, pp. 77–8.
62. *DMLH* 4, pp. 22–6 [210, of 1308], 124–6 [253, of 1312], 143–6 [264, of 1313]; 173–5 [281, of 1315], 204–5 [of 1317], 221–2 [309, of 1317].
63. D'Emilio, 'Women and Communities', 2015, p. 231–2.
64. *DHGE* XXV, 1994, p. 86.

Notes to Chapter 1

65 Willesme, 'Les Cisterciens à Paris', 1986, p. 135.
66 Berman, 'Cistercian Nuns', 1995, pp. 123–4.
67 Peugniez, *L'Europe cistercienne*, 2012, pp. 169–70.
68 Král, *Porta Coeli*, 1987, pp. 22–4; Vladík, 1994, p. 68.
69 *MU* 2, pp. 388–91 [1198].
70 Cowan and Easson, *Scotland*, 1976, p. 148.
71 *CRC* 2, pp. xiii-xiv.
72 *VCH, County of Dorset* 2, 1908, pp. 87–9.
73 Philly Ricketts at the Leeds Medieval Conference, 2002.
74 Roisin, 'L'efflorescence', 1943, pp. 350, 354.
75 Thompson 'Problems of the Cistercian nuns', 1978, p. 236; *Cf.* Roisin, 'L'efflorescence', 1943, p. 354.
76 Bouton, 'Nuns of Cîteaux', 1995, pp. 83–4; Cf. *DHGE* 11p. 918. XXX ? In Privat 1986?
77 Faust, *Die Frauenklöster*, 1984, p. 567.
78 *HEK* 2, p. 497 [521].
79 B. Barrière, *Cîteaux et les femmes*, 2001, p. 7.
80 Berman, *The Cistercian Evolution*, 1999, p. 231.
81 Jamroziak, *Cistercians*, 2013, p. 147; Berman, *White Nuns*, pp. 55–7.
82 Reimann, Heike, 'Cistercians Nuns in the High Middle Ages: The Cistercians of Bergen in the Principality of Rügen (North Germany)'. In: *Cîteaux* 25, 2004, pp. 233–5.
83 Charvátová, 'Bohême Mèdiévale', 1994, pp. 763–76; Hladík, 1994, p. 195. *CDEM* 2, pp. 302 [CCLXVI], 339 [CCXCIII], 381–4 [CCCXXIX–CCCXXX]: four German convents had this Latin name: *DHGE* XXIV, 1991, pp. 584–6.
84 Williams, 'East of the Oder', 1978, p. 242: Gahlbeck, 2002, pp. 628–9.
85 *Statuta* 1, p. 508 [1218/81].
86 *KDS*, p. 231 [218]; Peugniez, *L'Europe cistercienne*, 2012, pp. 1048–9.
87 *CDS*, p. 87 [149, of 1212], amongst several other references.
88 *CDS*, p. 168 [390, of 1262].
89 *CDS*, p. 126 [282, of 1224].
90 *CDS*, p. 122 [270, of 1222].
91 Kastner, 'Kloster Trebnitz', 1858, pp. 196, 205.
92 Wiszewski, *Cysterki Trzebnickie*, 1999, p. 706.
93 Wikipedia.
94 *DHGE* 29, p. 895.
95 *PU* 2, pp. 337–8 [1050], 372–3 [1097].
96 Williams, *Dünamünde Abbey*, 2020, pp. 20–1, 23, 16–17; Banga, *Rīgas*, 2007, p. 320; *RDD*, pp. 98–9.
97 France, *Scandinavia*, pp. 163–75.
98 Boyd, 'A Cistercian Nunnery', 1943, p. 81, quoting de Vitry's, *Libri Duo quorum Prior Oreintalis*.
99 J. F. Hinnebusch, *Historia Occidentalis de Jacques de Vitry*, Fribourg: Saint-Paul, 1972, p. 268. (In 1222 the nuns of Acre elevated their house in Cyprus into an abbey: Berman, *Women and Monasticism*, pp. 25–6).

100 Keble College, Oxford, MS 36.
101 Berman, *Women and Monasticism*, 2002, pp. 25–6 [3].
102 *CAR*, pp. 16–17 [X]; 94–102 [C–CIV], 177–9 [CLXXXVII–CLXXXVIII]; 232–4 [CCLXVII].
103 *PDC*, pp. 21 [16], 51 [31].
104 *DHGE* 13, pp. 795–6.
105 Connor, 'The Royal Abbey', 1988, p. 146.
106 Forey, 'Women and the Military Orders', 1987, p. 72.
107 *UKMR*, pp. 31–5 [2–7].
108 Jurgensmeier, *Hessen und Thüringen*, 2011, p. 225.
109 *UKSH* 1, pp. 203–4 [220].
110 *USD*, p. 65 [34].
111 Albe, 'Leyme', 1902, pp. 95–6 [8].
112 Berman, *Women and Monasticism*, 2002, p. 28 [5].
113 *HUK*, p. 462 [DL].
114 *MU* 1, p. 310 [1954].
115 *UKMR*, p. 38 [11].
116 *UKW*, p. 44 [5].
117 *PU* 2, 395 [1124, of 1278].
118 Schlegel, *Repertorium*, 1998, p. 401.
119 *CAAB*, p. 46.
120 *MPH* 6, p. 436.
121 *UZW*, as pp. 133 [168, of 1308], and 178 [290, of 1350].
122 *RT* 3, p. 525 [3348, of 1265].
123 *MU* 1, pp. 451 [2866], 465 [2964], 525 [3348]; *UKT*, pp. 302–3 [7–8]; 303 [9], 305 [13], 307 [17]; *RT* 3, p. 451.
124 Peugniez, *L'Europe cistercienne*, 2012, p. 79.
125 Peugniez, *L'Europe cistercienne*, 2012, p. 242.
126 Peugniez, *L'Europe cistercienne*, 2012, pp. 322–3, 326; Aurell i Cardona, 'Les Cisterciennes', 1986, pp. 235–6, 256, 261 (where a fourth, Beaulieu, is added. Beaulieu, originally a hospital, received a few nuns from St-Pons, but the archbishop of Arles making the gift, kept the jurisdiction of Beaulieu in his own hands, and forbade its attachment to the Cistercian Order. The authority of the abbess at Beaulieu was to be reserved to the cloister: this situation re-surfaced in differences with the archbishop in the early years of the fourteenth century): .
127 Aurell i Cardona, 1986, pp. 248–9.
128 Peugniez, *L'Europe cistercienne*, 2012, p. 79.
129 Peugniez, *L'Europe cistercienne*, 2012, p. 242.
130 Peugniez, *L'Europe cistercienne*, 2012, p. 218.
131 Peugniez, *L'Europe cistercienne*, 2012, p. 224; *DHGE* 21, p. 1013.
132 *DHGE* 10, p. 471.
133 Thompson, 'Problems of Cistercian nuns', 1978, p. 228.
134 *LCC* 2, pp. 348–55; Cf. Berman, White Nuns, p. 20.

Notes to Chapter 1

[135] G. Baury, 'Les moniales cisterciennes dans le Maine médiéval', In: *Annales de Bretagne st des Paysde l'Ouest* 120, 2013, Part 3, pp. 14, 16.
[136] Berman, *White Nuns*, p. 21.
[137] *Statuta* 3, pp. 21–30.
[138] *CAF*, pp. 184–6 [CLXXIII].
[139] Cawley, 'Mulieres Religiosae', 1992, p. 967.
[140] Roisin, 'L'efflorescence cistercienne', 1943, pp. 356–7.
[141] Ganck, 'Integration of nuns', 1984, p. 241.
[142] *Ibid.* p. 238.
[143] *Ibid.* p. 238.
[144] Roisin, 'L'efflorescence cistercienne', 1943, p. 370.
[145] *Ibid.* pp. 363–4.
[146] *DHGE* 15, p. 644.
[147] Cawley, *Send Me God*, 2003, p. 205.
[148] Roisin, 'L'efflorescence cistercienne', 1943, p. 360; Cawley, *Send Me God*, 2003, *passim*.
[149] Roisin, 'L'efflorescence cistercienne', 1943, pp. 363, 370; Cawley, *Send Me God*, 2003, *passim*.
[150] Roisin, 'L'efflorescence cistercienne', 1943, pp. 369–70.
[151] *Ibid.* p. 372.
[152] *Ibid.* p. 374.
[153] *Ibid.* p. 374.
[154] *Ibid.* p. 347.
[155] Freeman, 'A Cistercian Monk', 2010, p. 331.
[156] Roisin, 'L'efflorescence cistercienne', 1943, p. 348.
[157] Roisin, 'L'efflorescence cistercienne', 1943, pp. 375–6; McGuire, *Friendship and Community*, 2010, pp. 190–1.
[158] *Ibid.* pp. 371, 373–4.
[159] Lester, 'Creating Cistercian nuns', 2011, p. 19.
[160] *Ibid.* p. 35.
[161] *Ibid.* p. 36.
[162] *Ibid.* pp. 15–17.
[163] *Ibid.* pp. 57, 60.
[164] Jurgensmeier, *Hessen und Thuringen*, 2011, p. 225.
[165] Peugniez, 'L'Europe cistercienne', 2012, p. 300.
[166] *Ibid.* p. 366.
[167] Ganck, 'Integration of nuns', 1984, p. 236.
[168] *Ibid.* p. 237.
[169] *DHGE* 7, pp. 457 et seq., Oliver, 'Devotional Psalters', 1992, pp. 199, 201, 208, 210.
[170] Ganck, 'Integration of nuns', 1984, p. 244; Berman, 2002, p. 118.
[171] *DHGE* 7, pp. 457–8.
[172] Ganck, 'Integration of nuns', 1984, pp. 237–8.
[173] Ploegaerts, T., *Aywières*, 1924, pp. 1–8.

[174] Lachambre-cordier, 'Notre-Dame-des-Près', 2001, p. 251.
[175] Peugniez, *L'Europe cistercienne*, 2012, p. 510 DHGE 24, p. 774.
[176] *Ibid.* p. 534.
[177] *Ibid.* p. 535.
[178] *Ibid.* p. 620.
[179] Maegraith, *Gutenzelle*, 2006, p. 45.
[180] DHGE 6, pp. 269–70.
[181] Kiuhn-Refus, 1995, pp. 143–4.
[182] Barrière, 1983, p. 93.
[183] Peugniez, *L'Europe cistercienne*, 2012, p. 614.
[184] Ganck, 'Beatrice of Nazareth', 1988, pp. 327–8.
[185] Ganck, 'Integration of nuns', 1984, p. 242.
[186] CDVG, pp. 209–10 [159].
[187] *Ibid.* pp. 227–7 [129]; 'spelt': a health food.
[188] KHU, p. 218.
[189] Lekai, *The Cistercians*, 1977, p. 356.
[190] G. Veldeman, 'De Abdij van Zwijeke' In: *Cîteaux* 16, 1965, pp. 142–7.
[191] *Ibid.* p. 40.
[192] Jordan, 'Michery', 1985, pp. 314–15.
[193] Lester, 'Creating Cistercian nuns', 2011, pp. 132, 171.1.
[194] *Ibid.* pp. 129–30, 144.
[195] UAB, p. 6.
[196] Lester, 'Creating Cistercian nuns', 2011, pp. 130–311.
[197] *Ibid.* p. 65.
[198] CAM, pp. vi, 73–4.
[199] CAF 1, p. 114 [CXII].
[200] DAB, pp. 18–19.
[201] Schlegel, *Repertorium*, 1998, pp. 247–8.
[202] *Ibid.* p. 268; Köhler, *Klosters Nimbschen*, 2003, pp. 40–1.
[203] J. C. Carrick, *Abbey of Newbottle*, Edinburgh, 1907, p. 31.
[204] CAR, p. 201 [CCXXI].
[205] DHGE 18, p. 1115; Link, 1876, p. 587.
[206] UKM 3, p. 9 [1].
[207] Brunner, *Ein Cisterzienserbuch*, 2013, p. 612.
[208] Lester, 'Creating Cistercian Nuns', 2011, p. 41; Peugniez, *L'Europe cistercienne*, 2012, p. 128.
[209] *Statuta* 1, p. 405 [1213/4].
[210] Berman, *Women and Monasticism*, 2012, p. 39.
[211] DHGE 8, p. 1285; Brunner, *Ein Cisterzienserbuch*, 1881, p. 621.
[212] UKS, pp. 134–5 [5].
[213] Coomans, 'The Low Countries', 2005, p. 119.
[214] MB 7, Part 3, pp. 336–41.
[215] DHGE 8, pp. 1491–2.

Notes to Chapter 1

216 Connor, 'Royal Abbey', 1988, pp. 143–5; 'L'abbaye royale', 1988, pp. 322–3; *DHGE* 15, p. 960; 25, pp. 79–80; Albo, *Monasterio de Santa Maria*, 1950, pp. 52–62; Escrivá, *Las Huelgas*, 1944, pp. 75–108: pp. 370–1 - for a transcription of the bull of Gregory IX.
217 Albo, *Monasterio de Santa Maria*, 1950, pp. 54–5.
218 Kuhn-Refus, 'Germany', 1980, p. 139.
219 *Statuta* 1, p. 517 [1220/4].
220 *Statuta* 2, p. 36 [1225/7]; Ahlers, *Weibliches Zisterziensertum*, 2002, p. 69.
221 Degler-Spengler, 'Incorporation', 1995, p. 100; Baert, 'Moniales cisterciennes', 1962, p. 64.
222 Thompson, 'Problems of Cistercian nuns', 1978, p. 239.
223 *Statuta* 2, pp. 68 [1228/15], 76 [1229/7], 107 [1232/37; La Cambre, Belgium]; 116 [1233/27; Wauthier-Braine, Brabant]; 156 [1236/17, La Trésor S. Marie; France]; 180–1 [1237/63, Ter Beek, Belgium], to name but a few.
224 Ganck, 'Integration of nuns', 1984, p. 242.
225 Degler-Spengler, 'Incorporation', 1995, pp. 101–7.
226 *Statuta* 2, p. 275 [1244/7].
227 *Statuta* 3, p. 211 [1281/31].
228 *Statuta* 2, p. 419 [1255/43]. Perhaps a Venetian monastery.
229 *RBM* 2, p. 71 [180].
230 *UKNA*, pp. 506–7 [469].
231 Kratzke, 'North of Germany', 2005, p. 141.
232 *DHGE* 24, p. 583.
233 *DHGE* 24, p. 579.
234 Kratzke, 'North of Germany', 2005, p. 152.
235 *UKN*, pp. 2–3 [1].
236 *DHGE* 24, p. 814.
237 *DHGE* 21, p. 83; *RT* 2, pp. 146–7 [769, of 1187].
238 Jamroziak, *Cistercians*, 2013, p. 132.
239 *DHGE* 24, p. 885.
240 Wieland, 'Wechterswinkel', 1899, p. 295.
241 *DHGE* 25, pp. 621–2.
242 *RME*, p. 393 [365]; *DHGE* 25, p. 868.
243 *DHGE* 22, p. 255.
244 Kanior, 2000, p. 122; Wyrwa, *Monasticon Cisterciense*, 1999, p. 54.
245 Kratzke, 'North of Germany', 2005, p. 145.
246 *UKLB* 1, pp. 102–9.
247 *UKLB* 1, pp. 133–4, 1412, 161–2, 191–3.
248 *UKLB* 1, p. 191.
249 Faust, *Zisterzienser*, 1994, p. 251.
250 *DHGE* 1, p. 529; Peugniez, *L'Europe cistercienne*, 2012, p. 140; Richard, 'L'Établissement', 1953, pp. 100–1.
251 Peugniez, *L'Europe cistercienne*, 2012, p. 517.
252 Richard, 'L'Établissement', 1953, pp. 101–2.

253 Peugniez, *L'Europe cistercienne*, 2012, p. 183.
254 Ibid. pp. 260–1.
255 Ibid. p. 278; *Statuta* 2, p. 168 [1236/66].
256 Peugniez, *L'Europe cistercienne*, 2012, p. 393.
257 Jurgensmeier, *Hessen und Thuringen*, 2011, p. 602.
258 Peugniez, *L'Europe cistercienne*, 2012, p. 423.
259 Ibid. p. 424.
260 Ibid. pp. 425, 482.
261 DHGE 11, p. 565.
262 T. Ploegarts, *Les Moniales Cistercienne 3, Historie de l'Abbaye de Florival*, Brussels: Action Caholique, 1925, pp. 11, 13, 17–18; François, *Abdis Genta van Aarschot*, online, pp. 5, 25.
263 Peugniez, *L'Europe cistercienne*, 2012, p. 482.
264 Ibid. p. 459.
265 Ibid. p. 545.
266 Ibid. p. 578.
267 DHGE 24, p. 1295.
268 DHGE 14, pp. 519–20.
269 Peugniez, *L'Europe cistercienne*, 2012, p. 581.
270 Ibid. p. 582.
271 Ibid. p. 614.
272 Reimann, 'The Cistercians of Bergen', 2004, p. 235.
273 Peugniez, *L'Europe cistercienne*, 2012, pp. 711–12.
274 Ibid. pp. 755–6.
275 Ibid. p. 807.
276 Ibid. p. 817.
277 Ibid. p. 884.
278 Peugniez, *L'Europe cistercienne*, 2012, p. 1013.
279 Ibid. p. 222.
280 Ibid. p. 482.
281 Ibid. p. 1032.
282 Ibid. p. 1107.
283 DHGE 18, p. 1214.
284 15, p. 102.
285 Peugniez, *L'Europe cistercienne*, 2012, p. 241.
286 Ibid. pp. 366–7.
287 Ibid. p. 396.
288 *Statuta* 2, p. 161 [1236/39].
289 Ibid. p. 181 [1237/65].
290 MU 1, pp. 249 [1556], 251 [1568]; RT 3, p. 251 [1568, of 1247].
291 Peugniez, *L'Europe cistercienne*, 2012, p. 501.
292 DHGE 13, pp. 187–8.
293 DHGE 8, p. 1420.

Notes to Chapter 1

294 Peugniez, *L'Europe cistercienne*, 2012, p. 594.
295 *Ibid.* p. 657.
296 *DHGE* 24, pp. 707–8.
297 Peugniez, *L'Europe* cistercienne, p. 466.
298 Gascon, *Valldonzella*, 2013, p. 20.
299 Berman, *White Nuns*, pp. 57–60.
300 Albe, 'Leyme', 1902, p. 93.
301 Bouton, 'Nuns of Cîteaux', 1995, pp. 63–4.
302 Gol, *Vallbona*, 1973, pp. 13, 45–6, 49, 64.
303 *Statuta* 2, p. 68 [1228/16].
304 Bouton, 'Nuns of Cîteaux', 1995, p. 64.
305 *Ibid.* p. 76; *Statuta* 2, p. 352 [1252/32].
306 G. Despy, 'Les richesses de la terre'. In: J. Préaux (ed.), *Problemes d'Histoire du Christianisme* 5, 1974–5, p. 68; *ibid.* In: *Revue de l'Université de Bruxelles* 4, p. 410.
307 *CNC*, pp. 532–3.
308 *UKH* 1, pp. 2 [6, 7, 9]; 3.
309 Cf. *LCC* 2, p. 350.
310 *DHGE* 17, 1971, p. 1248.
311 *CDM* 3, pp. 747–50.
312 *UKMD*, pp. 2–6.
313 *AMO*, p. 11.
314 *Statuta* 2, p. 143 [1235/24].
315 *Statuta* 2, p. 148 [1235/40].
316 *Ibid.* p. 135 [1234/40].
317 *KDS*, p. 226 [213].
318 *Statuta* 2, pp. 156–7 [1236/20].
319 *Ibid.* p. 191 [1238/34]; Peugniez, *L'Europe cistercienne*, 2012, p. 578.
320 *Statuta* 2, p. 364 [1251/26].
321 *Ibid.* p. 161 [1236/39].
322 *Ibid.* pp. 203–4 [1239/7].
323 *Ibid.* p. 207 [1239/21]; Peugniez, *L'Europe cistercienne*, 2012, p. 514. [The inspecting abbots were those of Bronnbach and Langheim].
324 Peugniez, *L'Europe cistercienne*, 2012, p. 515.
325 *Ibid.* p. 534.
326 *Statuta* 2, 401 [10].
327 Bouton, 'Nuns of Cîteaux', 1995, p. 82. [Seemingly Marienmünster/Nonnenmünster in Worms].
328 *CDM* 2, pp. 76–7.
329 *RCH*, pp. 32–3.
330 Graves, 'Organisation', 1982, p. 333.
331 Graves, 'English Nunneries', 1979, pp. 495–6; Berman, 'Twelfth-Century Cistercian Nuns', 1999, pp. 860–1.
332 *UKF*, pp. 3–4 [7], 7 [14], 14 [32], 34 [54], 80 [124].
333 Peugniez, *L'Europe cistercienne*, 2012, p. 497; *DHGE* 18, p. 1117.

[334] *UKLH*, pp. 240–1 [22], 509.
[335] Thompson, 'Problems of Cistercian Nuns', 1978, p. 235.
[336] Ahlers, 'Weibliches', 2002, p. 152*n*; Steinwascher, 'Rinteln', 1986, p. 145.
[337] *UKR*, pp. 5, 25 [18].
[338] *UKR*, pp. 67 [76], 80 [93], respectively.
[339] *CHS*, pp. 90–1.
[340] *UKW*, pp. 82–3 [63, 65].
[341] *UKSG* 2, pp. 485–6 [488].
[342] Faust, *Die Frauenklöster*, 1984, p. 252.
[343] *DHGE* 21, p. 831.
[344] Köhler, *Nimbschen*, 2003, p. 144.
[345] Roden, *Strekrade*, 1984, p. 159.
[346] Jamroziak, *Cistercians*, 2013, p. 125.
[347] *Statuta* 2, pp. 321–2 [1247/36]; van der Meer, *Atlas*, 1965, p. 288.
[348] *DHGE* 21, pp. 858–9.
[349] Berman, *Women and Monasticism*, 2002, pp. 122, 203.
[350] Peugniez, *L'Europe cistercienne*, 2012, p. 767.
[351] Berman, *The Cistercian Evolution*, 1999, p. 40.
[352] *Ibid.* p. 196.
[353] *Ibid.* pp. 189–91.
[354] Peugniez, *L'Europe cistercienne*, 2012, p. 788.
[355] *Ibid.* p. 791.
[356] Mikkers XXX 1975, p. 367; Cf. *DP*, p. 352 [470].
[357] *MB* 4, Part 1, p. 446.
[358] *CCC*, pp. xiii-xiv.
[359] *DHGE* 9, pp. 1101–2.
[360] Albe, 'Leyme', 1902, pp. 94–5 [5–6].
[361] *CNC*, p. xi, XXX [465].
[362] Locatelli, 'L'Implantation Cistercienne', 1975, p. 212.
[363] Fort i Cogul, *Regesta*, 1965, pp. 90–4.
[364] Bouton, *Les Moniales Cisterciennes* 1, 1986, p. 87; Canivez, *L'Ordre de Cîteaux*, 1926, pp. 265–6.
[365] Kratzke, 'North of Germany', 2005, p. 145.
[366] Brunner, *Ein Zisterzienserbuch*, 1881, p. 626.
[367] *Ibid.* p. 623.
[368] Carville, *Norman Splendour*, 1979, p. 63; O'Dwyer, 'Crisis', 1976, pp. 14, 20, 58–9; Gwynn, *Medieval Religious Houses*, 1970, p. 140.
[369] *DHGE* 21, pp. 1378–9.
[370] VCH, *County of Lincoln* 2, 1906, p. 148.
[371] VCH, *County of Lincoln* 2, 1906, p. 150.
[372] VCH, *County of York* 3, 1974, pp. 178–9.
[373] Jamroziak, *Cistercian Order*, 2013, p. 135.
[374] *Statuta* 2, pp. 131, 135 (1234/26, 40).

Notes to Chapter 1

375 *UKMD*, pp. 74–5 [6, 8].
376 *Statuta* 2, pp. 173 [1237/27]; 237–8 [1241/40].
377 *Statuta* 2, p. 155 [1236/12]; Roisin, 'L'effloresence cistercienne,' p. 352.
378 Berman, *Cistercian Evolution*, 1999, p. 222. [Another convent with a heart burial was Wintney, England; before its high altar was interred the heart of Dame Diana Cobreth, a member of the founding family: VCH, *County of Hampshire* 2, p. 149].
379 Berman, *White Nuns*, 2018, 117–20.
380 *Statuta* 2, p. 155 [1236/12].
381 Peugniez, *L'Europe cistercienne*, 2012, p. 163; Berman, *White Nuns*, 2018, p. 133.
382 Berman, *White Nuns*, 2018, pp. 107–11, 132–3.
383 Berman, *White Nuns*, 2018, pp. 100–49, for a detailed analysis and description of this period.
384 *Ibid.* p. 135.
385 Peugniez, 2012, op. cit. pp. 263–4.
386 *Ibid.* p. 300.
387 *Ibid.* p. 302.
388 Berman, *Women and Monasticism*, 2002, p. 57; *White Nuns*, pp. 74–88.
389 Peugniez, *L'Europe cistercienne*, 2012, p. 224.
390 Jorge, 'Monastères au Portugal', 2001, p. 75.
391 Alegria, 'Les premières nonnes', 2001, p. 217; Boyd, *A Cistercian Nunnery*, 1943, pp. 85–6.
392 Peugniez, *L'Europe cistercienne*, 2012, p. 880.
393 ANT: PT/TT/MSMAR/G1M04/01/02/ and 03.
394 ANT: PT/TT/MSMAD/G3M03/02.
395 *DHGE* 29, p. 447.
396 France, *Cistercians in Scandinavia*, 1992, pp. 170–1.
397 Waddell, C., *The Primitive Cistercian Breviary*, 2007, pp. 35–7.
398 Peugniez, *L'Europe cistercienne*, 2012, pp. 31, 55.
399 *Ibid.* p. 202.
400 Reimann, 'Nuns of Bergen', 2004, p. 241.
401 *Statuta* 3, p. 239 [1287/9].
402 Bouton, 'Nuns of Cîteaux', 1995, p. 92.
403 F. van der Meer, *Atlas*, 1965, p. 300.
404 Peugniez, *L'Europe cistercienne*, 2012, p. 779.
405 *Ibid.* p. 807.
406 *DHGE* 11, p. 714.
407 Coomans, 'The Low Countries', 2005, pp. 69–71.
408 Hautcoeur, *Flines*, 1909, p. 19.
409 *DHGE* 14, p. 457.
410 Aurelle i Cardona, 'Les cisterciennes', 1986, p. 246.
411 Richard, 'L'Établissement', 1953, pp. 108–10.
412 *DHGE* 29, p. 895.
413 *PU* 2, pp. 389–90 [1114–15], 395–8 [1124], 419–20 [1159].

[414] *PU* 1, pp. 160–1 [818]; 167–70 [826, 827, 828]; 255–6 [946];342 [1056].
[415] *PU* 1, pp. 79 [699], 80 [700].197–8 [866].
[416] *PU* 1, p. 104 [734].
[417] *PU* 1, pp. 123 [763], 199–200 [868], 250–1 [938], 261 [953].
[418] *PU* 1, pp. 173–4 [833, of 1267].
[419] *PU* 2, p. 420 [1160].
[420] *PU* 1, p. 329–30 [1040].
[421] *PU* 2, pp. 389 [1115], 571; 329–30 [1040].
[422] *PU* 2, 487–8 [1254], 4, pp. 143–4 [2168].
[423] *PU* 2, pp. 372–3 [1097].
[424] *PU* 3, pp. 413–14 [1947].
[425] *PU* 2, pp. 395–7; 449–50, 590 [1373].
[426] *PU* 3, [1812], 4, pp. 44–5.
[427] *PU* 3, p. 379 [1903]. *Cf. PU* 3, pp. 379–81.
[428] Peugniez, *L'Europe cistercienne*, 2012, p. 79.
[429] *Ibid*. p. 71.
[430] *Ibid*.p. 239.
[431] Jurgenseier, 'Hessen und Thüringen', 2011, pp. 718–19.
[432] Hillebrand, 'Das Klosterbuch', 2015, p. 83.
[433] *CCH*, pp. 45–6 [II], 49 [VIII], 52–3 [XIII].
[434] *Statuta* 2, p.; 131 [1234/25], p. 166 [1236/61].
[435] *Statuta* 2, p. 166 [1236/61].
[436] *Statuta* 2, pp. 167–8 [1236/65].
[437] *Statuta* 2, p. 168 [1236/66].
[438] Peugniez, *L'Europe cistercienne*, 2012, p. 391.
[439] *DHGE* 22, p. 319; *MB* 2, Part 2, p. 520.
[440] D'Emilio, 'Widows and Communities', 2015, pp. 225, 228, 234, 251, 255, 260, 262–3, 265–6, 268.
[441] *OU* 2, pp. 213–15[270–2].
[442] *OU* 2, pp. 428–9 [532, of 1248].
[443] *Statuta* 2, p. 364 [1251/26].
[444] Berman, *Women and Monasticism*, 2002, p. 27.
[445] VCH, *County of Norfolk* 2, 1906, p. 360.
[446] *RFF*, p. 1.
[447] Scholten, 'Cistercienserinnen-Klöster', 1908, pp. 110–11; *DHGE* 21, pp. 1033–4. [The dates are open to question, as in 1258 the nuns of Roermond were forbidden to move 'from place to place' until all the necessary buildings had been completed: *REK* 2, p. 271 [2012].
[448] *MU* 1, p. 287 [1799]; *RT* 3, pp. 287 [1799], 311 [1968].
[449] *RT* 3, pp. 18, 31 [87, 146].
[450] *MU* 1, p. 315 [1989].
[451] *CDMC* 1, pp. 43–4 [38].
[452] Ziegler, 'A Rare Parchment', 2005, p. 314.
[453] Thompson, 'Problems of the Cistercian Nunneries', 1984, p. 235.

Notes to Chapter 1

454 Peugniez, *L'Europe cistercienne*, 2012, p. 152.
455 *Ibid.* p. 160.
456 *DHGE* 21, p. 1262.
457 *DHGE* 24, p. 1295.
458 *DHGE* 24, pp. 621–2; *UKI*, pp. 39–43 [1–2]. .
459 *DHGE* 25, p. 621.
460 *UKL*, pp. 31–4 [1–2]; Faust, *Die Frauenklöster*, 1984, p. 286.
461 Ahlers, 'Weibliches', 2002, p. 165n.
462 *UKL*, pp. 35–6 [4, 6].
463 *MU* 2, pp. 20–1 [692].
464 *MU* 2, pp. 29, 45.
465 Wieland, 'Wechterswinkel', 1899, pp. 321–9.
466 *DHGE* 8, pp. 1482–3.
467 Jamroziak, *Cistercians*, 2013, p. 131.
468 *VCH*, *Dorset* 2, 1908, pp. 87–8.
469 Freeman, 'Houses of a Peculiar Order', 2004, p. 255.
470 Reimann, 'Nuns of Bergen', 2004, p. 241.
471 Peugniez, *L'Europe cistercienne*, 2012, p. 429.
472 Bouton, 'Nuns of Cîteaux', 1995, p. 92.
473 *VDM.* p. 300.
474 Berman, *The Cistercian Evolution*, 1999, p. 191.
475 *Ibid.* pp. 29–30.
476 Peugniez, *L'Europe cistercienne*, 2012, p. 363.
477 *Ibid.* p. 365.
478 *Ibid.* p. 538.
479 *Ibid.* p. 559; *DHGE* 21, p. 1270.
480 *DHGE* 24, p. 581.
481 *DHGE* 22, p. 466.
482 *DHGE* 24, p. 811.
483 Peugniez, *L'Europe cistercienne*, 2012, p. 563.
484 *CHDM*, pp. 59–60.
485 Lester, 'Creating Cistercian Nuns', 2011, p. 73.
486 Berman, 'Dowries', 1993, p. 4.
487 Peugniez, *L'Europe cistercienne*, 2012, pp. 334, 340.
488 *Ibid.* p. 341.
489 *Ibid.* p. 57.
490 *Ibid.* pp. 377=79.
491 *DHGE* 21, pp. 1033–4; 22, p. 186.
492 *DHGE* 24, p. 85.
493 Baury, 'le Maine médiéval'. 2013, pp. 51–3.
494 *DHGE* 32, p. 44.
495 Barraud, 'Gomerfontaine', 1862, p. 585.
496 *UKM* 3, pp. 148–9 [37].

497 DHGE 32, p. 43.
498 Charvátová, 'Bohême Mèdiévale', 1994, p. 768; Jamroziak, *Cistercians*, 2013, p. 147.
499 Benešovská, 'Aula Sanctae Mariae', 2001, p. 59.
500 Reimann, 'Cistercians of Bergen', 2004, p. 238.
501 Peugniez, *L'Europe cistercienne*, 2012, p. 542.
502 Cooman, 'The Low Countries', 2005, pp. 69–71.
503 Peugniez, *L'Europe cistercienne*, 2012, pp. 235–6.
504 *Ibid.* p. 237; *CAM*, pp. v, 29 [XXXV].
505 *Statuta* 1, p. 458 [1216/41].
506 Peugniez, *L'Europe cistercienne*, 2012, p. 400.
507 *CDVG* pp. 5–6 [5].
508 Lester, *Creating Cistercian Nuns*, 2011, pp. 79–1.
509 Bermn, *White Nuns*, 2018, pp. 60–8.
510 Cf. Berman, *White Nuns*, pp. p. 51–5.
511 Berman, 'Women and Monasticism', 2002, pp. 47, 62; Lester, *Creating Cistercian Nuns*, 2011, p. 70.
512 *CNC*, pp. 279–80 [258].
513 Lester, *Creating Cistercian* Nuns, 2011, p. 155.
514 Peugniez, *L'Europe cistercienne*, 2012, p. 527.
515 *DHLT* 6, pp. 442–3, 449.
516 Berman, *Women and Monasticism*, 2002, pp. 21–2 [1].
517 *DG* 2, pp. 46–8 [6–8].
518 *CCG*, p. 3.
519 *CDVG, passim*.
520 *CAM*, pp. 96–102 [CIX–CXVIII], 111–12 CXXVII], 121–3 [CXXXI–CXXXIII], 125–6 [CXXXVI–CXXXVIII].
521 *CC*, p. 29.
522 *CNC*, pp. 5–32.
523 *OU* 2, pp. 348–51 [442].
524 *UKLT* 7, p. 458.
525 *UKH*, pp. 4–6 [19, of 1246].
526 Roden, *Saarn*, 1984, p. 24.
527 *UKGV*, pp. 4–7 [3, from Innocent IV)]; *CAF*, pp. 14 [XVII], 19–22 [XXII], respectively.
528 *CAF*, p. 173 [CLXII; dispensation of Clement IV in 1267].

Notes to Chapter 2

1 Bouton, 'Nuns of Cîteaux', 1995, p. 70.
2 *Statuta* 1, p. 485 [1218/4].
3 *PU* 4, p. 68 [2057].
4 Nichols, 'English Cistercian Nunneries', 1982, p. 151.
5 *CDVG*, pp. 117–19 [95].

Notes to Chapter 2

6. *PU* 1, pp. 160–1[818]; *PU* 5/2, p. 417 [2237].
7. *Statuta* 2, pp. 110 [119–20, 138, 144, 213, 254 [1232/52, 1233/42, 1234/51, 1235/26, 1239/52, 1242/49].
8. *Statuta* 2, p. 254 [1242/49, 51].
9. *Statuta* 2, p. 313 [1246/60]; Peugniez, *L'Europe cistercienne*, 2012, p. 395.
10. *Statuta* 3, pp. 97 [1271/24], 104 [1272/3]; Jordan, *Gender Concerns*, 2012, p. 90.
11. *Statuta* 3, p. 99 [1271/33].
12. van der Meer, *Atlas*, 1965, p. 297; Peugniez, *L'Europe cistercienne*, 2012, p. 538.
13. *DHGE* 4, p. 16.
14. Peugniez, *L'Europe cistercienne*, 2012, p. 128; Lester, *Creating Cistercian Nuns*, 2011, p. 188.
15. Peugniez, *L'Europe cistercienne*, 2012, p. p. 573.
16. *Ibid.* p. 657.
17. *Ibid.* p. 887.
18. *MB* 2, Part 2, p. 576.
19. Wieland, 'Heiligenthal', 1899, p. 164.
20. *CAM*, p. v.
21. *DHGE* 26, pp. 158–9.
22. Peugniez, *L'Europe cistercienne*, 2012, p. 31.
23. *Ibid.* p. 204.
24. *Ibid.* p. 119.
25. *Ibid.* p. 186.
26. *Ibid.* p. 224.
27. *CAAB*, p. 42.
28. *DHGE* 11, p. 565.
29. Peugniez, *L'Europe cistercienne*, 2012, pp. 377, 386.
30. *OU* 3, pp. 17–18 [24, of 1251].
31. *DHGE* 21, p. 1270.
32. Peugniez, *L'Europe cistercienne*, 2012, p. 45.
33. *VCH, County of York* 3, 1913, p. 167.
34. *DHGE* 13, p. 231.
35. Jamieson, 'St Mary, Haddington', 1952, p. 1.
36. *DHGE* 21, p. 1018.
37. Peugniez, *L'Europe cistercienne*, 2012, p. 482.
38. ANT: PT/TT/CSACMB/Mo3/001.
39. *Ibid.* pp. 169–70; Barrière, *Cîteaux et les femmes*, 2011, p. 168.
40. Peugniez, *L'Europe cistercienne*, 2012, p. 93.
41. *Ibid.* p. 99.
42. *Ibid.* p. 242.
43. *Ibid.* p. 349.
44. *Ibid.* p. 344.
45. *Ibid.* p. 226.
46. *Ibid.* p. 233.

47 *Ibid.* p. 267.
48 *AU*, p. 501 [222].
49 Peugniez, *L'Europe cistercienne*, 2012, p. 377.
50 *Ibid.* pp. 377, 399.
51 *Ibid.* p. 397.
52 *Ibid.* p. 379.
53 *Ibid.* p. 554.
54 *Ibid.* p. 573.
55 *Ibid.* p. 578.
56 *Ibid.* pp. 1079, 1081.
57 *Ibid.* p. 1053.
58 Gahlbeck, 'Der Neumark', 2002, p. 168.
59 Peugniez, *L'Europe cistercienne*, 2012, p. 355.
60 *PU* 1, p. 432 [553].
61 Peugniez, *L'Europe cistercienne*, 2012, pp. 458, 1069.
62 *DHGE* 29, p. 898.
63 France, *Cistercians in Scandinavia*, 1992, p. 173.
64 Wikipedia entry.
65 *PU* 2, pp. 337–8 [1050], 372–3 [1097].
66 Frohlich, *Die Zisterzienser*, 2010.
67 Kugler, 'Feldbach', 1980, p. 49.
68 Peugniez, *L'Europe cistercienne*, 2012, p. 79.
69 *Ibid.* p. 247.
70 *Ibid.* p. 55.
71 *Ibid.* p. 143.
72 Reimann, 'Cistercians of Bergen', 2004, pp. 33–5: *DHGE* 8, p. 450.
73 *PU* 3, pp. 52–3 [1478].
74 Guide leaflet at site.
75 Peugniez, *L'Europe cistercienne*, 2012, p. 241.
76 *DHGE* 9, pp. 1002–5.
77 *DHGE* 21, pp. 239–42.
78 *OU* 2, pp. 1250–2 [587].
79 *CAAB*, p. 42.
80 Bouton, *Bouchet*, 1979, pp. 16 24, 26.
81 *CNC*, p. 133 [111].
82 *CAM*, p. 197 [CCV].
83 *PU* 2, p. 362 [1082].
84 *DGA*, pp. 24–5.
85 *CDNE*, p. 38 [XXX].
86 *CDNE*, pp. 71–2 [LIV].
87 *UE* 1, p. 434 [711].
88 *UKMR*, p. 117 [131].
89 Online information.

Notes to Chapter 2

90. *DHGE* 9, pp. 1002–5.
91. *DHGE* 21, pp. 239–42.
92. *DHGE* 25, pp. 74–89.
93. Bouton, 'The Nuns of Cîteaux', 1995, pp. 20–1.
94. *DHGE* 24, pp. 584–6.
95. *CDEM*, pp. 190–1 [CLXXXV], 351.
96. *OU* 2, pp. 1250–2 [587].
97. Faust, Die Männer-und Frauenklöster, 1994, p. 139.
98. *DHGE* 26, pp. 158–9.
99. Coomans, 'Mémoire Dynastique', 2005, p. 106.
100. France, *Cistercians in Scandinavia*, 1992, p. 179; McGuire, *Cistercians in Denmark*, 1982, p. 3.
101. Holtmeyer, *Cisterzienskirchen Thüringens*, 1906, p. 146 [town plan].
102. Hervay, *Repertorium*, 1984, p. 110.
103. Fernandez, *San Clemente*, 1992, *passim*.
104. *UKGN*, p. 170 [25, of 1285].
105. Peugniez, *L'Europe cistercienne*, 2012, p. 160.
106. Domasłowski, J., *Kościoł i Dawny Klasztor Cysterek w Chełmnie*: Warsaw, 1983, pp. 82–3.
107. Sennhauser, *Zisterzienserbauten*, 1990, p. 259.
108. Ahlers, 'Weibliches', 2002, p. 1352n.
109. Jarck, 'Rinteln', 1984, p. 513.
110. van der Meer, *Atlas*, 1965, p. 294.
111. *MU* 1, p. 367 [2324].
112. *Kloster Burbach*, on-line.
113. *USM*, pp. 54–5, 61, 75.
114. *UBC*, pp. 157–8.
115. *CDEM* 2, pp. 246–7 [CCXXV].
116. *Kloster Burbach*, on-line.
117. C. Oefelein, 'Typiquemont atypique', 2001, p. 14.
118. *DHGE* 25, pp. 868–9.
119. *DNC* 1, p. 420.
120. *Statuta* 3, p. 136 [1274/52].
121. Römer-Johannsen, 'Goslar', 1984, p. 252.
122. Carville, 'Cistercian Nuns', 1995, pp. 67–8.
123. Jurkiewicz, *Szlak Cystersów*, 2006. p. 117.
124. D.H. Williams, 'Cistercian Nunneries in Wales', *Cîteaux* 26, Part 3, 1975, p. 164.
125. Lester, 'Creating Cistercian Nuns', 2011, pp. 1–2.
126. Peugniez, *L'Europe cistercienne*, 2012, p. 640.
127. *UKM*, p. 9 [1]; Peugniez, *L'Europe cistercienne*, 2012, p. 484.
128. *UKSH* 1, pp. 190–1 [205, of 1231].
129. *MU* 1, p. 362 [2286]; Schlegel, *Repertorium*, 1998, p. 396.
130. France, *Scandinavia*, 1992, p. 179.

[131] Warren, *La Bretagne*, 1991, pp. 204–5 (where a map).
[132] *UKL*, p. 40 [11, fo 1235].
[133] *PU 1*, pp. 327–8 [415].
[134] *PU 2*, pp. 79–80.
[135] *PU 4*, pp. 122–3 [2142].
[136] *UKLB 1*, pp. 206–8.
[137] *MU 2*, pp. 388–9 [1198].
[138] Luxatlas, 2016: plan by Jakob van Deventer, 1564.
[139] *UAB*, p. 4 [3].
[140] *Statuta 2*, p. 234 (1241/24).
[141] Jurgensmeier, *Hessen und Thüringen*, 2011, pp. 580–1.
[142] Ibid. p. 600.
[143] Ibid. p. 825.
[144] Ibid. p. 677; Cf. *UKEF*, p. 348 (of 1303).
[145] *DHGE* 15, p. 706.
[146] Ibid. p. 73.
[147] Lester, 'Creating Cistercian Nuns', 2011, pp. 61–2.
[148] *Statuta 2*, p. 174 [1227/30].
[149] *Statuta 2*, p. 189 [1238/26].
[150] *Statuta 2*, pp. 192–3 [1238/40].
[151] *Statuta 2*, p. 472 [1260/54]; Peugniez, *L'Europe cistercienne*, 2012, p. 417.
[152] *UKL*, pp. 44–6 [17–19], 56 [32], 99–100 [82]; Ahlers, 'Weibliches', 2002, p. 167n; Peugniez, *L'Europe cistercienne*, 2012, p. 466.
[153] *CCH*, pp. 58–9; Peugniez, *L'Europe cistercienne*, 2012, p. 368.
[154] *CAS*, p. 193.
[155] François, *Abdis Genta van Aarschot*, online, pp. 20–3.
[156] *CZT*, pp. 3–9, 14–18, 28–30 [II, III, V–VI, IX, XIX–XX, XXX–XXXI].
[157] *CZT*, p. 9 [IX of 1225].
[158] Coomans, *La Ramée*, 2002, pp. 19, 21.
[159] Ploegaerts, *La Ramée*, 1925, p. 18.
[160] *USD 1*, pp. 65 [35], 68 [38], 76 [47]; Wikipedia.
[161] *OU 2*, pp. 206 [263], 227–8 [287], 235–6 [295], 241 [304], 361–2 [457].
[162] *OU 4*, pp. 272–3 [431, of 1295], 286 [452, of 1296], 295 [466, of 1296]. The fields cost 8½ marks, 10 marks, and 5 marks and three shillings, respectively.
[163] Schlegel, *Repertorium*, 1998, p. 381.
[164] Bouton, 'Nuns of Cîteaux', 1995, p. 16; Peugniez, *L'Europe cistercienne*, 2012, p. 52, where reference is made to the site as 'inhospitable'.
[165] Bouton, 'Nuns of Cîteaux', 1995, p. 16.
[166] Peugniez, *L'Europe cistercienne*, 2012, pp. 55–6.
[167] Ibid. pp. 424, 436.
[168] *DHGE* 26, p. 440.
[169] Jurgensmeier, *Hessen und Thüringen*, 2011, p. 275.
[170] *DHGE* 26, pp. 158–9.

Notes to Chapter 2

171 Peugniez, *L'Europe cistercienne*, 2012, p. 115.
172 Albe, 'Leyme', 1902, pp. 98–9 [14].
173 Ziegler, 'A Rare Parchment', 2005, p. 314.
174 *AU*, pp. 486–90 [214–17]; *REK* 1, p. 56 [311].
175 *DHGE* 11, p. 587.
176 Ahlers, 'Weibliches', 2002, p. 155n.
177 Jordan, *Gender Concerns*, 2012, p. 91.
178 Jurgensmeier, *Hessen und Thüringen*, 2011, p. 63; *UE* 1, pp. 306–7 [500–1].
179 *UBC*, pp. 157–8.
180 *DHGE* 24, p. 586.
181 *DHGE* 25, p. 622.
182 *OU* 3, p. 48 [61].
183 Jurgensmeier, *Hessen und Thüringen*, 2011, p. 275.
184 *DHGE* 24, p. 747.
185 *DHGE* 25, pp. 85–6., pp.
186 *DSHG* 3, pp. 646–8 [XXIX–XXX].
187 Peugniez, *L'Europe cistercienne*, 2012, p. 539.
188 *DHGE* 22, p. 466.
189 Wehking, 'Die Inschriften', 2009, pp. 129, 131.
190 *OU* 4, p. 439 [686].
191 *UKWF*, 4:3, p. 686 [1431].
192 Peugniez, *L'Europe cistercienne*, 2012, p. 392; *Statuta* 2, p. 131 [1234/25].
193 *MB*, Part 2, pp. 458–9.
194 *CCG*, p. xxix; *DHGE* 22, p. 319.
195 *VCH, County of York* 3, 1913, p. 158.
196 *UKN*, pp. 1–2 [1].
197 Berman, *The Cistercian Evolution*, 1999, p. 44.
198 *DHGE* 21, pp. 1074–5.
199 *DHGE* 29, p. 947.
200 *Statuta* 2, pp. 349–50 [1250/20].
201 Lester, *Creating Cistercian Nuns*, 2011, pp. 1–2.
202 Peugniez, *L'Europe cistercienne*, 2012, p. 1052.
203 *PDC*, pp. 8–11 [5–8]; Peugniez, *L'Europe cistercienne*, 2012, p. 1119.
204 Peugniez, *L'Europe cistercienne*, 2012, p. 626.
205 *DHGE* 14, pp. 522–3 (for a fuller account).
206 Hervay, *Cisterciensis in Hungaria*, 1984, p. 158.
207 Peugniez, *L'Europe cistercienne*, 2012, p. 808.
208 Berman, *Women and Monasticism*, 2002, pp. 32–5, 135.
209 *Statuta* 2, p. 210 [1239/6].
210 *Statuta* 3, pp. 117–18 [1273/12].
211 *Statuta* 3, p. 71 [1269/15].
212 *Statuta* 3, p. 155 [1276/15].
213 *Statuta* 3, p. 277–1294/82].

214 *USB*, pp. 1516 [2, of 1247/48]; *OU* 2, pp. 397–8 [501, of 1247].
215 *USB*, pp. 23–4 [10–11].
216 *OU* 3, pp. 11–12 [15, of 1251]/.
217 *OU* 3, pp. 17–18 [24, of 1251].
218 *DHGE* 6, p. 1338.
219 *CAF* 1, pp. 11–12 [XIV]; *Cf.* pp. 82–3 [XCII, of 1251].
220 Noel, "L'Amour-Dieu," 1876, p. 148.
221 *UKG*, pp. 30–1 [28–9].

Notes to Chapter 3

1 *PU* 2, p. 434 [1176]: as that of Koszalin (P):but Rostock nunnery was dedicated to the Holy Cross [, and Trebnitz to St Bartholomew The Portugese nunnery of Celas, had St Anne, as patroness; Odivelas, St Dinis, after its founder, King Dinis; and Arouca, St Peter: ANT: PT/TT/GAV1/2/14;].
2 ANT: PT/TT/MSMAR/G3M10/15.
3 ANT: PT/TT/CSACMB/M03/001.
4 *UKI*, pp. 45, 78.
5 ANT: PT/TT/CSACMB/M03/001.
6 *PU* 3, No. 1830, of 1298]; *MU* 1, p. 367 [2324].
7 *ABB*, pp. 195–207.
8 *CKW*, p. 508.
9 Schlegel, *Repertorium*, 1998, p. 278.
10 Oefelin, 'SS Jacobi et Burchardi', 2005, p. 299.
11 Pearson, 'Spirituality', 2005, p. 330.
12 Kulke, *Zisterzienserinnenarchitektur*, 2006, *passim*.
13 Kratzke, 'North of Germany', 2005, p. 143.
14 *Ibid.* pp. 143–4.
15 Freeman, 'Cist6ercian Nuns and Art', 2014, p. 178.
16 Dimier, *Receuil des Plans* 2, 1949, *passim*.
17 *UKSH* 1, pp. 199–200 [213].
18 Kratzke, 'North of Germany', 2005, p. 162; *Cf. OU* 3, p. 212 [301].
19 Kratzke, 'North of Germany', 2005, p. 164.
20 *DHGE* 14, p. 806.
21 *DG* 1, pp. 33–4 [6].
22 Riggert, *Die Lüneberger Frauenkloster*, 1996, p. 70.
23 VCH, *County of Hampshire* 2, p. 149.
24 Jurkiewicz, *Szlak Cystersów*, 2006, pp. 80–1.
25 *UKL*, pp. 59–60 [34], 110–11.
26 *UKWF*, pp. 764–7654 [1614]; 'ad opera hortatoria'.
27 Williams, 2020, p. 22.
28 *UKWF*, 4: 2, pp. 565 [1252], 493 [1089].
29 *UKMR*, pp. 70–1 [62].
30 *CZT*, p. 86 [LXXXIII].

Notes to Chapter 3

31 *MPH* 6, p. 361.
32 Berman, *Women and Monasticism*, 2001, p. 23.
33 *CDMC* 1, p. 52 [45].
34 *VCH, County of Northampton* 2, 1906, p. 123.
35 Hervay, *Repertorium*, 1984, p. 193.
36 *PU* 3, pp. 26–7 [1443, of 1287].
37 Digitale Westfälische Datenbank: *Bennigshausen*.
38 D'Emilio, 'Women and Communities', 2015, pp. 235–6.
39 Berman, *Women and Monasticism*, 2002, pp. 108–11.
40 *HCM* 1, pp. 4–6; See also: Berman, *White Nuns*, 2018, 106.
41 *HCM* 1, p. 7; 2, p. 6; 3, p. 18 [XXII].
42 Peugniez, *L'Europe cistercienne*, 2012, *passim*.
43 Cooman', 'Low Countries', 2005, p. 78.
44 Peugniez, *L'Europe cistercienne*, 2012, p. 664.
45 Berman, 'Building in Wood, Brick .'., 2005, p. 38.
46 *OU* 3, pp. 39–40 [51].
47 *UKGV*, pp. 9–11.
48 *CAF*, pp. 194–206 [CLXXXII]; 229–31 [CCX, of 1279].
49 *MB* 2, Part 2, p. 457.
50 *DG* 2, pp. 50–2 [11, 13].
51 *DHGE* 25, p. 869.
52 *DHGE* 26, p. 440.
53 *UAB*, pp. 4–5, 17, 19, 35.
54 Steinwascher, 'Kloster Rinteln', 1986, p. 174.
55 804. *UKR*, pp. 26, 28, 30; 37 [42]; 52–3 [57, of 1296]; 68, 71–2 [77, 82].
56 *UKH*, pp. 37 [142], 114–15 [264, of 1320].
57 *UKH*, pp. 175–6 [358].
58 *KHU*, pp. 139–41; for a like example forBrenkenhausen (G) in 1278: *UKWF*, 4: 3, p. 728 [1521].
59 *OU* 4, p. 142 [208, of 1287]: for a like indulgence forOdivelas, Pt, see: *ANT*: PT/TT/BUL/0004/12 (of 1319).
60 *DHLT* 7, p. 457.
61 *DG* 2, pp. 50–2 [11, 13].
62 *DG* 2, p. 70.
63 Hautcoeur, *Flines*, 1909, p. 69; Pearson, 'Spirituality', 2005, pp. 328, 330.
64 *CCS*, p. 290.
65 *UKWF*, p. 525 [1154].
66 Bruiningk, 1904; Trops, 1943, p. 24.
67 Banga, *Rīgas Dievnami*, 2007, p. 320.
68 *PU* 1, p. 252 [940].
69 van der Meer, *Atlas*, 1965, p. 282.
70 Wikipedia; *PU* 3, pp. 418–19 [1953]; 4. pp. 391–2 (of 1309).
71 Desmarchelier, 'Églises de Moniales', 1982, p. 83.

72 *Ibid.* p. 81.
73 Mattson, *Riseberga*, 1998, p. 220.
74 *UKLH*, pp. 232–40 [9–10, 13–18, 20].
75 Jurgensmeier, *Hessen und Thüringen*, 2011, p. 253.
76 Mattson, *Riseberga*, 1998, p. 220; Jurkiewicz, *Szlak Cystersów*, 2006, p. 217.
77 Coester, *Cistercienserinnenkirchen*, 1986, p. 261; Wieland, 'Heiligenthal', 1899, p. 162; Jurkiewicz, *Slak Cystersów*, 2006, p. 217.
78 Coomans, *La Ramée*, 1925, p. 58.
79 Desmarchelier, 1982, pp. 79–119; Nichols, 1982a, pp. 159, 165.
80 Denison, E., *Ellerton Priory, Swaledale: Archaeological Survey*, Beverley, Yorkshire, 2011.
81 Dimier, *Receuil de Plans 2*, 1949, p. 154; *DHGE* 25, p. 74.
82 Hladík, *Porta Coeli I*, 1994, p. 95.
83 Broniewski, *Trzebnica*, 1959, pp. 22–4.
84 Grüger, 'Trebnitz', 1982, pp. 73–4.
85 Alvergnat, 2017, p. 104.
86 Peugniez, *L'Europe cistercienne*, 2012, *passim*.
87 *Ibid.* pp. 1030, 624, respectively.
88 Lewis, M., *Stained Glass in North Wales up to 1850*, Altrincham: Sherratt, 1970, pp. 7, 11, 39, 68–9.
89 Alvergnat, 2017, p. 234.
90 Kulke, 2006, p. 293.
91 D'Emilio, 'Women and Communities', 2015, pp. 283–4, 288, 300.
92 Hladík, 1994, p. 102.
93 *Ibid.* pp. 232, 240.
94 *Ibid.* pp. 272–3.
95 *UKH*, pp. 100–1 (241).
96 Coomans, *La Ramée*, 2002, pp. 48, 259.
97 Peugniez, *L'Europe cistercienne*, 2012, p. 813.
98 Kulke, *Cistercienserinnenarchtektur*, 2006, pp. 271–2.
99 Wikipedia on-line.
100 Kratzke, 'North of Germany', 2014, p. 162.
101 Oefelin, 'SS Jacobi et Burchardi', 2005, p. 304.
102 The phrase was coined by Lilian Grassi.
103 Coomans, *La Ramée*, 2002, p. 57.
104 Coomans, 'Low Countries', 2005, pp. 69–71.
105 Digitale Westfälische Datenbank: *Bennigshausen*.
106 Kratzke, 'North of Germany', 2014, p. 166.
107 Coomans, 'Mémoire Dynastique', 2005, p.
108 Alvergnat, 2017, p. 111.
109 Kratzke, 'North of Germany', 2014, p. 158.
110 Dimier, 'L'architecture cisterciennes', 1974, p. 152.
111 Mecham, 'A Northern Jerusalem', 2005, pp. 142–3.

Notes to Chapter 3

112. Oefelin, 'SS Jacobi et Burchardi', 2005, p. 304.
113. Kratzke, 'North of Germany', 2005, p. 151.
114. Coomans, 'Mémoire Dynastique', 2005, pp. 108, 115.
115. *Ibid.* p. 304.
116. Wikipedia: Kloster Brenkhausen.
117. Wikipedia on-line.
118. Peugniez, *L'Europe cistercienne*, 2012, p. 789.
119. Gol, 1973, *Vallbona*, 1973, Plates 8–14; p. 96.
120. Coomans, 'Mémoire Dynastique', 2005, pp. 109–10.
121. Coomans, 'Mémoire Dynastique', 2005, p. 116.
122. Peugniez, *L'Europe cistercienne*, 2012, *passim*; Wikipedia and other on-line entries.
123. *UKH*, p. 38 [143].
124. *USB*, pp. 37–8 [29, of 1274]; Cf. *OU* 3, p. 361; Faust, *Zisterzienser in Niedersachsen*, 1994, pp. 97–8.
125. *SU* 1, pp. 179–81 [247].
126. *CDP*, pp. 92–3 [LIV].
127. *CZT*, pp. 137–8 [CXIII].
128. *UKR*, pp. 106–7 [122].
129. *DCE*, p. 104 [1244].
130. *RBM* 4, Part 1, p. 130 [45].
131. *CDEM* 3, p. 54.
132. *CHDM* 2, p. 39.
133. *UKMD*, p. 188 [189].
134. *CZT*, pp. 137–8 [CXIII].
135. *PU* 2, p. 421 [1161].
136. *Statuta* 1, p. 485 [1218/4].
137. *Statuta* 3, pp. 18–19 [1264/3].
138. Peugniez, *L'Europe cistercienne*, 2012, p. 378.
139. *REK* 2, p. 167 [3187].
140. *Statuta* 2, p. 462 [1260/6].
141. Ploegaerts, *Aywières*, 1924, p. 25n.
142. *PU* 2, p. 104.
143. *PU* 1, pp. 432–5 [555, of 1252].
144. *UKGN*, pp. 184–6 [37]; *USM*, p. 107 [200, of 1296].
145. *VCH, County of Northampton* 2, 1906, p. 122.
146. *UZW*, p. 165 [254].
147. Peugniez, *L'Europe cistercienne*, 2012, p. 817.
148. Appuhn, 1981, p. 10 (illus.).
149. D'Emilio, 'Las Huelgas', 2005, pp. 225–32.
150. Peugniez, *L'Europe cistercienne*, 2012, *passim*; Cf. Appuhn, *Kloster Isenhagen*, 1981, p. 10 (illus.).
151. Siart, *Kreuzgänge mittelalterlicher*, 2008, pp. 23–40.

152 Peugniez, *L'Europe cistercienne*, 2012, p. 261.
153 *DHGE* 21, pp. 1033–4.
154 Nichols, 'An English Cistercian Nunnery', 1978, pp. 320–1.
155 Coomans, 'Low Countries', 2005, pp. 110–12.
156 D'Emilio, 'Women and Communities', 2015, p. 258, *n.* 117.
157 *UKLB* 1, pp. 286–7.
158 Peugniez, *L'Europe cistercienne*, 2012, pp. 261, 807.
159 Peugniez, *L'Europe cistercienne*, 2012, pp. 789, 1064.
160 Danion, 'Maubuisson'. In: Buchet, *La femme*, 1994, p. 13.
161 Wikipedia on-line.
162 Peugniez, *L'Europe cistercienne*, 2012, p. 822; Wikipedia on-line.
163 Coomans, 'Low Countries', 2005, pp. 100–1.
164 *NMD* p. 192.
165 Hervay, *Repertorium*, 1984, pp. 193–4.
166 Coester, *Cistercienserinnenkirchen*, 1986, p. 261.
167 Bell, 'Chambers, Cells, and Cubicles', 2004, pp. 188–9.
168 VCH, *County of York* 3, 1913, p. 181.
169 Faust, *Zisterzienser in Niedersachsen*, 1994, pp. 97–8.
170 *USD*, pp. 94–6 [66].
171 *Statuta* 3, pp. 239, 252 [1287/9, 10, 13; 328 [1314/4]; 376 [1327/37].
172 *CDN*, pp. 1427–9 [88].
173 Römer-Johanssen, 'Goslar Neuwerk' 1984, p. 268.
174 *CAF*, pp. 363–4 [CCCXXXV].
175 Ploegaerts, *La Ramée*, 1925 pp. 24–5.
176 *Ibid.* pp. 15, 25 (another grant of 1258, for the same purpose).
177 *MU* 2, p. 161 [879]; *UKN*, pp. 35–6 [XVIII].
178 *UKL*, p. 138 [135].
179 *OU* 3, p. 361.
180 *PU* 4, pp. 123 [2143], 157 [2184].
181 *UKE* 1, p. 790 [1422].
182 *UKWFn* p. 694 [1450].
183 *DSB*, p. 386 [L].
184 *CAM*, p. 110 [CXXV].
185 *UKGN*, pp. 170–2 [22].
186 Berman, *Women and* Monasticism, 2002, p. 26 [3].
187 *UKI*, p. 67 (23).
188 VCH, *County of York* 3, 1974, p. 179.
189 *Ibid.* p. 163.
190 *Ibid.* pp. 171–2.
191 *Ibid.* p. 179; *RJR* 1, 1913, p. 163 [452].
192 Williams, *Welsh Cistercians*, 2001, p. 152.
193 Rèpas, *Traja de Branco*, 2003, p. 401 [101].
194 *CDVG*, p. 57.

Notes to Chapter 3

195 Burton, 1979, p. 17.
196 *NPR*, p. 639.
197 *Ibid.* p. 375.
198 *RSL* 2, p. 41.
199 VCH, *County of York* 3, p. 163.
200 *DHGE* 26, p. 441.
201 *Statuta* 3, pp. 230 [1282/7]; 348 [1320/5].
202 *Statuta* 3, pp. 233-4 [1285/8, 1286/3].
203 VCH, *County of York* 3, 1913, p. 177.
204 Berman, 'Cistercian Nuns', 1995, p. 120; *CNC*, pp. 308-11.
205 *CCS*, p. 648.
206 VCH, *County of Warwick* 2, 1908, p. 82.
207 VCH, *County of Dorset* 2, 1908, p. 89.
208 Ploegaerts, *Aywières*, 1924, pp. 11-13, 14, 25.
209 Maricourt, 'Gomerfontaine', 1907, p. 449.
210 Barraud, 'Gomerfontaine', 1862, p. 581.
211 *Ibid.* pp. 583-4.
212 Berman, *Women and Monasticism*, 2001, p. 71 [35].
213 *UKO*, p. 25 [41].
214 *CAF*, pp. 409-45 [p. 444, for the pitancier].
215 *CAM*, p. 183 [[CXCI].
216 *UKO*, p. 36 [107].
217 ANT: PT/TT/MSMRC/No5/032.
218 *NBT, passim*.
219 *NRM, passim*, and p. 19.
220 *NWD, passim*.
221 *NDP, passim*.
222 *NMD*, p. 188.
223 *MB* 2, Part 2, p. 488.
224 *CDVG*, pp. 151-2 [121].
225 *SU* 1, pp. 166-7 [227].
226 *UKS*, p. 197 [43].
227 *DMF*, pp. 511, 513-14.
228 *UKH*, pp. 97 [235, of 1314]; 102 [243, of 1317].
229 *NSA*, p. 476; *CMF*, p. 22.
230 *UKLT* 8, pp. 74-6: a 'carrate'.
231 *CZT*, pp. 43-4 [XLVIII, of 1246].
232 *NBH*, p. 62.
233 *UKN*, pp. 62-3 [XXVIII].
234 *NMD*, pp. 305, 169, 309.
235 *CCC*, p. 67.
236 *CDVG*, pp. 190-1 [148].
237 *DG* 2, pp. 69-70.

238 CHDM 2, p. 97.
239 UKH, p. 97 [235].
240 Szwejkowska, *Bibliotheka Trzebnicy*, 1955, pp. 27–33; Cf. Grüger, 'Trebznitz', p. 72.
241 Overgaauw, 'Das Gravenhorster Fragment', 1993, pp. 21–6.
242 Jurgensmeier, 'Hessen und Thüringen', 2011, pp. 96, 245.
243 The original manuscript is British Library, Cotton Claudius D. iii. folios 140v-162v.
244 Mistele, 'Kalendar', 1962, pp. 55–68.
245 Williams, 2022, pp. 77–8.
246 CMF, pp. 16–24, 99–104.
247 NS, *passim*.
248 Pankoke, *Buchmalerei*, 1998, pp. 168–71.
249 Schneider, *Die Cistercienser*, 1977, p. 479. [It is now British Library MS 16950].
250 Coomans, *La Ramée*, 2002, pp. 37–8.
251 Faust, 'Zistercienser', 1994, p. 645.
252 Schneider, *Die Cistercienser*, 1977, p. 506.
253 Freeman, 'Cistercian Nuns and Art', 2014, pp. 181–2.
254 Löer, 'Kloster Welver', 1997, pp. 56, 62–3.
255 Anglès, *El Codex Musical*, 1931, *passim*.
256 Luaces, 'Cistercian miniatures', 2014, p. 233.
257 López-Vidriero, *Manuscrits e Impresos*, 1999, pp. 19–24.
258 Hughes, 'Medieval Liturgical Books', 1975, pp. 378–9.
259 Jordan, 'Musico-Liturgical Manuscripts', 1993, *passim*, and especially pp. 152–4, 164.
260 Heinzer, *Handschriften*, 1987, pp. 92, 311–17.
261 Coomans, *La Ramée*, 2002, pp. 37–8.
262 Schlegel, *Repertorium*, 1998, pp. 413–14.
263 Faust, 'Zistercienser', 1994, p. 256.
264 Wikipedia on-line.
265 Coomans, *La Ramée*, 2002, pp. 37–8.
266 Römer-Johannsen, 'Goslar',1984, p. 252, and online sources.
267 Faust, 'Zisterzienser', 1944, p. 645; *OU* 4, p. 445 [698].
268 Schlegel, *Repertorium*, 1998, p. 488.
269 Faust, 'Zisterzienser', 1944, p. 78.
270 Coomans, *La Ramée*, 2002, pp. 33–7.
271 Faust, 'Zisterzienser', 1944, p. 775.
272 Schlegel, *Repertorium*, 1998, p. 354.
273 Jurgensmeier, 'Hessen und Thuringen', 2011, p. 661.
274 DHGE 24, p. 495.
275 Jordan, 'Michery', 1985, p. 312.
276 ADY, H87, introductory notes.
277 CNC, *passim*.

Notes to Chapter 4

278 BL, Additional MS 46701.
279 *DSHG, passim.*
280 CNC, pp. 513–15 [459–60, of 1300/20].
281 Hervay, *Repertorium*, 1984, p. 110.
282 UKSG 1, pp. 392 [377, of 1208]; 395 [383, of 1210]; 401 [394, of 1214], and others.
283 UKMD, pp. 81–2 [18].
284 DHGE 7, pp. 469–70.
285 *CC, passim.*
286 *UKLT 7, passim.*
287 UKGV, pp. 78–9 [90].
288 *DSHG 3, passim.*
289 UKMD, pp. 154–5, 161, 208.
290 UKG, 104 [127].
291 *DMF, passim.*
292 UKR, pp. 97 [113], 105–6 [121].
293 *DNK, passim.*
294 Williams, D.H., 'Medieval Cistercian Seals'. In: *Archaeologia Cambrensis* 154 (for 2005, published in 2007), pp. 157, 174 (illustrations Nos. 64–8).
295 CHDM 2, pp. 77–83.
296 Baury, 'Cañas', 2008, p. 243.
297 Kratzke, 'Ornamenta Ecclesiae', 2014, p. 189.
298 CHS, pp. 76–7, 102–3.
299 Jurkiewicz, *Szlak Cystersów*, 2006, p. 149.
300 Kratzke, 'Ornamenta Ecclesiae', 2014, p. 196.
301 Cazabonne, 'Liturgical Life', 2014, p. 203.
302 *Ibid.* p. 206.
303 Freeman, "Cistercian Nuns and Art', 2014, pp. 178–9.
304 Wipfler, *Corpus Christi*, 2003, p. 67.
305 *Abbaye du Paraclete-des-Champs*, online.
306 Wipfler, *Corpus Christi*, 2003, p. 107.
307 *Ibid.* p. 125.
308 Freeman, 'Cistercian Nuns and Art', 2014, p. 178; Bartal, 'Where has your Beloved gone?, 2000, pp. 270–89.
309 Freeman, 'Cistercian Nuns and Art', 2014, p. 181.
310 Freeman, 'Cistercian Nuns and Art', 2014, p. 181.
311 Klack-Eitzen, *Heilige Röcke*, 2013, pp. 41, 52, 54.
312 Creutz, p. 112.

Notes to Chapter 4

1 Faust, *Zisterzienser*, 1994, p. 756.
2 *Ibid.* p. 361; UKLB 1, p. 292.
3 Roden, *Saarn*, 1984, p. 13.
4 DHGE 24, p. 583.

5   *UKWF*, 4: 3, p. 764 [1614].
6   *OU* 4, p. 55 [81].
7   *DGA*, p. 33.
8   *UKW*, p. 64 [36].
9   *UKR*, p. 65 [73].
10 Faust, *Zisterzienser*, 1994, p. 228.
11 *UKMD*, p. 174 [168].
12 *CCG*, p. 31.
13 Zeimet, *St. Katherinen b. Linz*, 1929, p. 19.
14 *UKI*, p. 67 [23–4].
15 *UKNA* 2, p. 234 [209].
16 *UKGN*, p. 172 [23].
17 *USB*, pp. 24 [13] 255 [116].
18 *PU* 1, pp. 327–8 [415].
19 Hervay, *Repertorium*, 1984, p. 110.
20 *UKG*, p. 30 [28].
21 *HUK*, pp. 462 [DL, of 1249: an indulgence of twenty days afforded to those lending 'helping hands' towards the completion of the cloister]; pp. 456–7: the site was given by George, advocate of Hamburg, and his wife Margarethe in 1247; 746 [DCCCXCIV, of 1296].
22 *CDG*, pp. 143–4 [106, of 1170].
23 As that of Harvesthude (Frauenthal): *HUK*, p. 461 [DXLVI].
24 *NPR*, p. 636.
25 *UKG*, pp. 16–17 [7].
26 *UKL*, p. 80 [56].
27 Noel, "L'Amour-Dieu," 1876, p. 144.
28 Alberti, *Valledemaria*, 2014, p. 231 [32].
29 Mouret, 'Convers et converses, '1986, p. 303; Bouton, 'Nuns of Cîteaux', 1995, p. 19.
30 Dąbrowski, *Klastoru Zarnowocu*, 1970, p. 61n; *MPH* 5, pp. 515, 517, 526.
31 Mersch, 'Conversi und conversae', 2008, pp. 64, 66.
32 Peugniez, *L'Europe cistercienne*, 2012, pp. 530–1.
33 Mouret, 'Convers et converses', 1986, p. 303.
34 *CNC*, pp. 308–13.
35 *UKR*, pp. 102–3 [117].
36 Berman, *White Nuns*, 2018, pp. 184–6; 'pocket money' is dealt with more fully in Chapter 6.
37 *CNC*, pp. 214–16 [198].
38 *CNC*, pp. 272–3 [252].
39 *CAAB*, p. 66.
40 *LCC (2)*, p. 353.
41 VCH, *County of York* 3, 1913, p. 177.
42 Ibid. p. 179.
43 Löer, *Kloster Welver*, 1997.

Notes to Chapter 4

44. *Statuta* 2, p. 104 [1232/23].
45. *Statuta* 3, pp. 105–6 [1272/10].
46. *RJR* 1, pp. 208 [583], 609 [216].
47. Lester, *Creating Cistercian Nuns*, 2011, pp. 108–9.
48. *Statuta* 2, p. 139 [1235/3]; *LCC (2)*, pp. 352–3.
49. Quoted by an author, but not mentioned in the published statutes.
50. *Statuta* 2, p. 139 [1235/3]; *LCC (2)*, pp. 352–3.
51. VCH, *County of York* 3, 1974, p. 164.
52. Comba, *Rifreddo*, 1999, pp. 53–4.
53. Lester, *Creating Cistercian Nuns*, 2011, pp. 15–17.
54. *Ibid.* p. 36.
55. *Ibid.* pp. 15, 42–4.
56. VCH, *County of Worcester* 2, 1971, pp. 154–5; also in 1319 to 'the white nuns of Whistones': *RTC*, p. 20.
57. Williams, 'Cistercian Nuns', 1975, pp. 158, 165.
58. Williams, *Cistercians in Early Middle Ages*, 1998, pp. 31, 62, 131, 133–4, 208.
59. *CP* 1, p. 247.
60. Steinwascher, 'Kloster Rinteln', 1986, p. 172; *CHS*, pp. 90–1.
61. Faust, 'Zisterzienser', 1994, p. 801.
62. *DHGE* 23, p. 894.
63. Schelgel, *Repertorium*, 1998, p. 400.
64. *OU* 2, pp. 448–9 [577].
65. Lackner, 'Medieval Hungary', 1995, p. 160.
66. *UKLH*, p. 509.
67. *OMA*, pp. 368–9, 374 [239–40, 246].
68. Aurell, 'Les Cisterciennes', 1986, pp. 235–6.
69. Schlegel, *Repertorium*, 1998, p. 421.
70. *CDEM* 2, pp. 339 [CCXCIII], 383 [CCCXXX].
71. *UKW*, pp. 41–2, 52 [1, 17]; *UKWF*, 4: 3, p. 790 [1674].
72. Schlegel, *Repertorium*, 1998, p. 251.
73. Steinwascher, 1986, 'Rinteln', p. 145.
74. *PU* 4, p. 241 [2309].
75. Steinwascher, *Hessen und Thuringen*, p. 283.
76. Wehking, 'Inschriften', 2009, p. 129.
77. Moldehauer, 'Zarrentin', 1963, pp. 50–1.
78. *UZW*, p. 142 [190, of 1318].
79. *CP* 1, pp. 129–30.
80. VCH, *County of York* 3, 1913, p. 164.
81. Ahlers, *Weibliches Zisterziensertum*, 2002, p. 192n.
82. VCH, *County of Warwick* 2, 1908, p. 82.
83. *DHGE* 22, p. 290.
84. Jordan, 'Gender Concerns', 2012, pp. 80–1.
85. Berman, *Women and Monasticism*, 2002, p. 43.

[86] *OU* 3, p. 390 [477].
[87] *UKL*, pp. 144–5 [143, of 1324].
[88] France, *Cistercians in Scandinavia*, 1992, p. 177.
[89] *UKG*, pp. 99–100 [1199].
[90] *UKR*, pp. 74–5 [86].
[91] VCH, *County of York* 3, 1913, p. 179.
[92] VCH, *County of York* 3, 1913, p. 177.
[93] Berman, *White Nuns*, p. 7.
[94] VCH, *County of York* 3, 1913, p. 181.
[95] *Ibid*. p. 181.
[96] *Ibid*. p. 164.
[97] *Ibid*. p. 168.
[98] Lekai, *The Cistercians*, 1977, p. 349; *DHGE* 25, 1994, p. 73.
[99] van der Meer, *Atlas*, 1965, p. 281.
[100] Williams, 2020, pp. 20–1.
[101] *DHGE* 24, p. 581.
[102] *DHGE* 14, p. 26.
[103] Peugniez, *L'Europe cistercienne*, 2012, p. 208.
[104] *DHGE* 21, p. 1262.
[105] Berman, *White Nuns*, 2018, p. 7.
[106] *UE* 1, pp. 385–6 [633].
[107] Dabrowski, *Klastoru Cysterek*, 1970, p. 29.
[108] *DHGE* 29, p. 987.
[109] *DHGE* 25, p. 868.
[110] *MB* 4, Part 2, pp. 536–7.
[111] *Ngn*, p. 136.
[112] *CDEM* 4, pp. 266–7.
[113] *PU* 4, p. 241 [2309].
[114] *RDD*, p. 99 [559].
[115] *DHGE* 23, p. 815.
[116] *DHGE* 24, pp. 587, 885, respectively.
[117] Lester, *Creating Cistercian Nuns*, 2011, pp. 15, 42–4, 58–9, 73.
[118] Mendigen Abbey, online.
[119] *MB* 4, Part 2, p. 518.
[120] *CNC*, p. 309 [287].
[121] Burton, *Yorkshire Nunneries*, 1979, pp. 21–3.
[122] VCH, *County of Northampton* 2, p. 122.
[123] Ploegaerts, *La Ramée*, 1925, p. 72.
[124] *DHGE* 26, p. 440.
[125] *CAM*, pp. 89–90, 105–6.
[126] *CAM*, p. 124 [CXXXIV, of 1246].
[127] Digitale Westfälische Datenbank.
[128] *PU* 3, p. 414–15 [1948].

[129] Jordan, *Gender Concerns*, 2012, pp. 80–1.
[130] *CAF*, p. 52 [LVI].
[131] Steinwascher, *Die Zisterzienser-Stadthöfe*, 1981, p. 190.
[132] *UKGV*, p. 20 [21].
[133] Berman, *White Nuns*, 2018, pp. 68–71.
[134] Berman, *Women and Monasticism*, 2002, pp. 83–4.
[135] *CDN*, pp. 127–8 [88].
[136] *CDN*, pp. 47–8 [37]; Jordan, *Gender Concerns*, 2012, p. 80.
[137] Ibid. p. 80.
[138] Ibid. P. 80.
[139] *CDRB* 1, pp. 247–8 [XII].
[140] *UKH*, pp. 63–4 [180].
[141] *CAAB*, p. 65.
[142] Jordan, *Gender Concerns*, 2012, p. 80.
[143] *UKMD*, pp. 218–19 [239].
[144] Graves, 'Stixwould in the Market Place', 1984, pp. 218, 222, 227.
[145] France, *Cistercians in Scandinavia*, 1992, p. 176.
[146] *PU* 3, pp. 355, 379; 4, pp. 44–5.
[147] Berman, 'Dowries', 1993, p. 8.
[148] France, *Cistercians in Scandinavia*, p. 176.
[149] Reiss, 'Lichtenthal', 1948, p. 237.
[150] Lecture by Sr Eleanor Campion, Mount St Bernard Conference, 1998.
[151] Bouton, 'Nuns of Cîteaux', 1995, pp. 20–1.
[152] *VCH, County of York* 3, 1913, p. 172.
[153] *MPH* 5, p. 513.
[154] *Statuta* 2, p. 231 [1241/5].
[155] *RSL* 2, pp. 231, 241.
[156] Lekai, *The Cistercians*, 1977, p. 356.
[157] Ploegaerts, *La Ramée*, 1925, pp. 27–8.
[158] *Statuta* 1, p. 320 (1206/5).
[159] Nichols, 1979, p. 139.
[160] Luddy, *Cistercian Nuns*, 1931, p. 16.
[161] *VCH, County of York* 3, 1913, p. 177.
[162] Berman, *White Nuns*, p. 25.
[163] *Statuta* 1, pp. 502, 505 [1218/4; 1219/12]; 2, p. 36 [1225/7]; p. 248 [1242/15]; 3, p. 293 [1298/9]; p. 374 [1326/6]; Bouton, *Les Moniales Cisterciennes*, 1986, p. 69.
[164] *Statuta* 2, p. 260 [1243/7].
[165] *Statuta* 3, pp. 239, 252–3 [1287/9, 10, 13].
[166] *CAF*, pp. 51–2 [LV]; *CCG*, p. 7; *RBM* 2, p. 114 [305, of 1261]; *CZT*, p. 45 [1] respectively.
[167] *CAMB*, pp. 21–2.
[168] *UKLT* 6, o. 466 [of 1256].
[169] *CAF*, p. 516 [CCCXCIII].

170 Digitale Westfälische Datenbank, Welver.
171 Albertí, *Valledemaria*, p. 246 [148].
172 VCH, *County of York* 3, 1913, p. 171.
173 VCH, *County of York* 3, 1913, p. 163.
174 Plogaerts, *La Ramée*, 1925, pp. 28–9.
175 *Statuta* 3, p. 288 [1297/4].
176 *UKSH* 2, pp. 38–40 [506].
177 VCH, *County of Northampton* 2, p. 125.
178 *RAO*, p. 167 [754, of 1329].
179 *Statuta* 3, p. 231 [1241/5].
180 *Statuta* 2, pp. 100–1 [1231/53], 231 [1241/5].
181 *Statuta* 2, pp. 271–2 [1243/65], 275 [1244/8].
182 Ahlers, *Weibliches Zisterziensertum*, 2002, p. 190n.
183 *RTC*, pp. 7, 10; *RWB*, pp. 16 [74], 115 [673].
184 *Statuta* 3, p. 342 [1318/3].
185 *UKLT* 6, p. 465.
186 *CC*, p. 29n.
187 Berman, *Women and Monasticism*, 2002, pp. 25–6.
188 *Statuta* 2, pp. 260, 275 [1243/6, 1244/8].
189 Digitale Westfälische Datenbank, Benninghausen.
190 Williams, 2002, *passim*.
191 *NMD*, p. 45.
192 *NBH*, p. 566.
193 *NSO*, p. 424; Williams, 2022, p. 64.
194 Williams, 2022, p. 32.
195 *NDP, passim*.
196 *NSA, passim*.
197 *NWD*, p. 219.
198 Berman, *White Nuns*, p. 25.
199 *Statuta* 1, pp. 502, 505 [1218/4; 1219/12]; 2, p. 36 [1225/7]; p. 248 [1242/15]; 3, p. 293 [1298/9]; p. 374 [1326/6]; Bouton, *Les Moniales Cisterciennes*, 1986, p. 69.
200 *Statuta* 2, p. 260 [1243/7].
201 *DHLT* 6, p. 454.
202 Jamroziak, *Cistercians*, 2013, p. 136.
203 Quoted by an author, but not found in the published statutes.
204 Ploegaerts, *Aywières*, 1924, pp. 24–5.
205 Mersch, 'Conversi und conversae', 2008, pp. 64, 66.
206 Berman, *White Nuns*, 2018, p. 211.
207 Carbonell-Lamothe, 'L'Abbaye de Vignogoul', 1986, p. 272.
208 *HCM* 3, pp. 20 [XXIX, bull of Urban IV, 1262]; 23–4 [XXXIV; bull of Clement IV, 1267], and finally pp. 24–5 [XXXV, of 1268]; *CAMB*, pp. 20–2.
209 *ADY*, H 787.
210 *CAF*, pp. 184–6 [CLXXIII]; Pearson, 'Spirituality', 2005, p. 328.

Notes to Chapter 4

211 Weissenberger, 'Wirtschaftesgeschichliche', 1960, p. 2.
212 *DHGE* 16, p. 1310.
213 *CAMB*, p. 66.
214 *RSL* 2, pp. 234, 239, 244, 251.
215 Wikipedia on-line.
216 *REK* 2, p. 88 [2714].
217 Framond, 'Vernaison', 1980, p. 151.
218 Jurgensmeier, *Hessen und Thüringen*, 2011, p. 56.
219 *CDM* 3, pp. 782–4.
220 *UKL*, pp. 317–18 [40].
221 VCH, *County of York* 3, 1913, p. 163.
222 *Ibid.* p. 163.
223 *Ibid.* p. 177.
224 *Ibid.* p. 161.
225 *USD* 1, p. 65 [34].
226 Jurgensmeier, *Hessen und Thüringen*, 2011, p. 709.
227 Faust, 'Zisterzienser', 1994, p. 276.
228 Richard, 'L'Établissement', 1953, p. 102.
229 *RT* 3, p. 525 [3348, of 1265].
230 *MU* 1, pp. 451 [2866], 525 [3348]; *UKT*, pp. 302–3 [7–8], 303 [9], 305 [13], 307 [17]; *Cf. MU* 1, p. 465 [2964, of 1261]; *RT* 3, p. 451 [2866], of 1260]. .
231 Peugniez, *L'Europe cistercienne*, 2012, pp. 788, 811.
232 van der Meer, *Atlas*, 1965, p. 302.
233 Barrière, *Obazine*, 1977, p. 111.
234 Weissenberger, 'Wirtschaftesgeschichliche', 1960, p. 2.
235 *DHGE* 5, p. 1327.
236 Hegner, 'Kleinbildwerke', 1994, p. 31.
237 Wikipedia on-line.
238 *DHGE* 25, p. 78.
239 Scholten, 'Cistercienserinnen-Klöster', 1908, p. 111.
240 *CAR*, pp. 107–8 [CXI, of 1250]; 174–5 [CLXXXIV, of 1261]; 262–3 [CCCIII, of 1291].
241 *DHGE* 14, p. 673.
242 Wikipedia on-line.
243 *UKL*, pp. 159–60 (No. 159).
244 Alvergnat, 2017, p. 54.
245 Krausen, *Bayern*, 1953, p. 58.
246 *DHGE* 25, p. 621.
247 *DHGE* 21, p. 1270; 24, p. 885.
248 *DHGE* 21, pp. 1378–9.
249 *Statuta* 1, p. 405 [1213/3].
250 *Statuta* 2, p. 36 [1225/7]; *LCC* 2, p. 352.
251 Lekai, *The Cistercians*, 1977, p. 350; Bonis and Wabont, 'Cisterciens et

Cisterciennes', 2001, p. 155.
[252] *Statuta* 1, p. 405 [1213/3].
[253] *Statuta* 1, p. 517 [1220/4].
[254] *Statuta* 1, p. 517 [1220/4].
[255] *Statuta* 1, p. pp. 520–1 [1220/21].
[256] *Statuta* 1, pp. 413–14 [1213/47]; the abbot of Tamié who had been deputed to inform Le Beton did not do so immediately, and was censured at the next year's General Chapter: *Statuta* 1, p. 419 [1214/5].
[257] Albertí, *Valledemaria*, 2014, p. 235 [67].
[258] *Statuta* 2, p. 40; *Cf.* pp. 64 [1227/45], 94 [1231/20].
[259] Lester, *Cistercian Nuns*, 2001, p. 115.
[260] *Statuta* 2, p. 36 [1225/7]; *Cf.* p. 68 [1228/15].
[261] *Statuta* 3, p. 293 [1298/2]; *Cf.* p. 298 [1299/2].
[262] Mecham, 'A Northern Jerusalem', 2005, p. 142.
[263] *Statuta* 1, pp. 415–16 [1213/59].
[264] *Statuta* 2, p. 117 [1233/30].
[265] *Statuta* 2, p. 116 [1233/27].
[266] CAR, pp. 97–9 (nuns not to leave after profession: Innocent IV).
[267] *Statuta* 1, p. 514 [1219/53].
[268] CNC, p. 309 [287].
[269] USB, p. 22 [10]; OU 2, pp. 1250–2 [587].
[270] *Statuta* 2, p. 36 [1225/7]; *Cf.* 2, p. 260 [1243/6].
[271] *Statuta* 2, p. 351 [1257/5].
[272] LCC 2, p. 351; *Statuta* 2, pp. 248, 260 [1242/17; 1243/6].
[273] VCH, *County of York* 3, 1974, p. 179.
[274] Boyd, *Cistercian Nunnery*, 1943, pp. 78–9.
[275] Ploegaerts, *La Ramée*, 1925, p. 27.
[276] Boudreau, 'With Desire I have Desired', 1995, p. 329.
[277] Ploegaerts, *Aywières*, 1924, p. 26.
[278] Freeman, 'Pastoral Care', 2011, p. 337.
[279] Lester, *Cistercian Nuns*, 2011, p. 116.
[280] Lekai, 1977a, p. 356.
[281] RFF, p. 5.
[282] Mötsch, *Thüringen*, p. 220 [K. 8].
[283] CAB, pp. 98–9 [XCVI, of 1301].
[284] *Statuta* 1, pp. 502, 505 [1218/84; 1219/12].
[285] *Statuta* 1, p. 517 [1220/4]; LCC 2, p. 352.
[286] *Statuta* 1, pp. 502, 505 [1218/84, 1219/12].
[287] UKG, pp. 33–4 [32].
[288] Cawley, *Send Me God*, 2003, p. 64.
[289] Goodrich, 'White Ladies', p. 144.
[290] UKLB 1, pp. 287, 292.
[291] Ibid. pp. 196–7.

Notes to Chapter 4

[292] *RBM* 4, pp. 122 [307], 168 [417].
[293] Jurkiewicz, *Szlak Cystersów*, 2006, p. 43.
[294] Hervay, *Repertorium*, 1984, p. 194.
[295] *DHGE* 16, p. 94.
[296] van der Meer, *Atlas*, 1965, p. 280.
[297] *Statuta* 1, p. 405 [1213/2].
[298] *Statuta* 2, pp. 106–7 [1232/34]; Peugniez, *L'Europe cistercienne*, 2012, pp. 391–2.
[299] *Statuta* 2, pp. 217, 238 [1240/9; 1241/44].
[300] *Statuta* 2, p. 232 [1241/11].
[301] *Statuta* 2, pp. 248–9 [1242/15, 16, 17, 18]; 260 [1243/6–7].
[302] *LCC* 2, p. 354.
[303] *Statuta* 2, p. 249 [1242/18].
[304] *LCC* 2, 353.
[305] *LCC* 2, p. 353.
[306] *Statuta* 2, p. 169 [1237/4].
[307] *Statuta* 2, pp. 36–7 [1225/8].
[308] Ostrowitzki, 'moniales de Rhénanie', 2001, p. 242.
[309] *CCS*, p. 290.
[310] Dodel-Brunello, 'Mégemont'. In: *Cîteaux* 37, Parts 3–4, 1985, p. 159.
[311] *HEK* 2, pp. 160–1, [163–4].
[312] *DHGE* 11, 1949, p. 619.
[313] *KDS*, p. 231 [218].
[314] *PDC*, pp. 21 [16], 51 [31].
[315] *Statuta* 3, p. 44 [1266/46].
[316] Berman, *Women and Monasticism*, 2002, pp. 25–6.
[317] *Statuta* 2, p. 150 [1235/47].
[318] *Statuta* 2, pp. 150–1 [1235/48].
[319] *Statuta* 2, p. 168 [1236/66].
[320] Peugniez, *L'Europe cistercienne*, 2012, p. 366.
[321] *Statuta* 2, pp. 174, 180–1 [1237/31, 1237/63]; Peugniez, *L'Europe cistercienne*, 2012, p. 413.
[322] *DHGE* 24, p. 974.
[323] *Statuta* 2, pp. 161 [1236/39]; 166 [1236/61]; 237 [1241, 36].
[324] *MB* 7, Part 3, p. 287.
[325] *DHGE* 22, p. 319.
[326] Roisin, 'L'efflorescence cistercienne', 1943, pp. 356 and *n*.
[327] *RFFK*, p. 7.
[328] *CDVG*, pp. 190–1.
[329] Edwards, J. G. (ed.), *Littere Wallie*, Cardiff: University of Wales Press, 1940, pp. 89, 132–3.
[330] *RFF*, p. 31.
[331] *CDEM*, pp. 331–2 [CCLIV].
[332] *DHGE* 9, p. 1004.

333 *DHGE* 8, pp. 1482–3.
334 Grélois, A., 'Abbé-Père et Abbesse-Mère', 2011, pp. 141–85.
335 *CAR*, pp. 232–7 [CCLXVII, of 1279]; 239–40 [CCLXXVI, of 1284]; 268–9 [CCCV, of 1292].
336 Peugniez, *L'Europe cistercienne*, 2012, p. 542.
337 *Ibid.* pp. 1048–9.
338 *Statuta* 2, pp. 375–6 [1252/1].
339 *Statuta* 2, pp. 389–90 [1253/1].
340 *Statuta* 2, p. 208 [1239/27].
341 *Statuta* 2, p. 423 [1256/10]; *LCC* 2, p. 349.
342 *Statuta* 2, pp. 146 [1235/32], 196 [1238/58], 229–30 [1240/72]. The pope had, in 1232, previously named the abbot of Aulne as Visitor of La Cambre: *Statuta* 2, p. 107 [1232/37].
343 *Statuta* 2, pp. 196 [1238/57], 214 [1239/57].
344 *Statuta* 2, p. 405 [1254/24].
345 Berman, *Cistercian Evolution*, 1999, pp. 195–6; *CDN*, p. 155 [102].
346 *CDN*, pp. 183–8 [112].
347 *DHGE* 9, p. 37.
348 *DAB*, pp. 16–17.
349 Ahlers, *Weibliches Zisterziensertum*, 2002, p. 186n.
350 *RJR* 1, pp. 199 [560], 211 [XXX], 235 [676].
351 Chadwick, 'Kirklees', pp. 353–4.
352 Berman, 'Building in Wood', p. 48.
353 VCH, *County of York* 3, 1913, p. 176.
354 VCH, *County of Warwick* 2, 1908, p. 82; *RGG*, p. 244.
355 *RGG*, p. 244.
356 VCH, *County of York* 3, 1913, pp. 179–80.
357 Burton, 'Yorkshire Nunneries', 1979, pp. 30, 33–4.
358 VCH, *County of Lincoln* 2, p. 150.
359 *Statuta* 2, p. 260 [1243/8].
360 *Statuta* 2, pp. 266, 270–1 [1243/37, 61–3].
361 Southern, R. W., *Western Society and the Church in the Middle Ages*, Pelican History of the Church 2, 1970, p. 317; *Statuta* 2, pp. 271–3 [1243/67].
362 *Statuta* 2, pp. 271–3 [1243/64, 66, 68].
363 *Statuta* 2, p. 271 [1243/64].
364 *Statuta* 2, p. 300 [1245/57].
365 *Statuta* 2, pp. 272 [1243/66], 326 [1247/31], 395–6 [1253/31].
366 *Statuta* 2, p. 281 [1244/37].
367 Schegel, *Repertorium*, 1998, p. 31, n. 98.
368 *Statuta* 2, p. 281 [1244/35].
369 *Statuta* 2, pp. 313–14 [1246/62], 326 [1247/61], 344 [1249/50], 359 [1250/55].
370 *Statuta* 3, p. 225 [1282/36].
371 *Statuta* 2, pp. 467 [1260/27], 468–9 [1260/32].
372 Dimier, 'Violences, Rixes et Homocides', 1972, pp. 53–5.

Notes to Chapter 4

[373] *Statuta* 2, pp. 357–8 [1250/55]; 374–5 [1251/73].
[374] *Statuta* 3, pp. 165–6 [1277/151].
[375] *Statuta* 3, pp. 64 [1268/39], 74 [1269/31], 85 [1270/24].
[376] *Statuta* 3, pp. 106–7 [1272/12].
[377] *Statuta* 3, p. 252 [1291/13].
[378] *Statuta* 2, p. 530 [1355/5].
[379] *Statuta* 2, pp. 39–40 [1225/23].
[380] *Statuta* 2, p. 208 [1239/29].
[381] Popielas-Szultka, *Klastory Cysterek*, 2006, p. 94.
[382] Degler-Spengler, 1995, 'Incorporation', p. 92.
[383] Dimier, 'Chapitres Generaux', 1960, pp. 268–70; Bouton, *Les Moniales Cisterciennes* 1, 1986, p. 50; Connor, 'Abbeys of Las Huelgas and Tart', 1995, pp. 41–2. [The abbesses were of Tart, Belmont, Poulangy, L'Estanche, Beaufay (Belfay), Collonges (Coulonges), Valbayon (Vauxbons), Champbenoît, Montarlot, Droiteval, Molèze, L'Esclache. Montreuil-les-Dames, Bussière, Rieunette, Lume-Dieu, Lieu-Dieu, Ounans and Corcelles. Montreuil, itself only founded in 1136, was able four years later to settle nuns at Fervaques, which became the first nunnery to be under the oversight of Clairvaux: Bonis and Wabont, 'Cisterciens et Cisterciennes', p. 155.
[384] Connor, 'Las Huelgas and Tart', 1995, pp. 40–4.
[385] Berman, 'Women and Monasticism', 2002, p. 8.
[386] Dimier, 'Chapitres Generaux', 1960, pp. 270–1.
[387] *Statuta* 2, pp. 252–3 [1242/40].
[388] Nichols, 'History of the Cistercian Nuns', 1987, pp. 202–3; for a good account of Las Huelgas, see: D'Emilio, 'Las Huelgas', 2005, pp. 191–282.
[389] Connor, 'Las Huelgas and Tart', 1995, pp. 30, 38, 40.
[390] *EOC*, p. 224 [1191/26n].
[391] *DMLH* 1, pp. 25–6 [13, of 1187]; 30–2 [16, of 1188]; 48 [24, of 1189]; 85 [47, of 1199].
[392] *DHGE* 25, 1994, pp. 73–4.
[393] Connor, 'The Royal Abbey', 1988, p. 136.
[394] *Ibid.* pp. 140–1.
[395] *DMLH* 1, pp. 83–5 [44–8, of 1189]; *DHGE* 25, 1994, pp. 73–4; D'Emilio, 'Las Huelgas', 2005, p. 198.
[396] Connor, 'The Royal Abbey', 1988, p. 132.
[397] Venarde, *Women's Monasticism*, 1996, p. 162.
[398] Boyd, *A Cistercian Nunnery*, 1943, p. 84.
[399] VCH, *County of York* 3, 1913, p. 179.
[400] *RJR* 1, pp. 177 [498], 213–14 [603], and 214n; 225 [648].
[401] VCH, *County of York* 3, 1913, p. 160.
[402] VCH, *County of York* 3, 1913, pp. 167–8.
[403] VCH, *County of York* 3, 1913, p. 175.
[404] VCH, *County of York* 3, 1913, p. 180.
[405] *Ibid.* p. 180.
[406] *UKH*, pp 86–7 [215].

407 E. Freeman, 'Nuns'. In: M. G. Bruun, *The Cambridge Companion to the Cistercian Order*, Cambridge: University Press, 2013, p. 103.
408 VCH, *County of Norfolk* 2, 1906, p. 371.
409 Peugniez, *L'Europe cistercienne*, 2012, p. 812.
410 Connor, 'The Royal Abbey', 1988, p. 146.
411 *DHGE* 16, p. 835.
412 *CDNE*, p. 190.
413 *CAAB*, pp. 410–11.
414 Williams, *The Tudor Cistercians*, 2014, p. 349.
415 *Statuta* 2, p. 295 [1245/30]; *LCC* 2, p. 354 [9–10].
416 VCH, *County of Dorset* 2, 1908, p. 88.
417 VCH, *County of Northampton* 2, 1970, p. 125.
418 VCH, *County of York* 3, 1913, p. 161.
419 Richard, 'L'Établissement', 1953, pp. 101–2.
420 Peugniez, *L'Europe cistercienne*, 2012, pp. 811, 829.
421 Fort i Cogul, *Regesta*, 1965, pp. 90–4.
422 *DHGE* 14, p. 457.
423 Ziegler, 'A Rare Parchment', 2005, p. 314.
424 van der Meer, *Atlas*, p. 300.
425 Cardona, 'Cisterciennes en Provence', 1986, pp. 246, 249.
426 Ploegaerts, *Florival*, 1924, pp. 33–4.
427 Ploegaerts, *La Ramée*, 1925, p. 21.
428 Willi, 'Lichtenthal', 1981, pp. 654–5.
429 VCH, *County of Worcester* 2, p. 156; *RDW*, pp. 111–14.
430 Chadwick, 'Kirklees', 1902, pp. 356–7.
431 *CNC*, p. 364 [333].
432 *Statuta* 2, pp. 334–5 [1249/2].
433 *Statuta* 3, p. 268 [1294/4].
434 VCH, *County of York* 3, 1913, p. 181.
435 *Ibid.* p. 172.
436 *DHGE* 21, p. 1270.
437 *Statuta* 3, p. 365 [1323/12].
438 Peugniez, *L'Europe cistercienne*, 2012, p. 212.
439 VCH, *County of Northampton* 2, p. 123.
440 VCH, *County of Lincoln* 2, p. 155.
441 VCH, *County of York* 3, 1913, p. 176.
442 *Statuta* 3, p. 296 [1298/9].
443 VCH, *County of York* 3, 1913, pp. 159–60.
444 *DHGE* 9, p. 1423.
445 *CDN*, pp. 157–65 [104–6], 243 [124].
446 Rèpas, *Traja de Branco*, 2003, pp. 249–52 [4a], 256–60 [7].
447 *CDMC* 1, p. 69 [88].
448 Kastner, 'Klosters Trebnitz', 1858, pp. 214–18.

Notes to Chapter 4

449 *DG* 2, p. 70; ? 'keeper of produce'.
450 Hervay, *Cisterciensis in Hungaria*, 1984, p. 198.
451 *PDC*, pp. 190–200 [122].
452 *ASC*, pp. 37 [141], 49 [222].
453 Guignard, *es monuments primitifs*, pp. 532–47.
454 *ANT*: PT/TT/MSMAR/G3M04/22.
455 *USD* 1, pp. 284–5 [254].
456 *CDN*, pp. 1427–9 [88].
457 Albe, 'Leyme', 1902, pp. 101–2.
458 *UKR*, p. 103 [117].
459 *UKF*, p. 12 [28].
460 Römer-Johannsen, 'Goslar Neuwerk', 1984, p. 268.
461 *VCH, County of York* 3, 1913, p. 171.
462 *CNC*, pp. 308–13 [287].
463 *Statuta* 3, p. 273 [1294/35].
464 *VCH, County of Northampton* 2, 1906, p. 122.
465 Mikkers, E., 'La Spiritualité Cistercienne'. In: M. Villers, ed., *Dictionnaire de Spiritualité* 13, Paris, 1988, pp. 776–7.
466 Boudreau, 'With Desire I have Desired', 1995, p. 328.
467 Ganck, 'Beatrice of Nazareth', 1988, pp. 322, 328–9.
468 Arblaster, 'Beatrice of Nazareth', 2013, p. 43.
469 Sullivan, M. A., 'The *Vita Beatricis*'. In: Nichols and Shank, *Hidden Springs*, 1995, pp. 352, 354.
470 Arblaster, 'Beatrice of Nazareth', 2013, pp. 44–5, 88.
471 Bussels, A., 'Saint Lutgard's Mystical Spirituality'. In: Nichols and Shank, *Hidden Springs*, 1995, pp. 216–22; L. T. Shank, 'Introduction', *Ibid.* p. 207; Jamroziak, *Cistercian Order*, 2013, p. 142; Newman, 'Possessed by the Spirit', 1998, p. 743; Ploegaerts, *Aywières*, 1924, p. 22.
472 Cawley, *Send Me God*, 2003, *passim*; Ploegaerts, *La Ramée*, 1925, pp. 27–8.
473 *DHGE* 4, p. 17.
474 Boudreau, 'With Desire I have Desired', 1995, p. 336; M. Cawley, 'Ida of Nivelles'. In: Nichols and Shank, *Hidden Springs*, 1995, pp. 305–17; Newman, 'Possessed by the Spirit', 1998, pp. 742–3; Newman, 'Crucified by the Virtues'. In: Farmer and Pasternack, 2001, pp. 198–9; Ploegaerts, *La Ramée*, 1925, p. 27.
475 Cawley, *Send Me God*, 2003, *passim*; Ploegaerts, *La Ramée*, 1925, pp. 27–89.
476 *CHDM* 2, pp. 98–9.
477 Mula, 'Emelina and Ascelina', 2011, pp. 44, 46, 52.
478 *CHDM* 1, p. 380; 2. pp. 44–5, 83–4, 185–6.
479 Jamroziak, *Cistercian Order*, 2013, pp. 141–2.
480 Luddy, *Cistercian Nuns*, 1931, p. 16.
481 *DHGE*.
482 *DHGE* 23, p. 746.
483 *Statuta* 2, p. 19 [1222/30]; Thompson, 'Integration of Cistercian Nuns', 1978, p. 239; Mouret, 'Convers et Converses', 1986, p. 288.

484 *NGn*, p. 138.
485 *NSN*, p. 332.
486 *CNC*, pp. 396 [361], 373–4 [339], respectively.
487 *CNC*, p. 138 [122].
488 *OU* 2, pp. 227–8 [287].
489 Burton, *Yorkshire Nunneries*, 1979, p. 17; VCH, *County of York* 3, p. 159.
490 *UKI*, pp. 74 [30], 77 [36], 79–80 [39], respectively; *RT* 2, pp. 357–8 [1976].
491 *UZW*, p. 160 [243].
492 *UKN*, pp. 13–14 [VI].
493 *CAF*, pp. 402–8.
494 Bouton, 'Les abbesses cisterciennes', 1994, p. 195. The printed statutes for 1218 do not include this provision.
495 Wehking, *Die Inschriften*, 2009, p. 129.
496 *Statuta* 3, p. 355 [1321/11].
497 *UE* 1, pp. 155–7 [271].
498 Ahlers, *Weibliches Zisterziensertum*, pp. 2002, 142–3n.
499 *CNC*, pp. xv, 208–13, 408–9.
500 *UKSG* 2, passim.
501 VCH, *County of York* 3, 1913, p. 166.
502 *Ibid*. p. 163.
503 *RJR* 1, pp. 203 [565], 204 [567], 211 [596]; VCH, *County of York* 3, 1913, p. 180.
504 VCH, *County of York* 3, 1913, p. 166.
505 Graves, 1984, p. 216.
506 *Statuta* 3, p. 49 [1267/10].
507 *UKL*, pp. 122, 172.
508 *CKW*, p. 260 [54], 263 [58].
509 Roden, *Saarn*, 1984, p. 72.
510 Cowan and Easson, *Scotland*, 1976, 145; *CCC*, p. 263 [58].
511 *CNC*, passim.
512 *DHGE* 16, p. 842.
513 *CAF*, p. 249 [CCXXIX]; Hautcoeur, *Flines*, 1909, p. 47.
514 Burton, *Yorkshire Nunneries*, 1979, p. 35.
515 Roden, *Duissern*, 1984, p. 103.
516 *UZW*, p. 160 [243].
517 Ronneberger, *Heiligen Kreuz*, 1932, p. 171.
518 *UKL*, p. 92 [72].
519 *UKLH*, pp. 25–6 [62].
520 *UKW*, p. 58 [27].
521 *CAAB*, p. 66.
522 *DMLH* 4, pp. 3–7 [201].
523 *KHU*, pp. 391, 393, respectively.
524 Noted by James France in a lecture at Mount St Bernard's Abbey, 1998.
525 *UZW*, p. 160 [243].

Notes to Chapter 4

526 *LFZ*, pp. 423–4.
527 *CAR*, pp. 51–2 [XLVI–XLVII].
528 *CAR*, pp. 239–2440 [CCLXXVI], 244 (CCLXXXI).
529 *DSHG* 3, pp. 641, 670, 675 [XVI, LXXXI, XCII].
530 VCH, *County of Northampton* 2, 1906, p. 121*n*, 123.
531 *CAR*, pp. 107–8 [CXI, of 1250], 132 [CXXIV, of 1252];, 139 [CXXII, of 1253]; 174–7 [CLXXXIV–CLXXXVI, of 1261]; 182–3 [CXCIV, of 1262]; 272–4 [CCCXII–CCCXIII, of 1292].
532 ANT: PT/TT/MSMAR/G5M07/20; PT/TT/MSMAR/G3M05/21; PT/TT/MSMAR/G1M02/06; PT/TT/MSMRC/MO1/009].
533 Rèpas, *Traja de Branco*, 2003, p. 261 [8].
534 Baury, 'Cañas', 2008, pp. 237–52.
535 Chauvin, *Belfays*, 1994, p. 97 [A. 56].
536 *UKMR*, p. 165 [192]; *Cf.* pp. 168–9 [197].
537 *UKR*, pp. 102–3 [117].
538 *UKLH*, pp. 277–8 [80].
539 *UKMD*, pp. 220–1 [242].
540 VCH, *County of York* 3, 1913, p. 171.
541 *Ibid.* p. 180.
542 *CNC*, p. 138 [122].
543 *UKL*, p. 40 [11]; Ahlers, *Weibliches Zisterziensertum*, 2002, p. 109.
544 *UKMR*, pp. 63–4 [50].
545 *CDBR* 1, pp. 249–50 [[XVII].
546 *UKS*, p. 238 [173].
547 *CDEM* 4, p. 217 [CLVI].
548 *UKMD*, p. 30 [31].
549 *OU* 3, *passim*; 4, *passim*.
550 *MU* 2, p. 47 [727].
551 Mötsch, *Thüringen*, 1999, p. 230 [K. 30].
552 *PU* 2, p. 421 [1161]; 3, p. 287 [1780, of 1296].
553 *UE* 1, pp. 197–8 [346].
554 *MU* 2, p. 48 [728]; *UKN*, p. 31 [15].
555 *UE* 1, p. 474 [770].
556 *OU* 3, p. 361.
557 *MU* 2, pp. 68–9 [757].
558 *MU* 2, p. 161 [879].
559 *DHGE* 25, p. 621.
560 *CKW*, p. 257 (No. 50).
561 Jurgensmeier, *Hessen und Thüringen*, 2011, p. 61.
562 *UKF*, p. 37.
563 *UKLH*, p. 563.
564 *MU* 1, pp. 479–80 [484].
565 Jurgensmeier, *Hessen und Thüringen*, 2011, p. 263.

[566] *UKW*, p. 33; Wikipedia online.
[567] Jurgensmeier, *Hessen und Thüringen*, 2011, p. 704.
[568] *Ibid.* p. 716.
[569] *Ibid.* p. 224.
[570] *UKR*, pp. 74–5 [86].
[571] *MUK*, pp. 1070–2 [656].
[572] *PDC*, pp. 147–8 [85]; he was probably Stephen Taparo, and the chaplains were Thomas and Peter.
[573] VCH, *County of York* 3, 1913, p. 180.
[574] *CDMC* 1, pp. 108–9 [94].
[575] *CDMC* 1, p. 192 [175, of 1229].
[576] *CDMC* 1, p. 192 [175, of 1229]. pp. 150 [132, of 1224]; 163–4 [145, of 1225].
[577] *DLMH* 1, pp. 297–8 [201].
[578] Gahlbeck, 2002, p. 317.
[579] *MB* 4, part 1, p. 446.
[580] *DHGE* 23, p. 746.
[581] Berman, 'Women and Monasticisim', 2002, p. 37.
[582] Aurell i Cardona, 'Les Cisterciennes', 1986, p. 261.
[583] *USM*, p. 255 [414].
[584] Mouret, 'Convers et converses', 1986, p. 288.
[585] *DMLH* 1, p. 121 [72].
[586] *DCB*, p. 46.
[587] *SU* 1, p. 131 [180].
[588] *Statuta* 2, pp. 399–400 [1254/5]; *LCC* 2, p. 355.
[589] *CAR*, pp. 268–9 [CCCV].
[590] Mouret, 'Convers et converses', 1986, p. 288.
[591] *Statuta* 3, p. 285 [1296/8].
[592] *KDS*, p. 226 [213]; *Cf. Statuta* 1, p. 502 [1218/81].
[593] *Statuta* 2, pp. 33–4 [1224/20], 37 [1225/8].
[594] *Statuta* 2, p. 76 [1229/7];; 3, p. 2 [1262/7]; *Cf.* Reimann, 'Cistercians of Bergen', 2004, p. 235*n*.
[595] *SU* 1, p. 131 [180].
[596] *Statuta* 2, pp. 399–400 [1254/5]; *LCC* 2, p. 355.
[597] *Statuta* 3, pp. 210–11 [1281/26].
[598] Roisin, 'L'efflorescence cistercienne', 1943, pp. 369–70; *DHGE* 32, p. 227.
[599] Lester, 'Creating Cistercian Nunns', 2011, p. 75.
[600] Burton, *Yorkshire Nunneries*, 1979, p. 21.
[601] Roden, Dusseren, 1984, p. 135.
[602] *MB* 4, Part 2, pp. 517, 551, respectively.
[603] *CKW*, p. 1260 (No. 54): 'degentis'; 286 (No. 96)./.
[604] *UKO*, p. 6 [16].
[605] *UKH*, p. 292 [523].
[606] Mouret, 'Convers et converses', 1986, p. 291.

Notes to Chapter 4

[607] Digitale Westfälische Datenbank: *Welver*.
[608] Mouret, 'Convers et converses', 1986, p. 291.
[609] *KHU*, p. 61.
[610] *DSHG* 3, p. 670 [LXXXI].
[611] Roden, *Dusseren*, 1984, p. 135.
[612] *UKM* 3, p. 161 [60]; 'textor', the alternative might be 'roofer'.
[613] *UKO*, p. 6 [16].
[614] *UKR*, p. 87 [102].
[615] *CDN*, p. 33 [18–19].
[616] *CAB*, p. 11 [XIV].
[617] *CAB*, p. 64.
[618] Lester, *Creating Cistercian Nuns*, 2011, pp. 175–6.
[619] *CDS* 1, p. 111[236].
[620] *CAR*, pp. 94–5 [C].
[621] *KHU*, p. 153.
[622] *UKLT* 7, pp. 224–6.
[623] *UKLT* 8, pp. 74–6.
[624] Faust, *Die Frauenklöster*, 1984, p. 230.
[625] Digitale Westfälische Datenbank, Benninghausen.
[626] VCH, *County of Northampton* 2, p. 122.
[627] Lackner, 'Early Cîteaux', 1981, p. 62.
[628] *KDS*, pp. 226–7; Reimann, 'Cistercians of Bergen', 2004, p. 235*n*; *SU* 1, No. 180: 'according to the custom of the Order clerks at their profession read their script before the altar, and making the sign of the cross place their deed upon the altar'.
[629] *LCC* 2, p. 355.
[630] *CDNE*, pp. 84–8 [LXIV].
[631] *Statuta* 3, p. 240 [1288/16]; *Cf.* p. 334 [1317/4].
[632] *CNC*, pp. 588–9 [506], 452–3 [415], respectively.
[633] *Statuta* 3, p. 285 [1296/8].
[634] *CDN*, pp. 183–8 [112].
[635] *Statuta* 3, p. 349 [1320/8].
[636] *Statuta* 2, p. 422 [1256/4].
[637] Lackner, 'Early Cîteaux', 1981, p. 62.
[638] *KDS*, pp. 226–7 [213]; Reimann, 'Cistercians of Bergen', 2004, p. 235*n*.
[639] *Statuta* 2, pp. 441–2 [1258/18].
[640] *Statuta* 2, p. 422 [1256/4].
[641] *DMLH* 4, p. 52 [223].
[642] *CDN*, p. 169 [107].
[643] D'Emilio, 'Women and Communities', 2015, p. 296, *n.* 249.
[644] Beam, *People of Medieval* Scotland, online.
[645] *OU* 4, p. 125 [178].
[646] *DAC*, 1978, p. 483.

647 *CNC*, pp. 155-6 [141].
648 VCH, *County of Worcester* 2, 1971, p. 157.
649 Chadwick, 'Kirklees', 1902, p. 325n.
650 Bouton, *Bouchet*, 1979, p. 25.
651 *CDVG*, p. 81 [67].
652 Roden, *Duissern*, 1984, pp. 105, 109.
653 *UKLH*, pp. 277-8 [80].
654 *CDNE*, pp. 84-8 [LXIV].
655 *CDVG*, pp. 233-6 [175].
656 *DCE*, p. 106 [XCIII].
657 *UKGN*, pp. 170-2 [22].
658 *RSL* 2, p. 253.
659 *RSL* 2, p. 241.
660 *LCC* 2, p. 350; *Statuta* 3, p. 334 [1317/4].
661 Lackner, 'Early Cîteaux', 1981, p. 62.
662 *LCC* 2, p. 350; *Statuta* 2, p. 92 [1231/6].
663 *Statuta* 2, pp. 113 [1233/12], 335 [1240/3].
664 Ahlers, *Weibliches Zisterziensertum*, 2002, p. 26n.
665 Thompson, 'Integration of Cistercian Nuns', 1978, p. 239.
666 *NV, passim*. They were: Argenton, Binderen, Differdingen, Florival (Bloemendaal), Maagdendaal (Linter), Muizen, Nazareth, l'Olive, Rotem (Rothem), Terbeeck, Val-duc, Vrouwenpark, Wauthier-Brain.
667 *NBM, passim*: Herkenrode, Maagdendaal, Muysen, Nazareth, Roosendaal, Val-St-Bernard, Vrouenpark, Zwijeke.
668 *CAF*, p. 172 [CLXI].
669 Ploegaerts, *Aywières*, 1924, pp. 24-5.
670 *Statuta* 2, pp. 169 [1237/2], 231 [1241/6], 335 [1249/3]; 3. p. 283 [1296/3].
671 *Statuta* 3, pp. 11 [1263/7], 32 [1265/2]; *Cf*. p. 240 [1287/16].
672 *Statuta* 3, pp. 349 [1320/7], 355 [1321/2], 399 [1332/8].
673 Y. Vanden Bemden and J. Kerr, 'The Glass of Herkenrode Abbey'. In: *Archeologia* 108, 1986, p. 190.
674 *DHGE* 23, 1989, p. 338.
675 *UZW*, p. 160 [243; Brother Ulric Vederlin was the confessor in 1333].
676 Rèpas, *Traja de Branco*, 2003, pp. 249-52 [4a].
677 *PU* 2, pp. 507-8 [1272]; *Cf*. McGuire, 'Cistercians in Denmark', 1982, p. 151.
678 VCH, *County of York* 3, 1913, pp. 171, 174, 176.
679 *Statuta* 3, p. 142 [1275/14].
680 *Statuta* 3, pp. 233-4 [1285/8, 1286/3].
681 VCH, *County of York* 3, 1913, p. 164.
682 *Ibid*. p. 177.
683 *Statuta* 3, pp. 409 [1334/10], 437 [1335/3].
684 Jamroziak, *Cistercian Order*, 2013, p. 141.
685 Chadwick, 'Kirklees', 1902, pp. 357-8.
686 Baury, 'le Maine Médiéval', 2008, p. 59.

Notes to Chapter 4

687 CZT, p. 86 [LXXXIII].
688 Coomans, 'Low Countries', 2005, pp. 100–1.
689 BL, Cotton MS Caludius III, f. 141.
690 NBT, p. 237.
691 NSS, passim.
692 NSA, pp. 520–1.
693 NT, p. 1648; UWKF 4:2, p. 1269 [1320].
694 CKW, p. 261 (Nos. 55 6).
695 NMD, passim.
696 UKI, p. 96 [91].
697 NWN, p. 390.
698 CNC, pp. 308–13.
699 France, *Cistercians in Scandinavia*, 1992, p. 177.
700 VCH, *County of York* 3, 1913, p. 172.
701 Ploegaerts, *Aywières*, 1924, pp. 11–13; pp. 14, 25, re 'the gate'.
702 Hautcoeur, *Flines*, 1909, pp. 29–30.
703 CAM, pp. v-vi; 54 [LXVII, of 1233], 63–4 [LXXVIII, of 1236].
704 CAM, p. 219 [CCXXVIII].
705 CCG, pp. 26–7, 29–30; Canivez, *Cîteaux en Belgique*, 1926, pp. 415–16; Cf. Dorpe, 1951, Groeninge, p. 86 [42].
706 Coomans, 'Mémoire Dynastique', 2005, p. 104.
707 CNC, p. 443 [407].
708 USD 1, pp. 77–8 [49].
709 *Statuta* 3, p. 212 [1281/34].
710 RFF, p. 25.
711 XXXX pp. 150 [132, of 1224]; 197–8 [181, of 1230].
712 Moldenhauer, *Zarrentin*, 1963, pp. 50–1.
713 USD 1, pp. 284–6 [254–5].
714 Ahlers, *Weibliches Zisterziensertum*, p. 192n.
715 Jamroziak, *Cistercian Order*, 2013, p. 137.
716 CZT, p. 86 [LXXXIII].
717 UKR, pp. 75 [86], 103 [117], respectively.
718 UKWF, 4: 3, p. 1115.
719 PU 4, p. 219 [2278].
720 Berman, *White Nuns*, p. 71.
721 D'Emilio, 'Women and Communities', 2015, pp. 272–3.
722 Trops, Heinrich, *Rīgas Sv. Marijas Magdalēnas*, University of Riga thesis, 1943. (Kindly communicated to me by the Very Revd. Andris Abakuks).
723 ANT: PT/TT/ MSMAR/G5M05/31.
724 DHGE 23, pp. 804–5; Creutz, *Bibliographie*, 1983, p. 112.
725 DHGE 13, p. 1003.
726 Schlegel, *Repertorium*, 1998, p. 169.
727 *Statuta* 1, pp. 320–1 [1206/5]; LCC 2, p. 351.
728 Nichols, 'Internal Organisation', 1979, p. 39.

729 VCH, *County of York* 3, 1913, pp. 164, 174, 177.
730 *UKMD*, pp. 220–1 [242].
731 *CNC*, pp. 568–9 [493].
732 *CDG*, pp. 236–8 [187].
733 *CNC*, p. 180 [168].
734 *Statuta* 2, p. 235 [1241/26].
735 *Statuta* 3, p. 268 [1294/3].
736 *Statuta* 3, p. 283 [1296/3].
737 Gol, *Vallbona*, 1973, pp. 89–90.
738 VCH, *County of York* 3, 1913, p. 177.
739 *UKR*, p. 67.
740 *DHGE* 15, p. 100.
741 Bouton, *Bouchet*, 1979, pp. 16, 24, 26.
742 *DHGE* 24, p. 1295.
743 Connor, 'The Royal Abbey', 1988, p. 132.
744 *DHGE* 25, p. 77.
745 *DHGE* 25, p. 622.
746 *DHGE* 6, pp. 269–70.
747 Cowan, *Medieval Religious Houses*, 1976, p. 238.
748 *REK* 1, p. 57 [321].
749 VCH, *County of York* 3, 1913, pp. 171–2.
750 VCH, *County of Lincoln* 2, p. 151; *CNC*, pp. 308–13.
751 VCH, *County of York* 3, 1913, p. 177.
752 Chadwick, 'Kirklees', 1902, p. 359.
753 VCH, *County of York* 3, 1913, p. 161.
754 VCH, *County of Lincoln* 2, 1906, pp. 150–2.
755 VCH, *County of Warwick* 2, 1908, p. 82.
756 *Statuta* 2, pp. 388–9 [1252/56–7].
757 Pearson, 'Spirituality', 2005, p. 330.
758 Coomans, 'Mémoire Dynastique', 2005, p. 135.
759 *MUK*, pp. 887–90 [533], 1118 [683]; Cf. *UKI*, pp. 65–6.
760 *RT* 2, pp. 146–7 [769, of 1187].

Notes to Chapter 5

1 Bouton, 1995, p. 19: 'The *The Life of Ida of Nivelles* mentions the nuns of La Ramée in Brabant as resting in the fields after harvest. The fields could have been in the enclosure, as in the twelfth century the meaning of 'enclosure' was still quite broad'.
2 Ploegaerts, *Aywières*, 1924, p. 9.
3 TNA, SC11/506.
4 *CAF*, pp. 89–91 [XCVII, XCIX].
5 *CNC*, pp. 37–8 [16].
6 *CNC*, pp. 206–8 [191–2].

Notes to Chapter 5

7. *CNC*, pp. 270–1 [250].
8. *CNC*, pp. 332–3 [304].
9. *CNC*, pp. 334–5 [307]; *Cf.* pp. 333–41 [305–6, 308–9, 312–13].
10. *OU* 3. p. 390 [477, of c. 1273].
11. Berman, *Women and Monasticism*, 2002, p. 23.
12. Berman, *White Nuns*, 2001, p. 96.
13. *UKSG* 1, pp. 392 [377, of 1208]; 395 [383, of 1210]; 401 [394, of 1214], and others.
14. Ibid. 3, pp. 888, et seq.
15. *UKLT* 7, p. 469.
16. *CAR*, passim.
17. Berman, *White Nuns*, 2018, pp. 208–12.
18. *UKH*, p. 195 [395].
19. *DMF, CCS*, passim.
20. *ANT*: Cloass PT/TT/*passim*.
21. *CDVG passim*.
22. *PU* 3, pp. 313–14 [1812].
23. *DCB*, pp. 59–60.
24. *NPR*, *passim*, and p. 639.
25. *NM*, *passim*.
26. *HUK*, p. 516 [DCXXVI, of 1258].
27. Berman, *Cistercian Evolution*, 1999, p. 193.
28. *HCM* 3, pp. 3–7 [II, IV, VI]; *CAF*, pp. 34 [XXXIII], 41–2 [XLII, XLIII, XLIV].
29. McGuire, 'Cistercians in Denmark', 1982, p. 160.
30. *CNC*, pp. 498–9 [452].
31. *UKMD*, p. 71 [2].
32. Landesarchiv Schleswig-Holstein, Mittelalterliche Urkunden des Uetersen-Klosters.
33. *DSB*, p. 374 [XVII].
34. *CC*, pp. 77–8 [LXXVII].
35. *OU* 4, pp. 311–12 [492].
36. *PU* 2, p. 527 [1302].
37. *CAF*, pp. 250–2 [CXXXV].
38. Kucharski, *Ołobok*, 2000, pp. 322, 327, 338.
39. TNA, SC8/309/15402.
40. *EMB*, pp. 127–9.
41. *HEK* 1, pp 386–7 [51].
42. *MU* 2, pp. 326–7 [1120].
43. *NM*, p. 658.
44. Coelho, *Expresiones*, 2006, pp. pp. 162–3.
45. *CDG*, pp. 144–5 [107].
46. *CDG*, p. 192 [148, of 1181].
47. *UKGV*, pp. 16–17 [16].
48. *UKNA*, p. 361 [329].

49 *UKMD*, p. 120 [81].
50 *UKW*, p. 59 [28].
51 *UKW*, pp. 74–5 [52, of 1309].
52 *CCS*, p. 674.
53 *RFF*, p. 37.
54 *CAR*, pp. 150–1 [CLIII, of 1257].
55 *CDBR* 1, p. 249 [XV].
56 *UKLH*, p. 243 [26].
57 ANT: PT/TT/MSMRC/M05/019.
58 *PU* 2, p. 252 [940].
59 *PU* 2, pp. 389–90 [1114–15], 395–8 [1124]. 419–20 [1159].
60 *UKF*, pp. 55–6 [90].
61 *CZT*, p. 86 [LXXXIII].
62 *CAB*, p. 28 [XXXVI].
63 VCH, *County of York* 3, 1974, p. 179.
64 France, *Cistercians in Scandinavia*, 1992, p. 173.
65 *UKLB* 1n p. 481.
66 *CAR*, pp. 153–4 [CLVI].
67 *DHGE* 22, pp. 634–5.
68 France, *Cistercians in Scandinavia*, 1992, p. 176.
69 *CZT*, p. 45 [l].
70 *CAMB*, pp. 21–2.
71 Digitale Westfälische Datenbank: Welver.
72 *PU* 3, pp. 379–80 [1904]; the deed was repeated in 1303: *PU* 4, pp. 91–2 [2092].
73 *PU* 3, pp. 380–2 [1905, 1906].
74 *PU* 4, pp. 44–5 [2027].
75 Popielas-Szultka, *Klastory Cysterek*, 2006, p. 65.
76 *DSB*, p. 385 [XLVII].
77 *SU* 1, pp. 179–81 [247].
78 *USB*, pp. 83–4 [89], 111–12 [119].
79 *MB* 3: 2, p. 456.
80 *MB* 2: Part 2, p. 459.
81 *UKL*, pp. 158–9 [159], of 1333.
82 *UE* 1, p. 238 [400].
83 *UE* 1, p. 238 [400].
84 *UKLT* 7, pp. 206–8.
85 *AU*, pp. 512–13 [232].
86 *AU*, pp. 524–6 [1245].
87 *CDNE*, pp. 77–9 [LX], 102–4 [LXXV], respectively.
88 *CDNE*, pp. 176–7 [CXV].
89 *CDNE*, pp. 158–60 [CVI].
90 *UKMR*, pp. 138–40 [163].
91 *UKH*, *passim*, and p. 99 [239].

92 *UKH*, pp. 41, 55–6; 146–7, 188 [382].
93 *CAM*, p. 66 [LXXXVII].
94 *UKSH* 1, pp. 253–4 [269].
95 *UKL, passim*.
96 *UKWF*, 4: 3, pp. 602–3 [1327]; p. 516 [1135].
97 Gahlbeck, 2002, pp. 168, 171.
98 Peugniez, *L'Europe cistercienne*, 2012, p. 212.
99 *OU* 2, pp. 213–14 [270–1].
100 *CAM, passim*.
101 Lester, *Creating Cistercian Nuns*, 2011, pp. 188–9.
102 *CAAB*, pp. 100–1.
103 Wieland, 'Heiligenthal', 1899, pp. 164–6.
104 *UKG*, pp. 13–25 [1–19].
105 *MU* 1, p. 547 [3492].
106 *UKT*, pp. 328–9 [62–3].
107 *UAB*, 0.
108 Charvátová, 'Bohême Mèdiévale', 1994, p. 769.
109 Kastner, 'Klosters Trebnitz', 1858, pp. 198–200.
110 Jurgensmeier, *Hesse und Thüringen*, 2011, p. 82.
111 *DHGE* 5, p. 1327.
112 *DHGE* 18, p. 1014.
113 *PU* 1, pp. 403–4 [522].
114 *UE* 1, pp. 126–9 [213].
115 *DHGE* 18, p. 1117.
116 Peugniez, *L'Europe cistercienne*, 2012, pp. 377–8.
117 *DHGE* 26, p. 465.
118 *DHGE* 19, p. 75.
119 Schlegel, G. (ed.), *Repertorium der Zisterzen*, 1998, p. 232.
120 *PU* 1, pp. 368–9 [476].
121 *CDVG*, pp. 59–60 [51].
122 Berman, *White Nuns*, 2018, pp. 158–74, 201.
123 Peugniez, *L'Europe cistercienne*, 2012, p. 812.
124 Connor, 'The Royal Abbey', 1988, p. 146.
125 *DHGE* 25, p. 78.
126 Berman, Women and Monasticism, 2002, p. 23; *DMLH* pp. 22 [11, of 1187], 56 [30, of 1192]; 176–8 [266, of 1231].
127 *UKSH* 1, pp. 159–60 [168].
128 *UKSH* 1, pp. 203–4 [220].
129 *OU* 3, pp. 131–2 [182].
130 *RFF*, pp. 2–3.
131 *UKS*, p. 193 [31].
132 *UKS*, pp. 202–3 [53, 57].
133 *DCB*, pp. 14–19, 23–4, 97–8.

134 *DCB*, pp. 24–5, 111.
135 *HEK* 1, pp. 366 [503], 489–890 [679].
136 *UKW*, pp. 47–8 [10–11]; *UKWF*, 4:3, p. 689 [1437].
137 *DSB*, pp. 371–2, 375.
138 *CDEH* 4, p. 250 [CCXXXIV].
139 *CDEM* 4, p. 39 (XXXI).
140 *CDBR* 1, p. 480 [11].
141 *UKLH*, p. 251 [41].
142 *PU* 4, pp. 224–6 [2288].
143 *CDG*, pp. 217 [171, of 1182; grant made by Peter Dominic, and his mother, Marina Romaniz]; 228 [179 of 1183; grant of Gonzalo Martínez].
144 *UKF*, p. 11 [25].
145 *OU* 2, pp. 234–5 [295, of 1232]; 382–3 [481].
146 *CDVG*, pp. 122–4 [99].
147 *UKBR*, pp. 95, 102, 124, respectively.
148 *CAM*, p. 122 [CXXXII].
149 *PU* 2, pp. 527–8 [1302], 531–2 [1309].
150 VCH, *County of York* 3, 1913, p. 172; *TE*, pp. 74, 299, 323, 325, 334.
151 *TE*, pp. 138, 178, 183–4, 213.
152 *TE*, pp. 276, 289, 303, 305.
153 *TE*, p. 276.
154 BL, Add Ch 20433.
155 VCH, *County of Worcester* 2, 1971, p. 157.
156 VCH, *County of Worcester* 2, 1906, pp. 154–5.
157 *RTC*, p. 47.
158 *CAR*, pp. 33–4 [XXVII, of 1224], 41–2 [XXXVI, of 1230].
159 ANT: PT/TT/MSMRC/MO1/008.
160 *OU* 2, p. 260 [333].
161 *OU* 4, p. 276 [436, of 1295].
162 *PU* 1, pp. 323–4.
163 *CAM*, p. 193 [CC].
164 *UKNA*, pp. 819–20 [784].
165 *DSB*, p. 398 [LXXXV].
166 Schlegel, *Repertorium*, 1998, p. 422.
167 *PU* 1, p. 298 [270].
168 *CNC*, pp. 284–8 [265, 268]; 306–7 [286], respectively.
169 TNA, E326/2878.
170 *CDEM* 3, pp. 266–7 (CCLXXV).
171 *PU* 2, p. 421 [1161].
172 Kastner, 'Klosters Trebnitz', 1858, pp. 195–200.
173 *CCC*, pp. 61–2.
174 *CCC*, p. 66.
175 *CDN*, pp. 146–8 [97, of 1280].

Notes to Chapter 5

176. *PDC*, pp. 75–80 [44].
177. Borrero, *El Archivo de San Clemente*, 1992, p. 28 [77].
178. *PU* 2, pp. 318–19 [449].
179. *PRU* 3, pp. 373–7 [492].
180. *ANT*: PT/TT/GV/15/2/4; PT/TT/ MSML/ G4M02/007.
181. *ANT*: PT/TT/MSMAR/G3M02/10 PT/TT/MSMAR/G5M08/27.
182. *CAM*, p. 46 [LVII].
183. *CAM*, pp. 155–6 [CLXV].
184. *USD*, p. 86 [58].
185. *USD* 1, pp. 193–9 [157], 200–3 [158–61].
186. *USD* 1, pp. 282–3 [252].
187. *CDEM* 7, p. 117 [169].
188. *CDN*, pp. 31–3 [26], 76–9 [64]; 96–101 [73]; 104–6 [76], respectively. For CDEM the Knights Templar, see also: pp. 112–18 [82–3, of 1264] and pp. 120–1 [85, of 1266].
189. *CAB*, p. 26 [XXXIV].
190. *DHLT* 6, pp. 455–6 [of 1251].
191. *CDEM* 3, pp. 369–70 [CCCLXVII].
192. *CDEM* 4, p. 377 [CCXCVII]; 5, pp. 40 [XXXIX], 105 [CII].
193. *CDEM* 3p. 202 (CLXXV).
194. National Archives, Kew, England: SC8/54/2694.
195. *UKM* 3, pp. 155–6 [51].
196. *PU* 7, p. 214 [4399].
197. *PU* 2, pp. 551–2 [822].
198. *Statuta* 3, pp. 472 [1260/49]; 100 [1271/46].
199. *Statuta* 2, p. 414 [1255/33 ?23]; 445 [1258/36]; 56–7 [1259/38, 44].
200. *Statuta* 3, p. 191 [1279/44].
201. *CDG*, pp. 521–2 [452].
202. *CAR*, pp. 56–7 [LIV].
203. *CZT*, pp. 78–80 [LXXVII].
204. *Statuta* 2, pp. 90–1 [1230/33]; *Cf.* Williams, *Cistercians in the Early Middle Ages*, 1998, p. 146.
205. *CDVG*, pp. 51–2 [45].
206. *UKD*, pp. 76–7 [85].
207. Albe, 'Leyme', 1902, pp. 98–9 [16].
208. *UKH*, pp. 127–38 [287–91, 293–4, 298–9].
209. *CNC*, p. 459 [422].
210. *PU* 2, pp. 329–30 [1040].
211. *PU* 3, p. 272 [1765].
212. *PU* 1, pp. 416–17 [543].
213. *CDRB* 1, p. 482 [VII].
214. *UKI*, pp. 111–14.
215. Berman, *Women and Monasticism*, 2002, pp. 70–1 [35].

216 *CAF*, pp. 46–7 [XLVIII].
217 *DHGE* 24, p. 581.
218 *CZT*, pp. 51 [LVII], 52–3 [LVIII].
219 *DVM*, p. 5.
220 Albe, 'Leyme', 1902, pp. 101–2 [12].
221 *CDN*, p. 89 [69].
222 *DSHG* 3, p. 650 [XXXVI].
223 *KD* 1, pp. 276–7.
224 *OU* 3, p. 81 [108, of 1254].
225 *OU* 3, pp. 147–8 [205–6].
226 Jurgensmeier, 'Hessen und Thüringen', 2011, p. 86.
227 *CDNE*, pp. 171–2 [CXII].
228 *CDNE*, p. 38 [XXX].
229 *CDNE*, pp. 71–2 [LIV].
230 *UE* 1, p. 434 [711].
231 *UKMR*, p. 117 [131].
232 *CNC*, p. 133 [111].
233 *CAM*, p. 197 [CCV].
234 *PU* 2, p. 362 [1082].
235 *UKSH* 1, p. 419 [466].
236 D'Emilio, 'Women and Communities', 2015, p. 270.
237 *DGA*, pp. 24–5.
238 *ASC*, p. 37 [141, of 1316].
239 Reiss XXX p. 237.
240 *CAF*, p. 490 [CXXIV bis].
241 Hautcoeur, *Flines*, 1909, p. 40.
242 Peugniez, *L'Europe cistercienne*, 2012, p. 235.
243 *Ibid*. p. 376.
244 Berman, *White Nuns* 2018, pp. 83–4.
245 *PU* 3, pp. 437–8.
246 Schlegel, *Repertorium*, 1998, p. 409.
247 Connor, 'Las Huelgas and Tart', 1995, p. 46.
248 *CNC*, pp. 47–8 [25].
249 *CNC*, p. xlii.
250 *CAAB*. 61.
251 Schlegel, *Repertorium*, 1998, p. 474.
252 Boyd, 'A Cistercian Nunnery', 1943, pp. 152–3. [There were about thirty tenants around 1250: *CAR*, pp. 110–12 [CXIV].
253 *CAR*, pp. 144–5 [CXLVII], 217 [CCALII].
254 *CNC*, p. 315 [290].
255 *UKL*, p. 117 [108].
256 *OU* 2, p. 392 [493, of 1247]. 2 weights of wheat, two of barley and one of oats annually.

Notes to Chapter 5

257 *OU* 3. p. 315 [459].
258 Popielas-Szultka, *Klastory Cysterek*, 2006, p. 62.
259 *UKS*, p. 238 [172].
260 *UKW*, pp. 61–3 [32, 33].
261 Berman, *Women and Monasticism*, 2002, p. 67.
262 *DHGE* 22, p. 466.
263 *VCH*, *County of Warwick* 2, 1908, p. 82.
264 Maricourt, 'Gomerfontaine', 1907, p. 449.
265 *MU* 2, p. 19 [601].
266 *UKWF*, pp. 696–7 [1456].
267 Cooman, 'Low Countries', 2005, p. 118.
268 *OU* 4, pp. 232 [355], 287–8 [454].
269 *DAB*, p. 64 [II].
270 *AU*, pp. 509–10 [229].
271 Chadwick, 'Kirklees', 1902, p. 321.
272 Berman, *White Nuns*, 2018, pp. 96–7.
273 *UKMR*, pp. 45–8 [22–3, 25–6]; 70–1 [61, of 1289; 63, of 1290]; 90 [92, of 1303].
274 *UKG*, pp. 42–3 [44].
275 *USB*, p. 77 [81].
276 *PU* 2, pp. 211–12 [884, of 1269].
277 *CDNE*, pp. 114–17 [LXXXII].
278 Hervay, *Repertorium*, 1984, p. 193.
279 *UKSG* 2, pp. 465–8 [458, 461].
280 *CAAB*, p. 63.
281 *CZT*, pp. 37–8 [XLI].
282 *UKSH* 1, p. 419 [466].
283 *CAM*, pp. 5–6 [VII].
284 *CCG*, p. 2.
285 *UKG*, p. 65 [72].
286 *CAF*, pp. 297–8 [CCLXXVI].
287 Roden, *Dusseren*, 1984, p. 113.
288 Goodrich, 'White Ladies'.
289 *UKN*, p. 122 [LXIII].
290 *CAF*, pp. 145–6 [CXXXV].
291 Wieland, 'Wechterswinkel', 1899, p. 297.
292 Barraud, 'Gomerfontaine', 1862, p. 582.
293 *CDNE*, pp. 16–18 [XIII].
294 Scholten, 'Cistercienserinnen-Klöster', 1908, p. 111.
295 Coelho, *Expresiones*, 2006, pp. 83–4.
296 *CMDC* 1, pp. 114–15 [100].
297 *DSB*, pp. 370–1 [III–IV].
298 *RFFK*, pp. 1, 7.
299 *CDNE*, pp. 59–60 [XLV], 61–2 [XLVII], respectively.

300 *CDNE*, pp. 148–50 [XCVIII–XCIX].
301 Berman, *White Nuns*, 2018, p. 201.
302 *UHLT* 7, pp. 457–8.
303 *MU* 1, p. 253 [1583].
304 *UE* 1, pp. 251–2 [421].
305 Mötsch, *Thüringen*, 1999, pp. 223–4 [K. 14].
306 *UKHB* 1, p. 63 [139].
307 Berman, *White Nuns*, 2018, p. 131.
308 Berman, *White Nuns*, 2018, pp. 204–5.
309 *RFF*, pp. 7, 46, 49.
310 Schlegel, *Repertorium*, 1998, p. 443.
311 *KHU*, pp. 75, 105, 153, 172, 174, 201, 218, 220, 232, 245.
312 *HEK* 2, pp. 552–6 [561].
313 Peugniez, *L'Europe cistercienne*, 2012, p. 77.
314 *KHU*, p. 308.
315 *ASC*, p. 33 [114, of 1309].
316 *CMDC* 1, p. 187 [170].
317 *PDC*, pp. 80–2, 89–91 [45, 49].
318 *PDC*, pp. 103–7 [58–9, of 1298–9].
319 *DMLH* 1, pp. 102 [57, of 1201]; 175 [109, of 1211]; 2, pp. 9–11 [260, of 1231]; 239–1 [437, of 1253].
320 Règpas, *Traja de Banco*, 2003, pp. 382, 385 [87].
321 *ANT*: PT/TT/MSMRC/M05/018.
322 *ANT*: PT/TT/MSMRC/M05/020.
323 Borrero, 'Archivo de San Clemente', 1992, p. 33 [113].
324 Berman, *Women and Monasticism*, 2002, p. 23; *White Nuns*, p. 44.
325 Berman, *White Nuns*, p. 44.
326 Peugniez, *L'Europe cistercienne*, 2012, p. 57.
327 Berman, *White Nuns*, 2018, p. 41.
328 '4 decim viginti'.
329 *CDN*, p. 187.
330 *CAS*, p. 220.
331 *VCH*, *County of Northampton* 2, 1906, p. 125.
332 *CNC*, pp. 399–400 [367–8].
333 *CNC*, passim.
334 *CNC*, pp. 305 [284], 386 [349].
335 *CNC*, p. 76 [55].
336 Chauvin, *Belfays*, 1994, p. 80 [A. 4].
337 Chadwick, 'Kirklees', 1902, pp. 322–3.
338 *HCM* 3, p. 8 [VIII].
339 Jordan, *Gender Concerns*, 2012, pp. 118–25.
340 Hautcoeur, *Flines*, 1909, pp. 30–1; *CAF*, pp. 36–7 [XXXVI].
341 Burton, 'Yorkshire Nunneries', 1979, p. 14; they were Keldholme, 12 sacks

Notes to Chapter 5

p.a.); Rosedale (10), Swine (8), Hampole (6) and Wykeham (4); Evans, *Pegolotti*, 1936, pp. 265–6.

342 Graves, 'Stixwould'. In: Nichols and Shank (ed.), *Distant Echoes*, 1984, *passim*; Berman, *White Nuns*, p. 43.
343 CNC, p. 131 [109].
344 CNC, pp. 33–4.
345 CNC, pp. xlv, 413–14 [382–4].
346 Berman, *White Nuns*, pp. 43–4.
347 TNA, E132/3/30.
348 UKH, pp. 134–5 [294].
349 UKN, p. 64 [XXIX].
350 Berman, *Women and Monasticism*, 2002, p. 70 [35].
351 OU 2, pp. 361–2 [457]; 3, p. 73 [95].
352 CAS, pp. 194, 220.
353 UKL, p. 84 [61].
354 UKG, p. 48 [52], 57–8 [61], respectively.
355 UKMR, p. 52 [31, of 1278].
356 MU 2, pp. 72 [762, of 1256] and 432–3 [1254, of 1272] respectively.
357 PU 4, pp. 19–20 [1998].
358 KHU, p. 203.
359 Schlegel, *Reperotrium* 1998, p. 502.
360 UKL, pp. 34, 83, 118–19.
361 OU 2, pp. 327–8 [418, of 1242].
362 RT 2, pp. 27–8 [150]. A photograph exists of American soldiers fishing near Ichtershausen at the close of World War 2: *Ancestry* magazine 19, Part 3, Provo, Utah, May-June 2001, p. 24.
363 UKSR, 1, pp. 67 [142], 407 [1089].
364 Borrero, 'El Archivo de San Clemente', 1992, p. 26 [63].
365 ASC, pp. 36 [134, of 1314]; 43 [180–2]; 180–1; 49 [222, of 1347].
366 PU 2, pp. 372–3 [688–9, of 1260], 395–8 [1124, of 1278]; 434–6 [1178].
367 PU 2, pp. 372–3 [1097, of 1278].
368 PU 3, pp. 33–4.
369 PU 2, pp. 108–9 (Żarnowiec), 372–3, 412 (Koszalin), 396 (Szczecin); 3. pp. 33–4 (Wolin).
370 PU 3, pp. 141–2 [1598, of 1291].
371 Schlegel, *Repertorium*, 1998, p. 381.
372 MU 2, pp. 432–3, cf. p. 401.
373 KD 1, 68–9, 78–9 (? 268).
374 Grüger, 'Der Orden der Zisterzienser', 1982, p. 95.
375 Wyrwa, 2000, p. 318.
376 Barraud, 'Gomerfontaine', 1862, p. 581.
377 *Ibid.* pp. 583–4.
378 CAM, pp. 3 [V], 7 [VIII, of 1227], 10 [XIII], 48 [LX, of 1233].
379 UKS, pp. 186–7 [11, of 1255].

380 *PU* 2, p. 139 [788].
381 France, *Scandinavia*, 1992, pp. 281–3.
382 Berman, *Women and Monasticism*, 2002, p. 23.
383 Ibid. p. 71 [35]; *White Nuns*, 2018, p. 81.
384 Berman, *White Nuns*, 2018, p. 203.
385 *HEK*, p. 441 [617].
386 *CAMB*, p. 8.
387 Berman, *Whute Nuns*, p. 59.
388 Berman, *Women and Monasticism*, pp. 108–11; 'Dowries', 1993, pp. 3–4.
389 Berman, *Women and Monasticism*, pp. 62–3, 65.
390 *PU* 2, pp. 4234 [1176], 456 [1213], 462 [1220].
391 *CDVG*, pp. 1 [1], 15–16 [13].
392 *CDVG*, pp. 7–8 [7].
393 *PU* 2, p. 456 [1213, of 1281], 462 [1220, of 1281]; 3, pp. 26–7.
394 *MU* 1, p. 484 [3085], 513 [3262].
395 *CZT*, pp. 20–1 [XXII, of 1230], 24 [XXV, of 1231]; 42–3 [XLVII].
396 *UE* 1, p. 389 [638].
397 Mötsch, *Thüringen*, 1999, pp. 230, 238 [K. 32, 55].
398 *DCE*, p. 85 [XLVII].
399 *DCE*, p. 107 [XCVI].
400 *REK* 3, p. 19 [103].
401 *DHGE* 9, p. 825.
402 *RT* 2, pp. 357–8 [1976]; *UKI*, p. 74.
403 *KHU*, p. 6.
404 *DGA*, p. 21.
405 *UE* 1, pp. 396–7 [648].
406 *DSHG* 2, pp. 383, 389, 393.
407 *UKB*, p. 640 [No. 63].
408 *UKI*, p. 88 [65].
409 Jamieson, 'St Mary, Haddington', 1952, p. 4.
410 Graves, 'Economic Activities of the Cistercians'. In: *Analecta S. O. Cist.* 12, 1957, p. 19n.
411 Waddell, C, 'Cistercian Institutes', !994, p. 33.
412 Cf. *DD*, pp. 1537–8 (of 1288).
413 *UKMD*, pp. 90 [33], 91–2 [35], 92–3 [37], 93–4 [38], 98 [44], 100 [47], 102 [50], 105–7 [57–8], 110 [64], 112 [68], 121 [834], 122 [84].
414 *UKMD*, pp. 92–3 [27].
415 Faust, 'Zisterzienser', 1994, p. 140.
416 Ibid. 'Zisterzienser', 1994, pp. 368, 448, respectively.
417 *UKN*, pp. 109–13 [LV]; 129–31 [LXIX, of 1328].
418 Faust, 'Zisterzienser', 1994, p. 768.
419 Schlegel *Repertorium*, 1998, p. 169.
420 *UKSH* 2, pp. 43–4 [509].

[421] UKSH 2, pp. 317–19 [730].
[422] PU 2, p. 182 [844, of 1267].
[423] PU 3, p. 81 [1514]. A 'last' may have equated to over 1600 kg [Volk, *Salzproduktion*, p. 1984, 117].
[424] Volk, *Salzproduktion*, 1984, p. 117n.
[425] RDD, p. 112 [651]: 'Rya', probably Rühn.
[426] UKW, p. 71 [47].
[427] USM, pp. 218–19, 227, [354, 364 'fontis'].
[428] Hiegel, C., 'Le Sel en Lorraine'. In: *Annales de L'Est*, 5th Series, No. 1 (1981), pp. 13–14.
[429] Digitale Westfälische Urkunden-Datenbank.
[430] Archiwum Państowe w Poznaniu: Ołobok Cystersi, A 1.
[431] Grüger, "Der Orden', 1982, p. 94.
[432] Dąbrowski, *Żarnowcu*, 1970, p. 66.
[433] Berman, *Women and Monasticism*, 2002, p. 23; DMLH 1, pp. 22 [11, of 1187], 56 [30, of 1192]; 176–8 [266, of 1231].
[434] DMLH 1, pp. 325–6 [223, of 1228].
[435] DMLH 2, pp. 17–18 (226).
[436] Borrero, 'El Archivo de San Clemente', 1992, p. 24 [43].
[437] Hallam, 'Salt-making', 1959, p. 100.
[438] CDEM 2, pp. 353–4 [CCCIV, of 1238].
[439] UKNA, p. 766 [735].
[440] PU 3, pp. 437–8 [640b].
[441] MUK, pp. 1054–5 [649].
[442] UKHB, p. 11 [33].
[443] VCH, *County of Northampton* 2, p. 122.
[444] TNA, E326/5474.
[445] DAB, pp. 59–60 [I].
[446] CAM, pp. 93–4 [CIV].
[447] CZT, pp. 39 [XLIII], 40 [XLIV], 47 [LIII].
[448] ANT: PT/TT/GAV/1/3/6.
[449] Dąbrowski, *Żarnowcu*, Gdańsk, 1970, p. 66.
[450] PRU 2, p. 138 [261]; PU 2, pp. 176–7 [837].
[451] PU 2, pp. 395–8 [1124], 434 [1176].
[452] CAM, pp. 49–50 [LXII]; 178 [CLXXXV].
[453] CAF, p. 50 [LII]; CDVG, p. 124 [101], respectively.
[454] Ploegaerts, *Aywières*, 1924, p. 18.
[455] Jurgensmeier, *Hessen und Thüringen*, 2011, p. 82.
[456] UKLT 7, pp. 454–5.
[457] CAB, p. 5 [V].
[458] MU 1, p. 245 [1529].
[459] DHGE 16, p. 835.
[460] Berman, *White Nuns*, 2018, pp. 154, 175–8.

461 *Ibid.* p. 156.
462 Peugniez, *L'Europe cistercienne*, 2012, p. 222.
463 Steinwascher, 'Die Zisterzienser-Stadthöfe', 1981, *passim*.
464 *Ibid.* p. 190.
465 *Ibid.* pp. 54, 58, 190.
466 Steinwascher, 1981, pp. 50–1, 129, 162,176, 188-89.
467 *Ibid.* pp. 52–3 (Fig. 14); 186–7.
468 *Ibid.* pp. 53–4, 172,175. (The properties are not plotted by Steinwascher).
469 *Ibid.* pp. 54, 59, 62, 67, 175.
470 *Ibid.* pp. 57, 190. 'sellatores'; 'leibzen'.
471 *Ibid.* pp. 54–7, 117, 151.
472 *Ibid.* pp. 176, 188–90.
473 *Ibid.* p. 86.
474 *UKSH* 1, pp. 195–6 [209, of 1231].
475 *MU* 1, p. 229 [1415].
476 *MU* 1, pp. 207 [1271], 253 [1583], 269 [1681].
477 *UKL*, pp. 50–1 [26], 80 [56].
478 *MU* 1, pp. 488–9, 518 [3099, 3295].
479 *UKO*, p. 5 [12].
480 *OU* 4, pp. 184–5 [282].
481 *HEK*, 2, pp. 51–2 [44].
482 *UKSG*, pp. 258–9 [223].
483 'sartaginis, cupe, caldarium'.
484 *CAM*, pp. 112–18 [CXXVIII].
485 Ploegaerts, *La Ramée*, 1925, p. 23.
486 Berman, *White Nuns*, pp. 59–60.
487 *KHU*, p. 188.
488 *USW* pp. 183–4 [223].
489 *UKE* 1, pp. 473–5 [845].
490 *UKWF*, 4: 3, p. 1270 [1373].
491 Coelho, *Expresiones*, 2006, p. 86.
492 Borrero, *El Archivo de San Clemente*, 1992, p. 25 [55].
493 TNA, C143/87/13; C143/21/30.
494 *PU* 2, 395–8 [1124; confirmed in 1278].
495 *PU* 2, pp. 446–7 [1199, of 1281].
496 *CCC*, pp. 34–8, 71–2.
497 Kinder, 'Blanche of Castile', 1976, p. 165 and note.
498 Peugniez, *L'Europe cistercienne*, 2012, *p. 157*.
499 Hautcoeur, *Flines*, 1909, p. 44; Cf. *CAF* 1, pp. 118–21 [CXVI and CXIX, of 1258].
500 Lester, 'Creating Cistercian Nuns', 2011, p. 62.
501 *CDNE*, pp. 180–1 [CXVII].
502 *PAS*, pp. 19–21.
503 *USB*, pp. 69–73 [70–1, 75].

Notes to Chapter 6

504 *UBC*, p. 211.
505 France, *Cistercians in Scandinavia*, 1992, p. 180.
506 *DHGE* 11, p. 565.
507 *VCH, County of York* 3, 1913, p. 167.
508 *RBM* 2, pp. 8 [72], 49 [130], 77–8 [193–4], 112 [302].
509 Hladík, 1994, p. 196.
510 *CDEM* 7, pp. 311–12 [129–30].
511 *RBM* 2, p. 112 [298].
512 *CDEM* 4, pp. 405–9 [CCCXX, of 1293].
513 *CDEM* 4, p. 32 [XXVI, of 1269].
514 *CDEM* 7, pp. 362–4 [CCLXXXV, CCLXXXVI].
515 *CDEM* 3, p. 95 (CXXVII).
516 *PU* 2, pp. 372–3 [1097].
517 *VCH, County of Lincoln* 2, 1906, p. 153.
518 *ANT: PT/TT, passim*.
519 Burton, *Yorkshire Nunneries*, 1979, pp. 15–16.
520 *VCH, County of Norfolk* 2, 1906, p. 369.
521 *VCH, County of Lincoln* 2, 1906, pp. 146–7; it was but one of theseven churches the nuns possessed.
522 *VCH, County of Lincoln* 2, 1906, p. 153.
523 *OU* 2, p. 237 [299]; *Cf.* p. 238 [301].
524 *UKL*, p. 95 [76].
525 *OU* 4, pp. 92–4 [140], 123–6 [178].
526 Williams, 'Cistercian Nunneries', 1975, p. 163.
527 *UKMD*, p. 183 [180].
528 *UKL*, p. 98 [80].
529 *CNC*, pp. 522–3 [466]; *Cf.* pp. 195–6 [181, of *c.* 1240].
530 *UKNA*, p. 530 [491].
531 *USB*, pp. 69–73 [70–1, 75].
532 *UKG*, pp. 30–1 [28–9].
533 *UKG*, pp. 30–1 [28–9].
534 *UKT*, pp. 313–14 [31].
535 *OU* 2, pp. 404–6 [513].
536 *UZW*, p. 142 [190].
537 *USB*, pp. 1516 [2, of 1247/48]; *OU* 2, pp. 397–8 [501, of 1247].
538 *DHGE* 6, p. 1338.
539 *CAF* 1, pp. 11–12 [XIV]; *Cf.* pp. 82–3 [XCII, of 1251].
540 Noel, "L'Amour-Dieu," 1876, p. 148.

Notes to Chapter 6

1 Albertí, *Valledemaria*, 2014, p. 156.
2 *Statuta* 3, pp. 328–9 [1314/4].
3 *Statuta* 3, p. 348 [1320/4].

4 VCH, *County of York* 3, 1913, p. 172.
5 VCH, *County of York* 3, pp. 175, 177.
6 *Statuta* 3, p. 355 [1321/13: 'varietatem modorum celebrandi'].
7 Baury, 'le Maine médiéval', p. 59.
8 Jurgensmeier, *Hesse und Thüringen*, p. 65.
9 *Statuta* 2, p. 530 [1355/5].
10 Goodrich, 'White Ladies', p. 139.
11 France, *Cistercians in Scandinavia*, 1992, p. 183.
12 VCH, *County of York* 3, 1913, pp. 171–2.
13 VCH, *County of York* 3, 1913, p. 177.
14 Chadwick, 'Kirklees', 1902, pp. 354–5, 361–2.
15 Chadwick, 'Kirklees', p. 358; CNC, pp. 308–13.
16 Chadwick, 'Kirklees', pp. 363–4.
17 VCH, *County of York* 3, 1913, p. 181.
18 VCH, *County of Northampton* 2, 1906, p. 123.
19 VCH, *County of York* 3, 1913, p. 175.
20 VCH, *County of York* 3, 1913, p. 181.
21 VCH, *County of York* 3, 1913, p. 171. 2, pp. 505–6 [514].
22 NPR, p. 638.
23 Berman, 'Cistercian Nuns', 1995, pp. 138–9, 155n.
24 NM, pp. 655–6.
25 CC, p. 151 [CXLVIII].
26 *Ibid.* p. 8.
27 UKSG.
28 Jordan, *Gender Concerns*, 2012, p. 84.
29 DVM, p. 23.
30 ECN, p. XXXXX.
31 CCG, pp. 36–7.
32 Lester, *Creating Cistercian Nuns*, 2011, p. 75.
33 France, *Cistercians in Scandinavia*, 1992, p. 177.
34 *Ibid.* p. 176.
35 *Ibid.* p. 176.
36 CZT, p. 86 [LXXXIII].
37 UKLH, pp. 252–3 [44].
38 CAF p. 529 [CCCCXV].
39 UKR, pp. 102–3 [117].
40 CZT, pp. 95–6 [LXXXVII], 107–8 [XCV].
41 CZT, pp. 117–18 [CI], *Cf.* pp. 119–20 [CII].
42 CZT, p. 124 [CV]: the nature of the 'quateron' is not cited.
43 CZT, pp. 137–8 (CXIII).
44 ANT: MSMAR/G3M13/30.
45 ANT: PT/TT/CSCS/010/0011/00786.
46 ANT: PT/TT/MSMAR/G7M04/21.

Notes to Chapter 6

47 *PU* 7, pp. 206–7 [4394].
48 Rèpas, *Traja de Branco*, 2003, p. 382 [86].
49 *Ibid.* p. 333 [48].
50 *UKS*, p. 205 [63].
51 *UKG*, pp. 90–1 [106].
52 *REK* 2, p. 292 [3436].
53 *USB*, pp. 69–73 [70–1, 75].
54 *UKLT* 8, pp. 77–91.
55 VCH, *County of York* 3, 1974, p. 160.
56 *CC*, pp. 116–17 [CXXIII], 125 [CXXIII], 139.
57 *CCG*, p. xxix.
58 VCH, *County of Hampshire* 2, 1903, p. 150.
59 *RTC*, p. 47.
60 Chadwick, 'Kirklees', 1902, p. 362.
61 VCH, *County of Northampton* 2, 1906, p. 126.
62 VCH, *County of Lincoln* 2, p. 157.
63 VCH, *County of Lincoln* 2, p. p. 157.
64 *RAO*, p. 66 [142].
65 *Statuta* 3, p. 512 [1348/11].
66 *UKT*, pp. 317–18 [40].
67 *DHGE* 21, p. 1270.
68 *MB* 2: Part 2, p. 576.
69 *DHGE* 23, p. 895.
70 Jamieson, 'St Mary, Haddington', 1952, p. 7; *DHGE* 22, pp. 1422–3.
71 Williams, *The Welsh Cistercians*, 2001, p. 37.
72 *DHGE* 16, p. 1310.
73 Aurelli i Cardona, 'Les cisterciennes', 1986, p. 261.
74 *DHGE* 7, pp. 162–3.
75 Peugniez, *L'Europe cistercienne*, 2012, p. 159.
76 Berman, *White Nuns*, 2018, p. 189.
77 *DHGE* 5, pp. 954–5.
78 Chauvin, B., 'L'integration des femmes à l'Ordre de Cîteaux. In: B. Barrière and M.-E. Henneau, *Cîteaux et les femmes*, Paris: Éditions Créaphis, 2001, p. 197; *DHGE* 7, p. 123.
79 Peugniez, *L'Europe cistercienne*, 2012, p. 115.
80 *Ibid.* p. 136.
81 *Ibid.* p. 140.
82 *Ibid.* p. 137.
83 *DHGE* 12, p. 1045.
84 Peugniez, *L'Europe cistercienne*, 2012, p. 119.
85 *Ibid.* pp. 120, 127, 129, 131.
86 *Ibid.* p. 152.
87 *Ibid.* p. 208.

[88] *Ibid.* p. 235.
[89] *Ibid.* pp. 185–6.
[90] *Ibid.* p. 241.
[91] *Ibid.* p. 299.
[92] *Ibid.* p. 341.
[93] *Ibid.* p. 449.
[94] *Ibid.* p. 1079.
[95] Peugniez, *L'Europe cistercienne*, 2012, p. 1086; Cf. *RBM* 2, p. 33 [84, of 1255]; *CDEM* 3, p. 202 [CCXXV, of 1255].
[96] *Ibid.* p. 170.
[97] *Ibid.* p. 187.
[98] Bouton, *Bouchet*, 1979, p. 34.
[99] *DHGE* 22, p. 320.
[100] Peugniez, *L'Europe cistercienne*, 2012, p. 805.
[101] *Ibid.* p. 295.
[102] *Ibid.* p. 144.
[103] *Ibid.* p. 68.
[104] *Ibid.* pp. 50, 344.
[105] *Ibid.* p. 179.
[106] *Ibid.* p. 190.
[107] *Ibid.* pp. 247, 303, respectively.
[108] *Ibid.* p. 293.
[109] *Ibid.* p. 305.
[110] *Ibid.* p. 582.
[111] *Ibid.* p. 773.
[112] *DHGE* 11, p. 107.
[113] Peugniez, *L'Europe cistercienne*, 2012, pp. 368–9.
[114] *Ibid.* p. 374–5.
[115] *Ibid.* p. 415.
[116] *Ibid.* p. 823.
[117] *Ibid.* p. 808.
[118] Hervay, *Cisterciensis in Hungaria*, 1984, p. 158.
[119] Berman, *Women and Monasticism*, 2002, pp. 132, 32–5, respectively.
[120] *CC*, pp. 168–9.
[121] *DHGE* 29, p. 358.
[122] Peugniez, *L'Europe cistercienne*, 2012, p. 1050.
[123] *Ibid.* p. 1064.
[124] *Ibid.* p. 202.
[125] *Ibid.* p. 582.
[126] *Ibid.* p. 569.
[127] *Ibid.* p. 581.
[128] Hervay, *Repertorium*, 1984, p. 111.

BIBLIOGRAPHY

PRIMARY SOURCES

ABB   *Archiv für die Bisthums Breslau* 2, ed. A. Kastner, Reiss, 1859.
ADY   *Archives départementales de l'Yonne.*
AMO   *Analecta Monasterii Ossecensis*, ed. C. Schoettgen, Dresden: Lieris Kravsianis, 1750.
ANT   *Arquivo Nacional Torre de Tombo [Lisbon], Class PT/TT/.*
ASC   *El Archivo del Real Monasterio de San Clemente*, ed. M. Borrero, Seville: Comisaría de la Ciudad de Sevilla Para, 1992.
AU   *Aachener Urkunden*, ed. E. Meuthen, Bonn: Peter Hanstein-Verlag G.M.B.H., 1972.
BL   *British Library, London.*
CA   *Codex Anhaltinus*, ed. Otto von Heinemann, Dessau: In Commission Bei Emil Barth, 1873.
CAAB   *Le Chartrier de L'Abbaye-Aux-Bois*, ed. B. Pippon, Paris: École des Chartes, 1996.
CAB   *Cartario del Monastero di Brione*, ed. G. Sella, Pinerolo: Novi-Ligure, Tip. Salvatore Raimond, [Corpus Chart. Italie XLIV], 1911; and in *Biblioteca della Societa Storica Subalpina.*
CAF   *Cartulaire de L'Abbaye de Flines*, ed. E. Hautcoeur, Lille: L. Quarré, Libraire, 1873.
CAM   *Cartulaire de L'Abbaye de Marquette* 1, ed. M. Vanhaeck, Lille: S.I.L.I.C., 1937.
CAMB   *Cartulaire de l'Abbaye de Maubuisson*, ed. A. Dutilleux and J. Depoine, Paris: Typographie Lucien, 1890.
CAR   *Cartario della Abazia di Rifreddo*, ed. S. Pivano, Pinerolo: Tipografia Chiantore-Mascarelli, 1902.
CAS   'Chartrier de l'Abbaye de Soleilmont', ed. L. Devillers. In: *Documents & Rapports de la Société Paléontologique et Archéologique de Charleroi* 7, 1875.
CC   *Cartulaite de Clairfontaine*, ed. P. H. Goffinet, Arlon: P.-A. Brück, 1877.
CCC   *Chartulary of the Cistercian Priory of Coldstream*, ed. C. Rogers, London: The Grampian Club, 1879.
CCG   *Chronique et Cartulaire de l'Abbaye de Groeninghe*, ed. F. van de Putte, Bruges: Imprimé Chez Vandecasteele-Werbruck, 1872.
CCH   *Chronique et Cartulaire de l'Abbaye de Hemelsdaele*, ed. C. Carton and F. van de Putte, Bruges: Imprimé Chez Vandecasteele-Werbruck, 1858.
CCS   '*Chartarum Coenobii Sonnefeldensis*', In: C. Schoettgen and others,

eds., *Diplomataria et Scriptores Historiae Germanicae medii aevi*, 3, 1760.

CDBR   *Codex diplomaticus Brandenburgnesis* 1, ed. A. F, Riedel, Berlin: F. H. Morin, 1838.

CDEM   *Codex diplomaticus et epistolaris Moraviae*, ed. A. Boczek, Olomuch: Typographia Aloysii, 2, 1839; 3, 1841; 4, 1845; 5. 1850.

CDG   *Colección Documental del Monasterio de Gradefes*, ed. T. B. Castro, Léon: Archivo Histórico Diocesana, 1998.

CDM   *Codex diplomaticus Moguntiaca*, ed. W. F. de Gudenus, Leipzig: Gottingae, 1743–68.

CDMC   *Colección Diplomatica del Monasterio de Carrizo* 1, Léon: Nonenque, Archivo Historico Diocesano, 1983.

CDN   *Cartulaire et Documents de L'Abbaye de Nonenque*, ed. C. Couderc and T.-L. Rigal, Rodez: Commission des Archives Historiques du Rouergue, 1950.

CDNE   *Cartulaqire de l'Abbaye de Notre-Dame de l'Eau*, ed. C.-Métais, Chartres: Archives du Diocese de Chartres 14, 1908.

CDP   *Codex Diplomaticus Poloniae* 1, ed, L. Rzyszczewski and A. Maczkowski, Warsaw, 1847.

CDRB   *Codex diplomaticus Regni Bohemiae*, ed. J. Friedrich and others, Prague: Academiae Scientiarum Bohemoslovacae, 1907–74.

CDS   *Codex Diplomaticus Silesiae* 1, ed, C. Grünhain, Breslau, 1868.

CDVG   *Recueil des Chartes et Documents de l'Abbaye du Val-Saint-Georges*, ed. É. Brouette, Achel, Belgium: Studia et Documenta, 1971.

CHDM   *Caesarius of Heisterbach: The Dialogue on Miracles*, London: George Routledge & Sons, 1929.

CHS   *Cronica comecie Holtsacie et in Schouwenbergh*, ed. S. Hohlt, Kiel: Solivagus Verlag, 2012.

CKW   *Cistercienserinnen-Heiligenblut-Kloster Waterler. (Urkunden. [1227–1690.])*, Geschichtsquellen der Provinz Sachsen 15, 1870.

CMF   *Le Cartulaire Médiéval de l'Abbaye de Fontenelle*, ed. J. Trotin, Valenciennes: Centre de L'U.E.R. Froissart, 1978.

CNC   *The Cartulary of the Priory of Nun Coton*, ed. A. E. Hyde, Dissertation Abstracts International, 1977.

CP   *Chronicon Portense*, ed, J. Pertuchius, Leipzig 1612.

CZT   *Cartulaire de L'Abbaye de Zwyveke-lez-Termonde*, ed. M. Alph and L. de Vlaminck, Gand/Ghent: Cercle Archéologique de Termonde, 1869.

DAB   *Documents et courte notice sur l'abbaye de Bival*, ed. J. Malicorne, Rouen: impr. De L. Gy, 1897.

DAC   *Dictionnaire des Auteurs Cisterciens*, ed. E. Brouette, A. Dimier and E. Mannnig, Rochefort, Belgium: Abbaye N. D. et St Remy, 1975-.

DCB   *Documento de Casbas, A. Ubieto, Valencia, 1966.*

DCE   *Description analytique et chronologique du cartuetteaire de l'abbaye de Epinlieu*, ed. L. Devillers: Mons,: Dequesne-Masquellier, 1866.

Bibliography

DD   'Diplomatarium Dobernanse'. In: E. J. de Westphalen (ed.), *Monumenta Inedita* 3, Leipzig, 1743.

DG   *Der Geschichtsfreund*, ed. M. Altdorf, Einsiedeln: Bei Gebr. Karl und Nicolaus Benziger, 1. 1843, 2. 1845.

DGA   *Diplomatische Geschichte des Adersleben*, ed. St. Kunze, Halberstadt: Berlag von Friedrich August Helm, 1837.

DHGE   *Dictionnaire d'histoire et de géographie ecclésiastiques*, ed. A.-H.-M, Baudrillat and successors, Paris: 1912-, now published by Brepols, Turnhout, Belgium.

DMF   'Annales Diplomatici Abbatiae Monialium in Frankenhausen', In: C. Schoettgen and others, eds., *Diplomataria et Scriptores Historiae Germanicae medii aevi*, 2, 1755.

DMLH   *Documentacio del Monasterio de Las Huelgas de Burgos*, ed. A. C. Garrido, Burgos: Fuentes Medievales Castellano-Leonesas, 1985–7.

DNC   *Diplomatum Nova Collectio*, ed. A. Miraeus, Brussels: Petrum Foppens, 1734-.

DNK   *Diplomatische Nachrichten von Jungfrauen-Kloster Marienpforte*, ed. C. F. Seyffarth, Torgau: Gedrucht bey Friedrich Samuel Rúdel, 1773.

DSB   'Reliquiae Diplomaticae Sanctimonialium Beutizensium', in: *C. Schoettgen and others, eds., Diplomataria et Scriptores et Historiae Germanicae medii aevi*, 2, Altenrberg, 1755.

DSHG   *Diplomataria et Scriptores Historiae Germanicae Medii Aevi* 2, ed. C. Schoettgen, Altenburg: Typis et Sumtibus Pavli Emanvel Richteri, 1755; 3, 1760.

DVM   *Diplomatorium Vallis S. Mariae*, e. 1892.d. R. Doehler, Görlitz: Izschaschel, 1902.

ECN   *Ein Cisterzienserbuch Novalis Sanctae Mariae*, ed. S. Brunner, Paderborn: Salzwasser Verlag, 1981.

EMB   *El Monasterio de Barría*, A.P. Moro, Bilbao, 2013.

HCM   *Histoire et Cartulaire de Maubuisson* 1, ed. A. Dutilleux and J. Depoin, Pontoise: Typographie de Amédée Paris, 1882; 2, 1883; 3, 1890.

HEK   *Hessisches Urkundenbuch*, ed. H. Reimer, Leipzig, 1. 1891, 2. 1892.

HUK   *Hamburgishes Urkundenbuch*, ed. J.M. Lappenburg, Hamburg, 1842.

ICE   *Inventarie des Archives de L'Abbaye Cistercienne d'Epinlieu*, ed. R. Wellens, Brussels: Archives Générales du Royaume, 1970.

KD   *Kodeks Dyplomatyczny Malopolski*, ed. I. Zakrzewski, Poznan, 1877-.

KDS   *Kodeks Dyplomatyczny Śląska*, ed. K. Maleczyński, Wrocław, 1955-.

KHU   *Kloster Himmelspforten Urkunden*, ed. E. Schöffler, Würzburg: Staatsarchiv, 2009.

LCC (2)   *Les Codifications Cisterciennes de 1237 et de 1257*, ed. B. Lucet, Paris: Éditions du Centre National de la Recherche Scientifique, 1977.

LFZ   *Das 'Stiftungen-Buch' (Liber Fundationis) des Cistercienser-Klosters Zwettl*, ed. J. von Frast, Vienna: Fontes Rerum Austriacarum 3, 1851.

MB   Monasticon Belge, ed. É. Brouette et al; 3, Part 2 (Liège: Centre National de Recherches D'Histoire Religieuse, 1966; 4, Part 1, 1964; Part 2, 1968; 7, Part 3, 1980.
MPR   Les Monuments Primitifs de le Règle Cistercienne, Dijon: J.-E. Rabutot, 1878.
MR   Mainzer Regesten, 1200–1250, ed. L. Falck, Mainz: GmbH Elmar Kolter (? n), 2007.
MU   Mecklenburgisches Urkundenbuch 1: 786–1250; 2: 1251–80; 3: 1281–96; editor not noted; Schwerin: Verein für Mecklenburgische und Aterthumskunde, 1: 1863, 2: 1864, 3: 1865.
MUK   Mainzer Urkundenbuch 2, ed. P. Acht; Darmstadt: Hessichen Historischen Kommission, 1971.
NBM   Obituarium Monasterii Loci Sancti Bernardi, 1237–1900 (Bornem), ed. B. van Doninck, Lierre, Antwerp, 1900.
NBT   Das Totenbuch des Cistercienserfrauenklosters Baindt, ed. L. Walter, O.Cist., In: Württembergische Vierteljahrshefte für Landes-geschichte, N.S., 26; Stuttgart, 1917.
NDP   Necrology of Notre-Dame-des-Prés, MS 0838, Médiathèque Simone Veil, Valenciennes.
NGn   'Gnadenthal', Cistercienser-Chronik 18, No. 207; May 1906.
NM   Abbaye de Maubuisson, In: Recueil des historiens de la France: Obituaires I, Part 2, Paris/Lille, 1902.
NMD   Nécrologe de l'abbaye de Marche-les-Dames, In: Analectes pour servir à l'histoire eccléiastique de Belgique 8, 1871.
NPR   Abbaye de Port Royal, In: Recueil des historiens de la France: Obituaires I, Part 2, Paris/Lille, 1902.
NPS   Das Nekrolog Cistercienser-Abtei Pairis, ed. J.B.M. Clauss, Mitteilungen der Gesellschaft für Erhaltung der Geschichte Denkmaler im Elsass, 22, 1908.
NRM   Het Necrologium der Adellijke Abdij van O.L. Vrouw Munster te Roermond, ed. J.B. Sivré, Toermond, 1876.
NS/NSA   Necrologium Saeldentalense, Bayerische Landesbibliothek on-line; Strum, J. (ed.), Necrologium Saeldentalense, Monumenta Germaniae, Necrologia 4, Berlin, 1920, pp. 473–524.
NSN   'Kloster Sonnenfeld', Cistercienser Chronik 13, No. 153, November 1901. [See also: CCS above].
NSS   'Een Necrologium der St. Servaas-abdij te Utrecht', In: Archief voor de geschiedenis van het aartisbisdom Utrecht, bijdragen, 27, 1901.
NT   Necrologium Tennenbacense, ed. F.L. Baumann, In: Necrologium Germaniae 1, Berlin, 1888, p. 338.
NV   Nécrologe de l'abbaye de Villers, 1574–1792, In: Analectes pour servir à l'histoire ecclésiastique de Belgique IX, 1872.
NWD   Necrologium Waldense, In: Necrologia Germaniae 1, Berlin, 1888.
NWN   'Johannis de Trokelow', In: Annales Edwardii II, Oxford, 1729.
OMA   O Mosteiro de Arouca, ed. M. M. de Cruz Coelho, ed. F.L. Baumann,

Bibliography

	Inn: Universade de Coimbra, 1977.
OU	*Osnabrücker Urkundenbuch*, ed. F. Philippi, Osnabruck: Verlag H. Th. Wenner, 1969.
PAS	*Polyptyque de l'Abbaye de Salzinnes-Namur, 1303–1307*, ed. L. Benicot, Louvain-Ghent: Centre belge d'histoire rurale, 1967.
PDC	*Le Pergamene di Conversano*, ed. D. Morea and F. Muciaccia, Codice Diplomatica Ba ed. R. M. Hainesrese 17; Trani, 1942.
PRU	*Preussisches Urkundenbuch* 1, Könisberg: Scientia Aalen, 1961; 2: ed. A. Seraphim, 1961; 3: ed. H. Koeppen, Marburg: N. G. Elwert Verlag, 1958.
PU	*Pommersches Urkundenbuch*, ed. R. Klempin, Stettin: In Commission bei Th. Von der Rahmer 1, 1868; 2: ed. R. Prümers, Stettin, 1885; 3: ed. R. Prümers, Stettin: Friedr. Nagelsche Buchhandlung, 1891; 4: ed. Georg Winter, Stettin, 1903.
RAO	*Calendar of the Register of Adam de Orleton, Bishop of Worcester, 1327–1333*, London: Her Majesty's Stationery Office, 1979.
RBM	*Regesta diplomatica nec non epistolaria Bohemiae et Moraviae*, ed. J. Emled, Prague: Typis Gregerranis, 2, 1882; 4. 1892.
RCH	*Repertorium Historicum Ordinis Cisterciensis in Hungaria*, ed. F. L. Hervay, Rome: Editiones Cistercienses, 1984.
RDD	*Regesta Diplomatica Historiae Daniae [2nd Series]*, 1, ed. A. Række, Forste vol. Copenhagen, 1880.
RDW	*The Register of the Diocese of Worcester: Registrum Sede Vacante*, ed. J. W. Willis Bund, Worcestershire Historical Society, 1897.
REK	*Die Regesten der Erzbischöfe von Köln* 1, ed. F. W. Oediger; 2, ed. R. Knipping, Bonn: P. Hansteins Verlag, 1901.
RFF	*Die Regesten des Frauenklosters Fraubrunnen*, ed. J. J. Amiel, Chur, 1854.
RFFK	*Die Regesten derFrauenkloster Feldbach und Tänikon*, ed. K. v. R., Chur, 1852.
RGG	*The Register of Bishop Godfrey Giffard* 1, ed. J. W. Willis-Bund, Worcestershire Hist. Soc. 1902.
RHE	*Revue d'Histoire Ecclésiastique* 39, 1943.
RJR	*Register of John Le Romeyn, Lord Archbishop of York* 1, Surtees Society, CXXIII, 1913. 2, 1917, ed. W. Brown.
RME	*Regesten zur Geschichte der Mainzer Erzbischöfe* 2, Innsbruck: Verlag Wagneisches Universitäts-Buchhandlung, 1886.
RPR	*Regesta Pontificum Romanorum, 1198–1304*, 1874–5.
RSL	'Registrum Epistolarum Stephani de Lexington, I–II', ed. B. Griesser. In: *Analecta Sacri Ordinis Cisterciensis* 2, 1846, and 8, 1952.
RT	*Regesta diplomatica necnon epistolaria historiae Thuringiae*, ed. O. Dobenecker, Jena: Verein für thüringische Geschichte und Alterhumskunde, 2, 1900; 3, 1925; 4. 1939.
RTC	*The Register of Thomas de Cobham, Bishop of Worcester*, ed. E. H. Pearce, Worcestershire Historical Society, 1930.

RWB A Calendar of the Register of Wolstan de Bransford, Bishop of Worcester, 1339–1349, ed. R. M. Haines, London: Her Majesty's Stationery Office, 1966.
Statuta Statuta Capitulorum Generalium Ordinis Cisrterciensis 1–8, ed. J.-M. Canivez; Louvain: Bibliothèque de la Revue d'histoire ecclesiastique, 1933–41, vols. 9–16.
SU Schlesisches Urkundenbuch 1–3, ed. H. Appelt; Graz-Cologne: Verlag Hermann Böhlaus Nachf., 1963.
TBC The Tax Book of the Cistercian Order, ed. A. O. Johnsen and P. King, Oslo: Universtetsforlaget, 1979.
TCS Twelfth-Century Statutes from the Cistercian General Chapter, ed. C. Waddell, Brecht, Belgium: Cîteaux, Studia et Documenta 12, 2002.
TE Taxatio Ecclesiastica Angliae et Walliae Auctoritate P. Nicholai IV, ed. T. Astle and others; London, Record Commission, 1802.
TNA The National Archives, Kew, England.
UAB Urkundenbuch der Abtei Bonneweg, ed. N. van Werveke, Luxemburg: Druck von Peter Bruck, 1880.
UBC Urkundenbuch des Bisthums Culm, ed. C. P. Woelky, Danzig/Gdansk: Verlag von Theodor Bertling, 1884.
UE Urkundenbuch des Eichsfeldes 1, ed. A. Schmidt, Magdeburg, 1933.
UHH Urkundenbuch des Hochstiftes Halberstadt, ed. G. Schmidt, Leipzig, 1883, vol. 1 and see later volumes.
UKB Urkundenbuch der Abtei Bonneweg, ed. N. von Werveke, Luxembourg, 1880.
UKBR Urkundenbuch der Stadt Braunschweig 1, ed. L. Haenselmann and H. Mack, Berlin, 1905.
UKD Urkundenbuch des Klosters Dobrilugk, ed. R. Lehmann, Leipzig: Verlag und Druck von B.G. Teubner, 1941.
UKE Urkundenbuch der Erfurter Stifter und Kloster 1, ed. A. Overmann, Magdeburg: Selbstverlag der Historische Kommission, 1926.
UKEF Urkundenbuch der Stadt Erfurt 1, ed. C. Beyer, Halle, 1889.
UKF Urkundenbuch des Klosters Frauensee, 1202–1540, ed. W. Küther, Cologne: Böhlau Verlag, 1961.
UKG Die Urkunden des Klosters Gravenhorst, ed. M. Wolf, Münster: Aschendorfísche Verlagsbuchhandlung, 1994.
UKGN 'Besuch einer urkundenliche Geschichte des Cisterzienser-Nonnenklosters S. Agnetis in der Neustadt Magdeburg'. In: L. von Ledebur (ed.), Allgemeines Archiv des Preussischen Staates, Berlin: Druck und Berlag von E. S. Mittler, 1835.
UKGV Urkunden der das Cistercienserinnen-Kloster Grafenthal oder Vallis comitis, ed. R. Scholten, Kleve: Druch und Verlag von Fr. Boss Wwe, 1899.
UKH Urkundenbuch des Klosters Heiligkreuztal 1, ed. A. Hauber, Stuttgart: Druck und Verlag von W. Kolhammer, 1910.

Bibliography

UKHB Urkundenbuch der Stadt Heilbronn 1, ed. E. Kupfer, Stuttgart, 1904.
UKI *ThurrngiaeSacra: Kloster Ichtershausen, Urkundenbuch*, ed. W. Rein, Weimar: Herman Böhlau, 1863.
UKL Urkundenbuch des Klosters Lilienthal, ed. H.-R. Jarck; Stade: Landschaftsverband der Ehemaligen Herzogtümer Bremen und Verden, 2002.
UKLB *Urkundenbuch des Stadt Lübeck 1*, Lübeck, 1843.
UKLH *Urkundenbuch der Langeln, Himmelpforten und Waterler*, ed. E. Jacobs; Halle: Druck und Verlag von Otto Hendel, 1882.
UKLT 'Urkunden archiv des Klosters Lichtental', ed. J. Dambacher. In: *Zeitschrift für die Geschichte des Oberrheins* 6, 1855; 7, 1856; 8, 1857.
UKM *Urkundenbuch der Kloster der Grafschaft Mansfeld*, ed. M. Krühne, Halle: Druck und Verlag, Otto Hendel, 1888.
UKMD *Urkundenbuch des Klosters Medingen*, ed. J. Homeyer, Hannover: Verlag Hansche Buchhandlung, 2006.
UKMR *Urkundenbuch des Klosters Mariengarten*, ed. M. Von Boetticher, Hildesheim: Verlag August Lax, 1987.
UKN *Urkunden des Klosters Neukloster*, ed. G. C. F. Lisch, Schwerin, 1841.
UKNA *Urkundenbuch des Hochstiftes Naumburg* 2, ed. H. K. Schulze, Cologne: Böhlau Verlag, 2000.
UKO *Die Urkunden des Klosters Oberschönenfeld*, ed. K. Puchner, Augsburg: Verlag der Schwäbischen Forschungsgemeinschaft, 1953.
UKR *Urkundenbuch des Klosters Rinteln*, ed. H.-R. Jarck, Rinteln: Verlag C. Bösendahl, 1982.
UKS *Die Urkunden des Klosters Seligenthal*, ed. A. Kalcher; Landshut: Verhandsungen des Historischen Vereines, 1893.
UKSG *Urkundenbuch der Stadt Goslar*, Goslar: Druck und Verlag Otto Hendel 1, 1893; 2, 1896.
UKSH *Urkundenbuch der Stadt Halle, ihrer Stifter und Kloster*, 2, ed. A. Bierbach, Magdeburg: Selbstverlag der Landes geschichtlichen Forschun gestelle, 1, 1930; 2, 1939.
UKSR Urkundenbuch der Stadt Rottweil 1, ed. H. Günter, Stüttgart, 1896.
UKT *Urkundenbuch des Klosters Teistungenburg*, ed. J. Jaeger, Halle: Druck der Buchdruckerei des Waisenhauses, 1878.
UKW *Urkunden des Klosters Wormeln*, ed. H. Müller, Aschendorff Münster: Historische Kommission für Westfalen, 2009.
UKWF *WestfälischesUrkundenbuch*, 4: 1, ed. R. Wilmans, Münster, 1872; 4:2, ed. H. Finke, 1880; 4:3, ed. H. Finke, 1884: 4:4 v[Indices] 1894.
USH *Urkundenbuch der Stadt Halle, ihrer Stifter und Kloster*, 2, ed. A. Bierbach, Magdeburg: Selbstverlag der Landes geschichtlichen Forschun gestelle, 1, 1930; 2, 1939.
USB *Urkundenbuch des Stifts Börstel*, ed. R. Rölker and W. Delbanco; Osnabrück: Selbstverlag des Vereins für Geschichte und Landeskunde von Osnabrück, 1996.

USD   *Urkundenbuch der Stadt Duisburg* 1, ed. J. Milz. Düsseldorf: Droste Verlag GMBH, 1989.
USM   *Urkundenbuch des Stadt Magdeburg*, 1, ed. S. Hertel, Halle: Druck und Verlag Otto Hendel, 1892.
USW   *Urkundenregesten zur Geschichte der Stadt Würzburg*, ed. W. Engel, Würzburg: Verlag Ferdinand Schöningh, 1952.
UZW   *Die Urkunden des Zisterzienserinnenklosters Wald: Regesten*, ed. M. Kuhn-Refus, Konstanz-Egginen: Edition Isele, 2014.
VDM   van der Meer, F., *Atlas de l'Ordre Cistercien*, Paris/Brussels, Éditions Sequoia, 1965.

SECONDARY SOURCES

Adelheid, M., 'Tanikon-Lilienthal'. In: *Cistercienser-Chronik* N. S. 149 (1980–3), pp. 71–94.

Ahlers, G., *Weibliches Zisterziensertum im Mittelalter*, Berlin: Lukas Verlag, 2002.

Albe, E., 'Notes sur L'Abbaye de Leyme'. In: *Bulletin Trimestrial de la Société des Études Du Lot* 27, 1902.

Albertí, J., *Santa Maria de Valdemaria, 1146–1580*, Estany, 2014.

Albo, J. A. R., *El Monasterio de Santa Maria la Real de las Huelgas*, Burgos: El Castellan, 1950.

Alegria, M., and F. Marques, 'Les premières nonnes Cisterciennes au Portugal'. In: B. Barrière and M.-E. Henneau, *Cîteaux et les femmes*, Paris: Éditions Créaphis, 2001, pp. 213–16.

Alvergat, M., S. Demaethe and G. Mallet (eds), *Moniales cisterciennes de Méditerranée occidental*, Saint-Guilhem-le-Désert, 2017.

Anglès, H. (ed.), *El Codex Musical de Las Huelgas*, Barcelona: Biblioteca de Catalunya, 1931.

Appuhn, H., *Kloster Isenhagen*, Munich, 1981.

Arblaster, J., and R. Faessen, 'The Influence of Beatrice of Nazareth'. In: *Cîteaux* 64, Parts 1–2, 2013, pp. 41–87.

Aurell i Cardona, M., 'Les Cisterciennes et leurs protecteurs en Provence rhodanienne'. In: Privat, *Les Cisterciens de Languedoc*, 1986, pp. 235–67.

Baert, J., 'Les Moniales Cisterciennes aux Anciens Pay-Bas Méridionaux'. In: *Collectanea Ordinis Cisterciensium Reformatum* 24, 1962, pp. 63–6.

Banga, V., et al., *Rīgas Dievnami*, Riga, 2007, p. 320.

Barraud, M., 'Quelques mots sur l'Abbaye de Gomerfontaine'. In: *Mémoires de la Société Académique du Département de l'Oise* 5, 1862, pp. 581–95.

Barrière, B., *L'Abbaye de Obazine*, Tulle: Imp. Offeuil, 1977.

Barrière, B., *Le Cartulaire de L'Abbaye Cistercienne d'Obazine*, University of Clermont-Ferrand II, 1989.

Barrière, B., 'Coyroux, Doublet Féminin de L'Abbaye d'Obazine'. In: *Les Religieuses dans Le Cloître et dans le Monde*, Acts of the International Colloquium of CERCOM; University of Saint-Etienne, 1994, pp. 131–8.

Barrière, B., and M.-E. Henneau, *Cîteaux et les femmes*, Paris: Éditions Créaphis, 2001.

Bartal, R., 'Where has your beloved gone?' In *Word and Image* 16, Part 3, July-September, 2000, pp. 270–89.

Baury, G., 'Les Fausses Quittances de Cañas'. In: *Cîteaux* 59, Parts 3–4, 2008, pp. 237–52.

Baury, G., 'Les moniales cisterciennes dans le Maine médiéval'. In: *Annales de Bretagne et des Pays de l'Ouest* 120: No. 3, 2013, pp. 49–64.

Beam, A., et al., *The People of Medieval Scotland*, on-line.

Bell, D. N., 'Chambers, Cells, and Cubicles'. In: T. N. Kinder (ed.), *Perspectives for an Architecture of Solitude*, 2004, pp. 187–98.

Benešovská, K., 'Aula Sanctae Mariae'. In: B. Barrière, M.-E. Henneau, *Cîteaux et les femmes*, Paris: Éditions Créaphis, 2001, pp. 55–71.

Berman, C. H., 'Dowries, Private Income and Anniversary Masses'. In: *Proc. Of the Annual Meeting of the Western Society for French History* 20 1993.

Berman, C. H., 'Cistercian Nuns'. In: E. R. Elder (ed.), *The Joy of Learning and the Love of God*, Kalamazoo: Cistercian Studies Series 160, 1995, pp. 121–56.

Berman, C. H., *The Cistercian Evolution*, Pennsylvania U.P., 1999.

Berman, C. H., 'Were there Twelfth-Century Cistercian Nuns?' In: *Church History* 68, 1999, pp. 824–64.

Berman, C. H., *Women and Monasticism in Medieval Europe*, Kalamazoo: Western Michigan University, 2002.

Berman, C. H., 'Building in Wood, Brick, Stone, Tiles'. In: Lillich, *Cistercian Nuns*, 2005, pp. 23–60.

Berman, C. H., *The White Nuns: Cistercian Abbeys for Women in Medieval France*, Pennsylvania U.P., 2018.

Berthier, K., 'Notre-Dame de Tart'. In: B. Barrière, M.-E. Henneau, *Cîteaux et les femmes*, Paris: Éditions Créaphis, 2001.

Bois, M., 'La Basilique Sainte Anne'. In: *Revue Dromoise* 83, 1980, pp. 75–82.

Böning, M., *Die Mittelalterlichen Glasmalereien In Kloster Neuendorf*, Berlin: Akademie VerlagGmbH, 2009.

Bonis, A., and M. Wabont, 'Cisterciens et Cisterciennes en France du Nord-Ouest'. In: B. Barrière and M.-E. Henneau, *Cîteaux et les femmes*, Paris: Éditions Créaphis, 2001, pp. 151–76.

Borrero, M., *El Real Monasterio de San Clemente*, Seville: Comisaría de la Ciudad de Sevilla Para, 1992.

Boudreau, C., 'With Desire I have Desired'. In: Nichols and Shank, *Hidden Springs*, 1995, pp. 323–44.

Bouton, J. de la Croix, *L'Abbaye de Bouchet en Tricastin*, Grignan: Abbaye d'Aiguebelle, 1979.

Bouton, J. de la Croix, 'L'Abbaye de Saint-Just-en-Royans'. In: *Revue Dromoise* 83, No. 416; June, 1980.

Bouton, J. de la Croix, *Les Moniales cisterciennes* 1, Aiguebelle Abbey, France; 1986.

Bouton, J. de la Croix, 'Les abbesses cisterciennes'. In: *Les Religieuses dans Le Cloître et dans le Monde*, Acts of the International Colloquium of CER-COM; University of Saint-Etienne, 1994, pp. 187–96.

Bouton, J. de la Croix, 'The Life oof the Twelfth and Thirteenth Century Nuns of Cîteaux'. In: Nichols and Shank, *Hidden Springs*, 1995, pp. 11–27.

Boyd, C. E., *A Cistercian Nunnery in Medieval Italy*, Havard University Press, 1943.

Broniewski, T., *Trzebnica*, Wrocław: Zakład Narodowy im Ossolińskich, 1959.

Bruiningk, H. von, 'Messe und Kanonisches Stundengebet', In: *Mitteilungen aus dem Gebiete der Geshichte Liv-, Est-, und Kurlands* 19, Riga, 1904.

Brunner, S., *Ein Cisterzienserbuch*, Paderborn: Salzwasser Verlag GmbH, 2013 (reprint of 1881 edition).

Buchet, L. (ed.), *La Femme, pendant le Moyen Âge et 'Époque Moderne*, Paris: CNRS Editions, 1994.

Burton, J. E., *The Yorkshire Nunneries in the Twelfth and Thirteenth Centuries*, York: Borthwick Papers, No. 56, 1979.

Campion, E., 'Cîteaux, Our Mother?' In: *Cistercian Studies Quarterly*, 34, Part 4, 1999, pp. 483–500.

Canivez, J. M., *L'Ordre de Cîteaux en Belgique*, Chimay, Belgium: Scourmont Abbey, 1926.

Carbonell-Lamothe, Y., 'L'abbaye de Vignogoul'. In: Privat, *Les Cisterciens de Languedoc*, 1986, pp. 269–81.

Cardona: *see* Aurelli i Cardona.

Carville, G. C., *Norman Splendour*, Belfast: Blackstaff Press, 1979.

Carville, G. C., *Cistercian Nuns in medieval* Ireland'. In: Nichols and Shank, *Hidden Springs*, 1995, pp. 63–84.

Cawley, M., '*Mulieres Religiosae* in Goswin of Villers'. In: *Vox Benedictina* 9, No. 1, Summer, 1992, pp. 99–107.

Cawley, M., *Send Me God*, Turnhout, Belgium: Brepols, 2003.

Cazabonne, E., 'Liturgical Life as Art'. In: Kinder, *Cistercian Arts*, 2014, pp. 201–6.

Chadwick, S. J., 'Kirklees Priory'. In: *Yorkshire Archaeological Journal* 16, 1902, pp. 319–68.

Charvátová, K., 'Les Abbayes de Nonnes Cisterciennes en Bohême Mèdiévale'. In: *Les Religieuses dans Le Cloître et dans le Monde*, Acts of the International Colloquium of CERCOM; University of Saint-Etienne, 1994, pp. 763–72.

Chauvin, B., *Mélanges à la Mémoire du Père Anselme Dimier* 3, Part 5, Pupillin: Arbois, 1982.

Chauvin, B., 'Belfays, abbaye cistercienne féminine'. In: *Les Cahiers Haut-Marnais* 196–9, 1994, pp. 58–106.

Chauvin, B., 'L'integration des femmes à l'Ordre de Cîteaux. In: B. Barrière and M.-E. Henneau, *Cîteaux et les femmes*, Paris: Éditions Créaphis, 2001, pp. 193–211.

Bibliography

Coelho, M. F., *Expresiones del Poder Feudal El Císter Femenino En Leon*, Léon: Universidad, 2006.

Coester, E., 'Die Cistercienserinnenkirchen'. In: A. Schneider, *Die Cisterciensia*, Cologne, 1986, pp. 358–65.

Comba, R. (ed.), *Il Monasterio di Rifreddo*, Cunea: Società Per Gli Studi Storici, Archeologici ed Artistici, 1999.

Conde, A. L., 'La tardias supervivencia de los monastrios dobles en la Península Ibérica'. In: *Studia Monastica* 32, Part 2, 1990, pp. 365–80.

Connor, E., 'The Abbeys of Las Huelgas and Tart'. In: J. A. Nichols and L. T. Shank, *Hidden Springs*, pp. 29–48.

Connor, E., 'The Royal Abbey of Las Huelgas'. In: *Cîteaux* 23, 1988, pp. 128–55.

Connor, E., 'L'abbaye royale de Las Huelgas'. In: *Collectanea Cisterciensia* 50, 1988, pp. 307–34.

Coomans, T. (ed.), *La Ramée*, Brussels: Éditions Racine, 2002.

Coomans, T., 'Moniales Cisterciennes et Mémoire Dynastique'. In: *Cîteaux* 56, 2005, pp. 87–146.

Coomans, T., 'Cistercian Nunneries in the Low Countries'. In: Lillich, *Cistercian Nuns and their World*, pp. 61–132.

Cowan, I. B., and D. E. Easson, *Medieval Religious Houses, Scotland*, London: Longman, 2nd edn., 1976.

Creutz, U., *Bibliographie der ehemaligen Klöster und Stifte*, Leipzig: St. Benno-Verlag GMBH, 1983.

Dąbrowski, K., *Rozwój Wielkiej Własnosci Klasztoru Cysterek w Żarnowcu* (with French resumé), Gdańsk: Gdańskie Towarzystwo, 1970.

Degler-Spengler, B., 'Incorporation of Cistercian Nuns' In: Nichols and Shank, *Hidden Springs*, 1995, pp. 85–134.

D'Emilio, J., 'The Royal Convent of Las Huelgas'. In: Lillich, *Cistercian Nuns and their World*, C.P., 20095.

D'Emilio, J., 'Widows and Communities : Cistercian Nunneries and their Architecture in the Kingdom of León. In: *Cîteaux commentarii cistercienses* 66, 2015, pp. 223–302.

Desmarchelier, M., 'L'architecture des églises de moniales cisterciennes'. In: Chauvin (ed.), *Mélanges Dimier* 2/5, 1982, pp. 102–20.

Dimier, A., *Receuil de Plans D'Eglises Cisterciennes* 2, Grignan: Abbaye Notre-Dame D'Aiguebelle, 1949.

Dimier, A., 'Chapitres Generaux d'Abbesses Cisterciennes'. In: *Cîteaux* 11, 1960, pp. 268–75.

Dimier, A., 'Violences, Rixes et Homicides'. In: *Revue des sciences religeuses* 46, Strasbourg, 1972, pp. 38–57.

Dimier, A., 'L'architecture des églises moniales cisterciennes'. In: *Cîteaux* 25, 1974, pp. 8–23.

Dobosz, J., and A. M. Wyrwa, *Cystersi w spolczeńswrie Europy Środkowej*, Poznan: Wydawnistwo Poznańskie, 2000.

Dorpe, B. van, 'De Abdij van Groeninge'. In: *Mémoires Cercle Royal Historique* et Archéologique de Courtrai, New Series, 25, 1951–2.

Elder, E. R (ed.), *Noble Piety and Reformed Monasticism*, Kalamazoo: Cistercian Publications, 1981.

Escrivá, J. M., *La Abadesa de Las Huelgas*, Madrid: Editorial Luz, 1944.

Evans, A. (ed.), *Francisco Balducci Pegolotti: La Pratica DellaMercatura*, Cambridge, Massachusetts,: The Medieval Academy of America, 1936.

Eydoux, H.-P., *L'Architecture des Églises Cisterciennes d'Allemagne*, Paris: Presses Universitaires de France, 1952.

Farmer, S., and Pasternack (ed.), *Gender and Difference in the Middle Ages*, University of Minnesota Press, 2001.

Faust, U., ed., *Die Frauenklöster in Nieder Sachsen, Schleswig-Holstein und Bremen*, St Ottilien: EOS Verlag Erzabtei, 1984.

Faust, U (ed.)., *Die Männer- und Frauenklöster der Zisterzienser in Niedersachsen, Schleswig-Holstein und Hamburg*, St Ottilien: EOS Verlag, 1994.

Fernandez, M. B., *Real Monasterio de San Clemente*, Seville: Comisaria de la Ciudad de Sevilla, 1991.

Ferrier, R (ed)., 'Cîteaux dans la Drome'. In: *Revue Dromoise* 83, 1980, pp. 49–154.

Fidler, R., and M. Schultebraucks, *Das Zisterzienser St. Mariae zu Welver*, Paderborn: Bonifatius Verlag, 2007.

Forey, A. J., 'Women and the Military Orders'. In: *Studia Monastica* 29, 1987: Part 1, pp. 63–92.

Fort i Cogul, E., 'L'eremitisme a la Catalunya nova'. In: *Studia Monastica* 7, 1965, Part 1, pp. 63–126.

Framond, M. de, 'Historique de l'abbaye de la Vernaison'. In: *Revue Dromoise* 83, No. 416; June, 1980, pp. 151–4

France, J., *The Cistercians in Scandinavia*, Spencer, Massachusetts, U.S.A: Cistercian Publications, 1992.

France, J., 'The Iconography of Bernard of Clairvaux and His Sister Humbelina'. In: Lillich, *Cistercian Nuns*, 2005, pp. 1–22.

François, F., Abdis Genta van Aarschot, online.

Freeman, E., 'Houses of a Peculiar Order': Cistercian Nunneries in Medieval England. In: *Cîteaux* 55, Parts 3–4, 2004, pp. 245–87.

Freeman, E., 'A Cistercian Monk Writes to a Cistercian Nun'. In: *Cistercian Studies Quarterly* 45, Part 3, 2010, pp. 331–52.

Freeman, E., 'Ælred of Rievaulx's Pastoral Care of Religious Women'. In: *Cistercian Studies Quarterly* 46, Part 1, 2011, pp. 13–26.

Freeman, E., 'Cistercian Nuns and Art in the Middle Ages'. In: Kinder, *Cistercian Arts*, 2014, pp. 175–86.

Fröhlich, R., *Die Zisterzienser und Ihre Weinberge in Brandenburg*. Berlin: Lukas Verlag, 2010.

Gahlbeck, C., *Zisterzienser und Zisterzienserinnen in der Neumark*, Berlin: Verlag Arno Spitz GmbH, 2002.

Ganck, R. de, 'The integration of nuns in the Cistercian Order, particularly in Belgium'. In: *Cîteaux* 35, Parts 3–4, 1984, pp. 235–47.

Bibliography

Ganck, R. de, 'The Biographer of Beatrice of Nazareth'. In: *Cîteaux* 23, Part 4, 1988, pp. 319–29.

Gascón, A. A. I., and M. G. I. Baro, *Monastir de Santa Maria de Valldonzella*, Montserrat, 2013.

Gayoso, A., 'The Lady of Las Huelgas'. In: *Cîteaux* 51, pts 1–2, 2000, pp. 91–115.

Giessler-Wirsig, E., 'Die Beziehungen'. In: *Zisterzienser-Studien* 4, Berlin, 1979.

Gol, J. P. I., *Abaciologi de Vallbona*, Santes Creus, 1978.

Goodrich, M., 'The White Ladies of Worcester'. In: *Transactions of the Worcestershire Archaeological Society*, 3rd Series, 14, 1994.

Graves, C. V., 'English Cistercian Nunneries'. In: *Speculum* 54, Part 3, 1979.

Graves, C. V., 'Organisation of an English Cistercian Nunnery'. In: *Cîteaux* 33, Parts 3–4, 1982.

Grélois, A., 'Abbé-Père et Abbesse-Mère'. In: *Cîteaux* 62, 2011, pp. 141–85.

Grüger, H., 'Trebnitz'. In: *Jahrbuch der Schlesischen F-W Universitat* 23, 1982, pp. 55–83.

Grüger, H., 'Der Orden der Zisterzienser'. In: *Jahrbuch der Schlesischen F-W Universitat* 23, 1982, pp. 84–145.

Grunder, K., A. Hidber and B. Sigel (eds.), *Zisterzienserbauten in der Schweiz*, 1 *Frauenklöster*, Zurich: Verlag der Fachvereine, 1990.

Gwynn, A., and R. N. Hadcock, *Medieval Religious Houses: Ireland*, London: Longmans, 1970.

Hall, J., S. Sneddon and N. Sohr, 'Table of Legislation Concerning Lay Burials'. In: *Cîteaux* 56, 2005, pp. 373–416.

Hallam, H. E., 'Salt-making in the Lincolnshire Fenland during the middle ages'. In: *Lincolnshire Architectural and Archaeological Society, Reports and Papers* N. S. 8, 1959–60, pp. 85–112.

Hautcoeur, E., *Histoire de L'Abbaye de Flines*, Lille: Giard, 1909.

Hegner, K., *Kleinbildwerke des Mittelalters in den Frauenklöstern des Bistums Schwerin*; Münster: Lit Verlag, 1994.

Heinzer, F., and G. Stamm, *Die Handschriften von Lichtenthal*, Wiesbaden: Otto Harrassowitz, 1987.

Hervay, F. L., *Repertorium Historicum Ordinis Cisterciensis in Hungaria*, Rome: Editiones Cistercienses, 1984.

Hillebrand, 'Das Klosterbuch für Schleswig-Holstein und Hamburg'. In: *Analecta Cisterciensia* 65, 2015, pp. 73–91.

Hladík, D., *Dějiny Kláštera Porta Coeli* I, Tišnov: Sursum, 1994.

Holtmeyer, A., *Cisterzienskirchen* Thüringens. In: Verein für thüringische Geschichte und Altertumskunde 1, Jena, 1906.

Hughes, A., 'Medieval Liturgical Books'. In: *Traditio* 31 1975, pp. 369–84.

Jamieson, J. H., D. E. Easson and G. Donaldson, 'The Cistercian Nunnery of St Mary, Haddington'. In: *Trans, East Lothian Antiquarian and Field Naturalists Soc.*, 5, 1952, pp. 1 – 24.

Jamroziak, E., *The Cistercian Order in Medieval Europe*, London: Routledge, 2013.

Jarck, H. R., 'Rinteln'. In: U. Faust, ed. *Die Frauenklöster in Nieder Sachsen, Schleswig-Holstein und Bremen*, St Ottilien: Eos Verlag Erzabtei, 1984, pp. 512–19.
Jordan, E. L., 'Gender Concerns: Monks, Nuns, and Patronage of the Cistercian Order in Thirteenth-Century Flanders and Hainaut'. In: *Speculum* 87, Part 1. January 2012, pp. 62–94.
Jordan, W. C., 'The Cistercian Nunnery of La Cour-Notre-Dame de Michery'. In: *Revue Bénédictine* 95, Parts 3–4, 1985, pp. 311–20.
Jordan, W. D., 'Musico-Liturgical Manuascripts'. In: *Cîteaux* 44, 1993, pp. 152–236.
Jorge, V. F., 'Monastères cisterciens de femmes au Portugal'. In: B. Barrière, M.-E. Henneau, *Cîteaux et les femmes*, Paris: Éditions Créaphis, 2001.
Jurgensmeier, F. and Schwordtfeger, E., *Die Mönchs und Nonnenkloster der Zisterzienser im Hessen und Thüringen*, St Ottilien: EOS Verlag, 2011.
Jurkiewicz, J. L., *Slak Cystersów*, Gdynia: Region, 2006.
Kaczyńscy, *Cystersi w Polsce*, Warsaw: Sport I Turystyka Muza S. A., 2010.
Kanior, M., 'Zakon cysterek i jego rozwój w Europie Środkowej'. In: Dobosz, Cystersi, pp. 109–22.
Kastner, A., 'Beilagel Erster Stiftungsbrief des Klosters Trebnitz'. In: *Archiv für die Geschichte des Bistums Breslau* 2, Neisse: Selbstverlage des Herausgebers, 1858.
Kinder, T. N., 'Blanche of Castile and the Cistercians'. In: *Cîteaux* 27, Part 3, 1976, pp. 161–88.
Kinder, T. N. (ed.), *Perspectives for an Architecture of Solitude*, Turnhout, Belgium: Brepols, 2004.
Kinder, T. N., and R. Cassanelli (ed.), *The Cistercian Arts*, Montreal: McGill-Queen's University Press, 2014.
King, A. A., *Cîteaux and her Elder Daughters*, London: Burns & Oates, 1954.
Klack-Eitzen, C., et al., *Heilige Röcke*, Regensburg: Verlag Schnell & Steiner GmbH, 2013.
Köhler, A.-K., *Geschichte des Klosters Nimbschen*, Leipzig: Evangelische Verlagsanstalt, 2003.
Král, A. B., *Podhorácké muzeum a areál Porta Coeli*, Brno, 1987.
Kratzke, C., 'The Architecture of Cistercian Nunneries in the North of Germany'. In: M. P. Lillich, *Cistercian Nuns and their World*, Kalamazoo, 2005, pp. 133–90.
Kratzke, C., 'Ornamenta Ecclesiae Cistercienses'. In: Kinder, *Cistercian Arts*, 2014, pp. 187–200.
Krausen, E., *Die Klöster des Zisterziensordens in Bayern*, Munich-Pasing: Verlag Bayerische Heimatforschung, 1953.
Kroebel, D., 'Les Moniales de l'Abbaye Cistercienne de Nonenque'. In: *Les Religieuses dans Le Cloître et dans le Monde*, Acts of the International Colloquium of CERCOM; University of Saint-Etienne, 1994, pp. 507–13.
Kucharski, G., 'Poczłątki Klastoru Cysterek w Ołoboku'. In: Dobosz, *Cystersi*, pp. 314–38.

Bibliography

Kugler, M. M., 'Feldbach'. In: *Cistercienser-Chronik* N. S. 149 (1980–3), pp. 47–70.
Kuhn-Refus, M., 'Les Cisterciennes en Allemagne'. In: Schneider *Die Cistercienser*, Cologne.1980.
Kuhn-Refus, M., 'Cistercian Nuns in Germany'. In: Nicholas and Shank, *Hidden* Springs, pp. 135–58.
Kulke, W.-H., *Zisterzienserinnenarchitektur des 13. Jahrhunderts in Südfrankreich*, Munich: Deutscher Kunstverlag, 2006.
Lachambre-Cordier, G., 'Les moniales de Notre-Dame-des-Prés'. In: B. Barrière, M.-E. Henneau, *Cîteaux et les femmes*, Paris: Éditions Créaphis, 2001, pp. 249–65.
Lackner, B. K., 'Early Cîteaux and the Care of Souls'. In: Elder, *Noble Piety*, 1981, pp. 52–67.
Lackner, B. K., 'Cistercian Nuns in Medieval Hungary'. In: Nichols and Shank, *Hidden Springs*, 1995, pp. 159–70.
Lekai, L., *The Cistercians*, Kent State U.P., 1977.
Lester, A. E., *Creating Cistercian Nuns*, Cornell U.P., 2011.
Lillich, M. P., *Cistercian Nuns and their World*, Studies in Cistercian Art and Architecture 6, Kalamazoo, 2005.
Link, G., *Klosterbuch der Diocese Würzburg*, Würzburg: J. Standinger'schen Buchhandlung, 1873.
Locatelli, R., 'L'Implantation Cistercienne en Bourgogne'. In: *Cahiers d'Histoire* 20, 1975, pp. 167–225.
Löer, W., 'Kloster Welver', In: *Gotische Buchmalerei aus Westfalen*, Soest: Mocker & Jahn, 1997, pp. 56–63.
López-Vidriero, *Manuscrits E Impresos del Monasterio de las Huelgas Reales de Burgos*, Madrid: Editorial Patrimonio Nacional, 1999.
Luaces, J. Y., 'Cistercian Miniatures'. In: Kinder, *Cistercian Arts*, 2014, pp. 223–38.
Luddy, A. J., *The Cistercian Nuns*, Dublin: Gill & Sons., 1931.
Maegraith, J. C., *Das Zisterzienserinnenkloster Gutenzell*, Verlag GmbH, Epfendorf, 2006.
Maricourt, Baron de, and A. Driart, 'Une Abbaye de Filles au XVIIIe Siècle: Gomerfontaine'. In: *Revue des question historiques* 81, 1907, pp. 447–82.
Mattson, A. C., *Riseberga Kloster*, Örebro: Ljungföretagen, Sweden, 1998.
McGuire, B. P., *The Cistercians in Denmark*, Kalamazoo: Cistercian Publications, 1982.
McGuire, B. P., *Friendship and Community, The Monastic Experience, 350–1250*, Cornell U. P., 2010.
Mecham, J. L., 'A Northern Jerusalem'. In: A. Spicer and S. Hamilton, *Defining the Holy*, Aldershot: Ashgate Publications, 2005, pp. 139–60.
Meier, P. J., *Die Stadt Goslar*, Stuttgart/Berlin: Deutsche Verlags-Anhalt, 1926.
Mersch, M., '*Conversi* und *conversae* in den Nonnenklöstern der Zisterzienser'. In: R. Oldermann (ed.), *Gebaute Klausur*, Bielefeld: Verlag für Regionalgeschichte, 2008, pp. 63–79.

Mistele, K. H., 'Kalendar und Nekrolog des Klosters Billigheim'. In: *Cistercienser-Chronik* N. F. 61–2 (December 1962), pp. 55–68.

Moldenhauer, R., 'Die wirtschafts und sozialgeschichtliche Bedeutung der Konversenkunde des Zarrentin von Jahre 1329'. In: *Cistercienser-Chronik* N. F. 65/66, December 1963, pp. 46–52.

Moro, A. P., *El Monasterio de Barria*, University of País Vasco, 2013.

Mötsch, J., *Fuldische Frauenkloster in Thüringen*, Munich: Urban & Fischer, 1999.

Mouret, D., and J. de la Croix Bouton, 'Convers et Converses'. In: Privat, É., *Les Cisterciens de Languedoc*. In: Cahiers de Fanjeaux 21, Toulouse, 1986, pp. 293–310.

Mula, S., 'Gossuinus's *Vitae* of Emelina and Ascelina'. In: *Cîteaux* 62, 2011, pp. 37–57.

Mycoff, D. A., 'The Legend of Mary Magdalene in a Twelfth-Century Cistercian Context'. In: *Cîteaux* 23, Part 4, 1988, pp. 310–18.

Newman, B., 'Possessed by the Spirit'. In: *Speculum* 73, 1998, pp. 733–70.

Newman, M. G., 'Crucified by the Virtues'. In: Farmer and Pasternack, 2001, pp. 182–209.

Nichols, J. A., 'An English Cistercian Nunnery'. In: J. R. Sommerfeldt (ed.), *Cistercian Ideas and Reality*, Cistercian Studies Series 60, Kalamazoo, 1978, pp. 319–28.

Nichols, J. A., 'Internal Organisation of an English Cistercian Nunnery'. In: *Cîteaux* 30, 1979, pp. 23–40.

Nichols, J. A., 'Medieval English Cistercian Nunneries'. In: Chauvin, *Mélanges* 5, 1982, pp. 152–76.

Nichols, J. A., and L. T. Shank, *Distant Echoes*, Cistercian Studies Series, 71, Kalamazoo, 1984.

Nichols, J. A., 'Early History of the Cistercian Nuns'. In: *Cîteaux* 38, 1987, pp. 102–3.

Nichols, J. A., and L. T. Shank, *Hidden Springs*, Cistercian Studies Series, 113, Part 1, Kalamazoo, 1995.

Noel, A., 'L'Abbaye de L'Amour-Dieu'. In: *Revue de Champagne et de Brie* 1, Paris, 1876, pp. 144–53.

O'Dwyer, B. W., 'Crisis in the Cistercian Monasteries in Ireland'. In: *Analecta Cisterciensia* 31, 1975, Part 2, pp. 267–304; 32, 1976, Parts 1–2, pp. 3–112.

Oefelein, C., 'Typiquemont atypique, l'abbatiale Saint-Jacob – Saint-Burchard d'Halberstadt'. In: Barrière and Henneau, *Cîteaux et les femmes*, 2001

Oefelein, C., 'The Cistercian Nuns' Abbey of SS. Jacobi et Burchardi'. In: Lillich, *Cistercian Nuns and their World*, pp. 283–306.

Oertig, Sr M. Beatrix, *725 Jahre Mariazell Wurmsbach*, Rapperswil: Kloster Wurmsbach, 1984.

Oliver, J. 'Devotional Psalters and the Study of Beguine Spirituality'. In: *Vox Benedictina* 9, No. 2, Winter, 1992, pp. 199–226.

Bibliography

Ostrowitzki, A., 'L'attitude des Cisterciens face aux moniales de Rhēnanie'. In: B. Barrière, M.-E. Henneau, *Cîteaux et les femmes*, Paris: Éditions Créaphis, 2001, pp. 239–48.

Overgaauw, E., 'Das Gravenhorster Fragment des *diaetis particularibus* von Isaac Judaeus'. In: R. Feldmann, *Die Klosterbibliothek Gravenhorst*, Munster: Universitäts-und Landesbibliothek, 1993, pp. 21–6.

Pankoke, E. (ed)., *Buchmalerei der Zisterzienser*, Stuttgart: Belser Verlag, 1998.

Parkes, M. B., *The Medieval Manuscripts of Keble College, Oxford*, London: Scolar Press, 19179.

Pearson, A. G., 'Spirituality, Authority and Monastic Vows'. In: Lillich, *Cistercian Nuns and their World*, pp. 323–64.

Peugniez, B., *Le Guide Routier de L'Europe cistercienne*, Strasbourg: Éditions du Signe, 2012.

Pigeon, M., 'Les femmes dans les *Vitae* des Saints de Savigny'. In: *Cîteaux* 35, Parts 1–2, 1984, pp. 73–82.

Ploegaerts, T., *Histoire de l'Abbaye d'Aywières*, Brussels: Action Catholique, 1924.

Ploegaerts, T., *Histoire de l'Abbaye de La Ramée*, Brussels: Action Catholique, 1925.

Ploegearts, T., *Histoire de l'Abbaye de Florival*, Brussels: Verbe et Lumière, 1925.

Popielas-Szultka, B., *Klasztory Cysterek Na Pomorzu Zachodnim W Średniowieczu*, Slupsk: Pomorska Akademia Pedagogiczna, 2006.

Privat, É., *Les Cisterciens de Languedoc*, Toulouse: Centre d'Études historiques de Fanjeaux, 1986.

Reimann, Heike, 'Cistercians Nuns in the High Middle Ages: The Cistercians of Bergen in the Principality of Rügen (North Germany)'. In: *Cîteaux* 55, 2004, pp. 231–44.

Reiss, L., 'Studien zur des Zisterzienserinnen-Kloster Lichtenthal'. In: *Zeitschrift für die Geschicte ds Oberrheins* 96, 1948, pp. 230–306.

Rèpas, M., *Quando a Nobreza Traja de Branco*, Leiria: Colecção História e Arte, 2003.

Richard, J., 'L'Établissement des Moniales Cisterciennes'. In: *Mémoires de la Société pour l'Histoire du Droit et des Institutions des anciens pays bourguignons* 15, 1953, pp. 83–129.

Riggert, I.-C., *Die Lüneberger Frauenkloster*, Hanover: Verlag Hahnsche Buchhandlung, 1996.

Roden, G. von, *Die Zisterzienserrinnenkloster Saarn, Duissern, Sterkrade*, Germania Sacra, N. F. 18, Berlin: Walter de Gruyter & Co., 1984.

Roisin, S., 'L'efflorescnce cistercienne et le courant féminin de piété au XIIe siècle'. In: *RHE* 39, 1943, pp. 343–78.

Rombouts, R., *Herkenrode 800 jaar*, Hasselt: Stadmuseum, 1982.

Römer-Johannsen, 'Goslar Neuwerk', In: U. Faust, ed. *Die Frauenklöster in Nieder Sachsen, Schleswig-Holstein und Bremen*, St Ottilien: Eos Verlag Erzabtei, 1984, pp. 250–80.

Ronneberger, W., *Das Zisterzienser Nonnenkloster zum Heiligen Kreuz bei Sallburg*, Jena: Verlag von Gustav Fischer, 1932.
Schich, W., 'Die Stadthöfe der Zisterzienserkloster in Würzburg'. In: *Zistercienser-Studien* 3, Berlin, 1979, pp. 45–94.
Schlegel, G. (ed.), *Repertorium der Zisterzen*, Kloster Langwaden: Bernardus-Verlag Langwaden, 1998.
Schneider, A. (ed.), *Die Cistercienser Geschichte Geist Kunst*, Cologne: Wieland Verlag, 1977.
Scholten, R., 'Die ehemaligen Cistercienserinnen-Klöster im Herzogtum Cleve'. In: *Annales des Historischer Verein für den Niederrhein* 60, Cologne, 1908, pp. 60–134.
Sennhauser, H. R., et al., *Zisterzienserbauten in der Schweiz 1: Frauenkloster*, Zurich: Verlag der Fachvereine, 1990.
Siart, O., *Kreuzgänge mittelalterlichter Frauenklöster*, Petersberg: Michael Imhof Verlag, 2008.
Steinwascher, G., *Die Zisterzienserstadthöfe in Köln*, Bergisch Gladbach: Jon. Heider Druckerei und Verlag GmbH, 1981.
Steinwascher, G., 'Kloster Rinteln'. In: *Niedersächisches Jahrbuch für Landesgeschichte*, 58, 1986, pp. 143–76.
Szwejkowska, H., *Biblioteka Klasztoru Cysterek w Trzebnicy*, Wrocław: Państwowe Wydawnictwo Naukowe, 1955.
Thompson, S., 'The problem of the Cistercian nuns in the twelfth and early thirteenth centuries'. In: D. Baker, *Medieval Women*, Oxford: Blackwell, 1978, pp. 227–52.
Thompson, S., 'Problems of the English Nunneries'. In: Nichols, *Distant Echoes*, 1984, pp. 227–52.
Toepfer, M., 'Die Konversen der Zisterzienserinnen'. In: K. Elm (ed.), *Beiträge zur Geschichte der Konversen im Mittelalter*, Berlin Historische Studien 2, 1980.
Trops, H., *Rīgas Sv. Marijas Magdalēnas*, University of Riga thesis, 1943.
Venarde, B. L., *Women's Monasticism and Medieval Society*, Cornell U. P., 1996.
Veyssière, L., 'Cîteaux et Tart'. In: B. Barrière, M.-E. Henneau, *Cîteaux et les femmes*, Paris: Éditions Créaphis, 2001, pp. 179–90.
Volk, O., *Salzproduktion und Salzhandel mittelalterlicher*, Sigmaringen: Jan Thorbecke Verlag, 1984.
Waddell, C., 'Cistercian Institutions', In: L. Pressouyre (ed.), *L'espace cistercien*, Paris, 1994, pp. 27–38.
Waddell, C., 'The Myth of Cistercian Origins'. In: *Cîteaux*, 51, 2000, Parts 3–4, pp. 299–386.
Waddell, C., *The Primitive Cistercian Breviary*, Fribourg: Academic Press, 2007.
Warren, H.-B de, *La Bretagne Cistercienne*, Nantes: Editions J.-M. Williamson, 1991.
Wehking, S., *Die Inschriften der Lüneburger Kloster*, Wiesbaden: Dr Ludwig Reichert Verlag, 2009.

Bibliography

Weissenberger, P., 'Wirtschaftesgeschichliche Nachrichten über einige bayrische Cist. - Frauenkloster'. In: *Cistercienser Chronik*, N. S. 51, Part 2, July 1960, pp. 1–10.
Wieland, M., 'Kloster Heiligenthal', and 'Kloster Wechterswinkel', In: *Cistercienser-Chronik* 11, 1899, pp. 162–7, 193–204, 257–2654, 281–99, 321–9.
Willesme, J.-P., 'Les Cisterciens à Paris'. In: *Cîteaux* 37, Parts 1–2, 1986, pp. 134–7.
Willi, D., 'Lichtental bei Baden-Baden'. In: Brunner, *Ein Cisterzienserbuch*, 1981, pp. 652–63.
Williams, D. H., 'Cistercian Settlement in the Lebanon'. In: *Cîteaux* 25: Part 1, 1974, pp. 61–74.
Williams, D. H., 'Cistercian Nunneries in Medieval Wales'. In: *Cîteaux* 26, Part 3, 1975, pp. 155–74.
Williams, D. H., 'East of the Oder'. In: *Cîteaux* 29, Parts 3–4, 1978, pp. 228–67.
Williams, D. H., *Cistercian Chronicles and Necrologies*, Gracewing, Leominster, 2022.
Williams, D. H., *Dünamünde Abbey*, Bakehouse Print, Abertillery, 2020.
Winkworth, M., *Gertrude of Helfta: The Herald of Divine Lone*, New York: Paulist Press, 1993.
Winter, F., *Die Cistercienser des Nordöstlichen Deutschlands*, Gotha: Friedrich Andreas Berthes, 1868–71.
Wipfler, E., *'Corpus Christi' in Liturgie und Kunst der Zisterzienser im Mittelalter*, Münster: Lit Verlag, 2003.
Wiszewski, P., 'Cysterki trzebnickie w społeczeństwie'. In: Dobosz, *Cystersi*, pp. 705–18.
Wyrwa, A. M., et al., *Monasticon Cisterciense Poloniae*, Poznan: Wydawnistwo Poznańskie, 1999.
Zeimet, J., *Die Cistercienserinnenabtei St. Katharinen b. Linz a. Rh.*, Augsburg: Dr Benno Filser Verlag, 1929.
Ziegler, C., 'A Rare Parchment from the Scriptorium of the Cistercian Nunnery of Saint-Bernard by Horn'. In: Lillich, *Cistercian Nuns and their World*, pp. 307–22.

Variant Names of Nunneries

After Frederik van der Meer, Bernard Peugniez, and other sources. Obvious equivalents, such as Bonus Locus = Bonlieu, are omitted.

Abbatia Nova	Gourdon (F)
Abundantia Dei	Salenques (F)
Ager Clavium	Schlüsselau (G)
Alba dominae	les Blanches (F)
Alesiensis	Fonts-lèz-Alais (F)
Almanarrae	Lamanarre (F)
Aqua	Eau-Lès-Chartres (F)
Aquiria/Aviria	Aywières (B)
Arcae	Arques (F)
Arcta Vallis	Engental (Swz)
Ascharia	Aschersleben (G)
Asunción	Carrizo (Sp)
Augia Ancillarum	Magdenau (Swz)
Augia Coeli	Himmelau (G)
Augia Macra	La Maigrauge
Augia Sancta	Magdenau (Swz)
Augia S. Mariae	Marienau (G)
Augia Virginum	Magdenau (Swz)
Aula B. Mariae	Eppinghoven (G)
Aula Dei	Nyekleaster/Godshof (Ho)
Aula S. Mariae	Blaetzheim (G)
	Saarn (G)
	Staré Brno (Cz)
Aula S. Petri	Blatzheim (G)
Aurea Cella	Doornzele (B)
Aurora	Frienisberg (Swz)
Badia di S. Pietro	Assisi (It)
Bartholomäus-Kloster	Blankenburg (G: Saxony Anhalt)
Battentium	Battant (F)
Beata Vallis	Seligental (G)
Beatae Genetricis Mariae	Blankenau (G)
Beatae Mariae	Herkenrode (B)

B. Mariae de antiqua Lera	Maria in der Leer (Koblenz, G)
B. Mariae in Deserto	Woestyne (G)
B. Mariae Fortis Consilii	Sterkrade (G)
B. Mariae et SS. Gervasii et Protasii	San-Giacomo di Veglia (It)
B. Mariae de Jerusalem	Spermalie/Nieuwland (B)
B. Mariae de Pratis	N. D.-des-Prés (F)
Beati Jacobi in Civitate	Halberstadt (G)
Belfait	Beaufays (F)
Bello visu	Beauvoir (F)
Bellum pratum	Beaupré (B); Beaupré (F)
Bellum riparium	Saint-Paul (F)
Benedicta Vallis	Benoîtevaux (F)
Benedictus Locus Regine super Tarrant	Tarrant (E)
Bethlehem	Elkersee (Ho)
Biachum/Biachium	Biaches-lès-Péronne (F)
Bitumen	Le Betton (F)
Blumental	Zehdenick (G)
Boevallis/Buevallis	Bival (F)
Bona Cella	Gutenzell/Gotteszell (G)
Bona Requies	Bonrepos (F)
	Marquette (F)
Bonavia	Bonneweg/Bonnevoie (L)
Bonus Fons/Bonifontis	Buenafuente (Sp)
Bonus Lacus	Bonlieu (F); (le)
	Vignogoul (F)
	Buonluogo (It)
Boschetum/Boquetum	(Le) Bouchet (F)
Braelia	Brayelle-les-Aulnay (F)
Brajacum	Braie/Bray (F)
Brassó	Szt Katalin (R)
Bunzium	Bons (F)
Bure	Lichtental (G)
Buxeriensis	Bussière (F)
Buyeval	Bival (F)
Calagurris	Calahorra (Sp)
Camera Beate/Sancte Mariae	La Cambre (B)
	Vrouwekamer (Ho)

Variant Names of Nunneries

	Marienkammer/Glaucha (G)
Campus Benedictus	Cham(p)benoît (F)
Campus Floridus	Baindt (G)
Campus Laudis	Lobenfeld (G)
Campus S. Michaelis	Michelfeld-Blotzheim (F)
Campus Silvae	Midwolde (Ho)
Campus Silvarum	Wald (G)
Campus Solis	Sonnefeld (G)
	Sonnekamp/Neukloster (G)
Campus speciosus superior	Oberschönenfeld (G)
Carpentoractensis	Sainte-Madeleine (F)
Castrum B. Mariae	Marienschloss (G)
Castrum Vetus	Châteauvieux (F)
Celi Thronus	Himmelthron (G)
Cella B. Mariae	Wormsbach/Marienzell (Swz)
Cella B. Mariae ad Clivum Calcarium	Kalchrain/Mariazell (Swz)
Cella Bona	Gutenzell/Gotteszell (G)
Cella Dei	Gutenzell/Gotteszell (G)
Cella Dominarum	Frauenroth (G)
Cella S. Johannis	Johanniszelle (G)
Cellas	Celas (Pt)
Chalaisium	Chaleis (F)
Cherium	Chieri (It)
Clara Stella	Lichtenstern (G)
Claretum/de Claretis	Les-Clarets (F)
Clarus Fons	Clairefontaine/Autelbas (F)
	Clairefontaine/Olizarowysław (Lt)
Clarus Locus	Clairlieu (F)
Clarus Mariscus	Clairmarais (F)
Clavassium	Clavas (F)
Coeli Corona	Himmelkron (G)
Coeli Hortus	Alzey (G)
Coeli Porta	Himmelspforten (G)
Coeli Thronus	Himmelthron (G)
Colengiae	Collonges/Colonges (F)
Commoda	Chumbd (G)
Congregatio Sacrarum Virginum	Wienhausen (G)

Consilii/Consilio Domus	Rathausen (Swz)
Consolatio B. Mariae	Consolation (F)
Corcellae	Corcelles (F)
Corona B. Mariae	Frauenkron (G)
	Patershausen/Marienkron (G)
	Nieuw-Mariëndael/Maria Kroon (Ho)
Corona-Virginum	Patershausen (G).
Cupersano/Cupersanum	Conversano (It)
Curia B. Mariae	Cour-Notre-Dame (F)
	Neydingen/ Mariahof (G)
Curia monialium	Eau-lès-Chartres/Panthoison (F)
Curia S. Mariae	Kentorp/Kentrup (G)
Dei Villa	Divielle/Villedieu (F)
Directa Vallis	Droiteval (F)
Ebersekensis	Ebersegg (Swz)
Elnonenca	Nonenque (F)
Esclachia	L'Esclache (F)
Eula	L'Eule (F)
Favarquiae	Fervaques (F)
Favasium	Favas/Fabas (F)
Felix Porta	Seligenporten (G)
Felix Pratum	Félipré (F)
Fenelhetum	Fenouillet (F)
Ferventes Aquae	Fervaques (F)
Filia Dei	(La) Fille-Dieu (Swz)
Flinae/Felinae	Flines (F)
Florida Vallis	Florival (B)
Flumen Frigidum	Fonte Laurate (It)
Fons Beate Mariae / Fons Calidus	Billigheim/Fuentecaliente (Sp)
Fons Salutis	Algemisí (F)
Fons Sancte Mariae	Marienbrunn (G)
	Burbach (G)
	Coesfeld/Hoven (G)
	Marienbronn (F)
	Marienborn (G)
	Differdange (L)

Variant Names of Nunneries

	Maidbronn (F)
	Fraubrunnen (Swz)
Fons Sommae	Fervaques (F)
Fonticulae/Fontinella	Fontenelle (F)
Frauental	Pohled (Cz)
Frisacensis	Friesach (A)
Furconium	Furcona (It)
Galilea	Vrouwenklooster (Ho); Piacenza (It)
Gaudium	La-Joie (Brittany, F) Île-de-France (Picardy, F)
Gaudium B. Mariae	Ter-Hagen/Maria-Vreugde/ Maria Bliscap (Ho)
Gomeri Fons	Gomerfontaine (F)
Grâce Dieu	Costejean (F)
Graefenthal	Grevendael/Neukloster bei Goch (F)
Gratia	La-Grâce (F)
Gratia Dei de eremo	Leyme/Grâce-Dieu (F)
Grenefeldensis	Greenfield E)
Hagensis	Ter-Hagen/Maria-Vreugde/ Maria Bliscap (Ho)
Heckenbachium	Heggbach (G)
Heiligengeist	Ybbs (A)
Heiligkreuzkloster	Eisenber (G)
Himmelgarten	Nordhausen (G)
Himmelpforte	Zarrentin (G)
Himmelpforten	Duissern (G)
Hispania	Espagne/Epagne (F)
Hoennepel	Hunnepe/ Mariënhorst
Hortus Coeli	Himmelsgarten/Alzey (G)
Hortus Dei	Olsberg (Swz
Hortus Floridus	Baindt (G)
Hortus S. Mariae	Mariengarten (G Cologne); Erfurt (G) Goslar/Neuwerk (G)/ Worms (G) Appiano (It)
Hospitalis Sancte Marie	Byloque (B)

The Early Cistercian Nuns, 1098–1350

Île-Dieu	Blanche (F)
Ilmena	Ilm/Stadtilm (G)
Insula S. Mariae	Les Isle/Îles (F)
	Marieninsel (G)
Insula Senardi	Villencourt/Willancourt (F)
Juncunda Vallis	Wonnental (G)
Karles	Kerlot/Kerley (F)
Lacus/Lacu Sancte Marie	Frauensee (G)
	Mariensee (G)
Libere Abbatiae	Parc-aux-Bois (F)
Lilium subtus Melodunum	Le-Lys, Melun (F)
Locum Vallis Coeli	Hemelsdaele (B)
Locus	Lieu/Lieu-l'Abbaye (F)
Locus Beate/Sanctae Mariae	Lokeren (B); Lieu-Notre-Dame (F)
	Pielenhofen/Bülenhofen (G)
Locus Dei prope Vergeium	Lieu-Dieu (F)
Locus Dominarum	Boulancourt (F)
Locus Imperatricis	Binderen (Ho)
Locus Regine	Tarrant (E)
Lorban	Lorvão (Pt)
Lousdunensis	Loosduinen (Ho.)
Lucida Stella	Lichtenstern (G)
Lucida Vallis	Lichtental (G)
Lumen Dei/Dieu	Favas/Fabas/Lumedieu (F)
	Grâce-Dieu/Leyme (F)
Machera ad Mosellam	Machern (G)
Macraugia	(La) Maigrauge (Swz)
Magdunum	Voisins (F)
Malodunum	Maubuisson (F)
Manuesca	Manosque (F)
Marchia dominarum	Marche-les-Dames (B)
Mariäkron	Rechentshofen (G)
Maria Saal	Stare Brno (Cz)
Maria Vallensis	Marienthal (G)
Maria-Vreugde	Ter Hagen (B)
Mariandorf	Marianowo (Pl)

Variant Names of Nunneries

Maria's Kamer	Vrouewekamer (Ho)
Marienberg	Börstel (G)
Marienborg	Hoven (G)
Marienbrunn	Burbach (G); Rulle (G)
Mariëndael	Ten-Daele (Ho)
Mariengarten	See Hortus Sancte Mariae
Marienhorst	Ter Hunnepe (Ho)
Marienkamp	Jesse (Ho)
Marienkron	Patershausen (G)
Mariënlof	Colen/Koben (B)
Marienpforte	Boitzenburg (G)
Marienrode	Isenhagen (G)
Mariensaal	Eppoinghoven (G)
	Saarn (G)
Mariental	Oslavany (Cz)
	Rottenmünster (G)
Marienthron	Grimma/Nimbschen (G)
Marienwerder	Seehausen (G)
Maylan	St Bernard-by-Horn (A)
Mazurae	Consolation (F)
Medius Mons	Mègemont (F)
Mercorium	Mercoire (F)
Miroir Notre Dame	Groeninge (B)
Molegesium	Mollêges (F)
Molesia	Molêze/Molaise (F)
Monasterium Beatae Mariae	Herkenrode (B)
Mons/Montes [in Ruga]	Bergen (G)
Mons Amoris	Fröndenberg (G)
Mons Aureus	Guldenburg (B)
Mons Beatae Mariae	Mont-Notre-Dame (F)
	Vinnenberg (G)
Mons Beatae Virginis	Varfruerga (Sw)
Mons Coelestis	Moncey (F)
Mons Pomarius	Baumgartenburg (A)
Mons Principis	Fürstenberg (G)
Mons S. Catharinae	Katherinberg (G)
Mons S. Georgii	Frankenberg/Georgenberg (G)
Mons S. Mariae	Bischofsrode (G)
Mons S. Nicolai	Adersleben (G)
Mons S. Ruperti	Rupertsberg (Bingen, G)

Mons S. Walburgis	Walberberg (G)
Mons Sion	Mont-Sion (F)
Mons Solis	Solberga (Sw)
	Soleilmont (B)
Mons subtus Laudunum	Montreuil-les-Dames (F)
Mons Vari	Fürstenberg (G)
Mont d'Or	Guldenberg (G)
Monte Sancte Marie	Menslage/Börstel (G)
Morsella	Moorseele (B)
Mouchiacum petrosum	Monchy-le-Péreux (F)
Mulne	Mülheim (G)
Musensis	Muizen (B)
Nazareth	Genezareth/Gennaard (Ho)
	Piacenza (It)
Nemus B. Mariae	Mariënbos (Ho)
Neukloster	Grafenthal (G)
	Sonnenkamp (G)
Neuwerk	Goslar (G)
Neuwerk-St-Maria	Nordhausen (G)
Nitidus Locus	Netleiu (F)
Nomen Dei	Namedy (G)
Nonnaticum	Nonenque (F)
Notre Dame au Bois	Lokeren (B)
Notre-Dame de Commiers	Vernaison (F)
Notre-Dame du Bon Conseil	Oudenaarde (B)
Notre Dame la Royale	Maubuisson (F)
Nova Civitas	Neuburg (G)
Nova Jerusalem	Spermalie/Nieuwland (B)
Nova Silva	Nieuwenbosch (B)
Novale/	Frauenroth (G)
Novalis Sancte S. Mariae	
	Isenhagen (G)
Nove Claustro	Sonnencamp (G)
Novum Claustrum	Gräfenthal (G)
	Neufchâtel-en-Bray (F)
Novum Opus	Goslar/Neuwerk (G)
Oisterloa	Oosteeklo (B)
Oliva	l'Olive (B)

Variant Names of Nunneries

Omnium Sanctorum	Oberwesel (G)
Oratio Dei	Oraison-Dieu (F)
Oriens	Orienten/Rummen (B)
Orto St Martini	Mariengarten (Erfurt, G)
Ortus	*See* Hortus
Pace Dei	Blankenberg/Zissendorf (G)
Pamele	Oudenaard (B)
Paracletus	Paraclet-des-Champs (F)
Parcus Dominarum	Vrouenpark (B)
Pax Dei	(la) Paix-Dieu (B)
Planis	Plan (F)
Pologeyum/Polengiacense	Poulengy (F)
Pomarium	Baumgarten (F)
Pons Dominarum	Pont-aux-Dames (F)
Pons Leonis	Löwenbrücken (G)
Pons Regis	Koenigsbrück (F)
Pons Salutis	Heilsbrück (G)
Porceto/Porcetum	Burtscheid (G)
Porregius/Porreium	Port-Royal-des-Champs (F)
Porretum/Perreium	Perray-aux-Nonnains (F)
Porta B. Mariae	Boitzenburg/Marienpforte (G)
Porta Coeli	Pielenhofen/Bülenhofen (G)
	Himmelpforten (Lower Saxony, G)
	Himmelpforten (North Rhine-Westphalia, G)
	Zarrentin/Porretum (G);
	Himmelspforten (Tišnov, Cz)
Porta Dei	Düsseren (G)
Porta Felix	Seligenp(f)orten (G)
Porta Marianus	Pielenhofen/Bülenhofen (G)
Porta Salutis	Heilsbrück (G)
Portus Beate Marie / Portus Sanctae Mariae	Bijloke (B)
Portus Regius	Port-Royal-des-Champs (F)
Pratea	La Prée (F)
Pratis	Notre-Dame-des-Prés (F)
Prato S. Marie/Pratis B. Mariae	Benden/Mariabenden (G)

The Early Cistercian Nuns, 1098–1350

Pulchra Augia	Schönau (G)
Pura Vallis	Eberseck (Swz)
Rameia	(La) Ramée (B)
Ramosa	Ramsen (G)
Reclinatorie beate virginis / Perreium	Perray-aux-Nonnains (F)
	Marquette (F)
Recta Vallis	Droiteval (F)
Refuge-Notre-Dame / Refugium Beate Marie	Ath (B)
Regiopontanum	Koenigsbrück (F)
Riuofrigido	Rifreddo (It)
Rive Sancte Marie	Stepnitz
Rivulum / Rivus Sancte Marie / Beatae Mariae	Marienfliess/Stepnitz (G)
	Marienfloss (G)
	Sterkrade (G)
	Marianowo (Pl)
Rosa Beatae Mariae	Ter Roosen (B)
Rosental	Börstel (G)
S. Agnetem	Lauingen (G)
SS. Albani, Cyriaci et Sociorum	Welver/Welffern (G)
S. Albert	Sestri (It)
SS. Alexandrie et Laurentii	Wienhausen (G)
S. Anna	Langendorf/Greislau (G)
	Vlotho/Segenstal (G)
	Tänikon/Liliental (Swz)
S. Annae	Klein Adwert/Sint Annen (Ho)
S. Antonio	Cortona (It)
St-Archangelus	Négropont (Gr)
S. Ashuldis	Sainte-Houd/Sainte-Hoilde (F)
S. Aspern	St-Apern (Cologne, G)
S. Bartholomaei	Blankenburg (Saxony-Anhalt, G)
	Trebnitz (Pl)
S. Benedetto	Conversano (It)
S. Benedicti	Castirs (Pt)
S. Bernaerds	Diest (B)
S. Bernardo	Vileña (Sp)
	Portalegra (Pt)

Variant Names of Nunneries

S. Burchard	Halberstadt/Neuwerk (G)
S. Catarina	Cingoli (It)
S. Catherinae	Eisenach/Katharinenkloster (G)
	Andernach-Namedy (G)
S. Catherinae et Pancratii	Wolmirstedt (G)
S. Christophori	Lafões/Alafões (Pt)
S. Columbae	Blendecques (F)
S. Cornelii	Machern (G)
S. Crucis	Blumental/Czedenik (G)
	Eisenberg/Kreuzkloster (G)
	Gotha/Heilig-kreuz (G)
	Rostock (G); Stachelberg (G)
	Zimmern (G)
S. Cyriaci	Frauenzimmern (G)
S. Dionysii	Odivelas (Pt)
S. Donati	San Donato Polverosa (It)
S. Félix-de-Montceau	Gigean (F)
S. Franca	Piacenza (It)
S. Gaudenzo	Rimini (It)
S. Georgii	Georgenthal/Jorisberg (G)
	Georgenzell (G)
	Georgenberg (G)
	Kelbra (G);
	Glaucha/Marienkammer (G)
	Leipzig (G)
	Niederschönenfeld (G)
	Ramsen (G)
	Rathausen (Swz)
	Ütersen (G)
S. Helenae	Löwenbrücken (G)
	Scala (It)
S. Iöris/Joris	Georgenbusch (G)
S. Jacobi	Althaldensleben (G)
S. Joannis	Vinnenberg (G)
S. Joannis Baptistae	Caravaggio (It)
S. Justi	Sant-Just (F)
S. Laurentius	Goion/Goujon (F)
SS. Leonard et Jacobi	Esholt (E)
S. Lupi ad Ligerim	St-Loup (F)
S. Margarethe	Beuren (G)

The Early Cistercian Nuns, 1098–1350

S. Maria ad Hortum	Mariengarten (Erfurt, G)
S. Maria in Indagine	Schmerlenbach (G)
S. Maria in Orto	Mariengarten (Goslar, G)
S. Maria Magdalena	Bival (F)
	Cistello (It)
	Plötzky (G)
	Reinbek (G)
	Tripoli (Ln)
S. Maria de Gora	Bergen (G)
S. Maria de Pratis	Pratis (F)
S. Maria la Real	Gradefes (Sp)
S. Maria del Salvador	Cañas (Sp)
S. Mariae Semper	Virginis Alt-Friedland (G)
S. Maria di Stivolato	Chieri (It)
S. Maria S. Theodore	Bamberg (G)
S. Maria de Valle Imperatoris	Binderen (Ho)
S. Maria de Verge/de Viridario	Modon (Gr)
S. Maria-S. Wilheim	Oberried (G)
S. Mariae	Frauenberg (Nordhausen, G)
	Szczecin (Pl)
S. Martin	Géronde (Swz)
S. Mauritii	Frauenpriessnitz (G)
	Fröndenberg (G)
	Carnoët (F)
S. Michaelis	Jena/Michaeliskloster (G)
	Reval (Es)
S. Nicolai	Witzenhausen (G)
S. Pauli de Frades	Almaziva (Pt)
S. Petri	Arouca (Pt)
	Cayssac (F)
	Poulangy (F)
	Worbis/Wurbitze (G)
S. Petrus S. Paulus	Oberweimar (G)
S. Pons	Gémenos (F)
S. Salvador	Bouças (Pt)
	Ferreira del Pantón (Sp)
S. Salvator	Aachen (G)
S. Salvatorem	Assen (Ho)
S. Salvatoris	Morseele (B)
S. Severo	Ravenna (It)

Variant Names of Nunneries

S. Sidonii	Saint-Saëns (F)
S. Sigismund	Orthez (F)
SS. Simonis et Judae	Wormeln (G)
S. Sulpicii	Saint-Sulpice-de-la-Pointe (F)
S. Theodori	Bamberg (G)
S. Thomae de Osech/Ernstburen	Sankt-Thomas an der Kyll (G)
S. Thomas	Halberstadt (G)
S. Tommaso	Cremona (It)
SS. Trinitatis et S. Margaritae	Wechterswinkel (G)
S. Udalrici	Sangershausen (G)
S. Walburgis	Markussra (G)
Sacra Vallis	Mehringen (G)
Sala Regia	Stare Brno (Cz)
Salicetum/Sartum	(le) Saulchoir (B)
Salsinii	Salzinnes (B)
Salvamentum	(le) Sauvoir (F)
San Luca	Milan (It)
San Salvatore	Monte Amiata (It)
Sancta Columba	Blendecques (F)
Sancta Crux	Eisenberg (G)
Sancta Maria de Gora	Bergen (G)
Sancta Maria de Salvatore	Canas (Sp)
Sancta Vallis	Heiligenthal (G)
Sancte Crucis	Rostock (G)
	Saalburg (G)
Sanctum Sepulchrum	Heiligengrabe (G)
Sanguis Christi	Wasserleben/Waterler (G)
Sta. Croce	Monte Favale (It)
Santa Cruz	Casarrubios del Monte (Sp)
Sartus Leodiense	Val-Benoît/Vaux Benoît (B)
Sayn/Sion	Seyne (Cologne, G)
Schola Dei	Ihlo (G)
Silva Benedicta	Sauvebenoîte/la Séauve (F)
	Wald (G)
Soleriae	Solières (B)
Solismons	Soleilmont (B)
Speciosa Vallis	Schöntal (G)
Speciosus campus inferior	Niederschönenfeld (G)
Speculum B. Mariae	Groeninge (B)
Spinoso Loco	Épinlieu (B)

The Early Cistercian Nuns, 1098–1350

Stagnum B. Mariae	Mariensee (Brandenburg, G)
Stanchia	L'Estanche/L'Étanche (F)
Steina in Augia	Steinen in der Au (Swz)
Stella Aurea	Güldenstern (G)
Stella B. Mariae	Mariastern-Gwiggen (A)
	Marienstern (G)
Stella praeclara	Lichtenstern (G)
	Termond/Zwyveke (B)
Tarretanse	Tarrant (E)
Tartum	Tart (F)
Thesaurus	(le) Trésor (F)
Throno S. Mariae	Grimma (G)
	Thron (G)
Thronus Coeli	Himmelthron (G)
Thronus S. Mariae	Nimbschen/Marienthron (G)
Trebnitium	Trzebnitz (Pl)
Tullino	Tullins (F)
Val des Virgines	Maagdendale (B)
Valle Beatae Mariae prope Tulpetum	Bürvenich (G)
Valle Christi	Rapallo (It)
Valle Coeli	Vivegnis/Verguines (B)
Valle Felici	Seligenthal (G; Bavaria)
Valle Rosarum	Börstel/Menslage (G)
Valle Sancte Crucis	Heiligkreuztal (G)
Vallis Angelorum	Engelt(h)al (G)
Vallis Baionis	Valbaïon/Vauboin (F)
Vallis Beatorum	Selingental (G; Baden)
Vallis Benedicta	Val-Benoît/Vaux Benoît (B)
Vallis Benedictionis	Vlotho/Segenstal (G)
Vallis Bona	Vallbona (Sp)
Vallis Bressiaci	Laval/Laval-Bénite/Val-de-Bressieux (F)
Vallis Catharinae	Kathariental (G)
Vallis Celi/Coeli/	Eesen/Eessene (B)
	Hemelsdaele (B)
Vallis Coelarum	Himmeltal (G)
Vallis Comitis	Grafenthal/Grevendael (G)
Vallis Dei	Brenkhausen (G)

Variant Names of Nunneries

	Gottesthal (G)
Vallis Directa	Droiteval (F)
Vallis Dominarum	Frauental (Cz)
	Frauental (G)
	Frauental (Swz)
Vallis Ducis	Valduc (B)
Vallis Felix	Seligenthal (G; Bavaria)
Vallis Florum	Florival (B)
	Blumental/Zehdenick (G)
Vallis Gratiae/Gratiarum	Gnadental (Baden, G; Hesse, G; Westphalia, G)
	Gnadental (Swz)
Vallis Guntheri	Guenterstal (G)
Vallis Liliarum/Lilii	Lilienthal/Wolda/Nordhausen (G)
	Tänikon/Liliental (Swz)
Vallis Nigra	Valnègre (F)
Vallis Nostrae Dominae	Val-Notre-Dame (B)
	Roosendael (B)
Vallis Profunda	Tiefental/Elisabethental (G)
Vallis Rosarum	Rosenthal/Menslage (G)
Vallis Salve	Valsauve (F)
Vallis Sana	Lavaysse/Lavassin/ Entraigues (F)
Vallis Sancta	Vallsanta (Sp)
Vallis Sancte Crucis	Marburghausen/ Kreuztal (G)
Vallis Sanctorum	Heilgenthal (G; Bavaria)
Val St Georges	Salzinnes (B)
Vallis S. Mariae	Oslavany (Cz)
	Pohled (Cz)
	Mariental (G; Baden);
	Marienthal (G; Hesse)
	Marienthal (Ostritz, Saxony, G)
	Marienthal (Saxony, G)
	Mergenthal (Saxony-Anhalt, G)
Vallis Sancti Petri	Mehringen (G)
Vallis de Swys	Steinen in der Au (Swz)
Vallis S. Trudonis	Terbeeck (B)
Vallis Vinearum	Val des Vignes (F)
Vallis Virginea	Frauenthal (Pomerania)

Vallis Virginum	Harvestehude/Frauental (G)
	Orienten (B)
	Maagdendaal (B)
	Notre-Dame de Pamele (B)
Vallis Viridis	Vallverte (Sp)
Vaux-Ste-Marie	Bellevaux (Swz)
Verneso/Vernaysium	Vernaison (F)
Vetus Vinetum	Vivegnis (B)
Via Coeli	Düsseren/Himmelsweg (G)
Villa Pacis	Friedenweiler (G)
Villarium Canivet	Villers-Canivet (F)
Villencuria	Villencourt/Willancourt (F)
Vinegolium	(le) Vignogoul (F)
Virginitas	(le) Virginité (F)
Viridarium	(le) Verger (F)
Vitriacensis	Saint-Jacques (F)
Vivarium	(le) Vivier (F)
Vivarium B. Mariae	Marche-les-Dames (B)
Vivennis	Vivegnis (B)
Vrouenhof	Waarschoot (B)
Walteri-Brania	Wauthier-Braine (B)

Index of Cistercian Nunneries

AUSTRIA
Friesbau 66
Gereuth 35
Saint Bernard-by-Horn 71, 144, 156

BELGIUM
Ath 72
Axel 58
Aywières 19–20, 24, 90, 93, 96, 25, 128, 133–4, 150–1, 170–9, 188, 210–11
Baudeloo 99
Beaupré 231
Bijloke (Byloque) 28, 58, 91–2, 95, 169
Bloemendaal 23
La Cambre 33, 59, 84, 86, 134, 161, 222
Clairefontaine 53, 55, 104, 121, 182, 230, 234, 238
Doornzele 125, 132, 237
Épinlieu 35, 47, 89, 129, 167, 213
Florival 23, 33, 69, 118, 144, 150–1, 162
Groeninghe 47, 54, 73, 80, 107, 119, 132, 171, 203, 231, 234, 237
Guldenberg 35, 98
Hemelsdaele 46–7, 60, 69, 132
Herkenrode 51, 59, 90, 168, 177, 188, 202
Hocht 35, 60
Little Bigard 66
Maagdendaal 50, 70–1, 81, 105
Mariëndael 238
Merelbeke 58
Mont D'Or 98
Nazareth 23, 47, 50, 118, 132, 150, 162
Nieuwenbosch 28, 58, 196
Nivelles 19–20, 23–4, 103, 115, 118, 129, 144, 151
L'Olive 30
La Paix Dieu 58, 132
La Ramée 19, 24, 60–70, 84, 86, 93, 103, 115, 118, 120, 128–9, 144, 150–1, 196, 220
Robertmont 35
Roosendaal 24
Salzinnes 19, 212, 220
Le Saulchoir 18, 69
Soleilmont 33, 47, 69, 207, 209
Spermalie 72–3, 82, 84, 185, 27
Swybeeck 66
Ter-Hagen 58, 132, 237
Ter Banck 22, 39
Ter Beek 132
Ter Bosch 28
Valduc 19, 50, 59, 114, 144, 202
Val-des-Virges 162
Val-Notre-Dame 58
Val-Saint-Bernard 47, 163
Val-Saint-Georges 25, 3, 55, 57, 98–9, 166–7, 180–1, 189, 191, 196, 217
Vivegnis 35, 37, 132
Vrouenpark (Parc-les-Dames) 35
Wauthier-Braine 127
Zwijveke 26, 66, 69, 80, 89–90, 96, 119, 169, 172, 184–5, 196, 198, 200, 202, 212, 217, 231–3

CYPRUS
Nicosia (St Mary Magdalene, St Theodore) 15–16, 94

CZECH REPUBLIC
Frauental 129–30
Mariasaal 94

Oslavany 13, 30, 64, 89, 114, 190, 193, 222, 231
Pohled 60, 129–30, 237
Pozsony 38, 73, 12, 238
Staré-Brno 52, 66, 188
Tišnov (Porta Coeli) 10, 13, 64, 66, 85–6, 91, 105, 111, 117, 119, 133, 158, 190, 195, 216, 222, 237, 239

DENMARK
Roskilde 62–4, 181, 231
Ryd 57
Slangerup 5, 4

ENGLAND
Aston 110
Basedale 73, 95, 147, 153, 156, 228
Catesby 54, 80, 90, 115, 146, 149–50, 156–7, 165, 179, 192–3, 216, 229
Codenham 35
Cook Hill 135, 192, 234–5
Cotham 41, 54, 62, 96, 103–4, 108–9, 115, 121, 124, 127, 145–6, 149, 153, 155–6, 158, 173–4, 176, 179–81, 193, 197, 199–201, 207–8, 224
Coton 36
Douglas (Isle of Man) 175
Ellerton 84–5, 141–2, 192, 234
Esholt 118, 144, 173, 176
Greenfield 41, 126, 147
Hampole 95, 110–13, 119–20, 124, 153, 168, 173, 207, 234
Handale 57, 94, 142, 155–6
Heynings 42, 118, 136, 173, 176, 234
Keldholme 59–60, 113, 141–2
Kirklees 135, 145, 166, 169, 176, 203, 207, 229, 234
Marham 37–8, 48, 57, 84, 91, 143, 223
Nun Appleton 117, 119, 135, 146, 158, 170, 175–6, 191, 221, 223, 227–30
Nunkeeling 142
Pinley 96, 112, 135, 176, 192, 202, 234

Rosedale 34, 141, 173, 228, 230
Sewardsley 120, 144, 207, 234
Sinningthwaite 94–5, 109, 113, 118, 124, 135, 147, 168, 173–6, 228–9
Stixwould 38, 42, 103, 117, 155, 208, 223
Swine 90, 93, 127–8, 135, 141–2, 146, 155, 158, 160, 163
Tarrant Keynes 11, 21, 35, 38, 49, 96, 128, 136, 143, 182, 191, 208
Wallingwells 142
Whiston(es) 120, 129, 135, 145, 192, 203, 208
Wintney 79, 100, 106, 169–70, 234
Worcester 110
Wykeham 141, 163

ESTONIA
Reval 15

FRANCE
L'Abbaye Blanche 78
Alamanare 161
Amboise 127
L'Amour Dieu 27, 62, 75, 108, 225
Argensolles 20, 58, 131, 151, 162, 187–8
Battant 62, 75, 225, 237
Beauvoir 60, 78, 134, 200
Belfays 5, 157, 207, 236
Bellecombe 70, 84
Belmont-aux-Nonnains 5, 236
Benoitvaux 139, 236
Bethlehem 235
Le Betton 53, 126
Biaches-lès-Péronne 18, 43
Bival 5, 26, 134–5, 203, 217
Blanche 5, 78, 110
Blendesques 17–18
Bondeville 5, 60, 135, 213
Bonlieu 19, 51, 63, 85, 133, 169, 228
Bon Répos 144
Bons 51
Le Bouchet 62–3, 125, 166, 175, 237
Brayelle 18

Index of Cistercian Nunneries

La Bussière 132–3
Camp-Souverain 60
Castejean 18
Clairmarais 51, 67–8, 73, 114, 221
Colonges 84, 137–8, 231
Consolation 9, 120
Corcelles 78, 237
La Cour-Dame-de-Michery 26
La Cour Dieu 2
La Cour Notre Dame 86, 103, 123, 180, 205
Coyroux 5–6, 40, 57, 125, 173, 185, 207
Divielle 59, 73
Droiteval 59, 78, 136–9
L'Eau 63, 84, 143, 203–4, 221
Eau-les-Chartes 44, 186
L'-Éclache 44, 61, 133
Élan 2
L'Étanche 45, 114, 138, 215
Favas (Fabas) 7, 18, 34
Fervaques 123, 143, 236
Flines 27, 45, 52, 56, 69, 75–8, 81, 83, 93, 97, 116, 119, 123, 154, 156, 162, 167, 170, 177, 179, 181–2, 184, 198, 200, 203–4, 207, 217, 221, 225, 232
Fontaine-Guêrard 33, 91, 143, 217
Fontaines-La-Blanche 19
Fontenelle 25, 100, 116, 129–30, 236
Fontes 84
Freisdorf (Freistroff) 34
Garriga 138
Goion 18, 34
Gomerfontaine 52, 96–7, 202, 204, 210, 236
Goujon 81
La Grâce-Dieu 22
La Jardin 22
La Joie 22, 26
Jully 4, 10
Koenigsbrück 44, 9, 137
Lamanarre 18, 109
Laval-Bénite 3
Lazières 18

Le Lieu Notre Dame 44, 61, 198
Le Lys 43
Marquette 59, 62–3, 93, 97, 102, 120, 170–1, 181, 186–7, 194, 199, 217–18
Maubuisson 10, 43, 60, 80–1, 85, 92, 105–6, 119, 122, 185, 207, 211–12, 222, 230, 237
Montarlot 139
Montrueil-les-Dames 54, 128
Mont-Sainte-Marie 37
Mortain 95, 123, 126
Mount Sion 18
Neufchâtel 135
Nonenque 40, 50, 93, 115–16, 126, 134, 146–9, 164–5, 187, 194–5, 198
Notre-Dame de la Joie 43–4, 60, 67
Notre-Dame des Prés 18, 21–2, 24, 37, 51, 68, 97, 110, 114, 116–17, 121, 164, 189
Notre-Dame-de-Sion 194
Obazine 5–6, 40, 57, 116
Orthez 18
La Paraclet 53
Paraclete-des-Champs 105
Parc-aux-Bois 17, 59, 62, 109, 123, 143, 156
Parc-aux-Dames 20, 81, 114–15, 136, 163, 180, 188
La Petrouse 74
La Piété-Dieu 21, 26
Port Royal (Paris) 53, 68, 95, 107, 116, 123, 134, 172, 181
Port Royal des Champs 43, 78
Poulangy 32–3
La Prée 2
Ravensburg (Pas-de-Calais)
Réconfort 46
Rosières 20, 84
Royaumont 43, 77
Sainte-Antoine-des-Champs 10, 28, 51, 65, 108, 112, 114, 117–18, 139, 189
Saint-Felix-de-Monceau 33, 74, 135, 238

Sainte-Hoïlde 60
Saint-Jacques-de-Vitry 26
Saint-Just 44, 51
Saint Loup 22, 110–11
Saint-Pierre-du-Puy 13
Saint Pons 13, 17–18, 77, 109, 114
Saint-Saëns 60, 135
Saint-Sulpice-de-la-Pointe 50, 60
Salenques 18, 113–14
Saulchoir 18
Tart 3, 10, 32–3, 45, 114, 125, 139–41
Le Trésor 36, 43
Val-des-Vignes 68, 163
Valloires 134
Valmagne 40
Valsauve 125–6
Val Virginal 36
La Vassin 51, 206–7
Vaubons 33, 86, 124–5, 144
Vergel 17–18
Vernaison 60, 70, 124, 163
Vic-du-Ciel 18
Le Vignogoul 40, 85, 123, 236
Villancurt 61
Villers Canivet 5
Villers-aux-Nonnains 13
Voisons 35, 71, 84, 116, 137
Yvetot 135
Woestine 17–18, 137, 236

GERMANY
Abbenrode 34, 79
Adersleben 63, 107, 200, 213
Aftholdsbach 58
Allendorf 124, 159
Althaldensleben 33
Anrode 63, 71, 100, 119, 188, 199, 213, 217, 228
Baindt 24, 97, 16, 175
Bamberg 5
Bennighausen 79–80, 83, 115–16, 121, 164–5, 172, 215, 233
Bergen 13, 34, 52, 81, 87, 138, 188, 190, 193, 215, 233
Bersenbrück 47, 72, 78, 82–3, 86, 103, 112, 154–5, 158, 166, 179, 182, 187, 189, 193, 201–2, 209, 223
Beuditz 28, 94, 116, 181, 185, 193, 204
Beuren 16–17, 22, 84, 124–5, 154, 159, 185–6, 205, 213, 222
Bickenkloster 35
Billigheim (Marienbrunn) 38, 49, 98, 100, 121, 133, 205, 216
Blankenau 33
Blatzheim 60
Boitzenburg 132, 195
Börstel (Menslage) 59, 64, 74–5, 81, 89, 91–4, 107, 127, 159, 185, 222, 225, 233–4
Bottenbroich 147, 218
Breitenbich 71
Brenkenhausen 88, 107
Burtscheid 50, 55, 60, 71, 101, 105, 186, 203
Caldern 48
Chumbd 114, 160
Dalheim 1, 60, 113, 218–19
Disibodenberg 34
Drolshagen 78–9
Düsseren (Duissern) 17, 70, 93, 124–5, 137, 148, 156, 163, 166, 171–2, 193–4, 203
Eisenberg 31, 33, 39, 67
Eisenach 67, 174
Erfurt (St Martin) 68, 94, 189, 220–1
Frankenburg 84, 159
Frankenhausen 46, 98, 104, 173, 180, 188, 215
Frauenberg 67, 78
Frauenroth 26, 54, 219
Fraupriessnitz Frauensee 27, 39, 61, 123, 149, 159, 184, 191, 219
Gevelsberg 116, 218–19
Georgenberg 50, 61, 124, 159
Glaucha 78, 222
Goslar (Neuwerk/Mariengarten), Gotha 63, 66–8, 93, 104, 112, 126, 149, 155, 180, 186, 191, 199, 203, 212, 219–20, 230

Index of Cistercian Nunneries

Grafenthal 48, 51, 55, 81, 91, 104, 116, 125, 183
Grana 73
Grimma (Nimbschen/Mariental) 31, 36, 64, 183, 197, 216
Graurheindorf 48, 114
Gravenhorst 50, 59, 75, 99, 104, 107, 112, 126, 129, 146, 188, 203, 209, 233, 235
Greislau 66
Gutenzell 24, 64, 169
Halberstadt 66, 77, 87–8, 111
Harvesthude (Frauental) 13, 17, 64, 107, 124, 214–15
Hedersleben 131, 222
Helfta 27, 31, 52, 67, 111, 118, 131, 152, 164, 169, 195, 235
Heggbach 24
Heiligengraben 86, 91, 105–6, 173, 190, 197–8
Heiligkreuz 17, 31, 136–7
Heilgenkreuz (Gotha) 86, 89, 98–9, 105–6, 114, 116, 142, 156, 180
Heiligkreuztal 36, 163, 196–7, 208
Himmelkron 50, 86, 108, 113, 126–7
Himmelau 13
Himmelpforten (Zarrentin) 25, 71, 82, 100, 107, 156, 163, 165, 205, 209, 221
Himmelspforten 31, 213
Holthausen 31, 51, 94, 114, 126
Horst 32
Hoven (Marienborn) 34, 48, 87, 105, 131, 175, 211, 213, 218–19
Ichtershausen 5, 31, 49, 66, 72, 77, 94, 107, 154, 159, 170, 175, 177, 198, 205, 209, 213, 216, 219
Ihlo 138
Ilm 82, 114
Isenhagen 32, 35, 59, 64, 66, 70–2, 79, 81, 87, 91, 102, 105, 107, 165
Itzehoe 12, 15, 70, 82, 95, 184
Ivenack 46, 94, 107, 116, 158, 197, 202, 209
Katherintal 196

Kelbra 48, 64, 66
Kölleda 39, 66
Krummin 14, 45, 61, 78, 185
Kiernack 73
Langendorf 107, 193, 224, 238
Lauingen 24
Lichtenthal 17, 49, 52–5, 83, 98, 102, 104, 117, 121–2, 144–5, 165, 180, 187, 195, 200, 205, 217, 234
Lichtenstern 52
Lilienthal 2, 31, 67, 69, 78–9, 94, 107, 112, 124, 155, 158, 169, 201, 209, 219, 223–34
Lübeck (St John) 32, 67, 92, 107, 129, 184, 215
Machern 37
Magdeburg (St Agnes) 40, 65, 94, 107, 161, 208, 215
Maidbronn 38, 50
Mansfeld 27, 48, 67
Marienborn 34, 70, 87, 105, 112, 131, 190, 195
Marienbrunn (Burbach) 65
Marienau 5
Mariengarten (Neuwerk) 17, 31, 39, 63–6, 68, 77, 102–3, 157–9, 188, 203, 209
Marienkammer 17, 67, 78, 120, 187–9, 199–200
Marienrode 72
Mariasaal 55
Marienkron (Patershusen) 34, 60, 124
Marienkamp 69, 87
Mariensee 71, 78, 137, 215
Mariental 25, 31, 38, 89, 103
Marksussra 100
Medingen 42, 72, 90, 104, 107, 114, 117, 154, 157–8, 173, 181, 183, 214, 223
Neuberg 33, 81
Neuendorf 91
Neukloster 31, 33, 45, 70, 73, 78, 85, 93, 98, 159, 209
Oberschönenfeld 24, 97, 164, 220

Pielehofen 108, 123
Plötsky 111, 193
Ramsen 34, 238
Reinbek 2, 46, 184
Rinteln 65, 82, 89, 104–5, 107–8, 111–13, 157, 160, 164, 172, 174, 232
Roda 66
Rohr 33
Rossleben 35
Rostock 11, 67, 77–8, 88, 104–5, 125, 184
Rottermünster 25, 136, 197
Rühn 81, 215
Rulle 70, 78, 81, 87, 101, 103, 153, 158, 191, 198, 201, 209, 220, 223–4
Rupertsberg 34, 237
Sankt-Thomas-an-der-Kyll 34, 49, 87, 131
Saarn 55, 107, 155, 175
Schledenhorst 125
Schönau 58
Seligenthal 28, 98–101, 108, 121–5, 158, 169, 190, 202, 211, 233
Sitzenroda 104
Sonnefeld 3, 72, 83–4, 93, 96, 103–4, 130–1, 153, 156, 163, 180, 183, 196, 198
Sonnencamp (Neukloster) 31, 33, 45, 70, 73, 85, 93, 98, 154, 159, 182, 204, 208, 210–11, 215
Stepnitz (Marienfliess) 116, 158, 189, 222, 238
Sterkrade 39, 125
Stunnenmunster 38
Teistungenburg 17, 125, 159, 188, 200, 224, 235
Tilgenkloster 238
Usedom 185
Uetersen 12, 181
Walberberg 49, 131, 218–19
Waterler 77, 84, 111, 126, 155, 157, 169–70, 182, 190, 231
Wechterswinkel 5, 31, 49, 112, 125, 134, 204

Wald 17, 61, 90–1, 97, 122, 125, 154, 156, 168, 224
Wanzka 81, 87, 103
Welver 79, 101, 109, 119, 163, 169, 185, 187, 233
Wetmar 66
Wienhausen 71, 81, 88, 91, 103, 106–7, 135, 156, 159, 182, 191, 215
Wöltingrode 111, 135, 175, 191
Wonnental 101
Wormeln 17, 39, 87, 107, 111, 156, 159, 190, 202, 208, 215
Zehdenick 209
Zimmern 52, 103, 108, 123
Zarrentin 49, 78, 81, 112, 114, 158–9, 172, 184
Zissendorf 35

HOLLAND
Bethlehem (Damme) 59
Binderen 132
Doornzele 132
Horst 72
Klaarkamp 2
Loosduinen 50, 52, 64
Marke 47, 73
Midwolde/Midwolda 33, 40, 70
Roermond 45, 48, 52, 78, 84–90, 97, 125, 174, 218
Ter Beek 132
Ter Hagen 47, 70
Ter Hunnepe (Marienhörst) 69, 73, 87
Utrecht (St-Servaas) 169
Vroukekamer 47, 174

HUNGARY
Brasso 111
Ivanics/Ivanić 34, 65, 104, 107, 238
Veszprémvölgy 38, 80, 92–3, 129, 148, 203

IRELAND
Barrymore 66

Index of Cistercian Nunneries

ITALY
Brione 59, 82, 128–9, 164, 184, 195, 217, 220
Buonluongo 35
Conversano 2, 16, 73, 85, 132, 148, 160, 194
Galilea 67
Nazaret 67
Rifreddo 16, 17, 125, 127, 133–4, 156–7, 161–2, 165, 180, 183–4, 192, 196, 201
San Donato 30
San Sepulchro 37
St John de Palude 30
Siena (Santa Maria della Visitatione) 34
Sezzadio 81
Venice (St Margaret, St Thomas) 58
Vesola 73

LATVIA
Riga 15, 79, 83, 113, 172–3

LEBANON
Tripoli 16

LUXEMBOURG
Bonneweg 26, 67, 82, 188, 23
Differdange 45, 144
La Piété Dieu 26–7

NORWAY
Bergen 7, 15, 64
Nonneseter 7, 15, 211

POLAND
Chelmno 65, 81, 84, 87, 105–6, 238
Kimbarówka 32
Koszalin 46, 61–2, 67, 77, 182, 191, 204, 221, 223
Łubnice 73
Marianowo 79, 81
Ołobok 14, 32, 73, 182, 198
Owińska 14, 32, 60–1, 187, 215
Szceczin (Stettin) 17, 45–6, 57, 63, 67, 80, 83–4, 90, 94, 99, 107, 112, 114, 159, 168, 183–4, 193, 197, 199, 203, 212, 217, 221
Toruń 32, 65–6, 71, 222
Trebnitz (Trebnica) 14, 32, 37, 77, 81, 85, 89, 98, 131–4, 148, 161–2, 165, 176–7, 185, 188, 191, 193, 210, 215
Wolin 14, 46, 61–2, 84, 116, 173, 181, 185, 201, 210
Żarnowitz (Żarnowiec) 14, 32, 80–1, 91–2, 105, 108, 114, 118, 194, 200, 210, 216–18

PORTUGAL
Arouca 44, 77, 95, 101–2, 111, 147–8, 157, 168, 180, 194–5, 206, 233
Celas 44, 60, 77, 91, 97, 157, 83, 192–3, 206
Cós 59
Lorvão 44, 60, 102, 194, 217, 223, 232, 239
Odivelas 77, 85, 89
Saõ Benito de Castris 36
Sémide 7, 34

SCOTLAND
Coldstream 11, 41, 60, 62, 99, 156, 166, 193–5, 207–8, 221
Haddington 7, 60, 213, 1
Manuel 235–6
North Berwick 7

SPAIN
Arroyo 78, 91–2, 144
Bonrepós 40–1
Buenfuente 35
Cañas 34, 45, 92, 102, 105, 140, 157, 206
Cambron 71. 196, 237
Carrizo 18, 47–8, 78, 80, 86, 92, 148, 160, 171–2, 200, 204, 206, 221
Ferreira del Pantón 34, 47, 80, 86
Gradefes 8, 47, 60, 78, 86, 107, 140, 166, 174, 183, 191, 196, 204

Las Huelgas 7–10, 29, 54, 63, 72, 80, 85–8, 91, 101–2, 113, 140, 143, 156, 160–1, 166, 172, 175, 179–80, 189, 195–6, 206, 211, 215–16, 239
Navelgas 40
Perales 140, 238
Rute 74, 238
San Arevolo-Ligaraja 125
San Felice 237
Santa Columba 60
Seville (San Clemente) 148, 200, 206, 209–10, 216, 221
Silvanès 40
Toledo (St Clement) 65, 205–6
Trasobares 45
Tulebras 7–8, 40, 140, 237
Vallbona 35, 40–1, 88, 92, 97, 125, 174, 239
Valledemaria 108, 119, 126–7, 227
Valldonzella 35
Vileoña 88
Villamayor 34, 91

SWEDEN
Gudhem 15, 116–17, 184, 211, 222
Riseberga 84, 231
Sko 15, 34, 112, 228, 231
Vreta 15, 44, 85

SWITZERLAND
Feldbach 61, 156
Fraubrunnen 36, 48, 64, 128, 134, 138, 171, 183
Frauenthal 86, 109
Gnadenthal 25, 63
Magdenau 25
Olsberg 34, 37, 68, 134
Rathausen 54, 79, 82–3, 99, 132, 148, 190
Selna 24, 65
La Voix Dieu 73
Wettingen 24

SYRIA
Acre 15–16, 94, 132
Antioch 15

TURKEY
Perchevo 15

WALES
Llanllugan 38, 86, 110, 223
Llanllŷr 38, 67, 110, 133, 192, 236

www.ingramcontent.com/pod-product-compliance
Lightning Source LLC
Chambersburg PA
CBHW030734250426
43671CB00035B/309